THE **ARCHITECTURE** OF THE **REAL ESTATE PRACTICE**

The Psychology & Art of the Real Estate Profession

SONNY R. MOYERS

Published By Sonny R. Moyers
dba The Renaissance Group
Denton, County, Texas
4340 Woodbine Ln.
Prosper, TX 75078

Sonny R. Moyers
MS Psychology
BS Management & Communications
Licensed Real Estate Broker - Texas
Sonny@SonnyMoyers.com
www.realestatebook.org

© Sonny R. Moyers 2022

First published 2023

Printed in the United States by IngramSpark
Moyers, Sonny, 2023

1. Real Estate Brokerage. 2. Behavioral Theory. 3. General Business. 4. Communications Theory.
ISBN 979-8-9887965-0-3 Hardback

Book Layout & Illustrations by Brooks Design, Inc.

$64.95
ISBN 979-8-9887965-0-3
56495>

9 798988 796503

DEDICATION

This book is dedicated to our esteemed clients, who have placed their trust in us throughout our real estate journey. Your unwavering support, loyalty, and confidence in our services have been the driving force behind our success.

Each page of this book is a tribute to the countless transactions we have navigated together, the dreams we have turned into realities, and the property we have helped you find and cherish. Your satisfaction and happiness have always been our top priority, and we are deeply grateful for the opportunity to have been a part of your real estate endeavors.

Your trust in us as your real estate agent has inspired us to continually strive for excellence, to stay abreast of industry trends, and to provide you with the utmost professionalism, knowledge, and guidance. The relationships we have built extend far beyond business transactions, and we treasure the friendships and connections we have forged with each and every one of you.

With us... It is all about You!

TABLE OF CONTENTS

PART ONE

PART TWO
FOUNDATIONAL CONCEPTS

PART THREE
FRAMING THE PRACTICE

PART FOUR

LAUNCHING THE PRACTICE

PART FIVE

MOVING ON AND MOVING UP

No book is ever the work of one person! Each person's knowledge is the sum of all they have learned from all sources of information during their lifetime. I would like to acknowledge a few people, some of whom are no longer with us but were instrumental in my success.

Some excellent authors provided me with knowledge along the way. Sidney M. Jourard, Peter Drucker, Mack Hanan, James Cribbin, Herman Heiser, Malcolm Gladwell, John Medina, and Daniel M. Wegner are among the most impactful.

I want to give special recognition to a small group of people, who each, in their own way, provided information that guided me in writing some of the material in this book. They include but are not limited to Judi O'Dea-Moyers, my wife, and my Partner. Ron Burgert, Betty Misko and Jack Matthews. I also want to include Coach Wally Bullington. A special thank you to the late Ebby Halliday, the founder and leader of Ebby Halliday Realtors, in the Dallas, Fort Worth area, for her guidance and support.

A heartfelt thank you to the late W. R. (Dick) Kendrick, the REALTOR® who first sponsored me to obtain my real estate license. I would not have finished my education had it not been for his support and mentorship.

I would also like to mention my parents, Willard P. and Joyce M. Moyers, who taught me so much and helped to instill in me a burning desire to succeed in business and life.

Inspiration must come from within, and each human being possesses potential greatness… **Find your greatness!**

Look to recognize inspiration when you sense that inspiration is in front of you.

READING GUIDE

This book is a comprehensive grouping of teaching lessons and concepts that include complex material created in a textbook style to be used as a reference manual for aspiring real estate professionals. The complexity is due to the fact that it explores the psychology and interpersonal communications skills and the business and marketing skills required to construct and manage a real estate Practice.

This is not a casual read to be skimmed through in one evening; rather, it is akin to a masterclass in real estate Practice development, interpersonal relationship management, client management, and numerous concepts and theories that are psychology based on human brain functions.

Some passages will warrant multiple readings and contemplative pauses to truly digest complex sections of the material. It is a resource you will frequently return to for guidance on various topics. This is not a "get rich quick book" about how to succeed without effort. The book is not about contracts, forms, or documents used in real estate. The real estate licensing process covers that material. It is a thoughtful book with numerous new ideas and practical solutions. It is different from any other book you will read about being a real estate professional.

The book features embedded links enabling readers to access exclusive video and audio content from the author. These exclusive videos serve as valuable supplements to the text, providing additional discussions and insights into the book's concepts.

Two fundamental premises form the foundation of the book. The first uncovers prevalent misconceptions among novice real estate agents. In particular, their tendency to initiate their careers without a strategic plan can lead to avoidable difficulties and setbacks. A holistic understanding of the challenges and rewards inherent in being a REALTOR® can greatly augment their probability of success.

The second premise underscores the dearth of insight many new agents have concerning the process of planning, building, and managing a successful real estate Practice. The book disentangles the fallacy that obtaining a license is a one-way ticket to success. Instead, it provides a lucid road map toward thriving in real estate sales. In line with this, the book advocates the concept of neuroplasticity, thoroughly elucidated in John B. Alden's book, "Rewire Your Brain."

An integral feature of this book is its abundant use of scripts (over 5,000 insightful words) to convey the language of real estate. Mainly narrated from the author's perspective, these scripts will empower agents with the language of problem-solving and collaboration, aiding them in making a memorable impression on their clients.

While the book primarily caters to new real estate agents, it also offers valuable insights for licensed assistants, office managers, and those already in a real estate career. It presents a broad perspective of the real estate industry, substantiated by extensive data and experience, making it equally relevant for those in both residential and commercial real estate.

At its core, the book aims to enlighten you with the essential tools to craft a Business Model for your real estate Practice. It encourages you to merge the lessons from the book with your unique style and personality, thereby crafting a unique and influential professional identity and brand. As you progress, you will adapt the language of the book to fit your personal style, swiftly becoming fluent in the language of real estate.

The book is arranged into five parts, each paralleling the stages of constructing a home. Part One provides insight into the current real estate industry and the challenges facing agents. Part Two sets the foundation of the real estate practice with Keystone Concepts. The Third Part, representing the framing and structure, introduces Structural Integrity Elements. Part Four, Launching the Practice, delves into operational concepts and philosophies of client management and proven strategies in marketing for the real estate industry. This includes a sample Business Model and provides insights on how to get your real estate Practice off the ground. This book isn't merely a road map to future success; it's a companion in achieving immediate victory. Part Five challenges you to "Move Forward" with your plan for success in the real estate industry.

The numerous client stories in the book provide insight into how the concepts and ideas presented were used in my real estate practice to help make my real estate career a success. The names of the clients have been changed to protect their privacy. The stories are real, and the results and outcomes stated are accurate.

I recommend a learning process called SQRRR. SQRRR stands for Survey, Question, Read, Recite, and Review. This learning method will help you best understand the book and digest the material as you identify how you will benefit after reading this inside the industry perspective from a very successful real estate agent. The book could be called a "Tell All Book," as it discloses the proprietary information and intellectual properties that I closely protected over my many years in the real estate business.

First, read about how I began my real estate career and met someone who helped **me become who I am** today

PREFACE

Inspiration… I believe it is an essential ingredient for art and any groundbreaking invention. In order to produce something that will not only make history but stand the test of time, every great artist needs significant inspirational moments, places, perspectives, or people. Inspiration doesn't have to be something extravagant. Inspiration uniquely strikes every individual and does not affect everyone similarly. It might surprise you that people can get inspired by walking in Paris or viewing the Sistine Chapel for the first time. For some people, a moment of inspiration might come from anything as simple as a walk through the Vatican Gardens, witnessing another person perform, or watching a little child at play.

I have been inspired many times in my life by different things, circumstances, and people. Every time inspiration arrives, it always moves me to take action. There comes a defining moment in which I realize an essential facet of myself. My experience has taught me that the best way to recognize an inspirational moment is to actively seek out situations that evoke feelings of fascination and awe in me. Sometimes I have a delayed reaction because my brain somehow perceives something, but it doesn't become consciously apparent to me until later.

I won't exaggerate if I say that different people and circumstances inspired every significant step that I have taken in life. My life would be a static world, and then suddenly, a defining moment would compel me to view things from a new perspective.

One of these moments occurred in my life on a steamy day in the middle of summer as I was relaxing by the pool in my backyard. I was inspired to write a concept described in the book when I looked at the billowing clouds above my head and saw the sun peeking through the clouds, spraying sunshine through the dark clouds in such illuminating glory. I had no idea why, but the light penetrating the clouds seemed to carry a message I could not disregard.

The words "Illuminating the Possibilities…" immediately popped into my mind for some unknown reason. They prompted a frenzy of thinking and creativity on my part. Based on all the inspiring moments I have experienced, I can safely say that inspiration is likely to strike you when you least expect it. I immediately knew that the visual image observed had special meaning for me. The visual image disappeared as quickly as it came, demonstrating that inspiration can be fleeting.

Let me tell you a story that still makes me anxious whenever I think about it. It was a bitterly cold winter evening in Abilene, Texas, and my wife and baby desperately needed food and essential supplies. We were completely broke, and I was scouring the dark alley behind our tiny garage apartment across from the university I was attending, looking, searching for any glass bottles to turn in to get a little bit of cash. Looking up at the ominous sky, I couldn't help but swear at God himself for our situation. At that moment, I was struck by a sudden realization: it wasn't God's fault that we were struggling. It was up to me to make a change. So, with a newfound determination, I made a promise that I still hold dear to this day. I promised that I would never let my family go without the necessities again and that I would do whatever it took to overcome any obstacles. And let me tell you, that promise has carried me through some of the most challenging times of my life.

I want you to benefit from the concepts and strategies in this book; to win in the real estate game. In late 2014, I attended an awards banquet where the best REALTOR® in Dallas would be named. I was among the three finalists for the award. We each had been interviewed by a panel of three judges who would decide who would win the McSam Award and be named the Best REALTOR® in Dallas for that year. Only one agent could win. The interview lasted for an hour. I had won many awards and was at the very top of the real estate profession in Dallas. This was different as I had to prove my value when competing with the very best real estate agents in the industry.

When my name was announced as the winner, I felt great satisfaction and, yes, relief. I was once again inspired to do something more. As I thanked those who had helped me win the award, I could feel the exhilaration and inspiration deep within me. Little did I know that the inspiration to share what had brought me to this point in real estate was the beginning of the plan to write this book.

PART ONE

CHAPTER 01 | MY JOURNEY TO REAL ESTATE

In a cold dark alley on a winter evening, I trudged through some trash and debris behind my garage apartment across from the University, searching the terrain for discarded glass bottles. I needed to find enough bottles to redeem and get money. Each clink of the bottles against my sack echoed an unwavering determination to buy food and essentials for my family, my beautiful infant daughter, and my young wife, hardly twenty years old. I swore to myself that I would never again be unable to take care of my family, and that dark, cold alley led me to meet one of the most influential people in my life.

W.R. (Dick) Kendrick would alter the course of my life and send me on a pathway toward success. I could never have envisioned that moment. Despite my financial struggles, I refused to give up on my dreams of a college degree and playing football for Abilene Christian University, where I had earned a full-ride scholarship. I was determined to find a way forward and carve out a better future for myself and for my family.

After getting through that problematic evening in February 1970, I began to search for a better solution to my financial problems. I refused to drop out of college and forfeit my scholarship. Perhaps I was just stubborn, but I had dreamed of earning a college degree and playing college football for as long as I could remember. I made some mistakes on the journey to that alley, but regret was not the solution to any problem.

Now, when I think of that fateful night in February, I am grateful for the hardships that led me to that dark alley and the chance encounter with a man who would change my life forever. Regret may have been an easy way out, but I refused to succumb to it. Instead, I forged ahead, carving my pathway to success.

Several days later, an advertisement in the Abilene newspaper was for a part-time apartment manager. I had first become aware of apartment management when, at sixteen, the apartment manager where we lived hired me to move furniture and watch the complex while he was out of town. Upon answering the ad, I met with David Granger, the manager of a twenty-six-unit apartment complex on the West side of Abilene, Texas.

Within minutes, David offered me the position; this seemed too easy. Being the Assistant Manager would provide an apartment with little to no rent, a telephone, and utilities for my family. Jumping at the opportunity, I found a way to move my small family and, without realizing it, began my career in real estate. David was a strange and distant man. He said little to me about the position, provided no training, and I wondered what he expected from me as the complex's Assistant Manager.

I questioned why he was acting so strangely, and my question was answered about two weeks after beginning the job. David knocked on my door, and when I invited him in, he declined but handed me an armload of books. He explained that the books included a checkbook for the complex, a box of keys, a pouch with cash and checks, and several other ledgers and documents. He explained that one of the documents provided the name of the apartment complex owner and his address and phone number. David was moving out, and I would never see or speak to him again.

Upon looking through the items David handed me, I found a pouch filled with several thousand dollars in cash and checks, along with the apartment complex's owner's name and number. I called his office and arranged a meeting with the apartment complex's owner. He was W. R. (Dick) Kendrick, the owner and designated broker at W. R. Kendrick Realty & Associates.

As I made my way to his offices, a sense of apprehension took hold of me. The moment I entered, the air felt heavy with expectation. Mr. Kendrick was seated behind his grand oak desk, peering at me over his wire-framed glasses.

I feared he would tell me to move out and replace me. He peppered me with questions like a machine gun firing relentlessly. He pelted me with inquiries about David and the circumstances. But then, to my surprise, he took a sudden interest in me. He asked about my background and how I became his Assistant Manager. He was surprised I had a family and attended ACU on a football scholarship. His deep southern Georgia drawl was soothing, and his voice had a calming effect on me.

For an hour, I talked, and he listened. He patiently listened as I revealed my lack of knowledge about business and managing an apartment complex. I confessed that I had never learned how to handle money or balance a checkbook. But to my surprise, Mr. Kendrick did not terminate me. Instead, he offered to teach me.

After about an hour, I explained that I had a class to attend and began to prepare to leave. He looked at me and asked me what on earth I was doing. I stood there, unsure of how to respond. But then, he made his request, asking me to sit back down.

And so, I did. And that was the moment when everything changed. He instructed me to take the books, money pouch, and keys and return to the apartment complex after class. He informed me that I was his new Manager and that I needed to give him an update in a day or two. It was the beginning of my apartment management and residential real estate career. W. R. (Dick) Kendrick and I had met, and my life would never be the same. I completed my time in Abilene and said a warm goodbye to my mentor and sponsor, thanking him for all he had done to help me. I had begun selling real estate in the summers instead of working in construction and learned about real estate by listening to the mesmerizing Dick Kendrick.

I left Abilene with a Bachelor of Science degree in management and a minor in communications. I had started on the ACU football team for four years and played defensive tackle on a National Championship football team my senior year. Most of this was made possible by Dick Kendrick and his efforts to help me succeed. Sometimes fate and circumstances bring people together in mysterious ways.

Embarking on a career in real estate is a fascinating adventure filled with opportunities like setting sail on a thrilling expedition that promises to meet amazing people, flawed people, highly successful people, and just plain everyday people. You earn the opportunity to meet an eclectic cast of characters.

The adventures I would have in real estate would take me to far corners of the world, to grand palaces that I could have never imagined seeing, and into situations that provided learning experiences that were rare and unforgettable.

A Twisted Path to Success

Pursuing a career in real estate is not just about fulfilling my aspirations but also about sharing extraordinary moments with the people around me. I'll never forget the time in late December 2014 when I found myself at a luxurious hotel in Dallas, Texas, surrounded by my wife Judi and many fellow REALTORS®

Twenty real estate agents in the ballroom were entered into a drawing to win a Mercedes Benz automobile. When I realized I had won, I couldn't believe my luck. To win, you had to accomplish particular sales objectives and then pick the right token to be declared a winner. Being there took talent, and winning took luck. Leaping up and down and smiling from ear to ear, I felt so lucky to have been on this particular journey. The keys were immediately given to Judi, and we could not believe that the E350 sedan was ours. Hearing this, you might think that the road I traveled was easy. It was not...

The road was twisted, with roadblocks, challenges, and some disappointments. The following chapter concerns the challenges you might face in your quest to become a successful real estate agent. You must be willing to navigate the challenges and overcome the odds to win recognition and rewards. Don't be afraid of either the successes or the losses. You will learn and grow from all of them!

Many REALTORS® are battling to achieve income and success despite enormous odds against them. This book begins with a look at the challenges that face new and aspiring REALTORS®. Don't be dismayed by the challenges of pursuing success in an overcrowded real estate world. You can be successful beyond your wildest dreams, as I was.

To do so, you must go where the brave dare not go.

As you read these pages, I hope you will be inspired to greatness - not just in the real estate profession but in any endeavor you are led to consider. This book is a road map to creating a practice that will withstand the test of time - one that will thrive even in the face of complex challenges, changes in economies, and the inevitable transformations that occur within you.

I sincerely believe that success is not just about what we achieve but how we achieve it. It is about building something that is enduring, will outlast us, and will leave a legacy for generations. This book is a guide to creating just such a practice - founded on principles of integrity, hard work, and a relentless commitment to excellence.

CHAPTER 02 | PLANNING TO SUCCEED...

Success in the real estate industry is inextricably linked to the status of the current situation. Assessing the present conditions in the real estate business gives vital insights into the health of the industry as a whole, as well as its tendencies and future possibilities. When making important choices about creating a real estate practice, this information is crucial for anyone interested in a real estate career.

Let me share a real-life learning experience that I had with brilliant executives seeking to build a real estate-related business.

Karen Hatfield was the Leasing Manager & Sales Director for a new company in Costa Mesa, California, attending an international convention I spoke to in New Orleans. Karen worked for a highly successful former President of a medium-sized corporation who had retired and started a real estate-related company. Preston Andersen, the owner, had leased a 25,000-square-foot facility in the pricey Costa Mesa, California area. They provided short-term lease apartments to small businesses. It was called a Business Center.

After the convention, Karen contacted me by telephone to ask about my visiting their offices in Costa Mesa and giving them advice. She was distressed as the business was struggling. She had a business degree from a reputable University and was devastated at her inability to make progress in her current role. Mr. Andersen was very unhappy with the results; she said they had to do something to turn things around. Things looked hopeless to Karen.

After sending a project proposal and agreeing to provide services, I flew to California and arrived in Costa Mesa. Karen met me at the airport and proceeded immediately to the building. A high degree of anxiety was visible to anyone who was observant. No one relishes being told that they are not performing and that changes must be made. I was empathetic with Karen, assuring her that I would be deliberate and fair in my analysis of the business and her. Over the next two days, I completed a Hybrid Information Transfer Study that indicated numerous problems with the business and its management. This business was a financial disaster for the owner.

I met Mr. Andersen on the first day but didn't spend much time with him until the end of the third day of my assignment, which included a read-out session to discuss my findings and recommendations from the review.

During my private visit with Preston Andersen, I observed a "doubtful, wait and see" attitude. He seemed uncertain of the benefits of my analysis and what I might recommend. He was not expecting my approach, which was consultative and collaborative in nature. Like many who had held influential positions in corporate life, he exhibited a cautious attitude and was somewhat aloof. I asked him to explain why he had chosen the business he founded, and he began to loosen up and talk about his prior life, the decision to establish the business, and the pathway he had traveled to this point. He was, by all outward appearances, troubled and dismayed. He had lost over $400,000 in the venture to this point.

He shared a lot of information, allowing me to understand the emotions I saw in him. He was devastated at his inability to make this business profitable. Distressed, he said, **"I have been successful in everything I have ever done. I ran a large corporation and can't believe I am failing. I don't think I should have tried this."**

I detailed my study methods, findings, and conclusions carefully, softening the blow of reality so as not to alarm him unnecessarily. Yet, my fiduciary relationship with him required me to speak frankly about my findings and opinions. I covered the financial results of the business objectively, which revealed monthly losses of around $20,000 per month for the past two years and a worsening situation going forward. Hearing it from someone else when he already knew the results seemed to draw him into the discussion. Clients who have deep emotions associated with bad results require time to absorb the blows. I gave him that time.

What might have been a thirty-minute meeting stretched out to several hours. I slowed everything down, and he let me do so. I talked about actions, strategies, tactics, and what was missing. I did not blame anyone, but he recognized that he was ultimately responsible as captain of the ship. I allowed him to realize this without saying it in condemnation. I tried to imagine how I would feel if I were him.

Speaking to him as a friend would speak to a disappointed colleague; with empathy and understanding of his situation, I remained firm in my findings and recommended actions. Using words like, we, team, group, and staff frequently, I allowed him to understand the problems and predict the actions needed. I took a partnership approach in relating to him rather than leaving him on an island by himself. At some point, he asked me, **"Sonny, what do I need to do?"** I gave him the recommendations without judgment and allowed him to reflect on his thoughts. He said, **"When can you begin to help me fix this?"**

He had deduced the bad news and the gravity of the situation without me "slapping him in the face" with the news. I illuminated his possibilities, and he trusted me to proceed. Within six months of working together, we had righted the ship, and the business began to become profitable and, over the next several years, became successful. It would take him four years to recover from the disastrous start of this new small business. Knowing how to begin is essential. Not knowing how to begin can be catastrophic. It is best to know the challenges in advance of starting a new venture. Finding out later makes it much more challenging to correct and adjust to get back on track. Preston and Karen became "Raving Fans" and clients for years to come.

Was He Qualified? Are You?

Even with a qualified educational background and excellent interpersonal skills, this experience serves as a real-life illustration of the obstacles, surprises, and possibilities that may occur. It opened my eyes to the need to maintain my flexibility and awareness in the face of challenging circumstances and the significance of seeking the counsel and direction of knowledgeable individuals who work in the real estate brokerage industry.

You face many challenges as a new and aspiring real estate agent. They can be overcome with a comprehensive plan established at the beginning of the practice that provides methods and concepts to create a more successful business and a more powerful **you**. To know how to overcome these challenges, there must be an exploration of the current situation and the environment surrounding the world of real estate so that your eyes are open and the pathway forward is illuminated. This could be called "An Estimate of the Current Situation." While there may not be as much capital invested at the beginning of a real estate Practice, the time one can waste is costly.

My goal in the following Chapter is to provide you with a clear understanding of the challenges you will face and prepare you to implement a plan of action to protect your capital from erosion and secure your success, thus avoiding a disastrous beginning as Mr. Andersen experienced.

While the statistics and information that follows are daunting, they must be evaluated as they provide a starting point for inspiring the creation of your unique Business Model. Self-assessment allows you to streamline strategies and tactics and construct your unique Business Model. You will combine your endowed talents and creativity with the ideas and techniques presented herein, thus creating a differentiated Business Model that embodies **you**.

Goals of This Book

You will be able to streamline your strategies and tactics if you take the time to analyze the market's current situation, which will, in the end, lead to the **construction of a business model** that is personalized to your particular set of skills and objectives. This self-assessment process is all about integrating your abilities and creativity with the insights received from studying statistics, with the goal of establishing a differentiated business model that genuinely defines who you are.

Although it may initially appear too overwhelming for you to handle, you shouldn't allow the numbers to discourage you. You can set yourself up for success and establish a business model that is individually adapted to your requirements and objectives if you pay attention to the facts connected to the recent results of agents in the real estate industry.

With this as the objective, fasten your seatbelt, and let's begin to explore the current situation in real estate sales.

CHAPTER 03 | AN ESTIMATE OF THE CURRENT SITUATION FOR REAL ESTATE AGENTS

When it comes to interpreting the data offered in the various reports, understanding the nuances of the real estate market can prove to be challenging. It is essential to consider that the United States alone is home to nearly 3 million licensed real estate agents, each of whom comes with their own unique set of experiences and knowledge. Some agents work full-time, some work part-time, and **others** become disillusioned and leave the industry due to financial constraints and limitations.

Most managers of real estate offices are licensed, and many licensed assistants in real estate work for full-time agents. We have had several that have worked for us. Most of them needed income, and once they became assistants never went back to full-time real estate sales but maintained their active license status. Many licensed agents work in positions where they are salaried and in companies such as relocation companies.

This book and my reason for review of the statistics below is to **focus on full-time active agents** attempting to build a career in real estate. For this reason, this book is based upon an assumption that someone working full-time in real estate expects to be profitable and successful over time.

Many older agents retire but keep their licenses active so that they can utilize their licenses for personal purchases in the future. This book was not written for them. To understand the current situation for agents, a review of important data from the most influential association of agents is required.

The National Association of REALTORS® is an association of Agents and Industry participants that permits using the trademarked term REALTOR®. This organization is known as NAR. The association produces a Member Profile Report each year that provides significant data about the real estate profession in the United States. It is most valuable in that the members of NAR are researched to provide information and are trusting in the organization as it is the most important source of information about REALTORS®. People licensed but not members of the Association are usually called agents and cannot use the term REALTOR® as it is a trademarked term. <u>The results of agents who are not part of NAR are not part of the statistics provided herein.</u>

The Member Profile report and other studies provided by NAR paints a picture of low profitability and marginal profit for a large portion of the participants in the industry. This might be surprising to you. Most people believe that real estate agents make a great deal of money. Most do not. The reports provide a great deal of information about the state of the industry and particularly about Agent profitability, income, and behavior. This report and prior years' reports should be required reading for anyone seeking licensure as a real estate agent. Why?

"Because… there is a Problem!"

New Real Estate Agents working in the business as a full-time occupation are failing at an alarming rate, evidenced by the following statistics. Twenty-one percent of all Agents affiliated with NAR are unsure if they will continue working in the industry for the next two years. In my opinion, the "net income" of a large percentage of REALTORS® is below a reasonable amount based upon the professional requirements that must be met. Net income is the money left over after all expenses and taxes have been paid. Suppose this amount of money does not allow for a sustainable lifestyle for the participant and the ability to invest proceeds back into the business. In that case, I consider this a failure, as few people can work without an income over a prolonged period.

Twenty-two percent of the 1,592,920 Agents affiliated with the National Association of REALTORS® earned less than $10,000 of gross income in 2021. If an Agents Gross Income is below $25,000, one must deduct expenses and taxes to compute "Net Income." There is little left to provide for living expenses and nothing left to reinvest into marketing and growing the business. (NAR Report 2022, p. 50)

Perhaps the most concerning statistic from the NAR report dealt with new and aspiring Agents. Fifty-seven percent of Agents with less than two years of experience made a Gross Income of less than 10,000 in 2021. One might think it is normal for a new agent to have minimal income in the first year after becoming a REALTOR®. Did they know this before they began a career in real estate?

According to the statistics, it might take new agents in the real estate sector up to two years before they begin to see significant earnings from their efforts. Although new agents likely go through this as a regular part of the learning process, it also indicates a problem inside the industry. The fact that new real estate agents have to work so hard for a significant portion of their early careers before generating a meaningful income is, in my opinion, a flaw in the system. This is also because this struggle's "opportunity cost" can sometimes be relatively high. Opportunity cost is the cost of lost opportunities due to a particular choice. In this scenario, rookie real estate agents having trouble making a living in the industry are missing out on opportunities to make money in other fields. This is a significant disadvantage. It could represent a high cost, both monetarily and emotionally, and it is one that the industry ought to work to reduce as much as possible.

If a person who could become licensed made fifteen dollars per hour for two years working full time, they would earn approximately $62,400. It is an opportunity cost to the person and represents a negative loss to them. The story of Preston Andersen provides a comparable story. He lost over $400,000 in his new venture during the first several years and gave up the opportunity to own and operate another business where he might have been more profitable. He also gave up the opportunity to have the $400,000 grow in an investment account. He also lost the time he could have spent doing something more beneficial to him.

Gross Income is the total revenue brought in by an agent before expenses. According to NAR, seventy-nine percent (79%) of REALTORS® with less than two years of experience who are Members of NAR had a gross income of less than $34,999 in 2021. Year three is not highly positive for many of the agents in the study group, so it seems they have not found the magic bullet even in year three. (NAR Report 2022, p. 50)

Net profit is the amount of money left over after expenses. Ninety percent (90%) of REALTORS® with two or fewer years of experience had a net profit of $49,999 or less in 2021. **To me, this indicates an industry-wide failure of the real estate agent recruiting process in that few candidates are advised to become knowledgeable about the real estate challenges before obtaining their licenses.** (NAR Report 2022, p. 50.)

The NAR Member Profile for 2022 indicates that <u>70% of all Agents, regardless of experience</u>, affiliated with NAR made less than $99,999 gross income in 2021. For many, this was after years of being an Agent. Only 18% of all REALTORS® nationwide had a net income over $100,000 in 2021. Only 4% of the REALTORS®, regardless of years in the business, had net incomes of more than $250,000 in 2021. (NAR Report 2022, p. 50.)

The 2022 Member Profile for the National Association of REALTORS® states that 31% of the Agents possessed a bachelor's degree. Yet, the failure rate is high, and profits are low for most. <u>How can this be explained?</u> Does this situation suggest that a degree is not enough for a person to be successful in real estate? If obtaining a license and having a degree is not enough for many, what is the missing ingredient that provides a pathway to success?

The report indicates that most sales Agents work less than thirty hours per week. The report did not indicate the average time spent per week by an Agent with less than two years of experience. Is the low number of hours worked reflective of the fact that <u>new and aspiring Agents don't know what to do, or is it that they have no one to work with? Both are possible</u>. It could be conjectured that faced with no Prospects and not knowing what needs to be done to find Prospects, many are lost and wandering in a real estate wilderness.

Many agents had a career before real estate, where they worked in a single-track system and often learned only one discipline in business, such as management, technology, or sales. I think few possess the many interrelated disciplines required to become successful agents. The NAR Report for 2022 states,

"REALTORS® enter the profession with a variety of prior professional experiences. Most often, their previous career was in management, business, or finance (15%), or in the sales or retail sector (14%)." (NAR Profile Report 2022, p. 72)

The following quote is taken from the NAR Report.

"In 2021, the rise of new members in the National Association of REALTORS® continued to increase. Membership grew from 1.48 million at the end of 2020 to 1.56 million at the end of 2021." (National Association of REALTORS® 2022 Member Profile Report, p. 5)

Based on this information, the Membership of NAR grew by approximately 80,000 agents between 2020 and 2021. The agents that left the industry for whatever reason were replaced with enough new participants to result in a net growth in membership of approximately 80,000 agents.

It seems likely that the number of Agents will continue to rise and that agent competition will increase, not diminish. Few Agents that are successful retire and surrender their license early in life. It is possible to practice real estate into your eighties if you desire to do so.

The report indicates that 15% of all REALTORS® are only somewhat sure about their future in real estate during the next two years. Some will likely leave the industry, and many will retain their licenses for personal use. The report further indicates that 6% or 95,000 plus agents affiliated with NAR are not certain about continuing in real estate for the next two years and are possibly on their way to another profession.

This could spell "Trouble" for unprepared Prospective agents.

New agents will face intense competition in the real estate world. According to the National Association of REALTORS®, the United States has approximately three million licensed real estate agents. The National Association of REALTORS® Member Profile Report for 2022 says that there are 1,592,920 Agents affiliated with the National Association of REALTORS® (NAR). Being affiliated with NAR is the only way to call oneself a REALTOR®. The 2021 census statistics say that there are 332,278,200 people in the United States.

Therefore, in 2022 there will be one licensed real estate agent for every 111 people in the United States of America. If you assume that the most likely active REALTORS® is affiliated with the National Association of REALTORS®, then there is one NAR-affiliated REALTOR® for every 209 people in the United States. The Census Bureau reports an average of 2.6 people per household in the United States. So, the approximate number of households would be 127,799,308 in the United States. Therefore, there is one active NAR REALTOR® for every eighty households. Many of the occupants of these households are not in the market for real estate as they choose to rent or cannot afford to purchase a home. This further supports the contention that real estate is not about the masses but the few. If an agent cannot find a few good clients, their success seems unlikely.

Taking this analysis to a more local level provides additional insight. According to NAR, in the State of Texas, where I practice, there are 152,556 Agents with licenses to sell real estate affiliated with NAR in 2022. The population of Texas in 2019 was approximately 29 million people, meaning that there are approximately 190 people for every REALTOR® in Texas. Some 29 million Texas residents include college students, elderly, or renters and, therefore, those not in the market to buy or sell real estate. Not all are Prospects. (NAR Monthly Membership Report, August 31, 2022.)

A real estate career appeals to many, and a REALTOR®, regardless of income, has no advantage in telling anyone they are marginally successful. Why would they? So why, then, are so many agents struggling in real estate? In the next chapter, we examine why so many agents are failing and considering a different career in the future.

CHAPTER 04 | WHY SO MANY STRUGGLE TO SUCCEED...

Many people aim to become successful real estate agents, and the road to accomplishing this goal can be fraught with obstacles. Building a clientele, keeping up with market changes, and negotiating regulatory requirements are all challenges that new agents must confront. However, new agents can gain significant insights and approaches for effectively navigating the market by first gaining knowledge of the common challenges they face and then learning from examples taken from real life. New real estate agents can gain a full grasp of the real estate industry, its obstacles, and the best strategies for overcoming those challenges to be successful in their careers by studying various case studies and examples.

A Case Study - Darren

Providing advice and guidance to a young man who sought to become a real estate agent provides an interesting case study for us to consider. Darren Warren shared his thoughts about becoming a RE-ALTOR®. His top three reasons for pursuing a career in real estate were:

- Significant Income
- Freedom and Flexibility in the Work Schedule
- Being his own boss...

Like many others, he has misconceptions about the industry and what it will take to become a successful real estate agent. Darren had no idea how much capital would be required to begin a career in real estate. He had no idea how to project how much money he would net on a $400,000 sale. I have met and interviewed many who have given me insight into what causes a person to choose a real estate career.

Although Darren is a naturally gifted and likable young man, becoming successful in the real estate business involves much more than simply charm and intellect. Although unquestionably advantageous, these characteristics alone are insufficient to ensure success as a real estate salesperson. To become a successful REALTOR®, you need to have the capacity to deal with the obstacles and intricacies of the industry, in addition to putting in a substantial amount of training and education time, as well as putting in a lot of hard work.

Real estate agents must understand various forms and contracts and have strong salesmanship and negotiation skills. They must also have good people skills and deal successfully with Prospects who may be quite emotional about buying or selling a property. It is because clients might become highly emotionally invested in purchasing or selling a home. Despite his natural talent and charisma, Darren could struggle with reaching this level of maturity and emotional intelligence.

The real estate business is highly competitive; success is not assured even for individuals with natural aptitude and people skills because of the nature of the business itself. Agents must be ready to invest the time and effort required to grow their client base, improve their abilities, and keep up with their field's most recent techniques and trends.

In a nutshell, although Darren may have some natural advantages because he is a likable and educated individual, to become a successful REALTOR®, he must be ready to work and learn the essential abilities. He may not be successful in reaching his objectives in this competitive and ever-changing profession if he depends solely on the natural skill and personality he was born with.

The question is; Does he have the maturity to deal with these circumstances, or must he rely upon his innate talent and personality to prevail?

Talent versus Environment—or is it both?

The age-old conflict of talent vs. environment is still intense in the real estate industry. To achieve success, is it necessary to have an innate skill set from birth, or is the environment that you grew up in that was the most critical factor? Or is it possible that a successful strategy in this fast-paced and competitive industry requires a blend of the two approaches? The answer isn't as straightforward as we'd want it to be, but one thing is certain: those that succeed in real estate can make the most of their inherent skills and the circumstances in which they found themselves. It doesn't matter if it's networking with clients, keeping up with the latest trends in the market, or merely having the determination and drive to succeed. To truly excel in their field, real estate professionals need an exceptional combination of their talent and their work environment.

Author Malcolm Gladwell points out that almost all the back stories of innately talented people who reached higher elevations of success also had a history of strife, challenge, and long hours of passionate work. Jack Matthews of Matthews Southwest is one of those who fly with the eagles in real estate as the developer of the highly successful Tribute Community, located in The Colony, a master-planned community in the DFW Area. Jack writes about his study of people and what motivates them, and what motivates him.

"What drives people is always interesting to me. Why, because I am still working on what my motivation is. A mix of a loving mother who was totally outmatched by a successful (not always) paranoid, tough and incredibly smart father. My father was way past tough on me and I took it as he was testing me. My guess, is my own mix of trying to help the little guy and do great things in the development world comes from my admiration of my mother and my competition with my father.

In this business, a guy who is not too smart can make a lot of money. But a guy who's smart will keep it. It is a matter of understanding the numbers, understanding the risks. The visionary part of me is expensive, but eventually and with patience, it pays off." (2023, Jack H. (Jack) Matthews, Matthews Southwest)

Meeting and working with people like Jack Matthews for fifty years in the practice of real estate provides excellent insight into what makes people successful.

It is common for novice real estate agents to have erroneous beliefs regarding the nature of the business, its procedures, and the steps involved in constructing a successful professional path. These misconceptions might harm them and slow their development as agents. Hence, new agents must be aware of these misconceptions and address them to comprehensively grasp the profession, its problems, and how to succeed.

Most new real estate agents believe that if they study, pass the real estate exam, obtain their license, and subsequently affiliate with a Brokerage Practice, they will be successful. They often believe that the office manager and/or broker will mentor and guide them sufficiently, helping them succeed. Many believe the real estate business is about being licensed and selling homes to different and unrelated people. Most new and aspiring agents have no idea of the fees and costs required to remain licensed.

New real estate agents erroneously assume that their broker will provide leads or that prospects will just call them once they know they are real estate agents. Additionally, many new agents assume that their office manager or broker will provide them with occasional prospects. However, the reality is that the office manager or broker is busy with their responsibilities and may not have time to handhold or micromanage a new agent.

Another common misconception is that the office manager or broker will provide them with significant time and training. While it is true that some brokers offer training programs, new agents often overestimate the amount of time and resources that will be dedicated to their development. In most cases, the broker will provide basic training, but it is up to the new agent to continue their education and development through additional resources and professional development opportunities.

Fifty-plus years of experience tells me that approximately 5-10% of the real estate agents in a typical office produce 80% of the revenues of that office. The other 90-95% of the agents in an office are left to fend for themselves and find a way to be successful regardless of their experience and education. The statistics in the NAR Report for 2022 suggest to me that my hypothesis is correct.

Due to the number of agents failing, there is a continuous cycle of recruiting new agents to replace those who have failed to achieve profitability and success.

Licensing is Not a Panacea

Licensing requirements in most states provide adequate contract training in using promulgated forms and general knowledge of real estate sales. They do not provide a broad spectrum of knowledge regarding the many business areas necessary for an agent to succeed. They do not provide client relationship management training.

While licensing and real estate standards and ethics education is essential, the statistics prove that licensing itself is insufficient to ensure becoming a successful REALTOR®.

While no statistics are available in the NAR reports about the number of agents that fail, most real estate brokers and managers who I know, if asked privately, will tell you that it is substantial. Perhaps most importantly, many Agents languish in a real estate career where they work hard but do not produce an income that allows them to grow their practice and make a comfortable living. Many leave active real estate but keep their licenses so that they can utilize them to make personal real estate purchases in the future. Many years of licensed agents leaving the business and keeping their licenses active when they are not active in the real estate business helps to explain why there are approximately three million licensed real estate agents in the United States but only 1.52 million active REALTORS® who are members of the National Association of REALTORS®.

Almost all who enter the residential real estate business do so because they want to sell homes. They have always liked real estate, and the idea of selling a home is exciting. They can imagine the fun of searching for a home with a client, having a nice business lunch, and touring with a buyer in a beautiful luxury automobile. They can imagine the excitement of attending a home closing and observing firsthand the satisfaction of a home buyer when the buyer sees their dreams come true. They often believe they will make a lot of money in the real estate industry. They can visualize the substantial check they will receive for doing something they genuinely enjoy doing. Most do not understand how agents are paid and how agents' expenses are handled. Few have researched the industry or reviewed the Industry Data cited in the previous Chapter. For this and other reasons, they do not know ENOUGH.

Many agents do not know how their practice will operate. Most new and aspiring real estate agents do not understand how revenue to a brokerage firm is divided or "split." In short, they do not know how much they will earn from selling a $500,000 home. They think they know... but they don't. Darren didn't either. Most do not know what organizational structure they should choose to establish their business.

They have yet to write out their reason for being in real estate and often cannot visualize how they will market themselves. They do not realize the intense competition they will face from other agents. They do not plan to build a practice, obtain clients, or sell homes. They do not know how to begin to develop a business model and focus almost entirely on the licensing process and choosing a Brokerage to affiliate with.

They do not understand how to manage clients, what will be involved in getting to the point of showing and selling Buyers, or how to identify Prospects and capture them as Clients. They are often confident that they will like the results they have seen other REALTORS® enjoy. Many cannot explain the difference between sales and marketing. This is essential in understanding how to be successful in real estate. Herman Holtz explains the difference in his book, *How to Succeed as an Independent Consultant.* He writes,

"In general, marketing is broader in scope. That is, while sales are the function or set of functions necessary to get orders, a great deal of earlier work was necessary to get into a position for pursuing and closing sales." (1983, p. 75)

The typical agent, including those who have been in the industry for years, has not clearly stated in writing why they want to do real estate, where they will do it, and how they will be successful. Proceeding without a blueprint is like attempting to build a home without a plan. Some start cutting lumber before they know what to do with the pieces.

Knowing so little about how to construct a Practice, they often cannot visualize how they will become successful because they do not know what to imagine. They have yet to identify why they would be chosen over the other available real estate agents in the area. They have not researched their competition and need to know the failure rate and reasons why other agents have tried and failed. Most have not read the various reports available from the National Association of REALTORS® or their State Association of real estate Agents.

Most aspiring agents who enter the real estate industry have never written a business plan and/or marketing plan. They do not know the difference between a business model, a marketing plan, a sales strategy, and a Client Management Program.

Many have ideas and expectations, but they have little knowledge of what will be required to succeed beyond the licensing process. Their business experience has usually been in a business or industry where they worked in a department such as sales, technology, or human resources. Perhaps they were successful as teachers in the public or private school system. Most ask what it takes to be a real estate agent and are told by their real estate agent that "it is effortless. You must take classes, take a license test, and affiliate with a broker."

Real Estate Sales—It's Easy—Not!

Many aspiring agents have degrees and credentials in a prior field and assume that this, along with possessing a license, provides them with the background and knowledge to become successful real estate agents and operate a real estate practice. Occasionally, real estate agents flatter their clients by praising them, not realizing that they might take it seriously! Easily achieving success is one of the many misconceptions aspiring agents have formed.

All the training that is provided in the pursuit of a real estate license is real estate specific. Little training is provided about the human behavior and attitudes of buyers or sellers or the emotions that buyers and sellers have in this endeavor.

Aspiring Agents often begin their real estate careers without a plan or the necessary understanding of concepts in real estate and interpersonal communications to assist them. They may know how to write a contract to sell real estate but do not always understand how to identify prospects and convert them into clients. They seldom expect to be confronted with highly emotional clients that require empathy, understanding, and great patience.

In his book *Perennial Seller*, Ryan Holiday writes about dedication to the effort of doing something. It should be considered by all who want to become successful real estate agents. He writes.

> *"The hard part is not the dream or the idea; it is the doing. It is the driving need that determines one's chances. You must have a reason—a purpose—for why you want the outcome and why you're willing to do the work to get it." (2017, p. 23)*

The NAR Member Profile Report is arguably the most accurate and complete resource for real estate brokerage industry information. They have access to information that is substantive, revealing, and informative. This report proves that becoming an expert and succeeding in real estate sales and marketing takes time. Gladwell, in *Outliers*, points out that even the highly talented, and some would claim musical geniuses of John Lennon and Paul McCartney, had a reason for their success outside their talent and charisma. He writes,

> *"In Liverpool, we'd only ever done one-hour sessions, and we just used to do our best numbers, the same ones, at everyone. In Hamburg, we had to play for eight hours, so we really had to find a new way of playing." (2008, p. 49)*

John Lennon—Genius?

As the story of John Lennon demonstrates, talent is only one factor in success. Hard work and determination are yet another. Sometimes, there is no understanding of how hard something will be. Jack Matthews faced enormous challenges, and talent and charisma weren't enough. It took determination. Jack explained that one of his biggest challenges was people telling him he couldn't do something. Being tenacious and committed to doing something despite the difficulty or challenges faced is required by most to achieve something of great value. Does Darren, the nineteen-year-old aspiring real estate agent, have the tenacity and drive to succeed? Can he not be "beaten down" by the negativity of those he may encounter?

Imagine an artist who stops learning and paints the same subject or scene each time they lift the brush to paint. Like the artist, the agent never finishes learning and, as a result, must always practice, hone their craft, and develop their expertise. The successful Agent must always be practicing the oldest and most successful formulas and the latest strategies, tactics, new ideas, techniques, methodologies, and technologies to remain proficient and an expert in real estate.

One can look around and find an Agent who has been wildly successful in a real estate career at an early age or after only a short period. How did they do it? How did they succeed when there were so many to compete with? Were they so innately talented and brilliant that they were instantly successful? Gladwell, in his book, *Outlier*, discusses in detail the 10,000-hour rule. This rule is an important measuring stick for the new and aspiring agent. If a new Agent works 40 hours per week for 50 weeks per year, they will spend two-thousand hours working in the business.

Time is Not Your Friend...

Based upon the 10,000-hour rule, the typical agent would be required to work for five years to become an expert in the real estate profession. Most do not enter the industry with an apprenticeship of five years in mind. Many will make some money along the way, but as the NAR report suggests, the amount they make could be insufficient to have them survive long enough to become an expert in the profession of real estate. While some can do so, most cannot, as demonstrated by the earning results in 2021 in the real estate industry, as reported by NAR.

Some might have found their way without a compass and should be congratulated. However, most aspiring real estate agents need a blueprint, a map, and proven philosophies and strategies to help them achieve their objectives and find long-term success in real estate. Some likely have a personality and magnetism that is so great that it doesn't matter what they know. Success will follow from their dynamism as they become top performers in real estate. Others without personal charisma and dynamism will work long hours and learn skills and knowledge to achieve greatness.

Two Premises

This book has two premises. The first is that too many aspiring real estate agents begin their careers with a flaw in their understanding of what the real estate brokerage business is about and what is required to succeed. They do not realize that without a plan, they will suffer and must fight to survive for months and perhaps years. Without understanding the rewards and challenges of becoming a REALTOR®, their likelihood of success is small.

The second premise is that new agents do not understand what it takes to plan, construct, and operate a real estate practice to succeed. Their thinking is flawed in believing that the pathway to being a successful agent is in the licensing process. So then, why do they fail? This book answers that question, and the remainder provides the aspiring real estate agent with a better understanding of the pathway to success in real estate sales. **This may require aspiring real estate agents to rewire their brains to succeed.** The book, *Rewire Your Brain* by John B. Alden will help us examine how to accomplish this.

Is a Career in Real Estate for You?

This book was written for new agents or aspiring and practicing full-time real estate agents who are not satisfied with their current results in the business but *desire* to be more successful. They must be willing to re-think and consider new ideas and concepts from an experienced and highly successful agent with significant credentials and experience in Management, Sales & Marketing, Business Planning, and Real Estate. The book is also meant for those who wish to improve their results and construct a long-term career that will provide an income more sustaining than what they are currently producing.

While this book primarily focuses on the Residential real estate sector, it also applies to those who lease and sell Commercial real estate and those who manage real estate salespeople. Others in the industry may wish to read the material to support those in the trenches of the business. <u>The social sciences basis of this book is universal to anyone who deals with clients and, most importantly, to the relationships that must be protected.</u> While the book is about real estate, it is also about people.

The material is conceptual and practical and provides scripts utilizing these concepts and statements that are the language of real estate. This material is written for agents willing to learn and apply the concepts and ideas presented. It is written for those agents who realize that success is not a matter of luck but rather a process of time, effort, and discipline in learning a profession as a REALTOR® and Agent. It is written for aspiring agents who don't have years to invest in the business to become profitable. The book is not intended to be an easy read but a comprehensive resource tool.

Success does not come from expectation alone! Success will come from the tireless pursuit of greatness. In the book *Good to Great*, Jim Collins writes about companies that strove to become and remain outstanding. He writes,

> *"Good is the enemy of great. And that is one of the key reasons why we have so little that becomes great." (2001, p. 1)*

So, what makes them Great rather than just Good? The relationships they build with people are a deciding factor.

Crossing the Divide

Sometimes the difference between good and great is a vast mountain range that must be crossed. Occasionally it is a small stream that must be crossed to be great. The difference between good and great may be several complex practices, and sometimes the difference is a series of small things that may not seem greatly important.

To achieve good is difficult, but to achieve GREATNESS in real estate takes a fanatical passion for helping others combined with a relentless pursuit of perfection while at the same time an understanding that perfection can never be achieved.

GREATNESS is not easily achieved. It will take time and patience as concepts and strategies are implemented. It is far better to begin a real estate career with an understanding of the challenges and an outline to success than to begin without a plan and discover that valuable time, money, and energy have been wasted. Jim Collins writes about Level 5 leaders in his book, *Good to Great*. These are leaders of what he believes to be truly great companies. He writes.

> *"Level 5 leaders are fanatically driven, infected with an incurable disease to produce sustained results. They are resolved to do whatever it takes to make the company great, no matter how big or hard the decision." (2001, p. 39)*

If you are passionate about becoming a successful real estate agent, you will most likely succeed if you maintain an open mind, have patience, and are willing to learn.

Avoiding Failure - Mitigating Risk

The material in this book is based on numerous sources of information. It is also based upon my experience working with many organizations in various industries, agents, and managers in the real estate profession, and most importantly, in a human laboratory with real people where there was an opportunity to study and explore human behavior.

It is a simple dilemma; proceed without regard for the results and facts stated, or study, learn, and apply great effort to realize success.

Does a career in real estate begin with a disciplined and practical approach? When reading this book, assume a willingness to take an informed, disciplined, and practical approach that provides the greatest likelihood of achieving goals! It can also be assumed that there is a willingness to devote time and effort to becoming a real estate professional and a business owner.

Getting Answers First

My client, Preston Andersen, who was written about earlier, COULD HAVE CONTACTED SOMEONE LIKE ME before signing his lease in Costa Mesa, California, and beginning his new business venture. He could have done the research that I did to understand the industry better before starting operations.

Why did he not do this? He was highly educated, had a history of great business success, and despite this, made a costly mistake in assuming that he knew. Most people who start a business have confidence and healthy self-esteem. He certainly was not lazy... He thought he knew. He was confident in his ability and trusted his experience and instincts.

When Preston listened to my final report explaining why he failed in his new venture, he was highly emotional but suppressed his despair. He fought back the tears and was devastated that he had lost hundreds of thousands of dollars of his retirement money on a small business that seemed to him to be quite simple.

Having a set of plans, blueprints, and guidance might allow an agent to shorten the time required to become an expert in the real estate industry. It might make the pathway easier for a brilliant, dedicated, and highly motivated person to reach success more quickly. It might mitigate risk. In writing this book, I aim to help you succeed and not experience the emotions that Preston Andersen felt.

The Keystone Concepts that follow are just that, a presentation of concepts and ideas, strategies and tactics that allow for the visualization of creating a Business Model. Scripts are provided that help to explain how the concepts can be utilized in actual contact with clients and prospects.

Part Two
Foundational Concepts

Chapter 05| Foundational Concepts of the Real Estate Practice

One of the early foundational concepts I struggled with at the beginning of our practice was establishing our values consciously and unconsciously in each Prospect's mind. Competition forced me to find solutions to differentiate us from the crowd to increase our perceived value to the client.

I wanted to create the perception in the prospect's mind that we were, without a doubt, the best choice for assisting the client in reaching their real estate goals. I sought to make such a powerful professional presentation that a Prospect would feel compelled to select us when we were competing with other agents.

This set me on a pathway to create a selling environment such that when we made a presentation, a prospect would be intrinsically motivated to abandon other agents and choose us. We had to be not just better but great, and a prospect had to believe this so profoundly that we could create an internal call for them to forget others. I called upon my experience in psychology and interpersonal communications theory to develop a strategy for building our practice to accomplish this objective of 'mind swaying a prospect' to choose us.

This "mind-swaying strategy" is later mentioned in the insightful writings of Malcolm Gladwell in his book, *The Tipping Point.*

Striving for greatness requires understanding the reality of the world around you. Let's explore the real estate industry further and examine how a practice can be designed to achieve Greatness.

Why—The Practice

"Practice" refers to the agent's real estate business for the following reasons. An agent is never finished practicing their art and improving their skills and must continue to learn and grow continually as they adapt to the many changes in the industry. Imagine an artist who stops learning and paints the same scene every time they lift the brush. The real estate industry requires constant learning, so the Agent must always be incorporating new ideas, techniques, and methodologies. In this book, "Practice" and "Business" are synonymous.

In the book, *Good to Great*, Jim Collins writes about companies that strove to become and/or remain great. This is the kind of attitude that an agent must have about their Real Estate Practice. Many agents who achieve success stop striving for greatness or to remain great. The real estate industry is as fluid as any industry in the world. Trends and clients change along with a changing economy, and agents must continue adapting to the industry as things progress. People transform, and how a real estate agent relates to and communicates with prospects must adapt to these changes in attitudes and preferences.

Visualizing a Plan

Architecture is defined as; The complex or carefully designed structure of something. The structure of the real estate practice begins with a set of plans and a design that can be called a **Business Model**. This is the starting point for the creation of a practice and the development of a blueprint. How does one visualize a design for a complex structure without knowledge of the building blocks that will be required? This book will provide you with the building blocks necessary to visualize the formation of your real estate practice.

Keystone Concepts used together are the foundation of the real estate practice. While they each stand alone, they all become part of a single structure and support each other. Because they are so interrelated, there may be times when discussing a Concept there is a correlation with other Concepts, and this may seem repetitive. This is done by design. Repetition combined with emotion is a winning combination in learning.

The more interrelated the concepts are, the more impactful they will become. Because they are interrelated, they often have connectivity, and therefore the Keystone Concepts together make a sound yet malleable foundation for the real estate practice.

Each significant concept provides strength and stability to the practice's foundation. When the concepts are combined in a single structure, they are flexible and robust. No individual concept is most important as they all contribute to the strength of the real estate practices foundation. This allows for constructing the framing above the foundation and supports further developing a real estate practice in a changing world.

A real estate agent must conceptualize and write a business model for their practice but may not possess enough knowledge and experience to formulate relevant strategies and tactics into a blueprint for success. How should a real estate practice be structured? How should the architectural plans be designed to assure long-term viability in the face of competition and change? What guiding principles or concepts will allow the agent to create a culture of service and professionalism within the practice? What should an agent do to compete with an army of hungry real estate professionals?

As discussed, Agents often begin their practice without a set of plans. The complex structure of a real estate practice needs to be explored more fully to assist the aspiring agent in creating their new enterprise. Failing to do so would permit an agent to proceed along the same pathway that thousands of others who have or will fail in the real estate industry have traveled.

By exploring and understanding in detail the way a practice is built, along with concepts and ideologies that structure the real estate practice, the agent and their practice can thrive and succeed. Much like a home is built with a plan, the real estate practice must be carefully conceptualized, planned, designed, and constructed logically and practically in concert with the ideals, intentions, and goals of the agent founding the Practice. The Keystone Concepts provide the agent a starting point to create a Practice's conceptual design.

Differentiating Yourself from Competitors

The agent needs to identify how they will be distinct from other Agents in the industry, how they will stand out, and how they intend to convince a prospect to choose them over other real estate competitors. Agents and people like Megan Masters must be noticeable and able to be identified in a crowd. As can be seen from the National Association of Realtors statistics that have been stated, the ability to stand out and differentiate oneself from others is essential to success. This can be called personal "Branding."

I recently met with an agent with four years of experience in real estate sales. After a short discussion, I asked her to describe her brand. She was stopped in her tracks and could not do so. You might think that this is the exception in the industry, but I assure you, it is much more likely the rule.

Robert E. Krumley, in his book, *Identity Branding*, provides some fascinating insight into this subject. His book's subtitle is "Distinct or Extinct." This book about branding is also very much about differentiating. He writes:

> *"How do you position yourself to become favorably viewed before you have met? You develop an Identity Brand, YOU, and then familiarize the Prospect with you through unique experiences in advance of your first personal contact. This can only be successfully accomplished if you have successfully identified, on an individual basis, the Prospects with whom you would like to do business." (2000, p. xiv)*

A Case Study – Megan Masters

A discussion about my client, Megan Masters, is appropriate now. Megan had an endless thirst for knowledge and self-improvement. I first met Megan at an International Convention in New Orleans in 1989. She was strikingly attractive and a little Avant-Garde. You couldn't help but notice her. She was distinguishably different. She carried herself with an air of confidence. She was different from the others who were attending the convention. She had branded herself to be noticed positively and powerfully. Megan Masters had a brand, and it was her, along with her obsessive attention to detail.

At this convention, my presentation provided information highlighting a research project I had completed in 1988. The presentation presented the attendees with a synopsis of what was found in their industry study. The study methodology used a "secret shopper" method as I visited real estate-related businesses like those at the convention and evaluated their sales and marketing systems, methods, and practices.

Little did I know from our first meeting that Megan was highly analytical, detail-oriented, and **driven to perfection**. One might think that a highly analytical and detail-oriented person might have difficulty in the real estate world where sales and marketing expertise is essential, but she didn't. This book will explain why this personality and analytical type of individual can excel in management, finance, sales, customer relations, client management, and marketing. Megan retained me to evaluate her business. I suspected that she would expect high marks from her team. The review completed at her business included an interview where I pretended to be Sam Reynolds, a Prospect.

The teaching case I used for the review had a fundamental rule that was adhered to without exception. If the person who interviewed me asked me a question, I had to answer it fully and completely upon the case profile. I did not offer answers if the sales executive that interviewed me did not ask important questions. I had learned from previous interviews that when a sales executive interviews Sam Reynolds and at the end of the interview is told that they failed to do something, they would strongly resist.

Refusing to Admit Weakness

If they failed to ask the appropriate questions and obtain the important data, they would deny and find excuses, saying, **"Well, I normally do that."** They might also say, **"Well, you didn't give me the time or opportunity to ask those questions."**

It is normal and logical for someone to refuse to admit they failed to do something. I would have expected nothing else, but I found teaching and improving performance challenging if the sales executive couldn't admit their missteps. Even though it may appear reasonable, this conduct may not be effective in a professional context, particularly in an industry driven by sales. If sales executives are hesitant to accept the areas in which they may improve, it can be difficult for a sales coach to assist those executives in improving their performance.

To solve this problem, a technique was developed that encouraged a development attitude rather than a fear of making errors to remove this anxiety. The idea of "Illuminating the Possibilities" served as the inspiration for the development of this strategy. This strategy motivates agents to reach their limits, try various approaches, and learn from their failures, leading to more substantial professional development and increased performance. Adopting this strategy enables agents to reframe their perception of their failures from those in which they should feel guilty to those in which they should find possibilities for personal development and advancement.

By allowing the unknowing sales executive as much time as they needed and answering every question, they asked truthfully, I avoided claims of an unfair process. I set up an interview process where they would find it difficult to deny or make excuses for their inability to fully understand the case before moving to a presentation stage. This was not a trap but a way of allowing them to realize without being told they had failed to do what was necessary to pass the test. This would be illuminating...

Sometimes the person interviewed knew it was a "role-play," and sometimes, they didn't. In Megan's case, her sales executive did not know that I was a secret shopper and that the case was not real but a role-play. This allowed for a true assessment of the sales executives' actions and results. After completing the role play, I would confess to being a Consultant for Megan and that I was assessing the sales process and methodology used at Megan's request. In prior studies, sometimes, this was met with dismay, but most times, not. I would then ask them how they thought they had done. Invariably they scored themselves in the very high to perfect range. I asked them if they felt that would close the sale. They usually felt they would. I asked them if they felt that they had connected with Sam in a trusting way. They almost always believed they had.

I would then review the case asking the sales executive to tell me everything they found out about Sam Reynolds and his needs and wants. After listing the information, they had uncovered, I asked them to go back and ask more questions and guided them in the process to ensure they obtained the detailed information they would have been given had they asked. This required additional time, and at the end of the repeated interview, the sales executive was most often astounded at what they hadn't asked and the information they would have obtained had they asked.

At this point, I would ask them to rescore themselves, and the score was usually significantly lower than they had previously stated. This allowed the sales executive to discover without me telling them that they had failed to understand the prospects' needs and wants fully. They also discovered that they would have found it impossible to close the sale without the information they had failed to obtain.

This coaching method allowed me to <u>illuminate</u> their deficiencies and avoid the inevitable denial that would otherwise occur.

Megan was surprised to hear the interview's findings, which caused her to seek greatness even more than before. When someone faces reality, they have an opportunity to change the future. This chapter will deal with reality and may cause some of you discomfort as she felt discomfort in realizing that her team had fallen short.

Over the ensuing years, I would come to admire Megan's relentless pursuit of perfection even when she knew that her organization was among the best in the industry. I learned to appreciate her unstoppable desire to be better than good and achieve greatness in her field of work. She was borderline fanatical about doing things the right way. <u>Megan learned early on that small things can make a big difference in how her clients perceive her company.</u> She was never satisfied with "just good" or "just successful."

What Does a Prospect See?

What makes one real estate Agent better than the others in the client's mind? Most of the public believes that all real estate agents are ubiquitous, offering similar services, skills, and abilities. Since licensing requirements, contract forms, and ethical standards are applied to every Agent, this lends credibility to the idea that all Agents are alike. This is further perpetuated by a large number of lookalike marketing strategies and tactics that Agents use because they are easy to find and use and don't require much effort. <u>They are so similar that they confirm the assumption that all Agents are alike.</u> How can an Agent ever be seen to be distinct in this sea of similar real estate salespeople? John Medina, the author of the book, *brain rules*, writes

"We do not see with our eyes. We see with our brains." (2012, p. 183)

He goes on to further explain,

"Visual processing doesn't just assist in the perception of our world. It dominates the perception of our world." (2012, p. 184)

Imagine walking into a crowded ballroom at a five-star hotel and seeing 399 people who all look alike, are dressed in grey, and all have the word "salesperson" stamped in red across their foreheads. It is so confusing to a Prospect, and they choose one or three and begin interviewing to select the most appealing.

The book *brain rules* also has an interesting commentary about vision. Medina writes:

"We actually experience our visual environment as a fully analyzed opinion about what the brain thinks is out there." (2012, p. 184)

To paraphrase, <u>what we see is not necessarily what we see. It is what we think we see</u>. Therefore, it should be considered that the visual information sent to the brain could be interpreted based on what the person seeing the environment thinks and has opinions about, not what they actually see. If their experiences guide them to form opinions, they become a reality. Therefore **"Perception is Reality."**

The book, *Consultative Selling*, discusses salespeople, their perceptions, and the traps that might be encountered. This provides insight into the way a prospect might see an agent and the perceptions they form:

"Stereotyping attributes a group's general characteristics to an individual. Stereotypes may be negative or positive. Either way, they encourage the salesman to prejudge a customer by shortcutting the perceptual process of getting to know him." (Hanan, Cribbin, Heiser, 2011, p. 28)

A client can also fall into traps and form perceptions that may be good or bad, but when viewing 399 options that are all similar, what will a client do? The Client might choose characteristics common to some of the Group and project those characteristics onto the entire Group of look-alike act-alike real estate Agents. While it might be possible to find an exception in the crowd, the Client might not take the time or expend the effort to find the exceptional Agent, and therefore believing that all are the same, just choose one.

Why would a home buyer, seller, or investor select one agent over another? Differentiation is defined as the act or process of differentiating oneself from others. Differentiating is doing things, writing things, or saying things that allow a Prospect to see clearly what makes the Agent different. This doesn't mean they necessarily believe that one Agent is better, but that they see a difference. They can consciously and subconsciously see that the Agent is different.

Differentiating accentuates the differences between two or more people and makes one distinct and easily identified. The differentiated Agent can become the one real estate agent in the crowd of 400 wearing blue rather than grey. They can become the one real estate agent in the ballroom with 399 other agents with **"interested in you"** printed on their foreheads rather than **"salesperson."** **Megan Masters was noticeable, visible, and distinctive.**

With the number of real estate agents in the marketplace being so high, this is certainly a challenging notion. How will an agent differentiate themselves from the other 152,556 real estate agents in Texas, for example? More importantly, if the Agent is in the DFW Area, where 7.1 million people live, how will it be distinct from the thousands of real estate agents living and working near their target audiences?

When a home buyer is looking for a home in a neighborhood and finds that all of them are similar, how would they choose one home over the other when they all look alike? Perhaps price, lot size, proximity to schools. These can be called differentiating factors. Differentiating factors are important to an agent because they position the agent in a certain way in the prospect's mind. Agents don't have many differentiating factors to make them look different unless they identify them and make them powerfully known to the target audience. Consultative selling and collaboration are two essential differentiating factors.

Krumley, in his book *Identity Branding*, talks about what marketing is and how it is ABOUT being different. He writes,

"Marketing is about building relationships. It is about doing different things than the competition, rather than doing the same things in different ways. If the competition is going left, you go right. If they are doing X, you do Y. It is about creating a distinct uniqueness that is pleasing to your specific market segment." (2000, p. xv.)

Money & Agent Selection

When selecting a real estate agent, prospects frequently center their attention only on the agent's fees or commission, particularly in situations where there are no readily apparent qualities that differentiate one agent from another. When such circumstances arise, Prospects seek the real estate agent with the lowest costs or fees. This hyper-focus on cost can be troublesome for agents because it reduces the value of the services they provide and the knowledge they possess. When a Prospect is only focused on the cost of the service, it can be challenging to persuade them that other aspects, such as an agent's expertise, understanding of the market, and service quality, are of equal significance. Research has shown that the customer's conviction that cost is the only issue that counts strengthens proportionately to the amount of time an agent spends discussing their professional service fee.

Consequently, it is extremely important to educate prospects on the value of services and the benefits beyond the cost of those services. Agents that can successfully convey their value are more likely to win over clients who are only focused on fees, ultimately leading to higher Practice performance and better client relationships.

The stereotype that real estate agents are all the same is reinforced when the Agent falls into the trap of talking about commissions and fees, thus reducing themselves to a commodity that is anything but unique. You are what you talk…

When focused on professional service fees and with the Agent discussing fees, they support the prospect's opinion that this is the most important consideration in making an agent selection. This could prevent the agent from presenting information about personal commitment, service, experience, education, or other differentiating factors allowing the agent to establish their uniqueness. Once fees or commissions are discussed, the water is contaminated. It is very difficult to decontaminate the water once this happens, and this prevents a Prospect from considering other factors that can differentiate the agent.

Differentiation is a dominant philosophy behind the strategies and tactics of a real estate Practice. This book explores the concepts and strategies for differentiating the real estate agent from the cast of thousands in the industry. So, the paradox is that an agent must differentiate themselves from other agents while at the same time finding ways to reveal to a prospect how the agent is like the prospect.

While reading this chapter, the term prospect often intermingles with the term client. Depending on the subject being discussed, the material being written assumes that a prospect and a client are the same in most cases. While the legal distinction between the two is evident, for concepts and discussions, please consider the two as synonymous except for the legal requirements when representing a client. In the formal sense, the primary difference between a prospect and a client is a signature on a form. This is not how the consultative agent thinks, as the consultative agent seeks to build relationships superior in client commitment over a signed agreement.

In this book, the prospect and client are never referred to as customers except in quotes from other parties. A prospect can begin as a contact and become a client, depending upon the mindset of the consultative agent. This may sound strange as what is "mindset?" Essentially, the consultative agent can bestow a client's rights on a prospect even when there is no agreement from the prospect that this is the case. After all, it is the agent giving rights and, simultaneously, having none. The agent takes the risk in this situation. The consultative agent would be more likely to expend more effort to capture a prospect with the hope of them becoming a client than most typical real estate agents would contemplate doing.

The Modern Real Estate Practice Foundation must be built on universal concepts and methodologies that allow for change, re-invention, and some degree of flexibility. Each concept and method of operation presented are discussed in detail and are considered Keystone Concepts in *The Architecture of the Real Estate Practice!*

While all the Keystone Concepts are important, some will be more important to each Agent/Owner depending upon the Agent's experience, education, background, and personal taste. All people are different, and each is endowed with a unique personality and uniqueness. The reader must choose how to integrate the concepts and combine them with their special style and personality to create the most powerful professional REALTOR® and consultant they desire to become.

The Keystone Concepts in this Section explain how agents can differentiate themselves from others and consciously and subconsciously establish perceived value in the prospect's mind, paving the way for winning in the competitive real estate arena. They also provide the foundation for the real estate practice and focus the agent on long-term success by developing and nurturing client relationships.

The Adaptive Unconscious Mind

A part of building long-term relationships with clients requires an understanding of concepts and ideas involving human behavior. This includes understanding why clients do what they do and how their opinions are formed. Daniel M. Wegner is credited with coining the Adaptive Unconscious phrase, which was first written about extensively in the early 2000s. He was an American social psychologist and a professor of psychology at Harvard University. In *The Illusion of Conscious Will*, he wrote about the Adaptive Unconscious. He described the unconscious mind concept as a mental process that affects judgment and decision-making. Exploring this unconscious mind postulate provides great insight.

"Unconscious action can also be understood in terms of what a person is thinking consciously and unconsciously at the time of the action. It is possible that both kinds of representation of action might contribute to the causation of the action, and in either event, would say that the real mental causation of action had taken place." (2002, p. 161)

Wegner seems to infer here that unconscious thought can spur conscious action. If a client were unconsciously thinking, **"Perhaps I have misjudged the situation, and I need to know more,"** they might consciously ask the agent for more details. In my story of inspiration and taking action in earlier chapters, it is easy to see that inspiration consciously caused me to take action.

It is entirely possible that my life has been unconsciously guided by many inspirations that caused me to take actions I was unaware of.

Much of the material presented in the Keystone Concepts is based upon understanding the Adaptive Conscious, Adaptive Unconscious Concepts, and subliminal thoughts and ideas. Applying these concepts in the Real Estate Practice and Profession is essential for success. It is a recognition that the adaptive conscious and unconscious are always present and that the reaction of people to various stimuli causes a reaction that may not be known to the person receiving the stimulus.

Is there a difference between the unconscious and the subconscious? Unconscious means not awake or lacking awareness. In the unconscious state of mind, the person is not aware of any way the thoughts are going on in their mind.

Subconscious, on the other hand, refers to thoughts, actions, or brain processes of which a person is aware of what they are doing but not actively aware of a particular fleeting thought that just pops into their heads for a millisecond. The thought is just below the level of awareness of the person. In the subconscious mind, this infers that the person is indeed partly aware of the thought processes. Therefore the hypothesis is that they are near the surface of consciousness and can comingle with the conscious thought of the person allowing for the formation of opinion. This is what happens when I use the term, Intuitive Thinking Rising.

When an agent reveals an issue or situation that the client was unaware of and the client, in a fleeting microsecond, thinks, **"I didn't know that,"** the client might still subconsciously form an opinion about the agent. This possible intimation of opinion helps the person's conscious mind form and evaluate thoughts and ideas. Much like seeing an immaculately dressed person and subconsciously noticing but not consciously thinking, wow, they are dressed perfectly. This is sometimes done without the intent of the client. They might not consciously think, **"I should take note of this as the Agent clearly understands a great deal about this situation."**

When the client is not involved mentally in a conversation, they may not particularly notice the comment or solution proposed by the Agent. Yet, a fleeting thought could still register with the brain and impact the client's opinion and actions. The unconscious thought can also be explained in an example. When a person is preparing to cross a street and senses danger from an approaching vehicle, and the person becomes aware of the danger and takes action to avoid injury, their unconscious mind could have been at work.

Many of the concepts in this book are based upon actions that the agent takes that affect both the unconscious and subconscious activities of the prospect's brain. **"Prospect Awareness without Awareness"** would be a good way to state this postulate. Whether agreeing or disagreeing with this hypothesis, the agent should consider that anytime they are in front of the client, everything they do and say can be seen and heard by the client, and an opinion formed or a previous opinion supported, whether that opinion is good or bad. Wegner, in his book, *The Illusion of Conscious Will,* further states,

> *"The third form of cognitive activation suggested by this analysis concerns a thought that is accessible but not conscious. Such deep activation describes the nature of much of our mental life, but it is the mental life of the unconscious." (2002, pp. 163-164)*

This indicates that what is going on in the unconscious is more important than one might have thought. It is not just the information being received or processed while sleeping. When a prospect has received a lot of information that has been seen but is not brought to the conscious mind, then they may have started forming opinions in the unconscious mind that, when brought forward to the conscious mind, causes the client to formalize opinions that might cause them to act. If the agent, by their actions, behavior, and attitudes, can place information in the prospect's unconscious mind, they might affect the outcome of an interview. Many of the concepts presented in this book assume that all that is presented to a client can in some way affect their actions or decisions.

Dick Kendrick & The Unconscious Mind

While people may not know why they feel or react in a certain way and may not even know they have reacted, they do. When Dick Kendrick offered me the position to manage his apartment complex in Abilene, Texas, he may not have made the decision consciously. His subconscious mind might have been at work and, after a few moments, risen to the conscious level, and that might explain his sudden action to retain me as his manager.

The client can see, hear, and register all that is happening with an Agent during a meeting. The Agent wants to believe that the ideas and words presented will cause the client to think and react in a certain way, even though they may not know that they are reacting in the manner hoped for by the Agent. The research I have done is practical and has been done over the past fifty years. This research was done while working with others and reviewing numerous sources of ideas and concepts that led to the formation of this hypothesis. The laboratory that I worked in was a real-life laboratory with real people.

Another Perspective About Unconscious Thought

The concepts of Adaptive Unconscious thinking are also covered at some length in a book written by Malcolm Gladwell. As discussed in the book, "*blink.*"

While the Adaptive Unconscious is frequently thought of when dealing with life-and-death decisions, such as moving out of the way of an oncoming automobile or train, it has been observed that people are affected by the Adaptive Unconscious in numerous ways. There is also an Adaptive Subconscious working in the human brain just below the conscious level but above the unconscious level. Subconsciousness is a way that is influenced by the part of the mind of which one is not fully aware. In short, people are aware of something, but it is not immediately conscious to them. This concept is also discussed in consideration of Data Slicing in Malcolm Gladwell's book, "*blink.*" The concept of "*blink*" also relates to ideas presented in the book, "*Rewire Your Brain*" by John Arden.

A person may not intend to focus or concentrate on thoughts. Still, thoughts and opinions are forming as this happens in the background and later, maybe in milliseconds, may become aware of the person. This Adaptive Subconscious, closely related to Adaptive Unconscious, is a powerful tool for the highly skilled REALTOR® to use in causing prospects to form positive opinions about the agent.

My observations over 50 years and thousands of interviews and conversations with others convince me that this is correct. Whether called Adaptive Unconscious or Adaptive Subconscious, the concept is similar. The brain works and forms thoughts and opinions without a person knowing that this is happening.

These concepts about the conscious and unconscious brain can be made simpler by the agent assuming that the other person sees, hears, and senses things that are obvious to them and also things that are not obvious to them at any given time. This makes the Agent "aware" of the client's "awareness" even when the client is not paying close conscious attention to the agent's actions.

This can partially explain the ability of a student or person to listen to a lecture but have their mind drifting away to an island in the Caribbean yet remember parts or complete portions of the lecture and be able to recall those thoughts when tested or asked to recall the ideas or thoughts. This concept of memory is also discussed at great length in the book *brain rules* by John Medina. The ability of a person to form opinions, make decisions, or approval or disapproval without intending to do so is a huge part of the concepts and strategies presented herein.

When a Prospect is confronted with specific behavior, information, and ideas, the prospect will form and make decisions subconsciously and perhaps unconsciously without a logical connection to their conscious thoughts. The opinion can be positive or negative toward the presenter. Therefore, the presenter should ensure that what is presented to the Prospect is most likely positive rather than negative.

Concepts and ideas are presented in this book that can help to form a positive impression with a prospect or client, whether the prospect or client is consciously listening or subconsciously hearing or seeing the information.

Fortunately for all of us, there is always an opportunity to learn and change. John Medina, the author of *brain rules*, writes:

> **"Some regions of the adult brain stay as malleable as a baby's brain, so we can grow new connections, strengthen our existing connections, and even create new neurons, allowing all of us to be lifelong learners. We didn't always think that." (2012, p. 253)**

Pouring the Foundation

The Keystone Concepts form the foundation of the real estate practice. Many require deep thought and perhaps the creation of new neurons in the brain to help create a different kind of real estate practice than may have been envisioned.

The agent must always remain aware of what the client is doing, possibly thinking, and how they are reacting. The agent must also recognize and be aware of the client's awareness… of them.

CHAPTER 06 | SELF-DISCLOSURE & RECIPROCITY

Self-Disclosure & Reciprocity is as close to a cornerstone concept of a real estate practice as one can imagine. It is the first concept I am writing about because it is, if not the most important, the most interrelated idea used throughout real estate practice. This concept operates with many other concepts and techniques written in this book. I have been teaching this concept internationally since the 1980s, and the theories presented were instrumental in my success in real estate and life.

A Case Study – Hego Hoffburg the Tugger in a Brown Suit

I was speaking at an International Convention, and there was a speaker's event after the first day. This allowed me to mingle with the other speakers. One of the topics that seemed to be most discussed that evening was a story about Hego Hoffburg. Several other speakers were talking about Hego and laughing at the situation he was creating. One speaker explained that a poorly dressed man was tugging at his coat sleeve after his presentation. When he noticed and turned to see who was tugging at his sleeve, he saw Hego for the first time. He was laughing at the appearance and demeanor of Hego. He discounted him as a nobody. He didn't give him the time of day.

Like many audience members at a presentation, some attendees have questions and huddle around the speaker after a presentation to ask additional questions. It seemed that Hego had numerous questions for many of the non-empathetic speakers.

One speaker elaborated that Hego had a strong accent, his suit was rumpled, and he seemed anxious to talk and obtain free advice. Listening without comment but promising myself that I would not treat Mr. Hoffburg the same way the other speakers had treated him if provided the opportunity. He approached me following my presentation the following day. The presentation was well received, and as usual, I was approached by several attendees with questions. Feeling a tug at my sleeve, I turned to see Hego standing slightly outside the group of people wanting to visit. He had penetrating brown eyes that seemed to offer a question mark. He was anxious, it seemed. The other speaker was correct in his description of Hego. He was dressed in a medium brown suit with a dull tie, and his clothes were askew.

He appeared to fear that I would brush him off as others had. After listening politely to his first question, glancing at his name tag, and without answering the question, I asked him a question in response, **"Hr. Hoffburg, may I please ask you for a small favor?"** He replied, **"Of course."**

I responded, **"I would like to answer your questions but would appreciate privacy. Would it be all right to meet in the lobby in thirty minutes? I will give you all the time you need and answer as many of your questions as possible."** He smiled a grateful smile and energetically nodded his agreement. We met later, and I listened to Hego and his brother Alfred as I began answering their questions. While keeping my answers brief, I asked him casual questions about his business and family. Soon, he was doing most of the talking while I, with large **"elephant ears,"** was listening.

Hego explained that he was from Buenos Aires and that he and his family owned a small building in Center City. He had three children that he was quite proud of and beamed when talking about them. He was likable and quite intelligent.

He wanted to get some information about the real estate business, particularly the ideas I had discussed. We spent more than an hour talking and visiting, listening, and responding to each other, and I found them both brilliant and their questions well thought out and specific. I answered all their questions and focused on their needs and wants.

At the end of the meeting, Hego asked me to travel to Buenos Aires and assist them in assessing a building their family-owned. The Hoffburg family owned a building in the center of Buenos Aires near the obelisk, which was almost unheard of as absolute property ownership in Argentina was restricted to the highly successful and wealthy. They also owned a ranch in Argentina's countryside encompassing over 4,000 acres of land. They were super wealthy and highly educated, and their family was connected with the Argentinian power structure as they provided goods and services to many influential people.

Hego and Alfred became clients, flew me to Buenos Aires for ten days, and never questioned my fees, expenses, or travel arrangement. They were almost the perfect clients. This is where the discussion of Self-Disclosure & Reciprocity, an interpersonal communications theory, begins.

Self-Disclosure & Reciprocity -The Concept

My master's degree thesis dealt with Self-Disclosure & Reciprocity. The writing of the paper changed my life for the better, and I hope learning about it will similarly change yours. I will continue to revisit my relationship with Hego throughout this chapter.

After their experiences with the other speakers at the convention, I am sure that Hego was wary of whom he spoke to and how they would react to his questions. It would not be unusual for him to be cautious and doubtful.

Sidney M. Jourard, in his book, *The Transparent Self*, wrote,

"The other man is a mystery. He is opaque. We cannot know in advance what he will do. We do not know his past, and we do not know what is 'going on inside him.' Consequently, he remains on guard when we are in his presence." (1971, p. 4)

If this is true, then the reverse can also be true. To the Prospect, we are a mystery… they cannot know in advance what we will or might do. They do not know our past and do not know what is going on inside of us… They do not know our motives, and consequently, they remain on guard when in our presence.

Sidney Jourard's statement is at the heart of the concept of self-disclosure and reciprocity. Self-disclosure and reciprocity have long been favorite subjects of psychologists. One of the reasons it is so popular is that it is primarily studied regarding the willingness of a patient to disclose to a psychotherapist.

I am quite sure that Hego Hoffburg was as uncertain of me as others were of him. Treating him respectfully and freely giving him my time established the beginning of a long and mutually beneficial relationship based on mutual respect, trust, and confidence. Disclosures of information about me further established a relationship of trust, laying the groundwork for open dialogue.

Taking the time to visit with them and allowing them to disclose and see me reciprocate with similar disclosures allowed them to move to a climate of trust and confidence quickly. This allowed Hego and his brother to listen to my message openly and trustfully. After this, what I said was heard differently than it might have previously been.

In the Journal of Experimental Social Psychology, Zick Rubin of Harvard University wrote the following:

"The tendency for self-disclosure to be reciprocal is probably the most consistent finding of laboratory studies in this area. The more intimately an experimenter, interviewer, our fellow subject reveals himself to the subject, the more intimately the subject tends to reveal himself in turn." (1973, p. 2)

In an article written by W. Morton Feigenbaum, the author wrote:

"Self-disclosure is widely recognized as an important process variable in psychotherapy. Outcome data have generally confirmed the view that patient self-disclosure in psychotherapy has salutary effects (Bratton,1961; Peres, 1947; Walker, Rablen,& Rogers, 1960) Jourard (1970, 1971) believes that the reciprocity principle operates in psychotherapy as in other interpersonal encounters and, therefore, self-disclosure by a psychotherapist encourages patients' self-disclosure." (1977, pp. 15-26)

Self-disclosure is recognized as an important communication method in psychotherapy and, in my opinion, the provision of real estate services to Prospects and clients. It has been a hallmark of my consulting and real estate practice for years.

Research data has generally confirmed the view that patient self-disclosure in psychotherapy has many benefits. Clients in real estate can likely benefit as well. Feigenbaum believed that the reciprocity principle operates in psychotherapy and other interpersonal encounters. Therefore, self-disclosure by a psychotherapist encourages patients' self-disclosure. To summarize, psychotherapist disclosures open the communications channels and elicit self-disclosure from a patient enabling the psychotherapist to treat a patient better. In a collaborative environment in real estate, when the client is allowed to talk and disclose, this can also be true.

When applied to the real estate business, the concept is as follows: <u>When disclosed to, a Prospect has a powerful psychological need to reciprocate with similar disclosures as those disclosures made to them.</u> If an Agent were to tell a Prospect about their pet, and if the Prospect has a pet, they are likely to reciprocate by talking about their pet. This is not just a thoughtful decision by the Prospect. It is a psychological need. Understanding this psychological need to reciprocate with similar disclosures is a fundamental objective of this chapter. Zick Rubin, in an article, also quoted Goulder, 1960, who wrote:

> *"When another person discloses personal information about himself to you, you are likely conclude that he likes and trusts you. By disclosing comparable information about yourself in return, you reassure him that his affection and trust are well-placed, that "I am as willing to let you know me as you are willing to let me know you." (1977, pp. 15-26)*

If the Agent discloses to a Prospect: **"I started in the real estate business about one year ago after a very successful career in teaching in the Atlanta schools. When I moved to the Dallas area, no teaching jobs were available, so I decided to try real estate. I like working with people and thought I could be helpful to my clients."** The Prospect is likely to reciprocate with information about their prior or current job, position, where they have lived, or career. Disclosure and reciprocal disclosure usually happen along the same level of intimacy. If a Prospect discloses something personal about themselves, the Agent is expected to reciprocate similarly. This may result in increased trust from both parties. Hego and Alfred saw my openness and willingness to answer questions without compensation, which represented an olive branch of friendship to them.

The "Passing Stranger" Effect

Many studies of self-disclosure and reciprocal disclosures examine the surprising phenomenon where people have disclosed themselves quite intimately to total strangers. The stranger who later leaves, never to be seen again, often displays the most surprising openness. This is believed because strangers who will never be seen again feel safe to disclose because they are unlikely to be hurt or have the information disclosed used against them. This is sometimes referred to as the <u>"Passing Stranger Effect."</u> One reason a person declines to disclose is fear of how the other party might use the information disclosed. Likewise, when a person reciprocates with disclosures, they are most often seen as demonstrating trust and therefore are deemed safe to the other party in the communication.

The "Mirror" of Communications and Modeling

This phenomenon can also be seen as "modeling." This is where a person tends to model the person speaking to them. An example of modeling might be when a speaker in a small group lowers their voice to almost a whisper and leans forward to the audience. There could well be a reciprocal leaning forward by the audience and an effort by the audience to listen more carefully to the words being spoken in a hushed tone. Modeling is also seen when an Agent discloses information about themselves that is appropriate for the situation, and the Prospect models their behavior and communicates by reciprocating with a similar disclosure about themselves.

In his article in the Journal of Experimental Psychology, *Disclosing Oneself to a Stranger: Reciprocity and its Limits*, Zubin also wrote,

> *"It has been observed that people sometimes disclose themselves quite intimately to total strangers, for example, to seatmates on a train or plane." (1975, 11,223-260, p.1)*

The tendency for self-disclosure to be reciprocal is a powerful communications strategy for the agent as it increases the likelihood of Prospect disclosure and allows the agent to understand the prospect better. There is an overpowering psychological need, not a desire, but a powerful subconscious need, to reciprocate when disclosed to by another person when the disclosures are appropriate to the situation.

Jourard, in his writings, made a powerful statement about the psychological need people feel to reciprocate when disclosed to by another person. He wrote,

> *"Researches I have conducted show that a person will permit himself to be known when he believes his audience is a man of goodwill. Self-disclosure follows an attitude of love and trust." (Jourard, S. M., The Transparent Self, 1971, p 5)*

An agent's mentality and desire to display trust and goodwill are vital components of establishing these relationships with clients. It is possible to make a deeper connection with Prospects by providing them with information about themselves, which also helps to build rapport and, eventually, fosters the development of long-term partnerships. When Clients believe their agent is interested in them and respects their requirements, this can serve as an impetus for developing a healthy relationship to both parties' advantage.

I have witnessed this phenomenon directly with clients such as Hego and Alfred, who responded favorably to my strategy of displaying interest in and respect for their requirements. Since I took the time to get to know my clients and was honest about the parts of my life that I didn't want them to know, I created a connection that eventually led to a fruitful working relationship. This strategy of creating trust and goodwill through self-disclosure is beneficial in the real estate sector and many other industries where it is crucial to build solid connections. If agents use this strategy, they may strengthen their relationships with their clients, develop a customer base that is loyal to their brand, and eventually achieve better success in their professions.

When I met with the pair, we had a great conversation, all sharing information, and this allowed me to understand a great deal about them. I did not act like a salesman. In short, I didn't sell. I related and understood. I sought to serve, and it showed in my actions and attitude. Serving with confidence that all will be positive takes faith.

Getting Too Personal Too Soon Can Disrupt Communication

Getting personal with Prospects or clients can be a blessing and a curse in any field where it is crucial to the business's success to create solid relationships. Although developing personal ties with others can help to strengthen rapport and trust, doing so too quickly or to an excessive degree can be detrimental and potentially interrupt good communication.

Agents need to strike a balance between the requirement to maintain a professional image and the need to engage with Prospects on a personal level. Moreover, they must ensure that clear communication is maintained at all times. In this context, it can be challenging to strike the right balance between personal and professional responsibilities, and representatives need to be aware of the possible pitfalls that might result from becoming too personal too quickly.

This phenomenon changes when the disclosure is too personal for the setting. When this happens, there is an often observed "retreat" by the other party who has been, in their opinion, inappropriately disclosed to by another person. This "retreat mechanism" can sometimes be seen visually by a change in body posture, stiffening, or movement away from the disclosure recipient. It can also be felt emotionally as the person who disclosed the information senses a withdrawal by the other party.

Withdrawal can be manifested by the failure of a person to reciprocate with disclosures. They could withdraw by remaining silent or changing the subject. With Hego and Alfred, they would have likely withdrawn if I had disclosed my desire to retain them as a client and spend days with them in Buenos Aires. Hego would then probably retreat and, after asking one or two questions, politely remove himself from the unpleasantness of my aggressive salesperson behavior.

The Timing of Self-Disclosure

The timing of the disclosure is also essential to understand. It seems that early disclosure by someone is highly effective in obtaining early disclosure by the person disclosed to if the disclosure was done reasonably and appropriately. This can break down resistance to disclosure by the other party. While Hego was highly outgoing, Alfred, his brother, was relatively quiet and introverted. Hego responded to me immediately, and his disclosures convinced Alfred that it was safe to disclose to me. This allowed Alfred to disclose and for me to reciprocate and build the relationship further.

The Effects of Timing of Self-Disclosure on Attraction and Reciprocity was also written about by Richard L. Archer and Joseph A. Burleson and published in the Journal of Personality and Social Psychology in 1980. This article analyzes the effects of early or late self-disclosure in the interview.

In this research, interviewers either disclose positive or negative facts about themselves early or later in the interview as planned before the communication. While the results of the study were not conclusive in some areas, it did indicate that early or late disclosure impacts the interviewee's perception. It concludes that disclosing should be timed to avoid disturbing the other person. This could mean disclosing at the wrong time and interrupting reciprocal disclosure and communication.

This may mean that when someone is disclosing, one should let them disclose while listening intently without breaking their pattern of openness. One should not interrupt disclosure until it is appropriate to do so. Allowing a person to continue to disclose without interruption can often result in the agent getting five answers without asking five questions. This is especially helpful in that it prevents the agent from appearing to qualify a Prospect and sending a product salesperson behavioral message that can be conversation-ending.

By obtaining five answers to one question, the agent can shorten the information transfer time and allows the sales executive to identify potential solutions more quickly and efficiently.

Getting Personal Without Offending

The more intimately an experimental interviewer or a fellow subject reveals themselves to the subject, the subject tends to reveal himself. Therefore, if a person were to disclose non-personal information early and then later disclose more personal information, the person has moved to a deeper level of trust in their willingness to disclose. Failure to reciprocate with a similar disclosure when a prospect discloses could be perceived by the other person as a **retreat** by the Agent. This could lessen a prospect's willingness to disclose further or cause them to reposition their disclosures to a less personal level of disclosure.

There are circumstances where a person might choose to move to a less personal level of disclosure and deliberately withdraw or retreat, causing the other party to move to a less personal level of disclosure. The agent must be aware of any action by the other party in the communication to feel uncomfortable with the agent's disclosures.

An agent disclosing to a prospect seems to be a cue to the prospect that it is time to reciprocate with a similar disclosure. When meeting with Hego, I said, **"I have been specializing in the real estate industry for years. My wife, Judi, is our Real Estate Group partner, and we have three Assistants. Judi and I are both Brokers, not just Agents, and therefore are held to a higher standard in the real estate industry. Judi was a special education schoolteacher in the Dallas Independent School District, and I have been a licensed real estate agent for many years. We both enjoy helping clients and guiding them collaboratively to reach their goals in real estate."**

This represents an early disclosure of an appropriate nature and would likely elicit a similar reciprocal disclosure by the Prospect as it did with Hego. When the disclosures continue, the need to reciprocate will build within the Prospect to a point where they might go so far as to interrupt the Agent. If they do, it would be a clear cue that they are reciprocating as expected, and they should be listened to carefully. Their immediate reciprocal disclosure of a similar nature is a clear example of reciprocity.

Building Trust

This relationship of trust can also be developed when a client believes that the agent will put them first in all matters. In the book *Consultative Selling*, the authors point out how this idea of building trust is important and allows the development of the consultative role of the agent. Not being seen as a product salesperson is important in establishing that the relationship between the client and agent will be one that will survive and continue after the sale of a product such as a home. When an agent incessantly talks about homes, buying, listing, and matters such as that, they can be seen as product-oriented salespeople with less interest in the person than they do in selling a product. By focusing on solving a problem or meeting a need or want, the real estate salesperson signals that their primary interest is in the client, not the sale of a product.

Creating trust with the client allows a salesperson (Agent) to cause the client to begin seeing the Agent as a consultant rather than just a salesperson. Additionally, the idea of the real estate agent becoming a consultative agent results from understanding the need to create trust and confidence with the client to meet their needs and wants and/or solve a problem.

The authors of *Consultative Selling* write,

"The intent of our approach is not to transform salesman into consultants. A salesman does not have to become a psychologist in order to perceive the major characteristics of his customer's personalities that influence their decision making." (1973, p. vii. Preface C)

Being a psychologist is not the same as being a consultant to the client and diagnosing business problems. The real estate agent can become a consultant to the client if the agent agrees that their goal is to assist the client in achieving their objectives rather than the agent selling a product such as a home. While the author talks about profit improvement, the agent should think of it as helping clients achieve their goals and that selling or purchasing a home is simply one transaction on a prospect's journey through life.

The process of modeling and trust building may operate simultaneously or separately. They often work hand in hand as the parties in the communication disclose and reciprocate with similar disclosures. Trust building will also elicit a deeper level of disclosure from both parties as they begin to trust each other, and the fear of reprisal or unfair use of the information disclosed diminishes.

For all agents, communicating with people and developing a strong relationship with them cannot be overstated. Building a relationship of trust and confidence can be called **"good positioning."** Positioning in sales terminology is often called **"creating a climate of trust and confidence."** This means being positioned with the contact so they can trust, allowing them to listen to the agents' message openly and trustfully.

Client's like Hego and Alfred are particularly "tuned in" to sales speak. When someone moves from a stance of greeting and getting to know them to a stance of, I want to sell you something, the dynamic changes. It is a signal to them that it is time to retreat. They don't want to be sold to, pushed, or treated as a money tree. The product salesperson will be relegated to the unimportant folder if they demonstrate the wrong attributes. This is why a consultative approach and a collaborative method are so rewarding.

Information is Power...

"Resistance to Disclosure" must be overcome by the Agent whenever possible to obtain relevant and essential contact information from the prospect and more information about their needs and wants. Because of the nature of the business, some of this information may be personal. When on the telephone, agents must keep the Prospect on the line long enough to establish trust and allow the prospect to disclose the information the agent needs to ensure proper follow-up. They have no reason to trust the agent; therefore, the agent must give them a reason, even if it is subliminal, to cause them to trust enough to disclose. Sometimes, words from the agent that can make it difficult for them to say **"no"** are helpful.

With Hego, I had a unique advantage. He and Alfred were right in front of me, and I could meet with them in person, share information, and observe them as they observed me. I had just been in front of a crowd in a highly positive situation and had made a positive first impression on them. They were open to disclosure! Being seen in a high-profile favorable situation, such as presenting at a meeting or convention, can create instant credibility. This credibility replaces the need for self-aggrandizement by the agent. As such, the agent can forego presenting their successes and focus entirely on the prospect's goals and objectives.

When communicating with a prospect on the telephone, the agent must recognize that the prospect wants information, and when they do, the agent has some power for a short period. That power has to be used appropriately. Suppose the agent provides the information to the prospect before the contact information is disclosed to the agent. In that case, the agent does not increase their power but reduces their ability to get the contact information. Once a prospect has what they want, there is little need for the prospect to continue the conversation, much less disclose contact information or reasons for buying or selling real estate.

In the example of Hego above, he wanted answers, and they were important to him. If I had just answered his questions while others were listening, I would have transferred the information to him and lost power. Perhaps he would have walked away satisfied with the answers. I made him feel important, and he opened the door for me to connect with him while I answered his questions. I shared information about myself through disclosure and gained time, time to connect with them. The agents' most important tool is their time. Having time for people to get to know and help them is the "key" to the client's brain and sphere of influence.

The agent has the most power before providing the information the prospect calls about. If the prospect wants the price and square footage of a home and the agent immediately and without asking for the contact information discloses the price and square footage, the agent has already lost power and is unlikely to get the contact information that the agent needs and desires.

The agent must be careful not to be pushed into providing information before obtaining what they need to stay in contact with a prospect. They must obtain the critical contact information to add to the Client Relationship Management system (CRM) and begin a dialogue that hopefully will result in a prolonged relationship of mutual benefit.

Handling a Prospect Telephone Call

Most Prospects who call for information about a property and speak to an agent they do not know frequently do not want to tell anyone who they are or what they are doing. There doesn't have to be a reason for this. They are just not trusting anyone that they might reach on the telephone. In person-to-person contact, they might have the same feeling. Still, in a face-to-face meeting, the resistance to disclosure is easier for the agent to overcome due to their ability to smile and indicate trust to the prospect.

Prospects generally do not want to be sold to, controlled, and forced to explain what they want. They often want information without risk or commitment and to get away without disclosing anything.

Occasionally, an agent will find someone on the telephone who is transparent. Other times, a caller might seek to avoid disclosure and be evasive. A caller might give fictitious information to avoid having to disclose themselves. Providing a false narrative eliminates the need for them to disclose and become connected to an agent.

Jourard, in his book, *The Transparent Self*, makes some interesting observations about patient behavior that should be considered here. He writes,

"It would seem that we can propose a hypothesis that could be tested, namely, that spontaneous self-disclosure in a therapist reinforces, or is a condition for, authentic disclosure and growth in the patient." (1971, p. 150)

To paraphrase, when an agent is open to disclosing about themselves, they reduce the fear the other person has and build trust, allowing the other person to disclose honestly and unfearfully. Self-disclosure by the prospect can be helpful to the prospect. It is helpful because by revealing themselves to the agent, the client allows the agent to assist them in reaching their goals. By allowing Hego to tell me about his family and his life in Argentina and reciprocating about my life and family, I was able to begin a relationship based on mutual trust. Hego needed answers and was anxious to get them. When I provided answers to his questions while simultaneously getting him to disclose, trust was built, and I also benefited by understanding the prospect more fully.

Overcoming Fear of Reprisal

While the real estate agent is not working with a patient, they are working with someone who might not want to disclose because of fear of reprisal. Through spontaneity and disclosure of the agent, the other person in the communications might be better served by encouraging them to disclose.

This natural resistance to disclosing information can be called **"Resistance to Disclosure."** Resistance to Disclosure is a natural state of being by Prospects for almost anything. The book, *The Transparent Self*, by Sidney M. Jourard is written in great detail. He writes.

> *"In its starkest, most operational meaning, resistance in a patient refers to his reluctance or inability to disclose his thoughts, fantasies, feelings, or memories as these spontaneously arise in the therapeutic session." (1973, p. 144)*

We are talking about clients who have problems that need to be resolved. These problems could be the need to sell or buy a home. Or it could be something more unknown by the prospect themselves. It could be a feeling or suspicion. Getting the client to talk and explain their problems is why the Consultative Agent motivates them to disclose. This will allow the agent to understand and potentially solve the clients' problems with their help and involvement in a collaborative way, even when the client isn't aware of the problem.

Occasionally, the resistance to disclosure is so personal that a client will or cannot disclose what they think or feel until the agent establishes a trust climate that the prospect can rely upon.

Advantage of Team Selling in Creating Trust

The book *Consultative Selling* makes some profound observations about the relationship between the client and salesman, in this case, the agent or agents. The authors write:

> *"As soon as a customer dislikes a salesman, he will tend to perceive all the ways in which he is different and exaggerate their importance. At the same time, he will perceive far less accurately any ways in which they may be similar." (1973, p. 24)*

Based on the information above, an agent team of at least two might have an advantage over a single agent because a client might find one of the two with characteristics that are more like themselves and, therefore, more agreeable to them. We found this to be true.

Our strategy was to quickly assess personalities in an interview and adjust our presentation plan to spotlight one partner over the other to maximize the likelihood of client receptivity. Over time, this became an unconscious strategy. Identifying a more analytically oriented client resulted in us making Judi, the more analytical partner, a more prominent player during presentations. I would have taken the leadership role if the client had a more outgoing expressive personality. This strategy proved to be highly successful for us. It proved to be a decisive differentiating factor as having both partners participating was presented as a benefit to the client.

It was unsaid but implied that the client could choose the Team member that was most similar to them to connect with more comfortably. One additional benefit of this dynamic is that when given a choice of choosing which of us to work with, it allowed the other agent to have the time to connect with and relate to a Prospect, thus assuring comfort with both agents in the future. Familiarity, in this case, is positive indeed.

We sometimes accomplished this "team dynamic" by stating: **"Highly successful agents find themselves unavailable sometimes. Judi and I are both Brokers, not just agents, we both can do all things in real estate and have a similar experience, so our partnership allows one of us to be available to our clients and ready and able to assist them most of the time. This allows our Group to provide a more personalized and responsive service to our clients. You should always feel comfortable reaching out to either of us for anything you need or want."**

In any situation or interview, the agent must be certain to listen carefully and relate to the Client so that they can mirror their behavior and not present any characteristics that the client might negatively perceive. By taking a Consultative approach, the Agent can be far less disagreeable.

This results from the agent focusing on the client's needs and wants rather than solutions such as a product sale of a home which could alienate the Client before the agent can be positioned correctly in a climate of trust and confidence. The watchword here is, don't sell. It may seem odd that a book about professional sales and marketing encourages not selling. We are committed to a consultative sales environment where problem-solving is the primary goal, and client purchases or selling decisions will likely follow.

The strategy of having two Agents make a presentation to a prospect provides the agents with a unique ability to create a liking and a bond of trust and confidence with the client.

In their book, *PRODUCTIVITY The Human Side*, Robert R. Blake and Jane Srygley Mouton explain this phenomenon thoroughly. When talking about joining Groups, they explain:

> *"The other explanation is that we seek out others who are like us. According to this view, we feel secure when we find that others share our points of view, and we feel threatened when others' attitudes, opinions, and feelings are different from our own." (1981, p. 34)*

A pair of agents have an opportunity to create "liking" by the client because they offer different personality types to the client. The collaboration further enhances the situation when two agents are working with a client, as the client can see the benefit of both personalities relative to the provision of services. Each of the two agents offers something beneficial.

The research cited supports the disclosure and reciprocal disclosure process and reveals an interesting opportunity for the collaborative agent. When an agent can relate to and share similar attitudes, opinions, and feelings through self-disclosure and reciprocal disclosure, they can create an affinity with a prospect. Having done so, by using a collaboration method, the agent can introduce ideas and opinions that might be different from a Prospect and be seen as stimulating.

This would support the differentiation strategy of the collaborative agent while at the same time arousing greater interest from a Prospect. The two concepts, considered together, can create a potent bond between a Prospect and the agent and make the agent's actions and words more meaningful.

Dealing with Two or More Prospects

The real estate agent often has meetings with and presentations to two or more prospects. This could be a couple, a couple with an important family member, or an individual client with close friends. This situation is different for using the concept of Self-Disclosure & Reciprocity. In some respects, it can be even more interesting and productive when more people are involved. When considering a presentation to two or more people thinking about selling a home, there is a strong likelihood that the concept of Self-Disclosure & Reciprocity will result in even more open disclosures than when presenting to an individual. When the agent begins their presentation with a statement in which multiple pieces of information are disclosed early, and where one of the Prospects reacts by reciprocating with similar disclosures, they could cue both the agent and the other parties that are part of the communication that disclosure is safe. Where the other participant receives this cue, there could be a landslide of information to follow.

The agent's cue to the first respondent is received. The first respondent reciprocates with disclosures to the agent, cuing the other respondent that they trust the agent enough to reciprocate. As a result, the second respondent trusts the opinion of the first respondent and opens the channels of communication with additional disclosures of their own. The snowball effect of this results in a very rapid development of trust. This allows the agent to position themselves quickly with both parties, enhancing the relationships.

This is especially helpful when one of the parties in the communication is highly analytical and typically less disclosing. In my conversations with Hego and Alfred, I found that Alfred became much more open when Hego led the way with disclosures. Playing off Hego's disclosures allowed Alfred to disclose more freely.

Communicating with a Non-responsive Party

Suppose that during a meeting or presentation, both parties do not reciprocate when disclosures are made to them. In that case, there is a possibility that a prospect or prospects are resisting because they have already decided to choose another agent and don't want to get too close to the agent they are interviewing. They may want pricing information. There could be other reasons, such as financial problems, a divorce, or some other factor that causes a failure to reciprocate. Regardless, the agent must continue to disclose and attempt to connect with the other parties through communication. The smart agent cannot be afraid to disclose even in the face of a non-responsive Prospect or Prospects.

When encountering this situation, the agent must avoid the feeling of negativity and rejection that they feel and continue to work to create a positive environment. This can be done by disarming themselves and assuring the person they are communicating with that it is safe to disclose. **"I find that many of my clients appreciate the collaborative partnered approach that I use in my business. I am here to solve problems, not sell homes. My way of working with clients is to focus on their needs and wants and help them to achieve their objectives."**

It is not unusual for an agent to be more analytical and possibly private than a highly expressive and outgoing Prospect. This provides a challenge to the agent. They must not be afraid to reveal.

The disclosure process changes when the agent has multiple people involved in a presentation. There are situations where a prospect might disclose to an agent quickly but might not do so to an agent while others are present. For this reason, all who attend the meeting with the agent must have an opportunity to speak and disclose early to add additional impetus for a prospect to feel comfortable and disclose. In a collaborative meeting process where all are included and contribute information to learning about a prospect, communication by all is enhanced because when multiple people disclose, the psychological need for reciprocal disclosure increases for all.

Enhancing the Need for Reciprocity

A delay strategy can increase the psychological need to reciprocate and is helpful to the agent to increase the psychological need of other parties. By deliberately delaying reciprocal disclosures by a prospect, the agent can increase the pressure and psychological need to reciprocate. This can have the effect of a buildup of the psychological need for a Prospect to reciprocate. Suppose the agent controls the beginning of the presentation for a short period allowing multiple disclosures by the agent to be received by the audience. In that case, they can prime the Prospect(s) for more profound and frequent disclosures.

When communicating with a highly outgoing, thinly masked prospect and another party who is not as outgoing and disclosing, the agent can create a strategy for increasing the willingness of the more reserved person to disclose. The agent can do this by remaining in a standing position temporarily. This makes it more difficult for a disclosing personality to interrupt the agent to reciprocate and forces a delay in the reciprocal process. Few Prospects seated while a presenter stands will interrupt the speaker. If the person standing discloses several times, the seated party may become anxious to reciprocate. The highly disclosing person, anxious to reciprocate, begins to disclose, and the less disclosing party is cued to do likewise as the disclosing party signals trust in the agent.

For example, the Agent might say from a standing position: **"I want to thank you for being here. Judi and I appreciate you taking the time to come to our offices. We have been in real estate for a combined 40 years, and we put great importance on the professional marketing of your home and how we will help you accomplish your goals. When we met at your home, we promised to provide you with a complete package of information about marketing your home and an analysis of your home value. This will help in determining a recommended listing price. We can also discuss the most likely time to sell your home. Our presentation today is in two parts. The first part is about our marketing program and how we collaboratively work with you to get your home sold at the highest possible price in the time frame that you have. Second, we delve deeper into the analysis of your home and our recommendations. If you don't mind, we will begin with the marketing program. Do you have any questions before we begin?"**

The agent can sit, and this action cues a prospect that it is time for them to talk, disclose, reciprocate, or ask questions. The agent must remember to use a visualization exercise at this time. By imagining that they are possessed with large eyes and large elephant ears and that their ears are raised, and their eyes intensely focused on the Prospect, the agent can suppress their desire to talk and allow the other parties to talk, reciprocate, and inform. They should focus their attention on everything that is said and can be seen at this time while simultaneously listening for appropriate times to disclose without interrupting the disclosures by the other parties in the communication.

When the agent allows a prospect, who may have developed a pent-up need to talk, to have their complete attention, the gates are opened to interpersonal communications with a prospect. The agent must give the parties to the conversation their full undivided attention and display active listening skills. There can be no effort by the agent to interrupt the outpouring of information that follows. The more the person discloses, the more likely the agent will have the opportunity to learn, relate, and empathize with a prospect

Social Conditioning – Sales Process

While most professional sales training emphasizes something called Prospecting, this method proposed changes in the methods of Prospecting in a significant way. Social conditioning may have caused people to expect certain behavior from a salesperson. When this behavior changes to avoiding agent speak, they are often surprised and impressed as the change allows them to be more important than what the salesperson has to say.

The typical salesperson has a list of information they would like to learn about a prospect. Working from this list can come across as a qualifying method. This is a product sales-oriented behavior and is not recommended. By priming the pump for disclosure, the agent allows a prospect to answer multiple questions without asking those questions. The agent must listen intently to the information provided, reflecting an attitude of interest and, at times, a lack of understanding to cause a prospect to expand on their thoughts or ideas. By writing down notes on a blank page, the agent signals the client that their responses are guiding the conversation rather than a pre-set agenda of the agent. A list of questions used to qualify is a clear signal of a salesperson's agenda.

I have found it helpful when finding out information about a client's needs and wants to ask a straight-forward question of the client, "Hego, do you mind if I take notes?" This causes the client to see that you are interested in what they have to say and that you have given them the power to disclose as they see fit. However, One must be careful that when permitted to take notes, the agent takes notes and demonstrates that what they have learned is vital to them.

If the agent moves to a presentation mode while this outpouring of information occurs, they can terminate the disclosure and cause a prospect to stop disclosing. This can sometimes be characterized as a retreat mechanism by a prospect.

Withdrawal Effect

The agent should be aware of the situation when a person demonstrates a retreat mechanism. This is often called a withdrawal effect. This is when a prospect declines to reciprocate when disclosed to, changes the subject, or provides some other evidence of discomfort. This should make the agent more intensely tuned in to other factors that could be working behind the scenes that would cause a prospect to be cautious or secretive.

Responsibility to Use Information Properly

Self-Disclosure & Reciprocity is an essential and far-reaching interpersonal communications technique for the agent. **It must also be used responsibly.** Prospects often tell the agent things they might not intend to share. It is incumbent upon the agent to keep confidential the information disclosed and remember the responsibilities of an agent to be highly ethical when working with a client as a fiduciary.

Most Important Concept

It could be argued that Self-Disclosure & Reciprocity is the most important concept for a Consultative Agent to master. It is used in almost all areas of client and Prospect interaction. In the following chapters, it will be referenced and referred to frequently. One more thought from Jourard adds dimension to the concept.

"Self-disclosure follows an attitude of love and trust. If I love someone, not only do I strive to know him, but I also display my love by letting him know me. At the same time, by so doing, I permit him to love me." (Jourard, S. M., The Transparent Self, 1971, p. 5)

Back to Hego Hoffburg

One final comment about Mr. Hego Hoffburg: on the seventh night that I was in Buenos Aires with Hego, he asked to take me to dinner and wanted me to visit his home before dinner. I, of course, agreed. It would have been very impolite to refuse.

After picking me up, we drove to one of the most significant buildings in Buenos Aires. After parking, we proceed to the penthouse floor and his home. I met Mrs. Hoffburg and was introduced to their three highly personable children. I could see that Hego wanted to impress me with his children, which was a psychological want I could help him realize. He smiled, and his eyes showed his great pride in his family. My being impressed with his children further demonstrated my openness to his needs and established a relationship of trust and liking.

The Hoffburgs lived in one of the most elaborate and impressive homes I have ever visited. They were among the super-wealthy in Argentina. Hego was dressed in a costly suit and looked the part of a highly successful person, as did his entire family. At the convention where we first met, he might not have wanted people to know his social status. I am very happy to have the opportunity to get to know him and his family, and I will never forget my time in Buenos Aires. Being a real estate agent brings you into contact with people you might never meet in a different profession. As luck would have it, the man in the rumpled brown suit inspired me.

CHAPTER 07 | KEYSTONE CONCEPT: THE THEORY OF THE MASK

It's possible that some Prospects won't feel comfortable expressing their honest thoughts and emotions, which can make communication more difficult and make it more challenging for service providers to fulfill their requirements. To overcome this obstacle, I recommend agents call upon the idea known as the Theory of the Mask. This idea proposes that prospects may conceal their genuine emotions by wearing a "mask" of politeness. Accepting and correctly interpreting their mask is essential for productive conversations with them. Agents can build stronger relationships with Prospects by learning to recognize the presence of the mask, allowing them to understand their Prospects better.

Poker Face – Steve Mark

Our experience with Steve Mark will give you a deep understanding of the potential problems of a Prospect wearing a mask. We had not met or spoken to Steve Mark until the meeting at his home with his estranged wife. She had declined to meet at our offices and asked us to meet her at her home instead. They were going through a difficult divorce, and Julianne called us and asked to meet about selling their home. Steve sat at the end of the table, at least two chairs away from us, and his **"poker face"** was set in stone. He kept his arms folded and said only a few words throughout the meeting. Our efforts to include him were met with a blank stare and no responses, not even the blinking of an eye.

It is not unusual for an agent to be involved in a situation like this; we have experienced this several times. The party in the divorce that arranges a meeting with any agent tends to cause the other party to be negative about anyone their counterpart recommends. While it is not unusual to experience this cold shoulder, one never becomes comfortable with the prevalent tension in the room. We made our usual "team" presentation and tried to establish ourselves as the experts in marketing and the collaborative agents we were. It is hard to collaborate with someone who won't speak or respond when spoken to, as Steve was.

After completing our presentation and answering a few questions from Julianne, she indicated that they were ready to move forward, and we began the process of preparing and signing representation agreements that allowed us to list their home for sale. There were no questions about our professional service fee (commission) for selling their home. Steve finally asked, **"Will you be sure and include me in all communications, negotiations, and discussions?"**

I looked at Steve and calmly reassured him in my most empathetic manner, **"Yes, of course, you both will be treated equally and included in all discussions, and anything said to either of you will be shared with the other. We will treat you with great respect and consideration as we know how difficult this is for you both."**

I further explained that we both had been through divorces and the process of selling a home and would be discreet in all we said and did. Steve looked at us and did not comment, and his **"mask,"** which was at least two inches thick did not budge. We left the meeting thinking that Steve had to be a cold individual and that he had the personality of a brick. We were wrong about Steve Mark and will share more as we discuss the **"Theory of the Mask."**

Sidney Jourard, in the book, *The Transparent Self*, writes about the masks people wear.

> *"In a society which pits man against man, as in a poker game, people do keep a poker face; they wear a mask and let no one know what they are up to. In a society where man is for man, the psychological iron curtain is dropped." (1971, p. 6)*

The Mask – A Visualization Exercise

The Mask is a vital visualization exercise for understanding how prospects hide their feelings and emotions when communicating. Everyone wears a mask when they talk to or meet someone they do not know or trust. Some people wear very thin masks, while others wear masks that are quite thick. The fact that the mask may be adapted to suit a person's gender and personality type is one of the intriguing aspects of this accessory. A person's career might affect how ready they are to divulge information, with occupations such as accounting often connected with more concealing behaviors. A person's perception of their safety and privacy is another issue that might affect the mask. Some people would feel more at ease if they didn't provide personal information like their name or contact details because they believe that this will shield them from future contact or communication that isn't welcomed. While teaching in Europe, I found that many other cultures wear a thicker safety mask than others, particularly in the United States.

When people are highly emotionalized, they tend to wear a mask that is quite thick, but sometimes, they remove their mask quickly and reveal themselves and all their vulnerabilities. This often happens when they trust and find that someone they are talking to is compassionate and understanding. Such was the case with Steve Mark. The agent must be sensitive to the problems and challenges people face daily and not harshly judge when they see dysfunction in relationships. The agent must avoid believing or feeling the situation has anything to do with them.

Several weeks after meeting Steve at his home with his estranged wife, we had a meeting with Steve at our offices. He was different outside his estranged wife's presence, and we had a very interactive and productive conversation. He was not at all cold and detached as we had thought. He was an intuitive and sensitive person. He shared his reasons for divorce with us; we listened and kept our thoughts and opinions to ourselves. We filed his comments away, never to be spoken of again.

Sometimes, training in sales and marketing provides professionals with a misconception about professionalism. They might see being professional as highly focused on the task at hand and insensitive to what is happening in a Prospect's mind. Jourard writes about this in *The Transparent Self* when talking about the training of medical professionals. He writes,

> *"I believe that professional training encourages graduates*
> *to wear a professional mask, to limit their behavior to the range*
> *that proclaims their professional status." (1971, p. 178)*

Jourard seems to believe that this professional mask is occasionally a barrier to communication with an already cautious person who wants information and might fear disclosing their situation. Jourard goes on to write:

> *"Patients are exposed not to human beings who have the expertise,*
> *but to "experts" who are dehumanized and dehumanizing." (1971, p. 178)*

Many real estate agents believe their task is to help someone sell or purchase a home. This is a clear indicator of the product salesperson. They are intensely focused on the product rather than the person they are talking with. Frequently they present themselves as the "expert" and forget to relate to a prospect in a more human way. Empathy is often forgotten.

Dealing With Client Conflict

With Steve and Julianne Mark, there was a bigger problem than just the home sale. There was a family breakup, and if the agent is so focused on solving the problem of selling the home, they can come across as cold and indifferent to the real problem that the clients are experiencing. This is one of the reasons that I try to deal with the real problem rather than just the symptoms that are present at the time. Selling Steve and Julianne's home was just one step in reorganizing their lives. Both would need to find another place to live and begin a new chapter in their separate lives.

Some callers who contact an agent are not as conflicted as Steve and Julianne. The agent never knows when they will receive a call that includes a situation. They must be aware of the possibilities and remain open to dialogue and empathy.

What must the Agent do to make someone feel comfortable enough to disclose their contact information and open their communications channels? Removal of the salesperson's mask of professionalism might help. This might seem to contradict the idea of professionalism having value. This is answered by the question, whose interpretation of professionalism is being considered? Professionalism without personalization can be cold and off-putting.

In an in-person meeting, a handshake and eye contact may be enough to disarm a prospect, but adding a disclosure at the same time helps accomplish the objective more quickly. It could be as simple as, **"Hi, I'm Smart Agent with The Renaissance Group. How are you today?"** This, combined with a friendly handshake and a nice smile, followed by paying complete attention to their response, is often enough to open the door to conversation. When on the telephone, there is an absence of a friendly smile or handshake. Therefore the agent must find a way to personalize the contact and open the communications channels.

The warmth in the voice, but most importantly, a keen sense of hearing and listening, is required. Empathy is an important variable in this regard. Demonstrating empathy can be a method of disarming the other person and, at the same time, having them perceive you as more than a salesperson.

The empathetic agent has a distinct advantage over many agents unaware of the value of empathy. Sometimes, agents are so focused on getting to the point, that they forget that the point is the client. For example, this book was not written to get to the point but to help the agent fully understand the complexity of the industry and the clients they will serve.

People Buy from People They Know & Like

If you agree that most people buy from people they know and like, then it is important to see and like a Prospect and for a Prospect to see and like the agent. The mask must be removed to see what is behind it and get to know the real person. Few people will remove their masks before feeling comfortable, so a strategy must be employed that causes them to be willing to remove their masks and trust. Practicing disclosing words and general information in a script that isn't delivered as a script will prepare the Agent to provide early disclosure and increase the likelihood of reciprocal disclosure.

While teaching in Germany, I learned firsthand that the masks people wore to my lectures were sometimes very thick. First, the attendee had to translate from English to their native language. Then they had to be willing to be seen, which required removing the mask. My lecture and exercises about Self-Disclosure & Reciprocity was one of the most popular.

Listening & Reciprocal Disclosure

With a Prospect, safe would be to feel protected, respected, listened to, and appreciated. If the other party in the communications discloses, trust can be gained as the disclosing person demonstrates trust by disclosing first. Hego Hoffburg must have felt this way when I spoke to him in the lobby. I wasn't worried about time or getting to the point but rather about establishing a relationship with Hego and his brother Alfred.

The practice of listening for times to reciprocate with disclosure is paramount. If the caller says, **"My children and I were driving by this property, and I was curious about the asking price, number of bedrooms, and if the property has a large yard?"** Immediate disclosure is beneficial to building trust between the parties in the conversation.

When a prospect can trust someone, they might be willing to remove a portion of their mask first and demonstrate openness. If the agent said, **"My name is Smart Agent, and I am a REALTOR® with The Renaissance Group. How are you today? I have three children. How many children do you have, and how old are they?"** They have begun disclosing basic information and sent a psychological signal to the other party that they are not afraid to disclose and are interested in the caller's situation. Asking a question at this point also interrupts the caller's original agenda and allows the agent to assert control over the direction of the conversation.

While actively listening for disclosure of any kind, a reciprocal disclosure must follow. It is imperative for the agent to immediately respond with their disclosures of information of a suitable kind whenever a client or Prospect discloses information to them. Without this kind of two-way information exchange, the other person may feel threatened or suspicious, which might end the dialogue. The ability of real estate agents to build a sense of trust and openness with their Prospects through disclosing personal information about themselves might encourage clients to feel more at ease when discussing their thoughts and emotions. This back-and-forth of disclosures paves the way for a Prospect to disclose themselves to the agent, making it possible for the two parties to engage in more prosperous and significant communication. In the long run, this may improve relationships and outcomes for everyone involved.

Disclosing at a Similar Level

It is not just about disclosing; it is reciprocating whenever disclosed to at a similar level of intimacy. If a Prospect says, **"I am moving here from out of town and want to find a home for my family…."** A reciprocal disclosure by the Agent of a similar nature, like, **"I understand your situation; when I moved to Dallas from California, I had to adjust to the way homes are built here in the Dallas area."** The reciprocal disclosure process is established, and the conversation will likely continue positively because a prospect will reciprocate further. The concept of Self-Disclosure & Reciprocity requires immediate reciprocity whenever disclosed to by another person, thus allowing the mask to be dropped and forming a relationship of trust and confidence to be built.

If a person feels comfortable and trusts another, they will most likely remove part of their mask but rarely remove it all. This depends upon the individual's personality, but only a few people are immune to this interpersonal communication technique. A relationship can be built if a prospect removes a portion of the mask and trusts. How does an agent get a prospect to remove their mask? Through Self Disclosure and Reciprocal Disclosure in a trusting and friendly way.

When the agent's motivations are client-benefit centered, disclosure by a client allows the agent to help the client. An agent that is afraid to disclose that they are excited about working with a client and demonstrating affinity is unlikely to be trusted. The agent must open their communication channels first to build trust and confidence.

Observation & the Brain

The brain observes through multiple senses, but the eyes sending information to the brain provides minor reactions, nuances, and much information. To feel safe, an agent may need to remove their mask first, even if it is a small amount of mask at a time. Removing the mask might be scary for the agent as well. Since the person is unknown, there might be fear and hesitancy to reveal. There could be a fear of rejection. However, to get to know the prospect, the agent needs to remove a portion of the mask and encourage reciprocity from the prospect. The agent, to be successful, must be willing to take the risk of rejection and experience discomfort when talking to a caller that appears cold or disinterested.

The relationship with Steve Mark developed with Steve becoming a long-term client. We are grateful he was willing to remove his mask and allow us to see the real person behind the **"Poker Face"**.

CHAPTER 08 | KEYSTONE CONCEPT:
THE "ONION SKIN THEORY"

The Onion Skin Theory is a concept that can assist in understanding the layers of a person's personality and figuring out how to connect with that individual. Each individual possesses numerous layers of their personality, similar to the layers of an onion, which may be peeled away to expose further information about the person's identity and what they want. Agents may create deeper relationships with their clients and deliver better service by gaining knowledge of this idea. When considered in this light, the Onion Skin Theory is an invaluable resource for anyone interested in enhancing their capacity for communication and developing more meaningful relationships with their Prospects.

This peeling away of the Mask that a person is wearing can be illustrated with a visualization exercise. This exercise explains how the Self-Disclosure & Reciprocity Concept works in communication. This provides another way of looking at how to cause the removal of the mask that a Prospect is wearing and might be more insightful for some.

Closing your eyes momentarily allows you to visualize a large yellow onion, thus beginning the exercise. This onion has a flaky and super thin outer layer, flaking off easily to reveal another layer. The outside of the onion is not very important but must be removed to see inside the layers of the onion.

The outer layer of the onion includes information that is not private. This includes where someone works, if they believe the weather is hot or cold, and other information. Simple basic un-threatening information makes up the outer layer of the onion. It could be considered meaningless information, yet it is part of the daily dialogue of most people. "How are you today?" And the response would be, "Fine, how about you?"

This might be normal communication between strangers. Does it mean that the person is fine? Not necessarily. They could be having a terrible, otherwise very bad, day. However, they might not be willing to share that with a total stranger unless the other person reveals their actual opinion of the day they are having.

If someone said, "How are you today?" And you replied, "Rotten... I was given a speeding ticket this morning, and when I got to the office, I realized I had forgotten my backpack. I am distraught with myself." The person asking might respond, "Oh, I am so sorry... I shouldn't have asked." You might reply, "No, thank you for asking, and I'm sorry if I dumped my problems on you."

"Oh, it's ok," the person says. "Last week, I had a day like that also."

You might reply, "What happened?" Up until now, the conversation has not been very personal. Because one person disclosed and revealed themselves, the stage is set for actual, meaningful communications between strangers that could result in a dialogue between people who get to know each other by removing the mask one piece at a time. Peeling away the onion involves listening, relating, and a willingness to take some minimal risk through disclosure.

Suppose I asked you to cut a large onion in half and hold one-half of the onion so that the inside can be viewed. In that case, we can see a metaphor that explains the Onion Skin Theory of Interpersonal Communications. The cross-section of the onion reveals levels of the onion from the fragile outer part of the onion to thicker layers of the onion as the sections move closer to the center of the onion. The layers become the thickest when the center of the onion is examined. The Center of the Onion, exceptionally large and thick, represents a person's deepest, most personal self. It includes the most personal fears, important dreams, and possibly heartbreak. It is truly the real person, and very few people know the center of the onion of an individual. Some people will not allow anyone to know the contents of the center of their onion.

As one moves out from the center of the onion, the layers become less dense, and each layer represents another stratum of a person's life. These layers are different, however, for each human being. Because each person is unique and has different motivations and life experiences, the layers vary significantly for everyone's symbolic onion.

One person's personal goals, like having children, might be closest to the center, while another person's business goals might reside in the center of the onion. As the outer layers of the onion are examined, they are thinner, less dense, and, therefore, less protected. People would be less fearful of disclosing information maintained in these outer layers. It is less likely that a person could be deeply hurt because of the disclosure of information on the outer layers of the onion.

As the extreme outer layers of the onion are examined, one can observe that these layers are fragile, less protected, and contain very little profoundly personal or private information. Therefore, these communication layers could be removed more easily because disclosing information about them isn't very personal, and there is little fear in sharing this information. Getting someone to disclose information on the outer layer is relatively easy as there is less fear or risk. Getting someone to disclose more profound information about the onion can be challenging unless the outer layer of the onion has been peeled away. Various pieces of the Mask that people wear are like the layers of an onion. Some must be peeled away before other pieces can be removed and trust earned.

Through many client interviews and conversations, I have found that needs are often easily identified. People generally know what they need but seldom know everything they want. When asking someone what they want, you encourage them to express a desire that may have been kept private for years.

If the relationship has progressed as hoped for, they might answer. When I asked, "What is it that, if you could have it, would be most satisfying for you?" The clients most often take time to reflect before answering.

In the next meeting, they often say, "I've thought about it, and I have always wanted an Art Studio to pursue my passion for art."

CHAPTER 09│KEYSTONE CONCEPT: INTUITIVE THINKING RISING…

In the world of real estate, there are moments of complete indecision and instant decision-making that can surprise and delight the real estate agent. Purchasing or selling a home is often one of the most significant financial decisions a person can make. It can also be one of the most emotional.

Many believe this is a complex agonizing, paralyzing decision process that takes extreme due diligence, research, investigation, inspection, and financial management that is seriously time-consuming. **It does not…** I have often been astonished at how quickly someone can make a huge and important decision, such as purchasing or selling a home.

Purchasing a property is not just about a business transaction but also a meaningful and formative event in a person's life. It is not only about the money involved in the purchase; it is also about the significant financial commitments that come with owning real estate. These obligations may include additional costs like maintenance, real estate taxes, insurance, and the initial cost of the home itself. Purchasing a property of any kind also necessitates adjusting to a new way of life and a different schedule each day, which may be extremely difficult. Bob Grenier was in the throes of making such a momentous decision.

Case Study – Bob Grenier

Bob was an engineer with a significant automotive company looking to own a home for the first time. It is a little unusual to get a sixty-five-year-old first-time home buyer. Bob was famous. He was considered a pioneer at the automotive company he worked for as he was one of the first Americans to be hired when it opened its doors in America. He had been with the company for years and could have already retired, but he loved to work. He loved the company. He was a dedicated employee and lived for what he did.

Bob was single, and he and I had much in common. We were almost the same age, and our birthdays were days apart. I first sensed Bob "blink" after we met. We hit it off from the minute we talked on the telephone! He made an instant decision to work with me. He was easy to work with and loved to teach me about the proper operation of my car. I listened intently to his suggestions about setting my parking brake and other vehicle operation and maintenance ideas.

The book, "*blink*," by Malcolm Gladwell describes an exciting phenomenon he calls "blink." Noted art experts are invited to view a statue, called a Kouros, worth millions of dollars. Several of the world's most excellent experts in Kouros had already authenticated the statue for the Getty Museum. When the statue was revealed, the renowned experts had varying reactions, but one blinked and said, "It's a fraud!" Some even felt nauseous but didn't know why they felt that way when viewing the Kouros. One commented it looked "fresh." The author writes,

> *"In the first two seconds of looking -- in a single glance, -- they were able to understand more about the essence of the statue than the team at the Getty was able to understand after fourteen months. blink is a book about those first two seconds." (2005, p. 8)*

One expert's reaction was both intellectual and emotional. This explains how he could be repulsed and nauseated. He was emotionally involved in the opinion. The object is confirmed fake, and the Getty Museum loses a great deal of money. How did the art expert know that the object was fake in the blink of an eye? It was his "gut" feeling, and he went with it. They could have been wrong, but they weren't. Of course, the Museum paid attention to the comments and reinvestigated to confirm authenticity. Eventually, it was confirmed to be a fake Kouros.

People like Bob Grenier often listen to and act on their " gut " feelings. His reaction to me, probably the first person to ever take the time to explain the benefits of home ownership to him, was practical and made sense. I suspect Bob had one of those "Wow" moments after hearing my explanation. He had lived in the Los Angeles area his entire life and had never envisioned becoming a homeowner. The prices of homes in his area may have been a part of this lack of motivation. It had not appealed to him, so he had never investigated the possibilities until now. His move to our area caused him to reconsider. Once he was given a picture in his mind, he blinked and said, **"Yes, it's time to be a homeowner."** His rapid cognition was not at all unusual. Several data points linked together caused him to decide almost instantly to move forward.

Rapid Cognition & Intuition

In his book, *"blink,"* Gladwell also writes about "rapid cognition" or "intuition," which is quite intriguing. Gladwell describes a concept in another paragraph called "thin slicing." This thin slicing to Gladwell uses data points to make a rapid decision based on prior experience. He writes,

> *"The answer is that when our unconscious engages in thin-slicing, what we are doing is an automated, accelerated unconscious version of what Gottman does with his videotapes and equations." (2005, p. 23)*

This might be commonly referred to as a "Gut" instinct. It might be both rapid cognition in concert with an emotional reaction. This could include a childhood memory or some other visualization recalled by the person seeing something that triggers them. Emotion heightens both awareness and perception. Contrary to widespread perception, emotions are not the enemy of real estate agents but rather their allies. Emotions are crucial in heightening the client's attention and increasing their awareness of the situation. Because of this elevated emotional state, Prospects are more susceptible to what they see, hear, and sense in the property they are interested in buying. It helps them make informed and confident decisions.

While working with Prospects contemplating the purchase or sale of a property, emotions will unavoidably be a factor. The degree to which these feelings are present will vary from client to client. These feelings can be used to develop an emotional connection with their clients and then utilize that connection to guide their Prospects more successfully through the process.

Blink and rapid cognition can help explain the well-known real estate axiom, "Curb Appeal." When showing homes to buyers and driving to a home for a viewing, it is not unusual for a client to say, **"This looks lovely"** or **"I'm not crazy about this one."** This is an example of an almost instantaneous reaction, a "blink." An agent should not ignore these reactions and must follow up on the statement regardless of its positive or negative nature to ensure they understand a Prospect's comments. One way to do this in the instance of negative comments is to say, **"Oh, do you still want to see this home? You should listen to your first reaction or gut instinct and proceed carefully. The inside of the home might change your mind, but if your first reaction is telling you this is not the home for you, we should pause a moment."** Then, at the opportune time, the agent could say, **"This reminds me of Malcolm Gladwell's book *"blink,"* let me explain."**

When explaining this concept to a Prospect, several goals are accomplished. It is unlikely that a Prospect has read Gladwell's book, and if they haven't, the agent has "demonstrated proficiency" in an area in which a Prospect doesn't expect an agent to have expertise. This is a critical perception-changing moment. Often the Prospect does not see an agent as much more than a friendly person with a real estate license. When teaching them something they do not know, the agent widens their perception window about the agent and allows a Prospect to see the agent differently and positively.

When a Prospect says, "I didn't know that!" the agent has likely increased their positive perception by the Prospect. Providing a Prospect information that they do not know, and did not expect an agent to know, increases their esteem and confidence in the agent and improves the agent's position with a Prospect. It can also differentiate the agent from others the Prospect may have met or dealt with. Perhaps no one has ever explained a "Wow" moment. In his book, *The Illusion of Conscious Will*, Wegner excitingly explains the phenomenon. He writes:

"The happiest inconsistency between intention and action occurs when a great idea pops into mind. The "action" in this case is the occurrence of the idea and tendency to say "Eureka!" or "Aha!" is our usual acknowledgment that this particular insight was not something we were planning in advance." (2002, p. 81)

While Wegner's quote explains how an idea pops into our heads and causes us to say "Wow" or "Aha," the explanation is similar. When someone presents an idea to us that we perceive to be a great idea, we might act by saying, "Wow." This new idea surprises us and makes a positive impression. Of course, it is sometimes customary to suddenly accept that the idea is our own. Yet, the impact has been registered in the brain.

The agent must remember that a Prospect sees and immediately begins to evaluate everything the agent sees and does. This is often done intrinsically, and the agent will not know that it is happening while it is happening. When acting differently and providing knowledgeable and relevant information, the agent can build trust and confidence with a Prospect. In his book, *blink*, Gladwell writes,

"This new notion of the adaptive unconscious is thought of, instead, as a kind of giant computer that quickly and quietly processes a lot of the data we need in order to keep functioning as human beings." (2005, p. 11)

A Prospect's reaction to seeing or hearing something can trigger thoughts and emotions. In the real estate business, it is often difficult to separate emotional reactions from reactions of just a business nature.

When the agent has the opportunity to teach something new to a Prospect, the agent can supply a "Wow" moment and demonstrate value in the relationship. The agent can pave the way for this teaching moment by saying,

"I find that my clients don't want to waste time looking at homes they don't feel they will like. While some prefer to go ahead and look at the homes when they have a negative first reaction to them, they often comment that it was a waste of time. While it is possible to change your mind when you see the inside of the home, which causes a negative first reaction, it is a low probability compared to seeing a home you love from the beginning. If you tell me you don't need to see a home that we approach, just let me know your thoughts. I don't want to waste your valuable time on a home you don't like, and we will most likely find a better choice during our time together. I have previewed all the homes I am showing you today, and if I know that the inside has special features that you should see, I will let you know, and you can decide whether to tour the home. We can also return to this home later if you change your mind! What do you think?"

The benefit is that the Agent avoids wasting a Prospect's time and reminds a Prospect that the agent believes their time is valuable. Just as importantly, the agent avoids squandering their own time. Every minute with a Prospect is of great value to an agent. Maximizing Agent productivity is extremely important to the agent's future success. The better use of time allows the agent to invest more time with prospects and clients.

The above mentioned method establishes the collaborative approach recommended for working with a Prospect. It allows a Prospect to see that the agent values the Prospect's opinion as equal to or higher than the value an Agent has for their own opinions. It supports the contention by the agent that they will always place a Prospect's wants and needs ahead of their own. A Prospect may have believed that the agent wants to sell a home, any home, and therefore the agent's opinions may need to be overseen. Collaboration builds trust with the Prospect and positions the agent as a highly knowledgeable and valued asset to a Prospect.

The concept of "blink" also tells us why photos, brochures, other media, and information on the Internet are so crucial to success. Just as in person, a Prospect often forms an opinion about a home from first seeing or reading about a home on the Internet. This explains why a Prospect might pick out a home to tour even when it fails to meet any of their described needs and wants previously shared with their agent. They may have blinked when they saw the photos and followed up on their gut reaction by asking to tour the home. They may ask to see the home even when it meets none of their home selection criteria.

The Agent is "Surprised"

Many agents are surprised when a Prospect who has asked only to see homes with four bedrooms in a particular neighborhood or doesn't have a swimming pool wants to see a home that doesn't meet their stated criteria completely. When a Prospect does this, the agent should listen carefully and take the Prospect seriously. Perhaps the property will be ruled out, but the agent must prioritize their request and give the Prospect's opinion importance. Failure to do so might send a negative message to a Prospect about the willingness to put their needs and wants first. In addition, when a Prospect finds that the property is lacking and has wasted their time, they may listen to their agent more carefully and give the agent's research and opinion more credibility. The agent might say, **"I am happy that we looked at this property you identified, as I have learned more about you and your wants. Thanks for bringing this one to my attention."**

The agent should also not be surprised that they want to buy a property that misses their stated criteria and hardly resembles what they said they wanted. The agent who is selling a product might be confused by this. The Consultative Agent is grateful that they have found what they wanted and that time was not wasted looking at properties that a Prospect wouldn't purchase. Agents should be careful in assuming that finding a home for a client is the most important reason for their existence.

The real estate professional must recognize that the home selection is a natural result of the agent providing excellent advice. Most of the time, who identified the home, has little to do with a Prospect's satisfaction. In a collaborative environment, the insurance Agent or Mortgage lender could bring a property to the agent or client's attention. This is the purpose of collaboration. Putting a Prospect first in every way is difficult, as the typical agent takes great pride in their knowledge and expertise.

Listening to the "gut" is only the beginning of a decision, but this is not just whimsical thinking or speculation. In the book, *Rewire Your Brain*, John Arden explains how the brain is structured to allow for fast decision-making. He explains,

> *"The human brain has a thousand times more spindle cells than our closest ape relatives possess. Many theorists regard this as one of the reasons we make snap judgments. These cells are so named because they look like spindles, with a large bulb at one end and a long, thick extension." (2010, p. 13)*

The agent might move forward with a client who has expressed a desire to go forward with a property by saying, **"Well, clearly your "gut" is telling you this might be the one. With that in mind, due diligence should be discussed."** Gladwell also discussed this in his book, *blink*. People generally are suspicious of forming an immediate decision or opinion without time, analysis, and deliberation. He writes,

"I think we are innately suspicious of this kind of rapid cognition. We live in a world that assumes that the quality of a decision is directly related to the time and effort that went into making it." (2005, p. 13)

The Agent who recognizes that a Prospect has come to a decision but is uncertain about the pathway forward might need reassurance that if they go forward, they will be safe. The Consultative Agent must explain how this safety can be maintained if a Prospect decides to act on their "gut" reaction.

Putting on the Brakes

Bob Grenier had a strong positive reaction when I explained to him on a conference call the fundamental benefits of home ownership. I suspect Bob had one of these **"Wow"** moments after hearing my explanation. He had lived in the Los Angeles area his whole life and had never envisioned being a homeowner. The prices of homes in his area may have been a part of this lack of motivation. It had not appealed to him, so he had never investigated the possibilities until now. His move to our area caused him to reconsider.

The Practice of real estate provides the Agent with numerous opportunities to observe situations that involve a "blink" on the part of a client. Understanding this concept allows the Agent to assist the Client in making good decisions, sometimes instantly, but almost always verified with comprehensive due diligence. The collaborative way of working with a client establishes the need and access to these other resources early in the process. This can be done by bringing those additional resources into collaboration with a Prospect in a Collaboration Hub.

The Agent can help clients satisfy their needs and wants and, at the same time, create a *"Raving Fan*!" To accomplish this, the Agent must demonstrate proficiency in real estate far beyond the client's expectations.

People generally tend to psychologically support an opinion they form, even in the face of dissenting opinions. The Agent must remember that a Prospect could form a positive opinion about a home and, despite later evidence that the home is less than desirable, refuse to accept this information. In this situation, the Agent could say, **"Just to reiterate, when you find a home and love it, you would want to proceed with due diligence, including inspections and appraisals. I will be there every step to ensure that the inspections and further due diligence are completed to your satisfaction and that the home you loved on the first visit is still the right home for you!"**

When the Agent brings negative information to a Prospects attention to protect them, the Prospect can see that the Agent is more interested in their success and good choices than they are concerned about making money. The consultative agent's goal is to help clients make good decisions about their real estate options. Homes may come and go; clients are hopefully here to stay.

With Bob Grenier, the above commentary is almost precisely how things happened. After touring several homes, we pulled up to a particular home, and Bob blinked. Upon entering the home, he said, **"I think this one is for me."**

Bob purchased that property, and the decision was made in the blink of an eye. He never looked back and still lives in that home today. We speak frequently, and he has retired and loves his home. He is a proud homeowner, and speaking to Bob always brightens my day because **I helped him make the move that changed his life for the better. This is one of the most satisfying accomplishments of being a REALTOR®.**

This discussion above demonstrates the benefits of Illuminating the Possibilities… for the client. Sharing this story and its commentary, the client sees a different side of the agent. They see that the Agent is interested in the psychology behind behavior and is well-read and knowledgeable. They learn something they didn't expect to learn from the agent. This opens their eyes and minds, both consciously and subconsciously, to the Agent's ability to expand their thinking. This is not what they expected. It is not just meeting their expectations but redefining what the Agent can do for them and what the agent can teach them. This is the "wow" moment in that it differentiates the Agent, establishes higher value, and can make a client into a "Raving Fan!"

Illuminating the Possibilities… is more than a concept. It is a philosophy for relating to and working with clients. Opening eyes, minds, and emotions regarding a decision is far more than just details and statistics about a property. It is about the home they have imagined and the safe place they want to create for their family. It is about helping them to make their dreams a reality.

CHAPTER 10 | KEYSTONE CONCEPT: "PROFESSIONALISM IS SYNONYMOUS WITH VALUE..."

Professionalism is not simply a catchphrase when it comes to constructing a successful career in real estate. Instead, it is the foundation upon which agent value is built. Prospects alike are searching for a relationship they can rely on, and maintaining a professional manner is essential to earning that confidence. Professionals can develop a reputation for quality that resounds with their audience if they commit to excelling in all aspects of their work, particularly communication, service, and devotion to quality. In a nutshell, professionalism is not only a trait but an essential factor in determining value.

Judi and I were searching for a way to differentiate ourselves from our competitors in the real estate world. We had a **"unique sales proposition"** in that we were both Real Estate Brokers, had extensive experience, were husband and wife, and had unique skills and talents that allowed us to provide superior services when compared to our competitors.

We wanted to create a higher perceived value of for our services and avoid discounting our fees to compete with other agents. Our fees were the highest compared to many other agents who tended to discount the fees and offer, in our opinion, a lower level of service. We were willing to risk losing some business opportunities to maintain our profit level and continue providing superior marketing services. We were willing to walk on the edge of the abyss to protect our reputation.

Creating an advantage for us over other agents when competing with us for listings in our very popular subdivision in Frisco, Texas, was a priority. The neighborhood was Starwood. I sought a method of creating such value that a Prospect would not ask for a fee discount. If they did ask, I wanted a way to demonstrate a benchmark level of service that competitors could not match.

There were over fifty real estate agents in our community of approximately one thousand homes. It was once one of the most popular neighborhoods in Frisco, Texas. The statistics cited earlier might be recalled at this point. Fifty agents seeking listings in a one-thousand-home neighborhood meant a Homeowner to Agent ratio of twenty households for every agent in the neighborhood. How could we differentiate ourselves when forty-nine other agents also professed to be "Starwood Specialists?" This did not count agents who lived outside Starwood but sought to do business in Starwood.

Industry Specialization & Neighborhood Specialization

To win in Starwood, we had to find a way to demonstrate that we were different and superior in the minds of a Prospect. We chose "marketing skill" as a primary differentiating factor.

Using an idea from my prior business experience, I decided to use an industry specialization approach to build our business model and brand us as the Starwood Specialist. Because of this strategy, we secured the domain name, StarwoodHomes.com and set up email addresses for each of us. Sonny@StarwoodHomes.com and Judi@StarwoodHomes.com

We were active in the HOA (Homeowner Association) and were mailing to and reaching out to the neighborhood in an organized and systematic way. We needed something more. We must create a distinct advantage over other agents when interviewing for a listing opportunity within Starwood. The competition was intense, and many were more successful than we were then. They were the Goliath, and we were the smaller David.

Creating the Mini Home Book

There exists a marketing strategy known in the real estate world as the *"home book."* This strategy called for the listing agents to create a three-ring binder that included comprehensive information about the home, neighborhood, schools, taxes, etc. It was envisioned that a prospect would sit down and review the Home Book for a particular home while visiting a home. This rarely happened. It was too much information and required too much time for Prospective buyers to review while touring several homes in a day. The Home Book always had "Do Not Remove from Property" boldly printed on its front. Most of the time, this book was poorly designed and looked thrown together and unprofessional. There was little risk of it being taken.

Faced with this harsh reality, I wanted to develop something to accomplish our objectives and Brand us as the Starwood Specialist. I showed a client a vacant home priced in the $400,000 range. The client remarked that the marketing materials were terrible. They were color printouts but of inferior quality with numerous typographical errors. The most surprising thing was that the picture of the home on the document was the wrong home. My client remarked, "I wonder if the homeowners know their agent is this incompetent."

This inspired me to immediately do something as it demonstrated to me that the documents in a home were not just about the property but also made a statement about the agent's ability or inability. Most agents prepare marketing materials for the home with little thought of their target audiences. They might think they are just reaching Prospective buyers or an agent showing a Prospective buyer. They are also reaching the homeowner, the homeowner's sphere of influence who visit the homeowner, and any **"neighbors"** who attend an **"open house"** or visit the property. The audience could be large and reach homeowners, buyers, and sellers in the neighborhood or area.

Additionally, I wanted to demonstrate that we were the most professional in our market area. I also sought to reach homeowners who weren't looking to sell their homes at the moment so that they could see what we had created and capture their attention before they needed or wanted to sell to make a move. To summarize, we wanted to create a way of:

- Differentiating Us from Our Competitors
- Protecting our Fee Structure to Avoid Discounting our Fee
- Increasing our Success in Listing Interviews
- Adding value to the Marketing Program for the Homeowners
- Presenting our "Professionalism in Marketing" in a Powerful Way
- Reaching future Home Sellers to plant a seed...

We were already utilizing PageMaker, a very high-end desktop publishing program for our marketing materials in the Consulting sector of our business. This Program later became Adobe InDesign. At that time, we were utilizing the staff at our office to provide Marketing Brochures for inside the home, which was either a one-page two-sided document, perhaps in color, or a two-page brochure. These were provided at no cost to us by the brokerage firm. The materials were created in a template and similar to most other agents placed in their listed properties.

These brochures were being created in a program that was not as robust as InDesign. They showed little creativity and provided nothing more than what other agents provided. They did not differentiate or demonstrate professionalism or proficiency beyond what others could do.

Being Different Makes You Noticeable

Differentiation can change the playing field significantly because most real estate Agents act similarly. Most are product-oriented rather than "Client Centered." When an Agent doesn't sell to them but listens to them and focuses on needs and wants rather than products, a Prospect sees a Consultative Agent willing to collaborate and listen. By demonstrating skills and attitudes that are far different, the Consultative Agent can redefine what the Prospect believes to be true about real estate agents. In the book *Consultative Selling*, the authors provide insight into how this can happen. They write,

> *"Consultative selling represents a day-and-night difference from product selling. It redefines the salesman and his job. It restructures his sales relationships. It repositions the sales function in the marketing mix to bring it more closely into line with the demands of a new selling environment..." (1973, pp. 7-8)*

By changing what the client sees and experiences, the Agent creates a scenario where the Client or Prospect finds a different look and feel to a consultation with a Consultative Agent. They can completely modify the dynamic of the whole process just by moving the focus of the conversation away from the product itself and toward the specific circumstances and goals of a Prospect. The client-centered agent, client goal centered on being more exact, can redefine how they are differentiated from the product-centered salesperson by establishing themselves as a consultant and advocate by creating a scenario tailored to the client's needs, preferences, and goals.

The best possible scenario for a Consultative Collaborative Agent in a competitive meeting is to have the other agents talk about buying and selling homes and about themselves endlessly. The typical product-centered Agent is ill-prepared to discuss important details with the prospect. They are often in a hurry to leave rather than listening when a Prospect wants to talk more about their needs and wants. The Consultative Agent has "time" and is willing to use that time to build a relationship of trust and confidence.

Competitively, the Consultative Agent seeks to present themselves as a more significant value while not claiming to be better than others. Demonstrating that they are different and not having to say better because it becomes apparent to the prospect from what they see, hear, and feel.

Professionalism is Synonymous with Value and is often an inexpensive and effective way to Differentiate oneself from competitors. Being perceived as a Consultative Agent is a differentiator that spells success.

As you read this chapter, we will explain more about how this strategy allowed us to become the most successful real estate agent in Starwood and gain market control in a few short years. As a result of our outreach marketing programs, we sold over 150 homes in Starwood over 15 years. We stopped counting the number of transactions, but if we had to estimate, the final number of homes sold before we moved and left that market was about 180 homes over seventeen years.

They would not tell the entire story. Each client obtained in Starwood provided significant opportunities beyond the professional service fee earned from selling properties in our neighborhood. Their spheres of influence were a fountain of income for our practice.

Setting the Bar Height

When real estate prospects see or hear a highly professional agent, they consciously and intrinsically associate more value with the agent. Professionalism means different things to different people. However, there are some behaviors that almost everyone can agree on that are indicators of professionalism. The audiences for a real estate agent vary significantly in personality, culture, age, family composition, financial status, as well as their opinion about the definition of professional behavior. Therefore, the agent must set the bar for professional behavior to satisfy most of the prospects encountered most of the time.

Fleeting Moments of Visibility

Fleeting moments of visibility are significant to the real estate agent. Most people can agree that some behaviors are attributable to highly professional people. Promptly returning phone calls is one example of a behavior that is often associated with professionalism. Being timely and fully prepared for a meeting is also considered professional behavior by most prospects. Dress is a different matter. How an agent communicates with others is also important to present professionalism.

Some people see professional dress as formal, while others are satisfied with a more casual dress code. The Agent cannot take chances in this regard. The Agent has limited opportunities to **"mind sway"** a prospect.

The real estate agent must present themselves in such a manner as to reach the highest percentage of people they may encounter. For this reason, they must dress to the highest level of expectation that they might encounter daily.

The more quickly an agent can establish their professionalism, the more likely it will be that a prospect can begin to accept the words the agent is saying as beneficial, meaningful, and valuable. This will allow them to both consciously or unconsciously form positive opinions about the agent.

> *"blink is concerned with the very smallest components of our everyday lives—the content and origin of those instantaneous impressions and conclusions that spontaneously arise whenever we meet a new person or confront a complex situation or have to make a decision under conditions of stress." (2005, p. 16)*

Gladwell makes a note of this quote above in his book *blink*. He points out that snap decisions are often made without much analysis or thought. Sometimes they are just a feeling, a notion, an opinion formed without consciously examining all the details. When someone is considering a move by buying or selling a home, there is likely a reasonable degree of self-doubt and stress involved. Under stressful situations, "snap decisions" can be made with amazing clarity.

To be precise, professionalism is Value! It is not just the words said, and that the client hears, it is also what they see, sense, and feel that is going on in their subconscious minds that is important. This is where the concepts of Adaptive Unconsciousness and Adaptive Subconsciousness come into play. An agent must consider both conscious and subconscious opinions that a prospect forms.

Malcolm Gladwell, the author of "*blink*" writes,

> *"For Georgios Dontas, it was the feeling that there was a glass between him and the work. Did they know why they knew? Not at all. But they knew." (2005, p. 11)*

When people see what is generally regarded as highly professional behavior, they just know it when they see it and consciously and subconsciously equate that behavior with higher value. The word intrinsic means; "belonging to the essential nature of a thing: occurring as a natural part of something."

Intuitive Thinking Rising

Individuals intuitively comprehend what defines professional behavior and ascribe more excellent value to individuals who exhibit such behavior. When considered in the context of this discussion, it implies that professional conduct is an essential component of a person's character and something that is inherent to them and comes easily to them.

Consumers are more inclined to place their trust in experts and conduct business with those who exhibit a high level of professionalism, competence, and dependability in their interactions. This demonstrates that professional behavior is not only innate to a person's character but also has concrete benefits in creating credibility and gaining trust among others.

Establishing higher value is vital in building relationships with buyers, sellers, and investors. Perceived higher value frequently overcomes a prospect's doubts about the agent they are interviewing. It also establishes value and overcomes prospects' doubts about what retaining an accomplished and talented Agent costs.

When an Agent wants to have the prospect believe that they bring a higher value than their competitors, the Agent must establish a higher value in the conscious, subconscious, and unconscious mind of the prospect from the very beginning of the relationship. This cannot be done without thinking about it and planning to demonstrate professionalism. All these small things accumulate to form an impression that the Prospect cannot avoid. Multiple exposures of evident professionalism create an internal feeling that an agent is the right choice for a Prospect.

Creating the Mini Home Book

This is where our story about finding a way to demonstrate professionalism and simultaneously accomplish the other goals stated at the beginning of this chapter comes into focus. To accomplish our objectives by creating a "Mini Home Book."

Our <u>Mini Home Book</u> was a Marketing Package available to anyone who toured our listings. It was also available on our website in a pdf format. The package was generally fifteen to twenty pages long, Velo bound with both a front and back cover, printed on high-quality paper, and included the following sections.

- A Professionally written **"Romance Story"** that described the property.
- A professional photographer took twenty or more color photos.
- Captions underneath each photo that was **"benefit-oriented."**
- Detailed information about each room and what each room contained.
- An Upgrade or Updated Items section.
- An entire page about the community, for example, Starwood.
- An entire page about the schools that supported the neighborhood.
- An entire page about the city.
- A brief but well-written profile about the Listing Agent.
- Photos of neighborhood events and activities.

To accomplish this objective, we had to expand our knowledge of the InDesign software. We chose this program because it was one of the best and a robust programs that few people other than designers and printers knew how to use. It was much more potent than most other programs used by agents or their offices. We did not believe that any other agents used the software. In presentations, we would explain,

"This twenty-page document is how we will present your home to the public. The Prospect touring your home can take this with them, and it is available online from our website in a pdf format. Your Marketing Package for your home would be similar, but each is personalized to your home and accentuates the positives that make your home unique.

When we finish the first draft of the document, we ask you to review it and provide us feedback and suggestions for improving it to get the best results. We will collaborate with you on the final version that is printed and placed in your home.

To prepare the document for distribution, we use special paper and cover stock for the front and back of the document. It is printed on our high-quality laser printer. It is nicely bound, and we find that Prospects who take this book tend to keep it, while other types of packages are frequently discarded. This package presents your home to a buyer in a powerful way and, perhaps most importantly, is so nice that they have difficulty throwing it away. They often keep it and continue to explore the material while driving around. This is the most complete and professional home Marketing Package we have seen. It takes between 30 and 40 hours for our team to build this, but we think it is worth the effort as it presents your home most positively."

We learned about using the InDesign program to build the Marketing Package for the homes we listed. Each page included required language, our neighborhood-specific contact information, and slogans that changed yearly, such as "YOUR STARWOOD NEIGHBORHOOD SPECIALIST."

Our "Mini Home Book" accomplished the objectives we had established. We were frequently asked how much it would cost for the Mini Home Book. We replied that it was included in our fee. We explained the development process and how the Prospect would be involved collaboratively.

The most common statement by prospects was, **"So, you will prepare something like this for our home!"** While holding up all the sample marketing brochures, one of us would say, **"Which would you rather have to market your home?"** Our marketing approach was different, and our marketing materials were unique and profound comparatively. We were the most professional. We accomplished our goal of differentiating ourselves from our competitors, established marketing excellence, secured a higher likelihood of success in listing appointments, spread the word about us throughout the Starwood community, and, most importantly, provided higher value to the homeowner while protecting our fee structure.

Impact...

One final note about the impact of the Mini Home Book: we often received a phone call over the years from someone who purchased one of our listings in past years. Upon meeting them for a listing appointment, they would bring out the Mini Home Book they received when touring our listed property. Invariably, they would say, **"Do you still prepare this?"** When this happened, we knew we had the inside track to winning a client as they were already fans.

Sometimes additional expense can be incurred that is worth the cost as it provides a differentiating factor that is worth the expense. We will continue to explain this profitable strategy's impact as we further explore the concept of "Professionalism is Value."

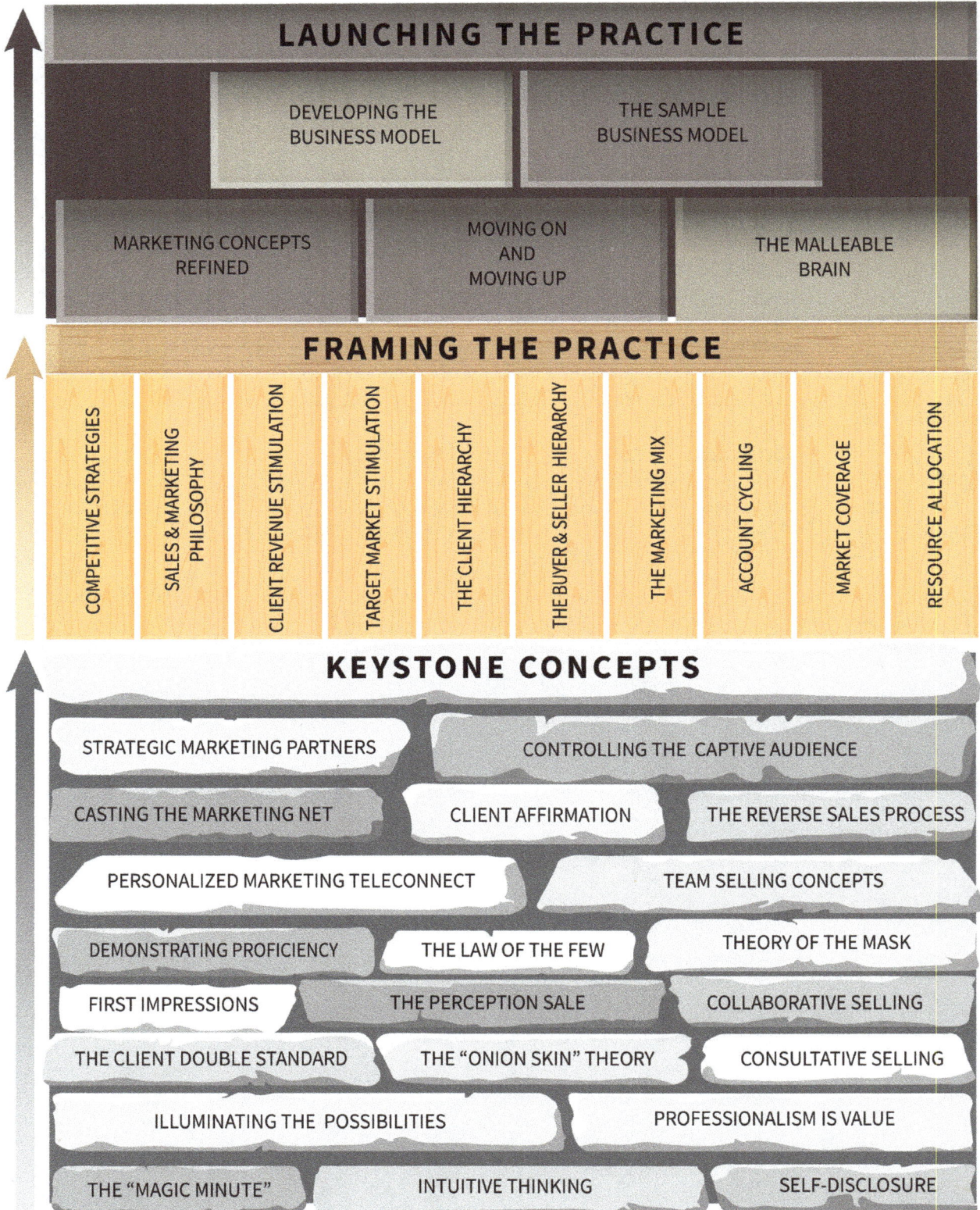

LAUNCHING THE PRACTICE

DEVELOPING THE BUSINESS MODEL

THE SAMPLE BUSINESS MODEL

MARKETING CONCEPTS REFINED

MOVING ON AND MOVING UP

THE MALLEABLE BRAIN

FRAMING THE PRACTICE

COMPETITIVE STRATEGIES

SALES & MARKETING PHILOSOPHY

CLIENT REVENUE STIMULATION

TARGET MARKET STIMULATION

THE CLIENT HIERARCHY

THE BUYER & SELLER HIERARCHY

THE MARKETING MIX

ACCOUNT CYCLING

MARKET COVERAGE

RESOURCE ALLOCATION

KEYSTONE CONCEPTS

STRATEGIC MARKETING PARTNERS

CONTROLLING THE CAPTIVE AUDIENCE

CASTING THE MARKETING NET

CLIENT AFFIRMATION

THE REVERSE SALES PROCESS

PERSONALIZED MARKETING TELECONNECT

TEAM SELLING CONCEPTS

DEMONSTRATING PROFICIENCY

THE LAW OF THE FEW

THEORY OF THE MASK

FIRST IMPRESSIONS

THE PERCEPTION SALE

COLLABORATIVE SELLING

THE CLIENT DOUBLE STANDARD

THE "ONION SKIN" THEORY

CONSULTATIVE SELLING

ILLUMINATING THE POSSIBILITIES

PROFESSIONALISM IS VALUE

THE "MAGIC MINUTE"

INTUITIVE THINKING

SELF-DISCLOSURE

CHAPTER 11 | KEYSTONE CONCEPT: THE "MAGIC MINUTE"

While consulting in Europe, I identified a teaching challenge. During my seminars, I found it difficult to explain to the attendees the kind of behavior expected when they first met a Prospect. My seminars not only included sales executives but their support teams as well. Many did not think of themselves as salespeople and were not accustomed to speaking directly with Prospects during a sales presentation. They often had an unfavorable opinion of the sales profession. Seeking to find a way to include all team members in the sales process, I introduced **"Team Selling"** concepts and the need for each team member to impress a Prospect with their commitment to providing outstanding service. I wanted them to leave their shells and impress the client with short comments. To accomplish this objective, I created the term "Magic Minute."

The "Magic Minute" is the first 60 seconds in which an Agent or team member can meet someone, talk to them on the telephone, or reach them when presenting to a person, group, or large gathering. In that sixty-second, they can change the outcome of the meeting.

While a person can make a great first impression by text or email, it is far more complex. Eye contact, facial expressions, body language, and verbal feedback are valuable and much more personalized when in person versus on the telephone. A video conversation via the telephone or computer is better than a text or email, but still not as valuable as a person-to-person meeting.

In the first 60 seconds of an encounter, the outcome of the interaction can be determined. The first impression is critical to success as first impressions are usually supported psychologically and are difficult to change. It can never be more important than in the first opportunity to speak directly with a Prospect.

If a great first impression can be made in the first 60 seconds of an interview, there is a high probability of winning the contest for Prospect respect and approval. Making a positive first impression ensures a positive response to almost everything spoken after the first 60 seconds.

The *Consultative Selling* authors further explain that one should make a great first impression. They cite an important concept called "The rule of primacy."

"Every salesman knows that he must make a positive first impression. Not all salesmen know why. According to the rule of primacy, the characteristics a customer first perceives in a salesman tend to be lasting." (1973, p. 23)

The discussion of "liking" has been written about in-depth in an excellent book, *PRODUCTIVITY The Human Side*. It seems clear that if a Prospect likes someone, they will most often associate with the person they can most identify with. In the first 60 seconds of an interview, if the Agent can reveal aspects of their personality that are like those of the Prospect, they can further enhance the impact of the first impression. This can often be done by carefully observing a Prospect's eyes and facial expression and determining their tendency to be outgoing or more introspective.

In the perfect "Magic Minute," an Agent or team member would be seen most favorably. They would best be situated in a position of power and prestige. Looking for opportunities to be in front of an audience and making a highly polished presentation allows a presenter to add more positivity after the first impression and to build a level of respect and liking that is essential to success.

People Buy from People they Know & Like

Do you buy from people that you know and like? Most people do. This is true in almost all sales endeavors. People like to buy from people they know and like and will go out of their way to do so. They will also avoid meeting with people they do not know and like and go out of their way to avoid them. Team Members, especially agents, need to make the Prospect know and like them, allowing them to feel comfortable from the beginning. This helps remove the mask that most people wear and allows them to be seen most favorably. Blake and Mouton wrote in PRODUCTIVITY The Human Side that people tend to join groups where those in the Group are similar in most ways to those considering joining a Group.

Being a part of a Group that contains people and personalities that a client likes is even more impactful than a single agent working alone. This explains why a Team in real estate can benefit an agent.

This is one of the primary reasons for working in Teams. If the real estate Team is making a presentation, it is an excellent strategy for the Team to deliver several "Magic Minutes." Delivering more "Magic Minutes" from various members of the Team during an event is incredibly beneficial. Numerous "Magic Minutes" often equate to more success! If each Team member makes a positive first impression, the positivity will accumulate in the mind of the Prospect. This is the reason and needs for Team Selling strategies and takes the positioning concept much deeper.

The Team being positioned and perceived by the prospect as professional adds power when compared to a competitor where the entire team is not involved. The book, *Working in Teams*, written by James H. Shonk, allows a prospect to join a Group of like-minded people who share the prospect's beliefs, opinions, and attitudes. A prospect can select both a Team and an agent.

Delivering a "Magic Minute" on a phone call is a high priority for the Agent and the Agents Team. In this text and Internet-driven world, it is easy to fall into the trap of responding to an email or text with a quick sound-bite message by text or email. An Agent needs to make people like them more than ever, and blurbs or short non-personalized messages seldom make people like someone. They deliver information but not personality. They can come across as terse and be taken negatively, creating a negative first impression. Always attempt to complete a phone call or set up a meeting to follow up after receiving a text or email. Looking for opportunities to interact with and provide a "Magic Minute" creates a positive first impression and is the goal of the agent team.

An opportunity to communicate with a prospect and get to know them is of immense value. It is typical for an Agent to spend a large percentage of their marketing budget to make the telephone ring or have an opportunity to begin communicating with a prospect. Regardless of how they reach out, the ultimate goal is to establish contact and deliver "Magic Minutes," where the agent can showcase their value proposition and build a personal connection with the prospect. Little is as important as a face-to-face meeting and making direct eye contact with a prospect. Anything that interferes with this should be avoided, but not at the risk of losing contact with a prospect.

Any opportunity to personalize the meeting and avoid short messages that do not allow an agent to make people like them should be avoided. The Consultative Agent has time to listen, collaborate, communicate, remove the mask, and build relationships of trust and confidence with the prospect. Calls should never be made when there is a limited amount of time.

Winning the Prospect

"Magic Minutes" result in more closed transactions and long-term relationships. In all future dealings with a Prospect, "Magic Minutes" must be delivered at every opportunity. For years, presentations consistently demonstrating professionalism increase the likelihood of winning a future opportunity.

If a Prospect interviews three agents and only one Agent has provided a "Magic Minute" to begin the meeting, and the two other competitors falter somehow and fail to deliver a "Magic Minute," the agent who delivers will have the inside track to success. If Team Members attend the meeting and deliver "Magic Minutes," the Prospect will think, **"All of these people are so involved and impressive."** "Magic Minutes" can distinguish between winning or losing in real estate.

CHAPTER 12 | KEYSTONE CONCEPT:
FIRST IMPRESSIONS

When Henry and Chelsea from Toronto asked me to meet them at their hotel before home touring, I was happy to do so to get the opportunity to meet with them in person. We had talked on the telephone several times, but each call was brief and confusing as Chelsea would not stop talking, and they constantly talked over each other. Henry and Chelsea were referred to me by one of our best "Raving Fans," yet they seemed uncertain about me. I wasn't sure why. I sensed something and was concerned. My apprehension was not alleviated upon arriving at their hotel.

They had secured a table in the lobby and were waiting for me when I arrived. Upon greeting me, they asked me to sit down. They explained that while I had been highly recommended, they were still interviewing three agents, and I was the last to meet with them. They would decide after our meeting and let me know if I had been selected. I had planned an overview tour for the day and did not know they were still deciding who would help them. After learning the morning plan, I calmed myself and began to answer their questions. I was pleased that I had brought a "gift" for them. It was a coffee table book about Texas filled with photos of interesting places in the state.

The first question they asked me would be pivotal and set the tone for the entire relationship. Henry asked me, **"Our move to Texas to purchase a home is significant to us, and we want to know why we should choose you over the other highly recommended agents we interviewed?"**

I took a moment to think through my response and looked back and forth at both of them while making eye contact. They were fully attentive, and after a "pregnant pause," I responded by saying. **"You should choose me to help you find your home because I don't sell homes. I help my clients make good decisions for their future and always consider that when recommending the purchase of a home, it is important to consider the exit plan, as most people will not live in a home forever. My sole purpose in being here is to help you make the right choices and guide you to achieve your goals, whatever they may be. I will always put you first."**

Chelsea continued the questions by opening the **"Finding a Home Guidebook"** I had shipped to them upon learning they were relocating to our area. She asked me why I felt school districts were so important when they did not have children.

I explained that in the early telephone conversations, Henry had indicated that a move back to Toronto sometime in the future was possible. Since many home buyers in our area are focused on schools, they should weigh this heavily when buying, as it will very likely be necessary when they sell their homes at some point in the future. She listened and seemed to agree that it was necessary. Henry nodded his approval.

After a few more questions, they suddenly informed me that they had decided and were ready to go on tour. They would notify the other agents later in the day. Chelsea thanked me for the book about Texas and mentioned that no one else had thought to bring a welcome gift. She smiled widely as we proceeded to the car.

Chelsea and Henry became loyal clients. Later, they confirmed that the other agents had focused all their comments on homes while I focused on their long-term goals and future. After looking at homes for three days, they purchased a newly constructed home in a beautiful neighborhood in the best school district in our area. It was a builder's **"Model Home"** and included many extras not typically included in a typical new home. Seven years later, they would call us and ask us to help them sell that home when they moved back to Toronto. They are still **"Raving Fans."**

The foundational idea behind the concept of first impressions strongly emphasizes the significance of establishing a favorable and long-lasting impression from the very first opportunity. Every encounter matters, whether it's a brief conversation over the phone or a face-to-face get-together. When meeting a new person or visiting a new location, people will likely form opinions within the first few seconds of their encounter.

So, why is it so important to make a great first impression? Hanan, Cribben, and Heiser wrote an impactful book about *Consultative Selling*, and this book provides us insight into the impact of making a poor first impression.

> *"Once a customer sees a salesman as incompetent, it will be very difficult for him to alter his initial reading. At every hint of personal or professional incompetence which the salesman gives, the customer's first impression will be reinforced." (1973, p. 23)*

Regardless of which culture or where they are in the world, most people have been told by their parents or someone important to them to "always make a good first impression." From the moment a Prospect sees the Agent, their eyes send information to their brain, and opinions and impressions are already being formed before the Prospect consciously realizes what they are seeing and what they think about what they are seeing. Some scientists believe that the brain, having received information, may have formed an opinion within the first 2 to 10 seconds, perhaps before the conscious mind of the Prospect thinks, **"I like this Agent,"** or **"I don't like this Agent."**

For this reason, real estate agents must pay close attention to every aspect, large and small. Real estate agents can differentiate themselves from rivals and set the groundwork for a transaction that will be fruitful if they can create a favorable first impression.

Psychologically, Prospects support their first impressions. One notable example of this is from the book written by Malcolm Gladwell, titled "*blink.*" In this book, renowned experts examine a historical artifact and declare the artifact to be authentic. They staked their reputations on the authenticity of a statue. Later, when it was proven that the item was a fake, the renowned experts said they believed it was real, wanted it to be accurate, and, as a result, were blinded by the first impressions. People support their first impressions, sometimes disregarding reality.

If a home buyer prospect or client approaches a home for sale from the curb and the home looks great, with the front yard nicely landscaped and a front door that is freshly painted and clean, they will form a positive first impression that will last until something significant happens to change their first impression. Sometimes they support their first impression to the point that it must be proven to them that it is incorrect. Their eyes have sent information to their subconscious minds, and opinion formation may have begun before the prospect can speak.

Gladwell, in the book, "*blink*" writes,

> *"The part of our brain that leaps to conclusions like this is called the adaptive unconscious, And the study of this kind of decision-making is one of the most important new fields in psychology." (2005, p. 11)*

Negative First Impressions

When a client forms the first impression about a home they are touring, the opinion is a first impression subconsciously and then is supported and affirmed consciously. Without realizing it, they will find things that support that first impression. When they approach the home and later enter, their eyes start transmitting information, and they may well think, **"See, I was right... this is a lovely home."** They will look for things that support that positive first impression. If the foyer and entry look great, the positive first impression will be carried forward into the rest of the home. When they see something needing attention, they tend to discount that condition and support their positive first impression. If a home has several positive first impressions in the first few minutes, a Prospect looks at the home positively despite blemishes that become apparent later. If they like the home from the curb, approach the front door and are impressed, enter the foyer, and are pleased with the appearance, it will be hard to convince them that the master bedroom might be too small.

If they enter a home having formed a negative first impression, they will likewise look for things that support that negative first impression. That is why many buyers will quickly decide about a home and decline to tour it before spending more than five minutes in the home, or in many cases, before they even exit the car to look inside the home. Curb Appeal is often used to describe this phenomenon, but it is possible that they "blinked," and the blink was not good. The first impression of a home buyer could be positive or negative, and if it is negative, they will likely leave the home quickly.

Likewise, when the Agent makes a great first impression upon meeting or greeting the Prospect, the Prospect will tend to give the Agent credit for everything they do well in the presentation and discount as less important those points of weakness that the Agent might reveal in their presentation. Later, when discussing professional service fees, the prospect might think, **"Yes, his fees are a little high compared to others, but he is worth it."** Remember that prospects like art experts tend to believe strongly in their opinions and, as a result, may become inflexible to change. When the prospect or client likes you, it is difficult for someone to convince them to choose another agent.

An agent who creates a great first impression is critical for convincing a prospect that the agent is the best choice to represent them. When an agent can provide multiple positive demonstrations of evidence of professionalism early in an encounter, this evidence can "accumulate" and create such a powerful positive first impression that the prospect is compelled intrinsically to select the Agent. An Agent that has previously met with a Prospect and created an excellent first impression may lose the battle for the Client because of this overwhelming positivity toward the new Agent. Therefore, a Prospect might say, **"Well, I thought I had made my mind up about choosing an Agent, but you have certainly made this difficult for me."**

Being First to Meet

Once an Agent has made a positive first impression, changing the prospect's mind is difficult. Being first to meet with a Prospect and creating a powerful positive first impression is far preferable to being last to meet with the Prospect. By being first, a benchmark standard can be set. Meeting with a Prospect after another very professional agent has presented requires the newly arrived agent to overwhelm the client with great impressions to unseat the first agent who won their praise.

The first appointment or phone call supplies the agent with an opportunity to create a first positive impression. If the Prospects' first impression of the agent is positive, they are likely to support that first impression as the interview or meeting continues. The noted experts in the book *"blink"* that believed the artifact was a fake also supported their first impressions and didn't back down when told they were wrong. Rather than admit they were wrong, they **"dug in,"** supporting the correctness of their opinion.

None of the experts who declared the kouros to be legitimately faced with differing opinions was willing to listen to others and concede that they were wrong. They wanted it to be correct and contended it was right until there was substantial proof otherwise, and they eventually conceded. <u>They were not happy to do so!</u>

The Two-Step Listing Approach

The agent should never give a prospect anything to be pessimistic about when they meet. The agent's essential goal is to look for ways to create a great first impression. A small gift frequently does wonders for a prospect's opinion of the agent! When the prospect forms their first impression, don't expect them to change their opinion quickly.

The "Super Bowl" for winning an opportunity to list a home is often secured from the first contact or interview and the impression formed at that time. The Two-Step Listing Presentation reserves the first meeting for making a great first impression and avoiding anything that could be perceived negatively. As a result, the odds are more favorable that a prospect will select the agent. This method is preferable because it avoids creating a negative first impression during the first meeting with a prospect, allowing the prospect to look for behavior and information that supports that positive first impression increases the chances of Agent success.

Visiting a Prospect's home and explaining that they need to replace the carpet, re-paint, or re-landscape is unlikely to make the Prospect like the Agent, even when the Prospect knows these things are true. Professionalism is synonymous with value because the highly professional Agent can convince the Prospect intrinsically that they are valuable. They cannot help but believe that an Agent is highly efficient and successful when making a positive first impression. The concept is supported because the Prospect does not make just a cognitive decision that the Agent is more valuable. Still, they also form a subconscious opinion that can be established in their minds. It can happen in their subconscious and unconscious mind.

This is where the "Mini Home Book" comes back into our discussion. The Mini Home Book was not created just for the homeowner or Prospective buyers. Every person who toured the home and carried this Mini Home Book from the home was presented with a professionally demonstrated package about us. Open Houses were open to neighbors and Prospective buyers who all had an opportunity to review the Mini Home Book and take it with them if they chose to do so. This allowed us to reach neighbors who might be clients in the future with a powerful and impressive display of our capabilities and professionalism.

Perhaps the most impactful use of the Mini Home Book was during the listing presentation itself. At the appropriate time in the presentation, we would introduce a Mini Home Book similar to the home we were interviewing for.

In addition, we brought several competitors' Marketing Brochures with us and allowed the homeowner to examine them all. This may sound risky as it placed information about our competitors before our Prospective client. We knew that it would not negatively impact our presentation to do so. Why? We knew that our materials would be so positively seen that there would be a clear difference perceived between what others provided and what we delivered. This was a differentiation strategy in full color before the Prospect. Perhaps we will continue our story about the Mini Home Book after discussing the "client double standard."

CHAPTER 13|KEYSTONE CONCEPT: THE CLIENT DOUBLE STANDARD

When meeting with a prospect, there is always a "client double standard" at work. Prospects frequently hold businesses and service providers to a higher standard than they would apply to themselves, and this phenomenon I refer to as the **"client double standard."**

For instance, it is permissible for the client to be late, not be dressed appropriately, or not have complete information available during the meeting or telephone conversation. The prospect judges everything most of the time and is greatly impressed by highly competent agents. A Prospect may feel frustrated if a service provider does not promptly pick up the phone to answer their call, even though a prospect is the one who does not pick up their phone when the service provider tries to reach them.

The ability to comprehend and acknowledge the existence of this double standard is essential to delivering outstanding service to Prospects and establishing solid connections with them. By doing so, people can meet a prospect's expectations and exceed those expectations, which helps them stand out from their competitors and fosters long-term client loyalty. Therefore "demonstrating proficiency" in the first encounter with a Prospect is important in imprinting that first impression on their impressionable minds. Proficiency is far more potent initially than later because of this tendency to support the first impression.

When an agent arrives late for a meeting, the client may look at their watch and observe that the agent is late, subconsciously noting, **"They should have been on time."** Other information can be found to support the negative first impression because the prospect is now tuned in to being critical. **"They should have been better prepared"** or **"They should have had better and more complete leave behind information"** are examples of supporting information that can paint the agent less positively. The client may believe that the agent should have dressed more appropriately but will seldom say this to the agent. Few people love confrontation, and the agent cannot expect transparency from a prospect unless a relationship of trust and confidence has been established. For example, a buyer touring a home where the owner is present and being asked by the owner for their opinion will seldom say, **"This is a terrible home, and there is no way I would buy it."**

Despite their negative first impression, it is more likely that they would say, **"It's a great home. Love what you did with the decorating, and we will keep it on our list."** No one wants to disappoint someone needlessly, so transparency cannot be expected. Because the agent will not know what the prospect is thinking, the agent must plan to demonstrate professionalism on the first visit and in the first minute with a prospect.

The agent is expected to take all the time that the prospect wants to listen to them about what is important to them. The client will fault the Agent for failing to have provided the correct information. Seldom will the Agent know that they feel this way, as people generally don't want to give anyone bad news.

Selecting a Buyer Agent

In the **"Competitive Arena,"** the Agent is judged and compared to the other agents who entered the ring. In the contest for a listing or to be chosen as a buyer representative, the prospective client decides which agent to choose for their real estate needs. The prospect will judge on timeliness, appearance, professional demeanor, personality fit, meeting preparation, information delivery, ability to answer questions, listening skills, and how the Agent differentiates themselves from the competitors. They will also judge intangibles that they cannot name. This includes how much they intrinsically liked the agent and felt they were listened to. They will evaluate how the agent relates to them when they are talking.

Internally, they will judge an agent harshly if they do not meet their expectations. The prospect probably believes that all Real Estate Agents are similar; therefore, the one chosen is not as important as determining a listing price and the professional fee that will be charged. The Agent must convince them otherwise! The Agent must "make them feel" that choosing them is the best decision they can make at that exact moment.

For these reasons, it should never be forgotten that on an appointment, the Agent is constantly being judged by the Prospect/Client even though no one is judging the prospect. The agent must be able to communicate directly with the prospect while making immediate eye contact and connecting with their unique and different personalities, regardless of what that personality might be. A prospect is not expected to compete while the agent is in the arena. The agent is!

CHAPTER 14|KEYSTONE CONCEPT: "ILLUMINATING THE POSSIBILITIES…"

Max and Sally were referred to me by a client who had referred me to several other prospective relocating buyers from California. Max wanted to rent a home until his wife, Sally, and their children could join him. He was looking for a property large enough for them to visit him for several weeks at a time, and they would join him permanently in approximately eighteen months. They had specific criteria that were not unusual, and there were eight to ten properties that met almost all their requirements. None met all of them.

After spending much time with Max and Sally on the TeleConnect calls, we planned a home-finding visit, and his family would join him. After preparing a touring plan for the properties on the list they sent, they chose seven to visit on the first day. Upon their arrival, I found Max and his family to be delightful. We toured the first four properties before lunch, and each was ruled out immediately. Since they would all need to live in the property for some time, once the family joined him, Sally insisted that the rental property had to be in the right school district and meet their living needs.

At lunch, Sally was somewhat perplexed and asked me what I thought about their plan of renting until they relocated. She expressed concern as the properties did not seem to be what she hoped to find. Max, an engineer, was also the financial planner for the family and was convinced that renting was the best option for them. I saw this as an opportunity to illuminate their possibilities for them. I had to wait for the right opportunity to do so.

I began by explaining a few of the challenges of renting a home. When they were informed that finding a home in the best school district available when they needed to occupy would be challenging, they began to question the renting option. It was also pointed out that renting a home of the quality they wanted would require at least a one-year lease term and restrict them from customizing the home to meet their needs, as they would have to leave any improvements with the property upon vacating the property. They would need Landlord's approval to make any changes. The Landlord could require that they restore the property to its original condition before vacating. They also were not guaranteed a second year of occupancy unless it was agreed to in the original lease, and that option to renew for an additional year might cost extra.

Max asked about other options. This was my opportunity to present. I began a detailed financial collaboration on the pros and cons of renting versus owning. This was concluded by summarizing why they would lose the opportunity to save money or earn by leasing versus buying. If they leased, the costs of buying other homes would escalate when they were leasing. If they purchased a home now at current prices, they would realize the appreciation in the home's value while waiting for Sally and the children to join them. They could change the property as they wished and not have to worry about renewing the lease in one year. The monthly cost to own would be less than the monthly cost to lease. Explaining that if they had the financial ability to purchase, they would be better off purchasing now and have the ability to get into the school district they desired.

Max was very participative in this discussion and asked me to quantify the financial impact of purchasing a home for $500,000 versus renting a home for two years. We agreed on some financial assumptions to be used. Nothing in our collaboration had anything to do with a particular home. This was a financial analysis only.

The children were getting seriously bored, so Sally took them outside to walk and allowed us time to talk in detail. Our discussion on the financial aspects took about forty minutes. When we were finished, Max suggested that we finish our tour of rental properties and allow him to consider the options. We toured the remaining three homes, which all fell short of the requirements. I provided them with four more rental properties to consider for day two, and Max asked if we could talk that evening and finalize a plan for the following day.

That evening, Max thanked me for the detailed information I had provided and asked me to modify their search plan and start showing them properties to purchase in the $500,000 price range that would meet their needs. The next day we proceeded as he suggested, and they found a wonderful newly constructed home in a master-planned community. The home was situated in one of the best school districts in the area, as Sally wanted. Sally and Max were fans, and less than eighteen months later, the family was reunited. In the two years following their purchase of the property, the property appreciated by approximately 16%, while they could pay less in monthly outflow and realize tax savings from the interest and real estate taxes they paid.

What Could Have Happened?

If I had told Max initially that his plan was flawed and that he would change his mind and purchase a home for over $500,000, what would he say? How would he have responded to me? This is why the "Illuminating the Possibilities" concept is so important to clients.

Illuminating the Possibilities… is providing information about something that someone does not know but does not realize that they do not know. Illuminating the possibilities… occurs when the Agent consults and collaborates with a Prospect and helps them understand the facts or information, allowing the client to discover the answers or solutions for themselves. This allows the Agent to illuminate a problem without being the messenger of bad news or adverse facts and avoids alienation of the client by the Agent being the purveyor of the bad news.

Don't Alienate the Prospect

The answers or solutions may be positive or negative. This Illumination of negative information to the client is most concerning to the Agent when the information or facts contradict the client's goals and objectives. For example, an Agent telling a Prospect that their home is worth far less than the Prospect believes to be the case is a sure example of how to alienate a Prospect.

When a Prospect is allowed to discover answers and solutions for themselves, they are easier to collaborate with than when the Prospect is told the Agents opinion without the client discovering the reality of the situation. Conflicts with a great deal of emotion frequently arise because the client is emotionally invested in the outcome of a decision. The answer should always consider whether or not providing solutions will make the agent feel better about themselves or make the client feel better about themselves.

Agents to be mindful that clients often have an emotional stake in their decisions and that this fact might lead to disagreements if unfavorable information is supplied to them. Due to this, it is essential to consider their communication has an effect on their clients' emotional well-being. It is not the appropriate strategy to provide solutions with the express intention of making the agent feel better about themselves; doing so may even make the client-agent relationship even more strained.

In order to have a good interaction, agents need to be proficient in delivering both positive and negative information in a helpful way while also considering the emotional impact on the Prospect.

The Agent looks to help the Prospect understand the situation by self-revelation rather than by the Agent directly providing the information. This is a differentiation strategy in that most Agents enter into a relationship with a Prospect as the "all-knowing expert" and often form a relationship that is not collaborative. It avoids the Agent attitude of "I know best what is best for you!" This "I know all the answers" mindset often results in a paradigm where the "all-knowing agent" that is wrong about the listing price for a home, for example, will own the decision to list at that price rather than share the listing price decision with the Prospect through collaboration.

Conflict Will Occur...

This collaborative approach will not avoid future conflict with the Prospect. It establishes an atmosphere that fosters conflict resolution productively. In the book *Interpersonal Conflict*, by Hocker and Wilmot, the reason to resolve conflict versus avoid conflict is explained.

"Our own position about conflict is similar to Wehr's (1979). We see it as a natural process, inherent in the nature of all important relationships and amenable to constructive regulation through communication." (1974, p. 6)

The collaborative process begins at the first meeting with a client and happens before any reasons for conflict, and therefore establishes a relationship of open dialogue and communications in a partnered relationship that resolves future conflicts more likely.

This highlights the importance of the agent understanding what the Prospect knows and what the Prospect thinks they know. It helps the Agent anticipate conflicts that are likely to occur and be prepared to resolve them with positive and productive methods. The Agent helps a Prospect to learn what they don't know without the Agent creating a negative reaction from the Prospect that could result in conflict. As a result, the client feels better about everything, including the agent.

Information & Misconception

As a result of the easy access to information in today's world, many potential buyers and sellers may feel they have a thorough knowledge of the real estate business and the procedures involved. Because of this misconception, some people are misled into thinking that they do not require the assistance of a real estate agent to navigate the market. It is not the ideal strategy to inform them that they do not have a great deal of knowledge and might appear to be condescending and alienate them.

One reason for this misconception is that access to vast information has led many to believe they are experts. A Prospect may, for instance, read articles online on how to negotiate the purchase of a property and then convince themselves that they can do it on their own. Yet, they might not realize that the articles they read may not apply to their situation. Furthermore, negotiating the acquisition of a property requires various skills and expertise that go beyond what they would have obtained from self-education.

Prospects may also be misled into believing they are qualified to represent themselves if they have a history of doing so. For instance, if they have successfully bought or sold a home in the past without the help of a real estate agent, they could believe that they do not need any assistance this time around. Their previous experiences may have led them to believe that they are capable of representing themselves in legal matters or that the services of an Agent are required only for access, information dissemination, or the creation of contracts. They might also have the impression that working in real estate is simple. They may have toured for days and seen numerous properties. What could an Agent teach them?

The real estate business is constantly changing, and the rules and contracts are often updated, making it challenging for an untrained individual to stay up-to-date.

An Agent telling the Prospect that they don't know enough to proceed without them is a risky strategy as they will most likely not believe that they are not prepared or knowledgeable enough and become negative toward the Agent. The experts that verified the Kouros in the book *"blink"* are a good example. They refused to admit that they were wrong when told they were, but later after overwhelming evidence, admitted that they ignored the warning signs that were there. I am certain that this was not a pleasurable experience for them to admit their error.

Suppose an Agent can illuminate, show, demonstrate, or otherwise prove to a Prospect that they do not know all the answers by collaborating with them and assisting the Prospect to discover the answers for themselves. In that case, the Agent can foster a partnered relationship of trust and confidence and does not insult or alienate the Prospect. This allows the Agent to create a "wow, I didn't know that" moment for the Prospect. This allows the Prospect to save face and accept that there is a better opinion than theirs. Their respect for the Agent is enhanced, and the Agent is perceived positively. In the case of Preston Andersen, he knew that things were wrong and just needed someone to confirm with him what he suspected. He also needed to have someone provide a clear pathway to move forward. Empathy was required to allow him to accept that he was failing and that there were solutions he had not considered. In *Consultative Selling*, the authors write,

> *"One outcome of a consultative selling relationship is the transformation of the salesman's customers into clients. This is far more than just a semantic difference. A customer is someone to be sold: a client is someone to be served. In a consultative relationship the client wins all the time. He does not win over the salesman; he wins with him. He cannot lose because the salesman will not let him." (1973, p. 14)*

Just as Prospects hate being told they are wrong, they love being told they are right when they are told this sincerely. One of the greatest compliments that an agent can give a client is the question, "What do you think about this?"

In the following example, the method of "Illuminating the Possibilities…" for a client is provided.

The Listing Opportunity – Contrasting Strategies

A Consultative Collaborative Agent, named Smart Agent, has thoroughly prepared for the Listing Presentation with sellers Peter and Martha Townsend. A review of the information and the development of a Comprehensive Market Analysis has been prepared and indicates a likely sales price of $825,000. Smart Agent has prepared a list of Active and Sold Properties for presentation to the Prospect on the collaboration center computer (Collaboration HUB) in the Agent's offices. The average sales time in the market for a home like the Townsends was between sixty and ninety days.

When Mr. and Mrs. Townsend arrived at the Agent's office, there was the normal greeting and a short get re-acquainted moment. Smart Agent toured them around the office and introduced the Townsends to several Team Members, and each Team Member contributed a "Magic Minute" to the presentation.

Smart Agent met the Townsends three days ago at Townsend's home for a tour and to gather information about the home and the Prospects to prepare for today's presentation. At that time, the Agent had presented a box of Godiva chocolates to the Townsends as a gift. During this first meeting, the Smart Agent refrained from talking about prices, time to sell, professional service fees, and repair or property improvement issues by explaining that all of this would be covered at the next meeting and requested up to ninety minutes for that presentation and discussion today. The Smart Agent told the Townsends, "If it is all right with you, I'll prepare a detailed presentation covering all this information when needed. Is that ok?" The Townsends permitted Smart Agent to proceed in this manner.

At that first meeting, Smart Agent had listened intently and learned that the Townsends had owned the property for 12 years, not made any significant improvements, and wanted to move to North Carolina to be near an ailing relative. Smart Agent took copious notes and focused on the floor plan, the condition of the property, and barriers that might affect the sale of the property. Smart Agent almost fell into a trap when Peter Townsend asked what needed to be done to prepare the property for sale. Smart Agent remembered to avoid this trap and said, **"You know, I need to look at my notes, think about your questions, and be prepared to answer those questions when we get together in a few days to review my analysis. Will that be all right with you?"** Peter replied, "Of course..." and, in a fleeting thought, believed that Smart Agent was comprehensive and disciplined."

Toward the end of this friendly first meeting, Smart Agent said, **"Well, you have a lovely home, and I need to prepare a detailed analysis for you, so it will take me a day or two to research and put together my analysis and marketing plan. It might be best if we meet at my office, as I have all my technology there, and we can review everything at my collaboration center at my office. It's very close by, and we could meet Wednesday or Thursday; which is better for you?"** They all agreed on a meeting date and time. Before leaving, Smart Agent looked at the backyard, noted the mature and overgrown landscape, and documented the front yard drive-up as being unimpressive when leaving the property. The property did not have a great deal of "curb appeal." The Agent was concerned that when the Townsends were told the reality about the value of their home, they might not be pleased or even become upset with this news.

The Townsends confirmed a meeting time and set a follow-up appointment at the office. Smart Agent is now fully and completely prepared with many answers and opinions. The Agent believes the list price should be no more than $849,000. There was a likely sales price of $825,000.

When encouraged to talk and share at their first meeting, Mr. and Mrs. Townsend indicated that they had gathered a lot of information about recent sales in their neighborhood and were convinced that their home was worth around $900,000. They had visited numerous Open Houses in the neighborhood even when the homes were not comparable to theirs. The Townsend's home had original appliances in the kitchen and finish-out in the owner's suite, had an older and overgrown landscape, and was dated in the Agents opinion.

The presentation began with the Smart Agent thanking the Townsends for their time and for the first meeting, which allowed the Agent to prepare thoroughly for today's presentation. Martha expressed her gratitude for the chocolates, and everyone was happy.

After giving a brief introduction about their background, experience, and credentials, as well as their knowledge of the local neighborhood, the Agent went on to explain that there were three parts to the presentation. This early disclosure of personal information demonstrated the Agent's willingness to be open and transparent with the Townsends.

The Smart Agent also set up the disclosure reciprocity process by disclosing and explaining the process used to evaluate and prepare for the meeting. This approach builds trust and demonstrates the Agent's professionalism and attention to detail.

The Agent then elaborated on the customized marketing plan developed for the Townsends' home. This could include various strategies such as virtual tours, professional photography, and social media campaigns designed to showcase the home's best features and attract potential buyers.

In the second part of the presentation, the Agent reviewed comparable properties that were currently on the market and had recently sold. This analysis helped the Townsends understand how their home compared to others in the area and what price range they could expect.

Finally, the Agent discussed pricing and the time required to sell the home and answered any other questions the Townsends had. This approach allowed the Townsends to have a clear understanding of the selling process and the expectations they should have.

The Smart Agent's approach to the presentation demonstrated their professionalism, expertise, and attention to detail. By providing transparency and customized solutions, the Agent built trust with the Townsends and established a solid foundation for a successful working relationship. Smart Agent avoided any discussion of professional service fees, costs of repairs, improvements, or details of the listing agreement. Smart Agent completed the opening presentation by saying, **"If you don't mind, I will answer any questions about price, time to sell, or other discussion areas after we review the analysis and comparable properties used for determining the recommended list price or range price. I will also discuss my recommendations for changes and updates to your home, as I know you are wondering about this. Is this ok with you?"** This confirmed that Smart Agent remembered the request for repair or improvement recommendations as well as the fact that Smart Agent promised to deliver pricing information and answer questions.

The Agent waited for agreement from the Townsends that delaying the price discussion was agreeable and then proceeded with the presentation. This "price put off" statement allowed the Smart Agent to avoid the most damaging factors until later in the meeting. This would allow sufficient time to allow the Townsends to discover some answers for themselves about their home and their home's value.

Smart Agent made a thorough presentation about their experience, education, support team, and how they worked collaboratively with clients. Smart Agent talked at some length about the differences between real estate Agents and pointed out that the Smart Agent was both a real estate Agent and a Broker. This was a significant differentiator as few Agents are also Brokers. Smart Agent explains that Brokers are held to a higher standard. Brokers are required to pass the additional test and must have some relevant experience. They can have other agents under their supervision and are expected to know more.

The Townsends did not understand the difference between an Agent and a Broker and said as much. The Agent listened carefully and explained the differences presenting the positives of a Broker/Agent compared to just a Sales Agent. At all times, the Townsends respected the Agent's request about the order of the meeting.

The Price Put-Off

Smart Agent obtained permission to delay discussing price and other issues until the Agent's credentials and marketing plan presentation could be completed. Smart Agent made a powerful and client-benefit-oriented presentation and avoided discussing the likely sales price, fees, or anything money-related. This included a discussion of necessary repairs and updates. There was no benefit in getting them upset early! They might shoot the messenger.

When the Agent moved to a presentation of the comparable properties, a significant amount of time was spent showing the Townsends photos of the sold comparable properties and active properties for sale. Smart Agent knew that the home needed some updates and did not want to tell the Townsends this but to let them discover this for themselves. The Agent noted the features and upgrades of sold properties, pointing out updated kitchens and bathrooms, as well as flooring and backyard environments. Smart Agent also showed evidence of landscape concerns without commenting about them relative to Townsend's home.

The presentation was very detailed, and Smart Agent was happy that there was a ninety-minute window. There was no rush, and the Townsends seemed comfortable with the pace of the meeting. Smart Agent did not have another appointment scheduled immediately following the presentation in case the meeting went long, as it did.

In my experience, an Agent must demonstrate to the Prospect that they are available for as much time as the Prospect needs. Many agents forget that telling someone they have another appointment can cause the Prospect to believe that the agent is too busy for them or that they are not as important to the agent. Allowing more than enough time sends a clear psychological message to the Prospect that they are essential and first on the agent's priority list. It also indicates how the Prospect who becomes a client will be treated later in the relationship.

This allowed the Townsends to see how their home compared, and it was evident to all that Townsend's home was dated compared to the examples provided and not equivalent to the homes that had sold recently of comparable size, age, and in the same neighborhood. The Collaboration Hub allows an agent to place multiple photos of properties on the screen and simultaneously allow for comparison. The Townsends often looked at each other and commented about how attractive the other homes were. Smart Agent was gentle, not making too much of a point about Townsends' home but focused on the comparable properties. At one point, Martha commented, **"You know I like stainless steel appliances, but they do show fingerprints, don't they?"** Smart Agent agreed that they show more fingerprints than the white appliances in the Townsend home.

Smart Agent never referred to Townsends' home and the home's condition or the dated kitchen, owner's suite, flooring, and back yard and front yard landscape deficiencies. Smart Agent smartly did not comment on these deficiencies but allowed the photos to do the talking. The Agent avoided talking about the Townsend home and how it compared, allowing the Townsends to see its shortcomings for themselves. Smart Agent also pointed out the drive-up appeal and the backyard environments of the sold comparable and on-the-market properties. The Townsends were deep in thought, particularly Mr Townsend. Smart Agent had determined he was the primary key decision maker for the property sale.

On the large screens in the presentation room, the Agent pointed out the comparable properties' drive-up photos and backyard environments and fully explained the details of improvements to the comparable properties. Smart Agent believed that any intelligent seller could see that the Townsend home was not updated compared to homes sold and on the market. At the end of each comparable property review, Smart Agent pointed out the sold price per square foot and the time on the market for each home. The average sales prices of comparable sales were provided.

Several times during this part of the presentation, the Townsends asked about their home and how much it would sell for. Each time, the Agent reminded them they would cover that in the next part of the presentation as agreed. Smart Agent said, **"You know, if it is all right, I'll finish this review, and then we can move on to a discussion about your home and pricing. I promise to give you a recommendation at that time. Is this ok?"** Smart Agent had been thorough and delivered on promises thus far, so not wanting to be rude, the Townsends agreed.

Try Not to Talk—Avoid Price

They also commented they had thought about making some improvements to their home but never done so; Smart Agent was silent and did not express an opinion of this strategy. Smart Agent was pleased they had allowed the presentation to be completed and felt good about how they absorbed the information about the other homes and their features and condition.

As Smart Agent completed the review of on-the-market and sold homes, the Townsends were quiet, clearly deep in thought, and anxious to hear Smart Agent's opinions. Smart Agent briefly reviewed the homes and presented a chart showing the sales price, sold price per square foot, and the time on the market to sell the properties. Then Smart Agent politely said, **"Well, Martha and Peter, thank you for allowing** me to present my marketing plan for your home. I appreciate your patience." All smiled, and Smart Agent proceeded. Mr. Townsend was surprised and thought, **"This is a very thorough presentation, well structured, and very informative, not at all like the other two agents we have interviewed."**

Finally, Revealing & Talking about Money

At this point, Smart Agent placed the Comprehensive Market Analysis on the screen and reviewed the computations showing a sales price range between $800,000 and $850,000. No other Agent called the CMA a Comprehensive Market Analysis. Mr. Townsend noted this and wondered, **'Why?'**

The Townsends, having had an opportunity to see what other more improved homes sold for, asked the Agent if making improvements to their home would be worth the money spent. The Agent, remembering the Townsends' goal of moving quickly to be with family, explained that significant improvements would take time, cost more than $60,000 in Smart Agent's opinion, and would delay the sale of the home and the ability for the Townsends to move as quickly as they wanted. Smart Agent mentioned that their goal of getting to North Carolina quickly was understood by the Agent.

The Townsends, having been told that their home was worth $50,000 to $60,000 less than they had thought, had already recognized that their opinion of value was incorrect and accepted Smart Agents' recommendation of listing the property at $849,000 and hoping to get at least $825,000 for the home.

Smart Agent illuminated the reality of the market to the Townsends, allowing them to discover that their opinion of value had been misguided. In the beginning, smart Agent had played it smartly as Mr. Townsend was convinced that he knew the market and the likely sales price. Smart Agent never told Mr. Townsend he was wrong or ill-informed, was well prepared, and the meeting took over ninety minutes, but the Townsends had more questions.

Being respectful, Mr. Townsend asked Smart Agent if there was enough time to go through the other questions that he wanted answers to, like fees and costs of selling. Smart Agent assured them that Smart Agent had all the time they needed. Smart Agent moved forward, prepared to listen to everything carefully and thoughtfully.

Dealing with Professional Service Fees

Smart Agent now answered the question about the professional service fee that Mr Townsend asked. **"My professional services fee is _% of the sales price. As you are experienced in selling and buying homes, I am sure that you know that the professional service fee of _% is split first with the Agent who represents brings the buyer but also with my Brokerage firm, so the share of the fee I receive is smaller than it might seem."** Smart Agent showed Townsends a chart showing the breakdown of fees received. Mr. Townsend noticed that Smart Agent was not at all concerned about discussing money and that Smart Agent appeared confident about what was being discussed.

Smart Agent was happy that the listing price recommended, likely sales price, fees, and repair recommendations were covered at the end of the collaboration as it allowed for a detailed non-controversial presentation of value and benefit. Emotional reaction and "pushback" had been avoided, and Mr. Townsend seemed ready to sign the listing agreement.

Impact

"Illuminating the Possibilities" is a powerful way of proving value, justifying the professional service fee, winning confidence, and creating **"I didn't know that!"** moments that cause a Prospect to hold the Agent in high esteem. An Agent should never say to a Prospect, **"You are wrong."** As a Consultative Agent, while correcting a Prospect, you should avoid insulting their intelligence and instead focus on assisting them in recognizing where they went wrong. The Agent is responsible for directing the customer toward accomplishing their goals and ensuring their success at each process stage. An example of this approach is when a client wants to purchase a home they cannot afford.

Sometimes, a client wants to buy a home in a particular area, but their budget might be limited. If they had their heart set on a property out of their price range, the agent might have to dissuade them from pursuing that area by explaining that fitting the home into their budget would be challenging. This can be done by guiding the client through the qualification guidelines for buying a home so that they discover for themselves their limitations.

This strategy highlights the significance of a Consultative Agent in assisting Prospects in achieving their objectives by providing advice and recommendations. The Agent can assist clients in making informed choices and avoiding costly mistakes by acting as a guide and facilitator. It is not the Agent's job to tell the client what they can or cannot do; instead, the Agent's job is to guide the client through the real estate market maze and assist them in making choices that best suit their situation.

The property listing presentation should be strategically based on what the Prospect thinks and what they feel and designed to allow the Prospect to realize, without being insulted, the real value of their property or other deficiencies that need to be addressed. The presentation should demonstrate a thorough knowledge of the client's needs and wants and the property's positives and negatives. It should demonstrate proficiency in comparing the property to properties of a similar type and condition. Most of all, the presentation should be respectful, collaborative, and conversational.

The listing presentation must be choreographed and rehearsed in advance. It must be constructed so that the Agent can control the presentation and ensure that the Agent can present their credentials and marketing plan to differentiate the Agent from competitors. It should avoid recommendations such as price, sales time, or repairs that will be likely necessary to sell the home. The listing presentation must first demonstrate the professionalism of the agent, the partnering collaborative attitude of the agent, and the commitment that the Agent will always do what is in the Prospect's best interest. It must be structured in such a way as to avoid recommendations about price and fees until the client has had an opportunity to discover the Illuminating answers that will allow him to save face with the Agent when talking about price, sales time, and repairs that might be necessary to move the property.

"Illuminating the Possibilities" with a Prospect requires remarkable tact and a demonstration of information that will illuminate the reality of the situation to the client. The Agent wants to do more than meet or exceed expectations; the Agent wants to redefine the expectations of what an Agent should be and clearly represent the difference between the typical real estate Agent and the Consultative Agent. The Agent seeks to make an overwhelmingly powerful presentation filled with such benefit and value that a Prospect is compelled to choose them. This partnered relationship can best be called **Consultative Selling**.

CHAPTER 15|KEYSTONE CONCEPT: COLLABORATIVE SELLING CONCEPTS

Jake Trimble was an upper-level executive for an insurance company at its Regional Offices in North Texas. He was referred to us by one of our fans and was hoping to find a home in our area. We arranged an overview meeting with him and prepared our team to confer immediately.

Upon arrival at our offices, Jake appeared to be friendly and all business. We met with him and our Team Members at our Collaboration Hub in our private offices, designed for someone technically minded but also involved in the professional sales function. Our Collaboration Hub was a Steelcase Corporation Collaboration Center with thirty-two-inch monitors and four data-sharing ports. This allowed others to connect to and share information via the monitors. According to the provider, Steelcase Corporation, they have never sold such a unit to a REALTOR® before. It was purchased to differentiate us from competitors during presentations to our Prospects and clients and to utilize it in the training and development of our team members. The technology cost was a little over $20,000.

After our introductory comments and visit, we got down to business. We were off to a good start as he seemed to enjoy collaboratively discussing his needs and wants with ample opportunity for him to talk. We had the entire day if necessary. He was hoping to purchase a home in the $700,000 price range. We will revisit Jake and his story after understanding more about Collaboration.

Understanding Collaboration

To understand the importance of Collaboration in the real estate industry, one needs to explore some interesting information about the human brain. The need for collaboration is all about the brain and coding that is believed by some to occur within a human being at conception. Genetics plays a prominent role in our discussion and may seem out of place when discussing becoming a successful real estate agent. The first requirement for opening the mind to this discussion is that the real estate business is, most importantly, about people. The collaborating consultative Agent wants to know how they think, believe, and feel.

To begin, an examination of some innovative thinking regarding Pride. One of the Seven Deadly Sins is Pride which is discussed in *Dante's Inferno*. Following is a quote from John Medina's book, *The Genetic Inferno*. It should be read carefully as it is essential to understanding why collaboration works so well with clients. Medina writes,

> *"For the past several decades, it has been fashionable for many researchers to think of the human brain as a "tabula rasa," a blank slate upon which the environment can write almost anything. This notion emphasizes the nurture side of the equation, the belief that human beings are a strict product of their environments, with genetics playing a secondary role (if indeed any role at all)." (2000, p. 276)*

What does all of this have to do with collaboration? It has to do with clients who have pride in what they have done and have deep emotions about what they are doing in the future. Medina goes on to write:

> *"This is a powerful analogy for showing how both nature and nurture work together to create a functioning human brain. Without the genetic hardwiring, the baby wouldn't even create an eye. But without the environment, the baby may never acquire vision." (2005, p. 277)*

Medina's argument seems to me to be that possibly all humans may be created with "self" and "ego" as part of their genetic makeup, and regardless of the environment around them and its relationship with the development of the view of self, one would be wise to consider the possibility that all humans are endowed at their creation with genes that impact the future person's view of self and ego. It is possible that people have genetic and environmental reasons to have pride and a high opinion of themselves. Most people who own homes or seek to own a home have great pride in becoming a homeowner or selling a home they have purchased. They also frequently have great pride in their choices relative to the home and a great deal of emotion involved in the decision to change their home ownership situation.

A person born into a family of low-esteem individuals and surrounded by environments similar to that for their entire lives seems likely to have low self-esteem like their parents. Yet, there are examples of many people with great self-value and esteem that accomplish amazing things and defy logic concerning the environment being the way people develop into who they are.

The collaboration process brings the client into an environment where the client's personality, including ego and self-esteem, is embraced and recognized as having value. This makes the client a participating partner in the process and recognizes their contribution to the success or failure of the project. Collaboration empowers a client by providing them with an essential voice in the process of selling or buying real estate.

Matrix Management

The Agent further supports this by recognizing that the client has supreme power over the outcome of a real estate transaction. Therefore, giving a client a seat at the table of collaboration and incorporating the Matrix Management style of business is an important development in how real estate services are provided in a collaborative consultative Practice. A brief review of the Matrix Management concept will shed light on this idea.

What is matrix management? The indeed.com website provides a simple and concise explanation.

> *"Matrix management refers to the organizational structure used by companies to distribute employee responsibilities and have them report to multiple managers. The two main chains of command within matrix management are the project manager and the functional manager." (2023, Indeed.com Website)*

Using the weak matrix system described, the Agent takes on the functional manager role, and the client or clients become the project manager(s). Team Selling requires interdependency and collaboration and encourages communication between Team Members and the client as an active participant to the extent that they want to be a participant. This allows a client to exert power in planning and decision-making and fulfill some of their self-esteem needs. Like the agent, the client is endowed with a view of self and ego, given respect, and deferred to. This facilitates a smoother transaction with less conflict and a greater appreciation for the Agent and the Team. This allows for the development of a **"Raving Fan"** mentality from the client. The term "Raving Fan" was taken from a book called *"Raving Fans"* by Kenneth Blanchard. Blanchard provides an interesting strategy for winning clients for life in this book.

Having dealt with the philosophy behind collaboration in real estate, time should be spent on what collaboration is, and how it has developed should be reviewed.

History of Collaboration

The concept of collaboration originated in the 19th century and derives from the Latin term collabora, and collaborate, "to work with others." Today, the Oxford English Dictionary defines collaboration as "united labor" or "cooperation" regarding "literary, artistic, or scientific work."

Surprisingly, very little has been written about Collaboration in the real estate industry. Real estate Prospects today are quite different from what they were in the past. They often know much about collaboration and its value in everyday life. They may have attended a university where collaborative learning was integral to the learning process. They also have more information and think they know more; as a result, they expect to be listened to and be a part of the process more than ever. While there are some exceptions, the Agent should consider that a collaborative approach is a better strategy than being "the all-knowing, do as I say" Agent of the past.

This is particularly relevant when meeting with a person who has attained a high level of business success, has a great deal of knowledge and experience, and has healthy self-esteem. They seldom want to be lectured to and most often expect to be involved in the collaboration process.

The hypothesis is that collaborative selling provides significant advantages over the historical and most often-used way that agents have previously worked with clients. This is based upon some "brainy" ideas presented in the book *brain rules* by John Medina. Collaboration provides some fundamental advantages, as he describes in his book.

"As you no doubt have noticed if you've ever sat through a typical PowerPoint presentation, people don't pay attention to boring things (Brain Rule #6). You've got seconds to grab someone's attention and only ten minutes to keep it. At 9 minutes and 59 seconds, you must do something to regain attention and restart the clock—something emotional and relevant." (2014, p. 2)

The collaborative Agent is fortunate that selling or buying real estate is often a highly emotional issue to most buyers and sellers, and therefore more accessible for a collaborative Agent to involve the client in the discussion, debate, and analysis. This positive aspect of having emotional involvement by the client is opposite to what most agents believe about the value of the client's emotions. When a person has deep emotional involvement in a subject, they tend to be more interested than when emotion is absent.

The client is uniquely invested in "home" or making a major move, whether buying or moving from a home. They usually have deep emotions involved in the process. Many agents profess that this emotion gets in the way of handling clients. Still, emotion is a Collaborative Agents friend in keeping the client attentive, engaged, and listening carefully to what the Agent is saying.

A transition from a presentation-focused lecture to a collaboration-focused interaction is required for a Collaborative Agent to successfully engage a client on a deeper level and create a solid connection with that client. This implies that the Agent not only provides the client with knowledge but actively includes the Prospect in discovering answers and solutions to their problems.

This approach of working together enables meaningful conversation, involvement, and feedback. The Agent may stop to ensure that the Prospect completely understands the information that has been delivered and may then allow the Prospect to provide feedback or ask questions to clarify any ambiguities. The Prospect has a greater sense of involvement and investment in the process, and they can express their thoughts, opinions, and feelings with the consultant, which eventually results in improved decision-making.

The Collaborative Agent can empower the client and allow them to take ownership of the process because they share the leadership role with the client. Because of this sense of ownership, the Prospect is motivated to actively engage in and contribute to determining the most effective solutions.

While helping a client locate the home of their dreams, for instance, a collaborative agent may pose questions to the Prospect such as **"What aspects of a house are the most important to you?"** or **"What are the major concerns you have regarding the process of purchasing a home?"** When the client is actively involved in the process, the Agent can better adjust their strategy to match their unique requirements and personal preferences.

About Power Imbalance

Collaborative Selling anticipates the Power imbalance that can be created when an "all-knowing Agent" provides services to a highly knowledgeable clientele with more information than ever. This is especially true when a client with healthy self-esteem believes that they do not necessarily need an Agent but must have one because they are not licensed to sell real estate. The collaborative selling process is all about sharing power, information, and knowledge to achieve more than can be achieved otherwise. It works hand in hand with a Consultative approach and a partnered relationship that establishes a long-term relationship with a client and their sphere of influence. This understanding of the importance of power in a relationship is described in the book, *Interpersonal Conflict* by Joyce L. Hocker and William W. Wilmot. They write about the normalcy of conflict rather than the aberration of conflict.

"One of the most common dysfunctional teachings about conflict is that harmony is normal and conflict is abnormal." (1974, p. 7)

Conflict will come about in almost all human endeavors. It is normal, and to deny that it will occur is unwise. All people have ideas and opinions, and behavior is based on their past experiences. Collaboration anticipates conflict and tries to turn normal conflict into a productive tool rather than a disruptive element.

Conflict is likely to exist in all relationships, whether personal or business-related. Denying that a problem exists because it is considered abnormal often causes more conflict and more emotions to be triggered. When working with people on something that is emotionally impactful to them, the likelihood of conflict is increased.

The agent working in a collaborative environment can better manage natural conflict resulting from client interaction. The client usually has important goals and therefore has great emotion involved in achieving those goals.

Frequently, <u>conflict arises because of an imbalance of power</u>. This is especially true when interdependent parties must rely on others to accomplish something important, such as selling or purchasing a home. Hocker and Wilmot, in the book *Interpersonal Conflict*, make this point clear.

"Conflict parties engage in an expressed struggle and interfere with one another because they are interdependent. "A person who is not dependent upon another—that is, who has no special interest in what the other does—has no conflict with that other person." (1974, p. 15)

They go on to write:

"Parties in strategic conflict, therefore, are never totally antagonistic and must have mutual interests, even if the interest only keeping the conflict going. Without openly saying so, they often are thinking, "How can we have this conflict in a way that increases the benefit to me?" (1974, p. 15)

Occasionally, the agent can overcome or reduce conflict by explaining to a client how they benefit from something. Explaining how they win is beneficial and keeps the agent on the same Team as the client.

Interdependence & Collaboration

By becoming interdependent on the client, the agent secures a different relationship dynamic that increases loyalty. Collaboration refers to "a coordinated activity during which participants collectively process, share knowledge or goals, and solve problems toward a joint outcome… such as selling a home or finding a new one.

Almost all Prospects know more, have more information than in the past, and frequently want to be more involved in the process. They want to work with Agents. However, they do not want to be shut out of the discussions of property selection and frequently have a list of properties they are sure they want to tour. Buyers often take pride in their knowledge of buying real estate and believe they have much to contribute to the process. They also want more power and think they have answers, and telling them otherwise is a poor strategy for any real estate Agent. In *Interpersonal Conflict*, Hocker and Wilmot further say,

"A move toward some equitable arrangement of power can lead the way to effective management (Wehr 1979). Parties can (1) limit the power use of the higher-power party, (2) empower the lower-power party, or (3) transcend the win-lose aspect of so many conflicts and create a collaborative structure." (1974, p. 92)

Who is the higher-power decision-maker in this situation? They are highly interdependent. Without the client, the Agent can sell nothing. The client has more power in that they have the power to terminate the relationship. Yet, they depend on the Agent to achieve their goals, and terminating the Agent will not always solve their problem. In this situation, regardless of how the Agent perceives the power balance to be, the Agent must give power to the client and allow them to exert their opinion unless that opinion is illegal or unethical in some fashion. In that situation, the Agent must withdraw. Therefore, collaboration and resolution of conflict is the best solution for all.

Most clients want to have an agent and use them in their transactions most of the time unless they purchase a newly built home. In this case, they may prefer to go forward without the assistance of an agent. Most Prospects do not understand why having an agent assist them when purchasing a newly built home from a builder is necessary. Telling them they need an agent doesn't work as they are confident they don't need the help. Demonstrating proficiency in the subject might open the window for them to consider why an agent is important when purchasing a "to be built" or "newly built" home from a builder. The collaboration process allows for more interaction and an opportunity for the agent to provide this demonstration.

They usually want someone to collaborate with to benefit from multiple points of knowledge and experience. Many Prospects have attended Universities where collaborative teaching environments were predominant or worked in an environment where collaboration is a way of working. This should be expected among many real estate clients an Agent meets.

Many Agents also recognize that many of these "highly knowledgeable clients" can present challenges because they don't know what they don't know! What does the statement; "they don't know what they don't know" mean? Having information and understanding the value of the information are two entirely different things. Sometimes too much information can mislead one into forming conclusions without a proper understanding of how the information is relevant. Unfortunately, forming an opinion based on the "thin-slicing data" can be problematic in real estate.

I Don't Need an Agent!

A knowledgeable client might believe that they don't need an Agent to help them but want one to collaborate with, especially on contracts, inspections, and sales or negotiation strategies. When an Agent sits with a client and fills in the blanks of a contract without explaining its nuances, the Agent reinforces the idea that it doesn't require much expertise or talent to be a real estate Agent.

Since the Prospect searching for a home is usually not paying a fee for Agent's services, and the Agent is willing to drive them around, take them to lunch, and make it easier for them, they will use the services of an Agent. They frequently believe that Agents are ubiquitous, pretty much alike, and many could do what the Agent does if licensed. Because they think they know, they assume they will have to pay an amount they have already determined for a home that meets their criteria. When these Prospects meet an Agent that works collaboratively, they usually recognize the difference, which is a positive factor for the Agent. Collaboration is an effective way for an Agent to differentiate themselves from their competitors while fostering an environment allowing the client to see the Consultative Collaborating Agent as a partner, not a salesperson.

When selling or purchasing a home, the client often has previous experience selling homes and retaining Agents and thinks they know what to expect in both instances. They often believe they will be able to sell their home for a dollar amount they have already considered. In the instance of purchasing a home, they may already have in mind properties that they want to consider and have an idea of how much they will be willing to spend. In essence, they may have a high self-opinion. After all, they have tracked all the homes in their part of town or neighborhood for months or years. They have truckloads of information that empower them to believe that they know!

Collaboration provides an environment that encourages discussion of issues and resolution of problems through joint problem-solving sessions such as monthly or weekly reviews. Conflicts that arise in real estate come in all different shapes and sizes. A husband and wife could disagree on a decision, a parent who is providing the funds for a transaction and wants to be satisfied but disagrees with their children's choices, or a decision by a client that confuses or frustrates an Agent.

Relationships that Survive Closing...

The Agent's goal is not just to sell a home but to build a relationship with multiple people that will survive closing on the purchase or sale of a home. Specifically, by working together, parties can accomplish something more quickly and with better results with less conflict than by operating alone. An Agent that understands and listens to the parties in the collaboration will most often have a more successful and more satisfying experience with the Prospect than that which would occur by failing to listen to all the parties in collaboration.

In the typical real estate transaction, the number of decision-makers is relatively constant, but the number of influencers can vary greatly. This can create conflict. Participants could be a couple, a couple with a parent or parents who want to help financially, or siblings who are influencers. There could be children that a Prospect wants to make happy, allowing them to provide input. There could be financial advisors or best friends who have experience buying or selling a home or investment property.

In this situation, there could be one Key Decision Maker or several Decision Makers, and the Decision Maker may not be the person who has signed a Representation Agreement and may not be on the Title. By working collaboratively, the Agent welcomes the interaction with others that the Prospect wants to be involved in, and this automatically provides the Agent access to the Prospect's sphere of influence. As the facilitator in the collaborative environment, the Consultative Agent serves the client in guiding them on their path to success.

The agent must understand who is to be collaborated with and facilitate the communication by how they respond and converse with the parties. The Prospect impacts this by introducing or describing how their associate, family member, or friend will be involved. In a successful collaboration, the setting up of the process results in mutually defined and shared goals and aims. The Agent's primary goal should be to provide great service to secure a long-term relationship with the Prospect and realize the benefits of several successful transactions over time rather than just completing one real estate transaction. In the case of influencers, there could be a Perception Sale that results in a future client or other sources of referrals.

To succeed in Collaboration, the Agent must know the Prospect's goals and how the Prospect and the other parties in the collaboration want to interact. This allows the Agent to understand the goals and what must happen to achieve these goals. What are the people who are collaborating hoping to achieve by working together to reach a goal? A better decision, a better price, or a faster resolution could all be the goals of the Prospect, and the Agent shares in achieving these goals. This often results in the Agent becoming a valuable consultant to the client.

Utilizing Subject Area Experts

The collaboration may involve other subject area experts, such as Mortgage Brokers, Insurance Agents, or Property Inspectors. The "Collaboration Hub" technology is based on recent changes and trends in business. In a collaborative environment, instead of the dominance of a single individual (All Knowing Agent), there are Subject Area Experts (SAE), and other parties involved, working with the client to create a better outcome.

When a Prospect successfully sells or buys a home, the Agent, Mortgage Lender, and other SAEs all stand to benefit. This helps to benefit the Strategic Marketing Partner program of the Agent. However, if the Prospect is unsuccessful, none benefit, and all most likely will lose. Knowledge is distributed among many participants, and participants are encouraged to take advantage of the availability of information, use others' ideas, and even allow others to use theirs. In the process, the Agent must operate under a new Paradigm.

This new Paradigm is that the Agent is not all-knowing, does not have all the answers, but instead uses their skills and experience as an adjunct to the Prospect's knowledge (recognizing and accepting the client's intellect and knowledge) to improve the possibility of success for the Prospect. Some Agents try to command what the Prospect does rather than collaborate to reach the desired outcome agreed to by the Prospect. This approach is likely to create conflict and inflame emotions.

The Prospect and other participants will likely feel empowered by a collaborative approach and take ownership in decision-making. Long-term client satisfaction is more likely secured.

This change sometimes requires a **"State of Mind"** change for the Agent. Having all the answers all the time can be challenging for any Agent! The Agent often believes that they are supposed to know all the answers all the time. It does not damage the relationship when Agent and Prospect jointly solve a problem or answer a question. In some cases, the relationship can be enhanced by this interdependency. Asking a client, **"What do you think should be done?"** can be seen by the client as recognition of their importance in the selling or buying process.

In his book *brain rules*, Medina wrote about the need for people to solve problems with the help of others and referenced man's history in the jungles as an example of this need to work in teams or groups. He wrote,

> *"Trying to fight off a woolly mammoth? Alone, and the fight might look like Bambi vs. Godzilla. Two or three of you together— coordinating behavior and establishing the concept of "teamwork"— and you present a formidable challenge. You can figure out how to compel the mammoth to tumble over a cliff, for one."* (2012, p. 13)

There is also ample evidence that this approach of team or collaboration with others for many would appeal to the self-perception of a client better than being told what to do and how to do it by someone new to them or someone that they may not hold in high esteem.

Suppressing the Desire to Provide Answers

One of the challenges of collaboration for some Agents is their unwillingness to suppress the desire to supply the answer long enough to allow the participants to discover. This is directly related to the Keystone Concept: "Illuminating the Possibilities" Allowing the Prospect to discover the answer allows the Agent not to need to provide the Prospect unwelcome news and run the risk of alienating the Prospect. While the Agent may know the answer, it is possible that waiting for others to know the answers also facilitates building relationships and securing future Client loyalty.

It is also important to understand that each situation or need may result in a different group of participants in the Collaboration Hub. Buyers and Sellers may need different Subject Area Experts (SAEs) to help them, but some may not need some of the available SAEs.

Encouraging the Prospect(s) to accept and support that they are important in solution development and decision-making is a winning strategy. A Prospect that doesn't have any knowledge of real estate may not bring great value but may be imperative in gaining affirmation. This will help them take ownership of the strategy, tactic, or decision that has been made. Later, when the team is successful, everyone will feel the satisfaction of a successful collaboration. However, if the TEAM is unsuccessful, the Agent does not have to take 100% ownership of the lack of success.

Collaboration is, therefore, like TEAM Building. Teams in collaboration may exist on a continuum from heavy involvement (Agent) to minimal involvement (Inspector). It is not just the desire to work closely with others that motivates the Collaboration initiative. Instead, it is the desire to differentiate oneself from other Agents in how an Agent operates and interacts with the client. The desire is to find approaches to deal with the evolving client who doesn't work with Agents the same way as clients did in the past.

The "Hot Seat" is Avoided

One of the benefits of this novel approach is a fresh attitude and a fantastic sense of relief that the Agent no longer must be all-knowing. Prospects, in general, are optimistic about the idea of Collaboration as an approach that is current and fresh and often expected by the Prospect. People are motivated when asked to be involved and participate in all aspects of a transaction. Like anything else, there will always be an exception to this rule.

A Prospect who does not want to be involved, who wants the Agent to be the all-knowing "tell me what to do resource," is still out there waiting. In this case, like others in the Collaboration Hub, the client may have little involvement. Despite their limited involvement, the Agent must communicate clearly and frequently the reasons why the subject area experts are participating in the collaboration. Communicating the benefit of having more ideas and opinions is a good strategy for the Agent.

Rooted in all of this is a simple assumption: Collaboration Teams are likely to have more success and faster results when working in a collaborative environment than when not. While the collaboration process may take more time and communication, it may also benefit the Agent in that the search and decision-making process would be shortened, and the Agent would be better able to utilize their valuable client contact time.

There will be a positive buy-in from all Team Members when decisions are made during collaboration. Team Members will want to work together more often after a successful collaboration that results in client success. This builds networks and facilitates the development of Decentralized Sales Organizations. This will foster a group success mentality and further bond Collaboration among TEAM members.

The real estate agent will be encouraged to share decision-making and not be reluctant to let some decisions be a decision by the collaboration group if they make sense. The Agent must always remain responsible for all actions to ensure they are ethical and legal. This will reduce stress for the Agent and result in a more enjoyable journey to client satisfaction and future referrals from a "Raving Fan."

Jake Relates to Collaboration

Let us return to our Prospect, Jake, for a moment. After explaining to Jake how we collaborate with our clients, in a moment of self-disclosure, he indicated that he had a Collaboration Hub like ours at his Regional and Corporate Office and was surprised to see our Collaboration Hub. We invited Jake to plug his computer in and share his research with us, but he declined, saying he would listen to our suggestions first. We had established our technical capabilities and differentiated ourselves from others. Jake and Terri became clients and purchased a home for over $750,000. He was a fan, and the fees we earned from his initial purchase more than paid for our Collaboration Hub. Much more importantly, Jake became our reference when talking with others. Several years later, after securing an extensive promotion, we helped Jake sell his home when he was promoted and moved to the Corporate Offices of his company.

Paving the Way to Better Communications

Struggling to get someone to communicate their needs, wants, problems, or motivations may be eliminated in the collaborative environment because the nature of the process is sharing and inclusion.

Collaboration is a structure for and a process to resolve common problems and explore new ideas in an open communication environment called the Collaboration Hub. In the Collaboration Hub, parties create a power-sharing relationship that encourages participation and joint decision-making. As such, the client also shares the responsibility of making the decision.

In a Collaboration Hub, subject area experts are brought together to share ideas and knowledge to facilitate a client having their needs and wants met. As a result, the sale or purchase of real estate happens. Certainly, Agents and participants in a Hub can recognize that the Prospect is an expert in their needs and, most importantly, their wants. This is not to assume that they don't have unknown needs and wants that can be illuminated for them. The agent serves as a consultant by assisting them in understanding their needs and wants and the relative value of each.

One of the keys to success in collaboration is for all participants to respect the other individuals in the Collaboration Hub. The Matrix style of management, where the Team Members see the client as a project manager, encourages Team Members to listen to and respect the client's ideas and concerns eliminating conflicts resulting from the client feeling ignored or unappreciated. Hub TEAM participants work together on the same tasks to understand challenges and opportunities. Communicating with each other goes beyond what they individually already know.

Impact

A final comment about Jake and his spouse, Terri: he recently called and asked for assistance moving back to our area. He wanted to ensure we could assist him and was adamant that we were his choice for support. We now represent him once again in a purchase contract to build a new home, and he continues to be a "Raving Fan."

CHAPTER 16|KEYSTONE CONCEPT: CONTROLLING A CAPTIVE AUDIENCE

Sandy was going through a divorce. She was devastated but had to find a place to live. We were in the process of selling her fashionable home in the Starwood neighborhood. She knew about us because of several years of seeing our names, receiving information from us, and talking to her neighbors. She was an absolute mess. She did not want a divorce and did not want to move from the custom home she had lived in for five years.

Her two daughters were in college, and one was with her when we toured a home that I felt would be right for her. She had been mostly uncommunicative during the search process as she was dealing with many emotional challenges. Upon approaching the home, with sad eyes, she said she liked the front of the home, and once we entered the home, she announced that it looked a lot like her current home, just smaller. She walked directly to the sofa, sat down, and cried uncontrollably.

While her daughter toured the home, Sandy and I sat quietly on the sofa. I said very little and listened intently while she told me how hard this was for her. I listened actively and allowed her to express herself, and she confided in me that this was the worst day of her life. I allowed her to weep and then calm down, and she began to rebound and asked me a few questions about the home. I explained that the builder who built her current home had built this home. It was smaller but very similar to her current home. After about forty minutes, she eventually asked me to take her on tour, and we proceeded with my original plan for touring the home.

Facing Challenging Situations

A real estate agent faces all kinds of situations and must be empathetic and recognize the deep human emotions that sometimes will be presented to them during their career. An agent must be **"aware"** and react to situations that can be unexpected. This is one situation of many in a long career with many clients and friends that need emotional support. Yet, the agent must not be deterred by these events and be responsive and professional in helping a client solve a problem. Sandy needed a home that met her psychological needs as well as her physical needs. Sandy needed an agent that was patient and empathetic to her situation. She purchased that home, and we have been in frequent contact ever since.

Adaptive, Unconscious, and Subconscious concepts play an important role in this chapter about Interpersonal Communications. While meeting with a captive audience in person, through video conference, or on the phone, the Collaboration Agent must make every effort to maintain control of the conversation while avoiding giving the impression that the Prospect is being manipulated in any way.

There is a reason for the Agent to remain in control. By being in control, the Agent can strategically postpone the provision of information and give them the opportunity to prolong the transfer of information in a positive manner, allowing them to interact with the Prospect and collect valuable contact information. This allows the Agent to establish trust and build a relationship with the Prospect. By demonstrating expertise and a willingness to collaborate, the Agent can change the Prospect's perception and be seen as a valuable asset.

While the Agent controls the conversation, they can create moments for transparency and reciprocity with the other party. When a Prospect provides information and discusses their objectives and concerns, the Agent can deliver individualized responses and prove that they can provide value to the relationship. Not only does the Agent have a greater understanding of the needs of the Prospect as a result of this, but the connection between the two parties also becomes more collaborative and productive.

For example, an Agent is meeting with a potential home buyer. The Agent can obtain information about the requirements and preferences of the Prospect by asking open-ended questions and attentively listening to the answers provided by the Prospect. This enables the Agent to show homes that provide value to the Prospect while meeting the parameters specified by the Prospect. The agent may build a relationship of trust with the Prospect, ultimately leading to a successful transaction if they demonstrate their competence and readiness to collaborate.

Being in control is not meant as a "negative act of control" but rather a benefit to the Prospect as it allows the agent to serve. It is often important for the real estate agent to manage emotion to further the client's interest. Using collaboration and interpersonal communications strategies, the agent can overcome the "Resistance to Disclosure" and partner with the Prospect. This passive control has no ulterior motive as it is meant to allow the agent to help the client achieve their goals and objectives and solve client problems along the way.

Control & Sales Speak-A Contrast in Style

Controlling the Prospect will allow the agent to obtain contact information that will allow the agent to stay in touch with the Prospect. When a Prospect calls, they most often have an agenda, a list of things they want to know, and these things they want to know are usually highly important to them. They are focused on getting answers and are anxious to get them without delay or endure **"sales speak."** They expect to find a product-oriented salesperson on the other side of the conversation. To say that they have tunnel vision is an understatement. A Consultative agent is different from most real estate agents because you operate as a consultant and collaborator. You can benefit the Prospect more when you are given the opportunity to serve.

They also have expectations that guide them when talking with an agent. They expect the standard approach of a product salesperson to meet and greet, present, overcome objections, and try to close a sale. Not doing this changes the dynamics of the conversation, and it goes against what the client expects. It allows the agent to connect in a different way than the Prospect thought they would be communicating.

In John Medina's book, *brain rules*, the author discusses the **"Alerting or Arousal Network."** This concept has broad application to the idea of controlling a captive audience. Medina wrote,

> *"In Posner's model, the brain's first system functions much like the two-part job of a museum security officer: surveillance and alert. He called it the Alerting or Arousal Network. It monitors the sensory environment for any unusual activities. This is the general level of attention our brains are paying to our world, a condition termed "intrinsic alertness." (2014, pp. 110-111)*

In a telephone call to an Agent, where the caller is requesting property information, the Prospect, with expectations in mind, is presented with such an alert, as described above, except it is no danger. The Consultative Agent follows the normal pattern of meet and greet but suddenly departs from the expected by not presenting or moving into a product sales role. The agent flips a switch and begins to express interest in the client and their needs and wants without following the sales pattern expected of a product-oriented salesperson. This is done by the Agent saying, **"Now that we have had a chance to visit, perhaps you could tell me a little about your goals and objectives and what you are hoping to accomplish regarding real estate?"**

A Prospect expects to hear a sales pitch and plea to be retained. This change from the expected sends an alert and arouses the brain in that this is different and unusual. The client suddenly finds themselves talking about what is important to them and what they hope to accomplish rather than listening to a sales pitch from the agent about properties that the agent wishes to sell. The agent focuses on Prospect needs rather than products.

Intrinsically, without knowing why, the Client starts to pay attention to this different approach by the agent and loses focus on their initial goal of obtaining information and hanging up. It is unlike what they have found in conversations with other Agents. In other conversations, they may have been provided information without empathetic interaction and moved on without further discussion. They have not always been treated with the caring attention of someone who is not in a hurry to make a sale but is more interested in building a relationship by solving a problem for the caller.

There is also a difference in the power balance as suddenly the Agent seems less concerned about what the agent wants and more about the Prospect's needs and wants. The consultative agent doesn't sell, and they accept a Prospect's power position. They understand, listen, relate, and avoid moving into a sales presentation until they understand a Prospect's motivations. The Agent seeks to control by focusing on the Prospect rather than themselves. Since Prospects are most interested in their needs and wants, this encourages discussion and collaboration. When small things are disclosed, the Prospect tends to reciprocate and reveal. This approach is empowering to the Prospect and results in their reciprocal disclosure.

Balance of Power & Positive Control

Maintaining control involves "Power" and who has "Power" at various points during a conversation or meeting. A Prospect has the ultimate power in that the Agent seeks to know and connect with the Prospect to build a relationship. The Agent needs the Prospect more than the Prospect needs the Agent. The balance of "Power" during the conversation will wane and flow depending on how badly the Prospect wants or perceives they need the information the Agent possesses.

By focusing on the Prospect, the Agent seeks to avoid answering specific questions about their services, fees, agreements, and perhaps a particular property. As Prospects provide information, the Agent can dole out the answers as the Prospect and Agent share information about themselves through self-disclosure and reciprocity.

The Agent has some power in that they have the information wanted and can either provide it or not. Withholding the information for a moment to obtain contact information is often necessary for the Agent to remain in contact with a Prospect. The agent should withhold some information for as long as possible without offending or alienating the Prospect. If the Agent feels that alienation is possible, they should disclose accordingly to maintain contact with the Prospect.

At some point, the Prospect will realize that they have not obtained the information they were hoping for and will go back to the pattern of discussion that they expected. They will ask the Agent to move forward and answer their questions. By delaying, the Agent buys time, obtains client-specific information, and can proceed with knowledge and understanding in a problem-solving consultative manner. The Prospect has a problem that needs to be solved. They need to buy or sell a home or investment property. What is their problem, and how can the Agent solve the problem?

Having learned more about the Prospect and what they need, the Agent is ready to begin solving problems and becoming a Consultative Agent. The client has done most of the talking and disclosing, and now it is appropriate for the Agent to disclose more information to the Prospect based on what they need and want. The agent might say,

"Thank you for sharing that information so I can stay in touch. Let's explore further what you would like to accomplish." This once again signals a different approach than what a Prospect is expecting.

The Goal – Meeting Face-to-Face

If this communication was by telephone and has determined where the Prospect needs assistance, the Agent can now move forward with setting a face-to-face appointment with the Prospect. This should be the ultimate goal after receiving a call from a Prospect. Getting a chance to meet the Prospect in person expands the relationship quickly.

If the phone call was to express interest in having an agent help sell a home, the agent can move to a home visit appointment to meet with the Prospect but still must have contact information to follow up. In any situation, the goal for the Agent is to set a meeting in person with the Prospect. Many opportunities in real estate begin with a telephone conversation. Mastering the art of controlling a Prospect and securing an appointment is a requirement for long-term success in real estate sales, brokerage, and consulting.

In almost all instances, there are some things that an Agent can expect a Prospect to want to know, and the Prospect will be seeking immediate answers. Providing immediate answers to these questions is not to the advantage of the Agent.

- Who pays the commission for your services, and how much is that Commission?

- Whom do you work for, and will you be loyal to me?

- How much will it cost for what I want, and how much can I negotiate?

- How soon can I accomplish my objective and close on the sale or purchase?

- How much cash will it take for me to be able to close?

- If selling my home, how much can I sell for, what repairs or improvements will I need to do, and how much will it cost me to sell?

Talking about money is a losing strategy for the Agent. Discussing the likely sales price for a Seller or the purchase price for a Buyer is seldom positive for the Agent, as there is no sure way of knowing how the client will react to the information. There is nothing positive about telling a client what services cost. It also makes it appear that the Agent is focused on money rather than assisting a client. When the Prospect is focused on money, and the agent follows, there is an inability to make other things such as client care, marketing, experience, and credentials more important. A fundamental rule is to never talk about money until required. It is important to convince a Prospect to agree to delay the money discussion whenever possible. The Agent would like to avoid price with the Prospect's approval. Gaining that approval to delay is essential.

A Prospect has likely thought about these money questions numerous times before the conversation and is poised to pounce on the Agent quickly, hoping to get what they want immediately. The caller can escape without commitment to satisfy their need to obtain the information. It is, therefore, essential that the Agent take control from the very beginning and avoid a power struggle with the Prospect by controlling the dissemination of the information that the Prospect wants, allowing the Agent an opportunity to make a powerful presentation that will consciously and/or subconsciously make a Perception Sale to the Prospect. It is also essential for the Agent to get approval from the Prospect when asking to put off answering a question. This allows the Prospect to feel they are in control and have power.

When an Agent has the information others want, they have the power! When information is shared too quickly, power is diminished.

Here is an example of an Agent losing power quickly: The caller says, **"I am calling about a home at 4340 Woodbine Lane in Prosper. Can you tell me how much it costs and if it has a pool?"** The Agent responds, **"Of course, that home is listed at $455.000 and does have a pool. Can I get your name, please?"** The caller has what they want and could say, **"I'm fine, I was just curious, thank you!"** and then hang up. This will deny the Agent an opportunity to identify the caller and obtain their contact information. This could block follow-up with the caller by the Agent. It also fails in allowing the Agent to arouse interest from the caller, thus securing time to position themselves as a problem-solving resource to the caller.

While the agent often has caller identification and knows a name and a phone number, they have not done anything to break down the "Resistance to Disclosure," so it is far better to have the caller provide or confirm the information willingly. This will make a follow-up contact feel more comfortable.

When a caller calls about a property, they have what might be called SITUATIONAL INTEREST. This kind of interest is short-term and must be addressed quickly and moved to a different form of interest to allow the Agent time to connect with and relate with a caller. Jeanne Ellis Ormrod, in her book, *human learning*, explains situational interest as follows:

> *"Situational interest is sometimes of the "catch" variety: It engages you for a short time (as the Llama engaged me), but you quickly move on to something else, and so cognitive processing and learning are apt to be limited." (2012, p. 463)*

When the Agent can catch the caller and move them to a different kind of learning, they arouse interest and engagement. She explains another kind of learning, which she calls the "HOLD" variety. She writes.

> *"Other instances of situational interest are of the "hold" variety: You stay with a task or topic for a lengthy period—say, for an hour or more. Hold-type situational interest and enduring personal interests are ultimately more beneficial than catch-type interest." (2012, pp. 463-464)*

By controlling the Prospect for a longer time, the Agent can introduce topics, ideas, and information that moves the caller from a "CATCH" mentality to a "HOLD" mentality. This allows the agent to connect mentally with a common interest for both parties. The Prospect's interests are vital to gaining their full attention.

Transferring information that the Prospect wants and the resulting power transfer to the Prospect is unfavorable for an Agent unless done strategically. One of an Agents goals is to keep power in any communication as it allows the Agent to extend the conversation and increase the opportunity to connect with a Prospect personally and gather information about the Prospect. Buying time allows the agent to connect, demonstrate proficiency, and arouse personal interest.

For that reason, giving up information too quickly can cause an Agent to lose power and result in an inability for the Agent to get the vital Client information they need. Holding on to information when it is known that the Prospect wants it is a way of passively controlling the Prospect and staying connected with the Prospect long enough for the Agent to obtain information and build a relationship. This is best accomplished in a consultative way, with a Prospect's needs and wants to be paramount to the agent.

Using Power Phrases

"Power Phrases" provide the Agent with badly needed techniques to achieve this. These phrases are about the balance of power in a meeting or conversation. "Power Phrases" are spoken phrases that allow an Agent to control a Prospect yet not cause the Prospect to feel that the Agent is controlling them. This is often accomplished by the Agent gaining Prospect approval to delay providing the answers they called about.

Power phrases make it difficult for the Prospect to say no to something an Agent requests or says. Power Phrases are diplomatic ways of saying, **"Not now. I'll get to that later."** Power Phrases allow an Agent to put off giving answers that the Prospect wants until the Agent has fully and completely delivered their **"I can help you"** message. "Power Phrases" buy the Agent time.

Using "Power Phrases" in meetings with prospects allows money discussions to be delayed. It thereby avoids talking about contracts, representation agreements, fees, repairs, and updates needed until ready to do so. Most importantly, "Power Phrases" allow an Agent to postpone providing unpleasant news or information until the Agent has helped the Prospect discover or learn that they need help. For example, telling a calling Prospect that the home they called about is sold.

Power Phrases are psychologically loaded words, phrases, and combinations of phrases that, when used, make it difficult for the Prospect to say **"No."** This inability to say "no" results from the Agents language used in concert with the "Information is Power" concept.

Most people, even when anxious for answers, will try to be respectful and kind when asked politely to agree to something if the request is reasonable and permission is asked. Approximately 50% of Prospects are generally agreeable by personality type and may find it almost impossible to demand something when politely asked to wait for the information. Somewhat disagreeable people will be willing to go along if they are promised to get the information they desire in a reasonable timeframe. For this reason, Power Phrases, more than anything else, must be polite, friendly, and used with a smile and promise of delivering the information the Prospect wants! Power phrases used with the concept of Demonstrating Competency provide the Agent with a tool chest that can make the Agent desirable while arousing interest in the person they are communicating with. Demonstrating competency mixed into a conversation or meeting takes the Prospect's mind off their pursuit of information. It causes them to forego their need for answers because they get substantial ideas and information from the Agent.

Power Phrases include but are not limited to the following:

- Please
- Thank You,
- If it is ok with you, may I…
- If you don't mind, I would like to…
- I'd appreciate it if…
- Can you help me with something, please?
- May I ask you for a favor?
- If it is all right with you, I would like to…
- Great, thank you for that… I really appreciate this
- Remember, we agreed to get to that in a little while…
- I want your advice on something, Who, What, Where, Why, How, etc.
- You probably already know this…
- As you know…

Power Phrase Combinations are even more psychologically powerful… when a promise to answer the Prospect's question is given or implied! This is not a trick in that the Prospect really wants the information and, when faced with not getting the information or politely going along as asked, will usually do so if they believe the Agent is sincere about later giving them what they want.

As a result, when promising to provide the answers and deliver the information, the Prospect most often tends to believe that it will happen. If the answers are not eventually given, the Prospect could be alienated. In the statement below, the Agent promises to answer the questions and leave open the possibility that the information will be provided. Many Prospects would prefer not to ask about fees or money as it makes them uncomfortable. They do not want to appear cheap by attempting to negotiate.

"If you don't mind, I'd like to talk about our marketing program, our analysis of your needs and wants, and then answer all other questions that you might have if I have not already answered them for you during my presentation… Is that all right with you?"

On rare occasions, the client interrupts the presentation because they realize they still don't know what will be charged for services provided. A Prospect often worries about this and is anxious to get an answer. A Prospect seldom interrupts a speaker when the speaker delivers a positive and powerful message that is benefit-oriented to the Prospect. When the Agent is saying enthusiastically and positively something valuable to them, they don't want to lose out on the ideas being presented. Therefore, at the beginning of the presentation, control should be established. If the Agent is standing, it would be almost impossible for the person to interrupt and stop the presentation.

However, if the Prospect should interrupt the presentation and say, "Smart Agent, I have one question I would like to get to!"

The Agent could respond, "Sure, Jack; what is your question?" "I want to know what you charge. What is your commission for selling our home?"

"I see. Well, if you remember, we agreed to wait until I had finished my presentation on our marketing program. That would allow you to understand all that I do to market your home, and then the professional service fee has relevance because you know what you'll be paying for. Does that make sense? So, if you don't mind, please allow me to complete my marketing and analysis part of the presentation, and then we can talk about all your questions, and I promise to be fully open with you regarding all of this. Is that ok with you?"

Most prospects in the real estate industry do not choose an agent because they appear weak. Instead, they are looking for an agent who will strongly advocate for them and help them achieve the best possible outcome in a transaction. By staying in control of the interaction, the agent can demonstrate their mental toughness and ability to fight for their client's interests.

Suppose a prospect is looking to purchase a property in a competitive market with many other interested buyers. In that case, they want an agent who can assertively negotiate and secure the deal. This can instill confidence in clients that they have chosen a capable and effective agent.

Remaining in control demonstrates the strength and, in most cases, assures the Prospect that the Agent is tough and mentally disciplined enough to help them win. It shows their ability to navigate a challenging situation and get the desired outcome. Most Prospects respect mental toughness in an agent and want a "tiger" on their side of the negotiating table.

While the Prospect may still insist on an answer, it is unlikely. However, if they do, they might say, "Well, I want to know what you charge right now…"

"Fine. Well, Jack, my fee is _% of the sales price. So, the exact amount depends on how much I can sell your home for. Naturally, if I can get you a higher price for your home, you win. The ability to get the most money for your home is directly related to our marketing and how we support the value of your home. That is why the marketing program that I provide is so important. Our marketing efforts are directly related to your sales price. In addition, the fee I receive is much less than you might think because other agents and brokerage firms share in this _% fee. I hope that answers your question, and I will gladly go into more detail in a few minutes. Is this ok?"

The statement above provides an excellent reason why an Agent avoids talking about a specific or professional service fee, as the Agent doesn't know the exact amount that will be charged until the final price is determined. This is a very insightful example of a combination of Power phrases with a promise to provide.

It would be difficult to stop a presenter and say, "No way, give me what I want to know, or I am going to leave right now!"

This is why it is essential to remember that it is so difficult for a Prospect to say "no" or demand because the Agent is being polite and asking for permission. They have permitted to delay the discussion until later. A Prospect has an overriding concern: not getting the information they want and wasting their valuable time. Their fear of not getting the information they want is the power that allows the Agent to avoid unpleasant topics until a foundation for the professional service fee has been constructed. Making a powerful, filled with-value presentation, which proves that the Agent is the most qualified and valuable resource to the client, is the strongest argument for supporting the real estate professional service fee. The longer the conversation goes on, the more invested a Prospect becomes in getting the information they want. This causes them to stay connected with the Agent.

A collaborative, consultative approach and fully and completely differentiating the services provided will allow the Agent to support their fee structure. When a Prospect has already formed a positive opinion about the Agent, and the presentation supports that opinion, it is easier for the Prospect to accept the fee and see the value in doing so.

When the rules and agenda for a meeting are established up front, the Agent can almost be guaranteed the time to finish the presentation of other than price information before talking about unpleasant things like money.

Example:

"Bob, thank you for taking the time to meet with me today and discuss your real estate needs. It is a great compliment when asked to assist clients with an important topic like selling their residence. There are three parts to my presentation today. The first concerns our marketing and how we present your home to the public and Prospective buyers. We examine how we collaborate with you on the marketing process.

The second is a detailed look at the comparable properties that have sold and your competition on the market for sale today.

We will then cover a detailed analysis of our pricing model and our recommendations about how much your property will likely sell for to a qualified buyer. We can then discuss any other questions you have about the time it should take to sell your home, how to prepare it for the market, our services, and any other questions you might have.

So, if you don't mind, I'll begin with an overview of our marketing program!"

This statement demonstrates the "Price Put Off!" Strategy. The statement clarifies that a Prospect will get all the answers they want at the appropriate time. This "promise to provide" is the carrot that allows the Prospect to accept this approach and allow the presentation to move forward. The Agent's strength, demeanor, and confidence make them feel comfortable that the Agent is not afraid to disclose and that they will be satisfied at the end of the meeting. The Agent should remember that the Prospect has the ultimate power. They can "hang up" or "walk away!"

There is a significant difference when a Prospect talks over the telephone or on a Zoom call. First, they are not as Captive as in a face-to-face meeting. An example earlier in this chapter revealed how to lose power in a telephone conversation with a Prospect wanting information. The following dialogue demonstrates how to maintain power, control the call, and obtain the information needed while attempting to build a relationship.

"This is Smart Agent, a licensed agent with the Renaissance Group. How may I help you?"

"Yes, I'm calling about the home at 4340 Woodbine Lane in Prosper. Can you give me the price and tell me if the home has a pool?"

"Of course, I'll be glad to help you with that. My name is Smart Agent (Disclosure). May I have your name, please?" (Seeking reciprocal disclosure)

"My name is John (Disclosure), and I was driving in the area and was curious about this home." (Disclosure)

"Great, thank you, John. While I was looking that up for you, I saw your phone number on my phone. Are you calling from your cell phone? And is this the best number to reach you if we get cut off?"

(Disclosure, Seeking Reciprocal Disclosure)"Yes, it's my cell (Disclosure), and it's the best number for me. How much is the home listed for?" (Seeking Reciprocal Disclosure)

"John, the information just came up on my computer. What is your last name, if you don't mind?" (Disclosure – I have the information you want-promise given)

"It's Reynolds, but..."

"Ok, well, the price is $455,000, and it does have a pool... What made you interested in that home, if you don't mind me asking? (Disclosure)

"Well, my kids go to school in the area, and we are moving from Chicago. How long has it been on the market?" (Disclosure, Seeking information)

"Let's see, I work in that area a lot, and I am not surprised to see that it was on the market for about 30 days and is currently under contract with an Active Option contract... are you familiar with that type of contract?" (Disclosure)

"Oh... No, what is that?" (Wants more information)

"Well, in Texas, an Active Option contract gives the buyer the right to examine the property in an Option Period and cancel the contract if they change their minds or find something that causes them to back out. This is important because you might be able to see the property still if you want to, and I could try to get an appointment if you like. Are you working with an Agent?" (Disclosure, Demonstrating Proficiency, Seeking Reciprocal Disclosure)

"No, we just moved here, and we are staying at an extended stay hotel, but I need to find a home asap." (Disclosure – Urgent Need)

"Well, John, that sounds challenging with a family and all. I often work in this area and know of several other homes that are still on the market and similar to the one you called about. If you would like, I can meet at my office near the property you called about and share that information with you. Are you working with an Agent?"

"No, I have talked to a few Agents but have not signed with anyone yet."

"Ok, that's fine, John... Why don't we meet at my office? I have an excellent book called "The Finding a Home Guidebook" that explains Option Contracts, and I can show you the book, and we can talk about properties that meet your needs. We have an excellent Collaboration Hub in my office, and we can get more acquainted. Which would be better for you, this afternoon or tomorrow? I'm sure you're weary of that hotel room."

This conversation provides insight into how control and power are used to provide a strong reason for the Prospect to meet. Controlling the Prospect provides the Agent time to open doors to meetings and relationship-building through collaboration.

It is now fitting and appropriate for the client to listen to the Agents presentation. Still, the Agent must remember that there are only about ten minutes to do so before the Prospect starts to lose interest and their mind wanders back to the information they were seeking. The consultative agent knows that moving into a collaborative role will prolong the Prospect's attention and avoid early disclosure of information that could negatively affect the consultative relationship with the client. This is where a carefully planned and rehearsed presentation about non-product information can be presented. The Agent is mindful of the fact that the Prospect wants answers to several questions that Prospects usually want to be answered.

Property Call – and Call Prospect Capture

Quincy called about a property that another agent in our office listed. How they got to me is a good question. They did not request the listing agent and wanted to know the sales price and some specific information about the home. Quincy was a first-time home buyer.

I wanted to secure a face-to-face meeting as soon as possible. Here is an example of how to accomplish the objective. After using the techniques described in this chapter, I obtained the critical contact information but did not yet answer all of Quincy's questions, so I still had some power.

"Quincy, it may take me some time to get the answers you want, and I might need to call the listing agent to confirm some things. You said that you are driving around. Perhaps you could swing by my office near the home you called about. I could provide you with all the information you need and the Seller Disclosure and Survey information simultaneously. Can you be here in about 15 minutes? When you are here, I will also show you the "Finding a Home Guidebook," which would be very helpful to you as a first-time home buyer. Is that ok with you?"

Quincy did as I suggested and became a client. Controlling the Prospect is essential in converting callers from visitors to clients.

What is the Intent?

If control intends to help solve problems, provide guidance, and put the other person's best interests at heart, it may be perceived positively. A real estate agent that cannot control a Prospect has little chance of survival in a real estate jungle of 1,520,920 REALTORS®. Had I not been able to control the situation and my emotions, Sandy, a client written about earlier, might have reacted badly to touring the home she eventually purchased. She has lived in that home for years and completely recovered from her difficulties. Control requires restraint. It requires patience and empathy for the situations that a client finds themselves facing.

CHAPTER 17 | KEYSTONE CONCEPT: THE PERCEPTION SALE

D anny and Carla Brecken had received our mail in the Starwood neighborhood for about three years. Our signs had been in the neighborhood on homes we had listed for sale, and we were actively involved in many neighborhood activities. Yet, we had never met. In April, we received a call from Danny asking for tax protest information. We had offered to provide such information on one of our mailers to the neighborhood. We delivered the tax protest information to his home and had the opportunity to meet Danny and his wife, Carla, for the first time. This began our relationship with Danny and Carla.

The following year Danny asked us to provide tax protest information again, and we provided it promptly. We took the information to his home rather than sending it by email. This gave us another opportunity to see them both again. They were very friendly and appreciative. We stayed in touch but never pressed him about selling his home. We called and asked about his tax protest, and he was ecstatic as he had won significant concessions both times and thanked us for our support.

Entrenched Ideas

As we proceed through this chapter, we will revisit Danny and Carla's journey and our part in turning the pages to a new chapter in their lives.

Most clients have entrenched ideas about what an Agent does or does not do. They think that they sell homes. When an Agent allows the Client to see them differently, it is often illuminating to the Client. For example, sending information to your clients about vacation homes or farm and ranch properties might make a perception sale because they had no idea that the Agent has expertise in these other areas. Providing information about insurance issues and major loss concerns can surprise clients as they are unaware that an Agent knows or even cares about their insurance needs. If an agent provides information about insurance issues or major loss concerns, it can showcase their knowledge and expertise in an area the client may not have expected. This can help an agent and the Prospect create trust and rapport with one another.

When an agent intentionally does something to change the client's perception of them, it is called a "Perception Sale."

What is "perception?" One can see, hear, or become aware of something through the senses. The senses are a biological system used by an organism (in this case, humans) to gather information about the world and respond to stimuli.

The real estate agent makes a "Perception Sale" by offering a service or information that causes a client to recognize that an Agent has provided something of value and benefit. Providing this service does not necessarily make the Agent money. Still, it seeks to change a client's perception, allowing the client to see the Agent as a valuable resource that might be able to help them or someone they know in the future.

When a real estate agent assists a client with finding a rental property, even though the agent will receive little income for this service, the client may appreciate the agent's willingness to help and view them as a trusted advisor for future real estate transactions.

Similarly, suppose an agent provides information about local schools, parks, and amenities in the area to a client who is new to the neighborhood. In that case, it can help them become more comfortable and establish a connection.

When speaking to someone or assisting someone by putting them first without compensation or expectation, the Agent can make a Perception Sale that will substantially impact the Agent's long-term revenue. While a "Perception Sale" could produce income and profit, the position is to worry about client success, not revenue or profit for the Agent! This is a problem-solving consultative strategy.

Perhaps the most powerful "Perception Sale" is a sale that changes the perception of the Prospect that the Agent is a product salesperson. Most clients perceive that Agents sell houses and are commissioned salespeople who are highly motivated by money. They most likely don't see the Agent as a problem-solving consultant focused on client success. Even after working with a problem-solving consultative agent, they may have forgotten how the Agent works and need to be reminded. When they see a different approach and attitude, it is something they don't expect, which benefits beyond measure. This builds client trust in the Agent!

Danny and Carla might have been surprised that we did not ask about helping them sell their home and that we failed to act like a typical salesperson. We stayed in touch, and our marketing programs ensured they noticed us and our success in Starwood. They even attended a **"wine-tasting event"** we hosted at home. Danny was quite talkative, and we became fast friends and continued to build the relationship.

In the book *"Consultative Selling,"* the authors write.

> **"The conversion process by which a customer becomes a client is a consultative salesman's most continuing and demanding task. It is his principal educational burden." (1973, p. 15)**

Elongating the relationship with the client beyond closing is essential for long-term success. One of the most powerful positions an Agent takes is to worry about the client's long-term success after purchasing a home. This can be demonstrated by the Agent saying,

"Bill, one of the things that I counsel my clients on is the need to look for an exit strategy anytime they make a home purchase. Most of my clients will not live in a home forever and, at some point in the future, will need to sell the home and purchase another. In any case, they want to sell the property on time and realize the benefit of increased equity. I always recommend that when a property is chosen, the client explores the likelihood of disposing of the property profitably in the future. I call this an exit strategy."

This is an excellent way of demonstrating the consultative role as it moves the client from perceiving that the Agent wants to sell a home and make a commission to perceiving them as a consultant who wants to help a client be profitable.

An Example of a "Perception Sale"

Home prices in the DFW Area have risen dramatically in the past few years. Clients who purchased homes in the past five years could have experienced a 75% increase in their property values. Some clients have been happily living in their homes for several years and are not in the market to buy or sell after having experienced this incredible growth in the value of their homes. They may not realize how being underinsured could impact them in the future.

They may realize that their property taxes have gone up substantially as they received a tax statement but focused on the tax bill, not the home's estimated value. They have seen increases in their homeowner's insurance costs but don't fully understand why. Many people don't pay much attention to these things as they are so busy with their everyday lives.

This TeleConnect contact aims to provide the client with a reason to see the Agent as a consultant and problem-solver. It is to encourage future contact because the client benefits from their relationship with a Consultative Agent. It is to remind them of the great experience that they have had since the home was purchased. This contact will also support the "Raving Fan" relationship that has existed in the past and needs to be maintained.

Here is an example Agent script for the contact. After reaching the client and reconnecting and visiting for a few moments, the Agent might say,

"Jack, it is so great to visit with you and hear how happy you have been in your home. I want to thank you for allowing me to help you!

I have been receiving many calls from Clients and Friends recently about the fantastic increase in the value of their homes that they have experienced. You may have also noticed this for your home. These calls and their questions caused me to be concerned that many of my clients are not up to date on their insurance coverage in the case of a total loss from a fire or storm. Do you have a moment for me to explain my concerns?"

Excellent, thank you... well, I'm sure you have an insurance policy with a maximum payout for a total home loss. The insurance company usually calculates these total payouts based on information about the construction cost of building a similar home in your area.

Unfortunately, they don't specifically know your home and, as a result, primarily use square footage and construction date to compute your home's replacement costs. These computer models are frequently wrong or lag behind the market and could result in you being underinsured because of the replacement cost value of your home in a rising market.

As you know, I DO NOT offer insurance, but I am concerned about you being adequately insured. I would hate to have you suffer a significant loss and want to ensure you avoid this risk. So, here is what I recommend you do!

I suggest you should get in touch with and have a review meeting with your insurance agent, asking them to provide you with the maximum amount you could receive in the event of a total loss of your home. The loss value does not include the cost of a swimming pool or outbuildings unless the event damages them. In many policies, a base coverage such as $300,000 on the dwelling and perhaps a rider adds up to 50% if necessary to rebuild your home. So, in this example, the maximum payout might be $450,000. If the cost to replace your home as it is built is $525,000, you would be exposed to $75,000 in out-of-pocket cash. That is a lot of money.

Some might take the risk and not raise their coverage; this is called self-insuring. This is entirely up to you based upon comparing the increased premium you might incur to the risk.

You have a swimming pool and an outdoor kitchen area with excellent value, so the total market value of your property dwelling minus the lot and pool and outbuildings might be $600,000. If you need help computing this, just call me after you review the CMA. Remember that the document I am sending you looks like I am talking about selling your home. Rest assured. I know you are not ready to sell or move. How does this sound?

If you allow me, I will send you a Comprehensive Market Analysis showing your home's market value, which is important in determining the total replacement cost value of your home. This will allow you to compare what you are insured for versus the approximate market value of the home. The model that the insurance Practice uses may not give you value for the upgrades and changes you have made to the home in the past year, as it is generally based upon a square footage construction cost amount for the average home. The more your home is updated, the more you are likely to be out of balance in this replacement cost calculation.

This is where you will need to use your judgment or ask others for help. If you want me to come by and review this, just let me know. Does all this make sense?"

This is how to make a "Perception Sale." The client sees that the Agent does more than sell homes. They see that the Agent has their long-term needs in mind and isn't concerned just about money. They see the Agent as someone committed to their success. This approach can also demonstrate proficiency in areas other than selling homes and adds value to their relationship with the client. Several positive statements from Clients will be made in this process, and after the Client thanks them, the Agent should say, "Don't forget, I appreciate you trusting me to refer your friends and associates who need help in real estate. Please keep me in mind in the future."

Thank you & Silence

Some clients will say thanks for the information and not respond. Don't be misled… They may already know what you have told them, but if they don't, they may not want to admit that they don't. The impact of your consultative call will be internalized by the Client and help in protecting the relationship with the client from competitors. Their conscious and unconscious mind may remember the effort on their Agent's part. They may also mention the Agent's activity when talking to friends and associates, opening the door for a referral to someone else.

When the Agent adds "Perception Sale" projects to the marketing and client care program, they accomplish an important client retention goal. They provide good reasons to stay in touch with the client over the years, cementing the relationship and protecting the account and their "Raving Fan" status. Every follow-up plan with a client should include these contacts so that the client doesn't get weary of endless sales messages from the Agent. Clients do not like receiving many calls with the sole purpose of qualifying them for another purchase or simply asking for referrals. Provide benefit and value as a problem-solver for the client, and they will want to talk.

Never-Ending Sales Messages--Ugh

It is easy for a long-time client to get weary of endless messages and solicitations about buying or selling a home. It is often five to seven years between transactions because that is the average time people take to move. Seeing and hearing sales solicitations for five years can be tiresome.

When long-term clients are bombarded with numerous product sales messages and pitches regarding buying or selling a home, they may become annoyed and lose interest in listening. Because the typical period between transactions is anywhere between five and seven years, Prospects may be subjected to constant sales pitches over a prolonged period, which might irritate them.

If a real estate agent persistently sends emails or flyers advertising homes for sale, a client who has worked with the agent for a significant amount of time may start to disregard them or even unsubscribe from further contacts. The client may get the impression that they are being inundated with excessive information or that the sales representative is solely concerned with making a sale rather than giving value.

It would not be unusual for a client to become exasperated with endless sales talk. Changing the subject and sending information about something other than agent success can be quite effective. Once an agent earns trust, the need for "self-aggrandizing" about their success ends for a while or possibly forever.

Real estate agents must balance staying in touch with long-term clients and not swamping them with too many sales communications. Finding this balance is a difficult task. As an alternative to concentrating primarily on making sales, real estate agents may provide clients with other valuable resources, such as up-to-date market information, information on upcoming local events, or helpful advice about homeownership. Agents may enhance their relationships with long-term clients and remain at the forefront of their client's minds for future transactions by providing communication that is both meaningful and customized.

Perception Selling broadens the relationship with the Client and encourages the Client to open their sphere of influence contacts to the Agent. While the Agent is waiting for the Client to decide to move into other real estate, the opportunity to work with their sphere of influence is a winning strategy that could be available now. When an Agent has time available and can focus on Perception Selling, significant progress can be made in identifying future business opportunities.

Trait Linkage

Selfless behavior and the provision of beneficial ideas and information makes an exciting contribution to Perception Selling. In their book *Consultative Selling*, the authors describe trait linkage.

"One good trait deserves another: Through a mental structure process known as trait linkage, a customer who attributes one good trait to the salesman will also tend to attribute other good traits." (1973, p. 24)

Unfortunately, this mental structure can confirm what a Prospect thought to be true when stereotyping real estate Agents as product salespeople that are all similar in most ways. By always looking for a sale, the Agent may present a negative trait to a Client. A Perception Sale can be a perception-changing strategy and differentiate the Agent.

A Perception Sale can also cause clients to want to share the Consultative Agent with others as they want their friends and associates to have an equally positive experience. Perception selling can build multiple positive images of the Agent. This experience, over time, builds relationships of trust and confidence. The "Raving Fan" that recommends the Agent allows the Agent to begin a relationship with a new client with a positive perception and eases the challenge of proving value to a new Client as they have already heard about how the Agent works and the benefit the referring party substantiated.

Opportunity to Serve Presents Itself Again

Danny and Carla called us and asked us to meet with them. They had talked to another client about us and gotten a raving review from a "Raving Fan." This supported their previously formed positive opinion about us, and we proceeded to help them list and sell their home. They wanted to purchase another home, and we assisted them in finding and contracting to build a home in another fashionable neighborhood in Frisco, Texas. They referred us to several of their friends and associates, and we frequently listed them as a reference when interviewing other Starwood homeowners.

Developing the relationship with Danny and Carla took time, effort, and constant communication in a patient-consultative way. The money we spent on staying in touch was minimal compared to the financial gain we received from helping them with their real estate needs. We also benefited from a relationship that lasted for years. We have now helped them move again; recently, I talked to Danny. He mentioned our long association, and I again thanked him for his support and friendship.

We did miss the mark in one area of attention. We knew their son was attending University, but we didn't pay enough attention to him. Later, when he became highly successful in the stock brokerage business, we did not get the opportunity to represent him. Our client management program had not been successful in this regard. We did not pay enough attention to Danny and Carla's sphere of influence.

Danny and Carla provided testimonial letters to us and are still friends. This demonstrates the need to recognize that the "Raving Fan" will not always push for your success unless you try to motivate them to do so.

When Magic Happens

The road to success for an agent is sometimes littered with lost opportunities. When a client who is a "Raving Fan" is also a "Connector" who reaches out to others, **Magic Happens**. You must be available and reachable when that magic happens.

CHAPTER 18 | KEYSTONE CONCEPT: DEMONSTRATING PROFICIENCY

Michael Carlton was a client who had purchased several homes with us being his Agent. He had referred numerous people to us and was a "Raving Fan." He was also a Connector. He collected friends like some people collect sports memorabilia. The business he had helped us achieve was more than ten million dollars in production. The revenue earned over several years by our Practice was more than $250,000. He was a VIP in our client ranking system.

We frequently contacted Michael and kept up with him and his family. Their two children were on our list of people to call on birthdays. Our client management program was constantly working to ensure the relationship stayed intact.

I called Michael to see how he was doing (TeleConnect Call) and brought his attention to something happening in our neighborhood of Starwood. He was very friendly and, at the end of the call, asked me if I had time to meet with him for lunch. He needed some advice. We met at a local barbecue restaurant that was his favorite. After catching up on things, Michael got to the point. He was the financial manager for a non-profit organization, and they were considering moving their offices. He was concerned about a decision the head of the non-profit was considering in commercial real estate.

I listened to his concerns and avoided attempting to solicit the opportunity to represent his organization in finding space. I kept my comments focused on solving his problem. His concerns were warranted. He had a problem, and I could help him solve that problem.

Answering all his questions about leasing commercial space, I explained that, in my opinion, his non-profit organization, which an Agent did not represent, was indeed getting ready to make a mistake. I explained why, and he listened carefully. I provided detailed information and demonstrated professionalism and extensive commercial real estate lease knowledge. The meeting was longer than two hours, and I had the rest of the day available if necessary.

I Paid the Check

The conversation ended with Michael telling me that he would think about all that I had said, and he thanked me for my time and all the information I had shared with him. I paid the check for over forty dollars, and we said goodbye.

This chapter primarily focuses on the Prospect but applies when working with clients. A Prospect can become a client with a signature, so there are moments before and after signing an agreement when the relationship is somewhat muddled.

I Didn't Know That

Demonstrating Proficiency is accomplished by presenting or providing information to a prospect that allows them to see the Agent as a valuable resource with information or ideas they do not have, thus proving to the prospect that the Agent provides them an economic and personal value. Proficiency is a high degree of competence, skill, or expertise

In demonstrating the knowledge and ability to help someone, the door is opened for the Prospect to be committed to the Agent by signing a Representation Agreement, Listing Agreement, or some other form of representation. One of the best things an Agent can hear from a prospect is, **"I didn't know that!"**

At the beginning of a conversation with a Prospect, an agent can instill confidence in their competence, skill, and expertise by demonstrating their proficiency. Likely, claiming experience, skills, or knowledge won't be enough to persuade a Prospect that an agent is competent.

For instance, a real estate agent who claims to be an expert in the field may not be able to persuade a prospect if they have heard similar claims from many real estate agents operating in the same market area. Similarly, simply having a designation that supposedly demonstrates one's level of expertise may not be adequate evidence of one's ability.

Shallow Proof Doesn't Prevail

Instead, prospects are more likely to be impressed by demonstrated proof of expertise. Case studies, testimonials, or even just instances of successful transactions that the agent has closed in the past are all things an agent might provide to prospective clients. They can also provide valuable insights, advice, or market analyses demonstrating their understanding and knowledge of the real estate industry.

Claiming to be an expert is shallow proof, as many others can also produce written evidence of being a designated expert in some real estate area. Prospects do not necessarily trust "designated" expertise versus "demonstrated" expertise. It is not that a designation for being an expert in a particular area of real estate is not valuable. It is simply that demonstrating proficiency is far more powerful and effective when combined with the designation than attempting to prove it with a piece of paper or a designation logo. When agents believe that a designation is enough, they often fail to differentiate themselves by demonstrating their expertise.

In multiple Prospect interviews and discussions, numerous Agents will all produce written documentation and logos displayed on their business cards proclaiming their expertise. Few will find a way to demonstrate that they are experts in such a way as to convince a Prospect that they are highly proficient. Winning the contest with a Prospect is best achieved by demonstrating expertise rather than claiming expertise. It is incumbent upon the Agent to look for ways of proving their proficiency and thus making a "Perception Sale" that is confidence creating.

Demonstrating Proficiency eliminates the need for claiming expertise, as the Prospect has been given evidence of the Agent's proficiency. It is challenging to demonstrate proficiency when an Agent is not proficient. The Agent must be prepared for each Prospect interaction by delving into ways of demonstrating to the Prospect and their unique situation that the Agent is more than boastful but is proficient.

There are impactful ways that an Agent can demonstrate proficiency and "mind sway" the opinion of the Prospect that they are different from and better than the other Agents in their area or those that claim to be proficient.

Demonstrating Proficiency

A new or aspiring Agent is holding an "Open House" for another Agent in a neighborhood where the new or aspiring Agent wants to specialize. A Prospect enters the "Open House," and the new Agent meets the Prospect highly professionally. As the Prospect tours the home, the Prospect will most likely ask for the price as the Agent has intentionally not provided any information that gives them the Listed Price of the home. Intentionally not providing high-interest information to a Prospect is effective because it induces interaction between the Prospect and the Agent, allowing for disclosing and reciprocal disclosure.

The Prospect says, **"So, what is the asking price for this home?"** The Agent smiles and says, **"Oh, of course, let me give you that information! This home is currently priced within 2% of the average sales price of homes sold in this neighborhood over the past four months.**

The square footage of this home is 3,299 square feet, and that puts this home right in the middle of the average square footage of homes in Overland Park. Overland Park has 350 homes, but only 251 are on interior lots as this one is and, therefore, not as desirable, as evidenced by the average sales price of homes on interior lots in the neighborhood. The sales prices are trending lower, however, as the last two sales have been at slightly less than the average price of similar homes sold in the past four months. If you don't mind, can I get your email address to send you this information? The home is priced at $499,000. Is this in your price range?

I specialize in this neighborhood and know a great deal about it… do you have other questions?"

The agent, to remain faithful to the idea of building trust, must, at some point, reveal the asking price of the home. However, given the information above, some prospects might be ready and willing to set an appointment. Don't risk alienation but withhold the sales price as long as possible.

In the above script, without telling the Prospect that the Agent is an expert, the Agent demonstrated proficiency in both the home and the neighborhood and has established expertise and neighborhood specialization. The <u>Proficiency Demonstrated</u> concept works directly with "Information Is Power" and "Professionalism is Value." The Keystone Concepts are seldom used independently and are best used in concert with each other to create credibility, a positive image, and proficiency that is difficult to refute.

My Business Card Says It All...

When the Agent provides the Prospect with a card that shows that the Agent has various designation logos, the Prospect is unlikely to believe that the Agent is qualified. Many do not have any idea what the designations mean, and the Agent's claims of expertise are shallow indeed. Demonstrating Proficiency isn't just about real estate matters. Proving to a Prospect that the Agent is a professional and qualified can be done in several ways on many different subjects.

Bill is a Buyer Prospect and has signed a Representation Agreement with the Agent. The Agent and Bill are touring homes the Client has expressed interest in seeing. The Agent and Bill have toured the three homes chosen by Bill already, and Bill has been disappointed in them as they didn't appeal to him. At the fourth stop, they pull up to the home, and the Buyer Prospect remarks, **"Hey, this is much more appealing to me... I can't wait to see this one."** The Agent is delighted as this was one of the homes that the Agent added to the showing list, but the Prospect had **not** requested to tour.

As they approach the home, the Agent notices that the attractive front door has been refinished and looks great. The landscape has been nicely trimmed, and the beds are mulched. The Agent comments, **"This one is off to a good start. Look at the care they have taken on the landscape and front door. It has been my experience that when this much care has been taken on the front of the home, the inside of the home doesn't usually disappoint."**

The Prospect has already noticed and nods approval as they enter the home. As they proceed, the Agent is impressed with the home's appearance, sees a well-appointed formal dining room, and remembers that the Prospect indicated no use for a formal dining room. The Agent says, **"Well, I remember that you indicated that a formal dining room isn't needed, but this dining room looks nice."** This demonstrates to the Prospect that the Agent has listened and was bringing up one of the stated needs and likes previously indicated to the Agent. The Prospect, visibly impressed, says to the Agent, **"You know, I could get used to that, and I like the way it is open via that walkway to the kitchen area."** This does not surprise the Agent as the Agent knows that people often support their first impressions and overlook inconsistencies when their first impression is positive.

The Agent stops and faces the Prospect, preparing to make a point. The Agent makes sustained eye contact establishing control, and begins, **"This reminds me of a story I should share with you. There is a book by Malcolm Gladwell, a psychologist. The book is titled "*blink*." Have you read it?"** The Prospect replies, **"No, I haven't...."**

The Agent continues, **"Well, in this book, the author talks about a phenomenon he calls blink, which is basically about trusting your first instincts or "gut" reaction when you see something and blink, either liking it or hating it. I thought I saw you blink when we were touring the second home we saw today. That was a negative blink? Am I correct?"**

The Prospect says, **"I didn't like that home at all."** The Agent continues, **"So, in his book, Gladwell makes the point that when you see something and blink positively, you should trust your instincts but also proceed to complete due diligence to confirm your opinion. I believe that you like this home. Let's look further and see what you think in a few minutes! ok?"**

The Prospect likely thinks, **"It appears my Agent is well-read, understands human behavior, and is tuned in to my likes and dislikes. I like that, hum, very impressive! "My Agent is smart and professional."**

Regardless of the tour's outcome, the Prospect has been impressed with the Agent's proficiency and focus on their needs. Demonstrating Proficiency builds respect and trust. Later when the Prospect says, **"I like almost everything about this home… what do you think?"** The Smart Agent will give their opinion with absolute openness, including any negative factors the Agent has observed to be present. This demonstrates to the Prospect that the Agent is not just pushing a positive narrative about the home.

The Agent continues, **"I always prioritize their needs while collaborating with my clients. I have found that helping my client to make a great decision is the most important thing I can do. The home they choose usually takes care of itself as they know and trust what they like. Before touring today, I researched all the homes we were scheduled to tour. This one seemed interesting to me. The photos were good, and the information provided was excellent. Here is the Seller's Disclosure about this home.**

I also noted a list of upgrades and things that the homeowners made to the home since they purchased it four years ago. This was interesting to me as the upgrades and improvements were substantial, so it caused me to wonder why they would sell so soon after moving into this home. Many studies show that most homeowners stay in a home they purchase for 6.5 years on average. I called the listing Agent, with whom I have a professional relationship, and asked why the Seller was moving. The owner has a job transfer to Phoenix and needs to move quickly. All this tells me this might be a good opportunity for you."

"Wow, I didn't expect all this. Thanks for doing the legwork!" Says the Prospect. **"Do you think I am being hasty about making a quick decision when I have only seen four homes?"**

The Agent replies, **"Well, I always put my clients first, but part of that is paying attention to their feelings about a home. If you love this home, I wouldn't want you to delay and miss out on getting this home if you feel strongly about it. The good thing is you can purchase the home under a contract to purchase with an Option Period if the Seller agrees, and that allows you the ability to hold the home off the market while you do due diligence and confirm that it is the right one for you.**

Under that circumstance, the Option Contract in Texas provides you, if negotiated, 7 to 14 days to think, evaluate, inspect, and if you choose to terminate the contract without explanation to the Seller. This gives you the best of both worlds. You put the home on ice while you continue to look and complete your investigation of the home. The Option Contract usually requires an Option Fee of between $250 and $1,000, which is negotiable. The home appears to be in average to good condition. I would think the lower end of the Option Fee scale is in play. I would collaborate with you and present an offer on your behalf, and while we wait, we could continue to look at other homes. Your thoughts Bill…."

Bill replies, **"I remember reading about the Option Contract in the "Finding a Home Guidebook" you provided me. That sounds great. Do you think we should write it now or continue to look at the homes we have scheduled?"**

"I would go with your opinion (I trust you) there. Perhaps I should call the Agent while we are on our way to the next home on tour and find out if they are working on any offers?" Says the Agent.

The Prospect says, **"Perfect, let's find out right away, I blinked when I walked in the front door, and I hope no one is serious about this home!"**

The Client often picks up on the Agents language and plays it back. It is proof that the Agent has made a lasting impression. When a Prospect starts using the words, we, let's, what do you think, etc., it is apparent that the client is beginning to accept the role of the Agent as a trusted team member and a collaborative Agent. While it is clear to all that the client is the decision maker, this mindset change is important to note. Sharing power is both a client and agent result in collaboration. When a client asks an Agent to provide recommendations, it demonstrates trust in the agent.

Incoming Call Opportunities

Demonstrating Proficiency is equally important when talking to a Prospect on the phone. This could be a return phone call or when you receive a property call from a Prospect. It could be on any call to a Prospect or Client.

Here is an example of using the "Demonstrating Proficiency" concept when an agent receives an incoming call about a property from a Prospect.

The Agent answers the phone, saying, **"This is Smart Agent with The Renaissance Group,"** The caller wants information about a particular property advertised on the Internet and has specific questions that couldn't be answered with the information available.

"I want to get some information about a property you have listed for sale."

The Agent replies, **"Great, thank you for calling. My name is Smart Agent. I am a REALTOR®. If you don't mind, can I get your name, please?"**

The Agent recognizes that the cellular phone has captured their phone number and name but wants to break down the "Resistance to Disclosure" that usually exist with a Prospect. The caller gives their name again and confirms that the phone number is their cell and the best number to be reached on but is just beginning to look. The caller explains that they need to know the size of the Owner's Suite Bedroom as they have a disabled Mother who will need a hospital bed and a full-size bed in the bedroom.

The Agent realizes the opportunity to demonstrate proficiency and replies, **"I have been in that home because I tour all homes listed in our office. The Owner's Suite is large but not large enough for your description. I am familiar with the size of a hospital bed as I have a relative in the same situation."**

This disclosure makes the Prospect feel better, but the Agent needs to keep the Prospect talking and offering to help, so the Agent says: "I just noticed that the home you called about is under contract and will probably close in the next 30 days."

The Suspect says, **"Huh, it seems every time I find a home that might work, it seems to be under contract. Very frustrating."** Hearing that the caller has a problem, Smart Agent comments, **"I realize it is as I have helped several clients recently that had difficulty finding a home. We developed a great strategy to deal with the inventory shortage in homes…."**

The Prospect questions, **"Really, what strategy is that?"**

The Agent continues, **"I have a system that allows me to set you up to receive an email with any property that comes on the market, becomes available again because of a contract termination, or has a price reduction. This allows my client and I to get real-time information and respond accordingly. By the way, are you working with an Agent?"**

The Suspect replies, **"No, I thought I would find the home myself and get someone to help me if I need assistance."**

The Smart Agent replies, **"I understand, that is one way to search, but my research shows that in 92% of the home purchases in this area, a REALTOR® represented the Buyer. That means most homes in our area are sold with an Agent representing the Buyer. A Buyer might as well have an Agent as almost 100% of the time, the Seller pays the fee for an Agent representing a Buyer, so there are no costs to you.**

It could cost you valuable time not to have someone who works just for you and is devoted to finding the right home when it first comes on the market. Being first is often essential to success in finding the home you want. My buyers usually find a home within 30 days of their home search. The average time to close a home is about 45 days, so it will not happen fast once you find the perfect home. How long have you been looking for a home?"

"Longer than that…" says the Prospect.

The Agent now believes that this is a legitimate Prospect, and there seems to be good dialogue, so the Agent offers, **"There is a home in a neighborhood near the home you called about that has a super large Owners Suite. It might work depending on your price range and if you like the home. I could show it to you right away. It was under contract last week, but the Buyer could not get financing approval, and it came back on the market yesterday. I toured it right before it went under contract. Want to look at it? I could show it to you immediately if I can get an appointment. What do you think?"**

What do you think? Oh, fine. I understand. Exactly. Is this ok? These phrases encourage Prospect interaction as they shift the need for a response back to the other party and encourage elaboration on the other parties thinking.

"I am not sure, but I could see it today. What are they asking," Says the Prospect."

Don't give a price to the Prospect until you must avoid alienating the Prospect. One rule of thumb to keep in mind. It is permissible and often necessary to walk on the edge but don't fall into the abyss.

"Let me check to confirm, but it is under $500,000. Yes, it is at $495,000, but it was originally listed for $525,000 before it went under contract, which makes me believe that the first contract was under $500,000. We can meet there, but let me call and see if I can get an appointment. If I show you the home, I will, of course, expect to be your Buyer Agent! Is that agreeable to you? I will need your address and email address to prepare a Representation Agreement to represent you. Is this ok?"

Comprehensive Market Intelligence Demonstrates Proficiency

An Agent needs to have a comprehensive understanding of the real estate market and the capacity to recall pertinent information quickly to capture a Prospect in the marketing net successfully. In addition, the Agent needs to be able to demonstrate their skills in a way that will persuade the Prospect that they are both competent and knowledgeable.

For example, an Agent who can provide the latest market trends, including average home prices and selling times in a particular neighborhood, can impress a prospect with their market knowledge. Similarly, an Agent who can provide prompt and accurate solutions to the questions that a Prospect may have regarding the process of purchasing or selling a home may exhibit their level of competency and experience.

These specific examples of demonstrated expertise have the potential to generate a perception sale, which may ultimately transform clients into "Raving Fans." Clients are more likely to refer an agent to their friends and family if the Agent can demonstrate to a Prospect that they are dealing with an agent who is knowledgeable, talented, and efficient. In the long term, this could increase the number of successful transactions. One thing is certain, in my opinion. Clients don't often refer people without Agent encouragement to do so!

Knowing the market and accessing information from memory combined with the ability to show the Prospect that the Agent is highly proficient is essential in capturing a Prospect in the Marketing Net. These example demonstrations of Proficiency will be the kind of perception sales that will make clients love their agent.

Michael & the Boss

You may wonder how the situation with Michael and the non-profit organization worked out. Well, let me explain.

A few days after our lunch meeting, Michael asked me to meet with him and the CEO of the non-profit organization he worked for. He was best friends with the top man and wanted me to explain in more detail what I had told him at lunch. I, of course, agreed and asked if I could bring barbecue. He said no thanks, but we set a time and date for the meeting.

Jack, the head of the non-profit, was also a client. I had been referred to Jack by Michael and had sold him and his family their current home, also in Starwood. Jack had a very substantial ego, and I did not look forward to explaining that he was making a big financial mistake. I was lucky; his best friend and his Chief Financial Officer, Michael, had already told him, and he was ready to listen.

Jack was personal friends with the Landlord, with whom he was considering signing a lease for ample space in a low-rise building. Despite all the marketing information shared over the past several years, Jack either didn't know or didn't want to see that I was an expert in Tenant representation in large commercial buildings. Fortunately, Michael explained this to him. After another two-hour meeting with Michael and Jack, Jack agreed to consider other options. The non-profit organization signed a Tenant Representation Agreement with me, and I began to show them office space.

After several weeks of touring buildings, Jack liked a more expensive building than the original option he had considered. The building had a diesel generator that would power his call center even with power disruptions and also provided expansion options for his fast-growing non-profit. The final space selected was more than 25,000 square feet and leased for ten years. My professional service fee was more than $285,000. Most importantly, the solutions provided were far better than the original plan would provide. The diesel generator in the building was instrumental in the success of the non-profit. Jack was already a fan but now became a "Raving Fan" and referred numerous other prospects to me in the future. Michael was a hero to Jack, and his relationship with Jack continued as they were now better friends than ever. Michael was grateful for my help, and we continued communicating for years.

Don't Ignore the Signs

Never miss an opportunity to demonstrate proficiency in small and large ways. This is selling without selling, informing without pretense, and Client Care with a capital C. The presentation of proficiency is cumulative in time with a client. It all adds up to trust and admiration. Even after the Agent completes a transaction with a Client, the Agent must continue demonstrating proficiency. The more it is demonstrated, the more the Client feels confident referring the Agent to their sphere of influence.

Once again, Demonstrating Proficiency is a powerful concept, but even more powerful when combined with the other Keystone Concepts. In the situation discussed above, consider how the "Perception Sale Concept," as well as the "Casting the Marketing Net," concept along with the "blink" concept are interrelated as well as interdependent, as are most of the Keystone Concepts.

CHAPTER 19 | KEYSTONE CONCEPT: "CASTING THE MARKETING NET..."

Elizabeth Deluca was an important person I wanted to know. She owned and operated a successful business in Cherry Hill, New Jersey. I was scheduled to make a presentation in Midtown Manhattan at a large hotel, and I wanted her to attend so we could meet. How could I get her to register and attend my presentation?

When I called her office, I was surprised she took my call, but she might have thought I was a prospect. She responded with a question. I explained that I was a real estate agent and marketing and sales consultant specializing in her industry. **"Have you ever owned a business like mine?"**

I explained, **"No, I had not owned a business like hers, but I had researched and studied her industry for several years."**

I suspect she then asked me the following question with a wry grin.

"I have been working in this business for almost twenty years. What could make you think you could teach me anything about my profession?"

As we have already learned, everyone has an ego, some from birth, and to open their minds to advice; they often need a demonstration of benefit.

I replied very positively and friendly, **"Well, Elizabeth, I realize that I probably don't know as much about your business as you do. However, why don't we play a little game?"**

She suspiciously replied, **"Ok-----what is the game?"**

I explained that I would be speaking in Midtown Manhattan in several months and would like her to attend my presentation so we could meet. I made the following proposal.

"Here is what I invite you to do. Ask me the hardest, most difficult, and most perplexing question that you can think of about your sales and marketing challenges or your lease agreement with your building. It can be anything that you can imagine. If the question is answered satisfactorily and provides good advice, you will attend my presentation. If I fail to answer your question satisfactorily, I will apologize for wasting your time, and you can forget about my speaking engagement. What do you think?"

She paused momentarily and then asked me to wait while she thought about my proposal. When she came off hold, she said, **"Ok, that's a deal. I have a question for you about overcoming an objection."** The objection was one that I was frequently asked about during my many presentations to her industry participants.

I asked Elizabeth to role-play the scenario with me while I pretended to be her, and she pretended to be the prospect. I proceeded with the role play and dealt with the objection in a way I had done numerous times before with other owners like Elizabeth. There was a bit of silence while I explained the solution to her problem.

After a short pause, Elizabeth told me she would attend my presentation in Manhattan. The rest of the story is of great satisfaction to me. Elizabeth and I became good friends, and as her consultant, I provided significant advice to her for years. I assisted her in re-negotiating her Commercial lease with her building, and Elizabeth became a "Raving Fan" and was provided as a reference to other prospects.

Overcoming Call Reluctance

Some agents may feel like they cannot help someone who owns a multi-million-dollar property because they have never owned one. It is important to keep in mind, however, that clients are looking for solutions to the problems they have with their real estate, and the agent who can provide these solutions will be welcomed into the client's inner circle regardless of whether or not they have personal ownership experience.

The "Net"

This brings us to the importance of casting a net over a prospect and keeping their attention long enough to demonstrate the benefits of working with an agent. Real estate agents specializing in luxury properties can demonstrate their expertise by providing insights into the current market for high-end properties and showcasing their expertise in navigating the specific challenges of buying or selling a luxury home.

"Casting the Marketing Net…" is a visualization concept that helps the Agent create a different mindset in the prospect's mind. Mindset is defined as; an established set of attitudes held by someone. When in this different mindset, there are specific strategies on the part of the Agent that are used when first talking to a Prospect. By visualizing the "Net," the Agent establishes a mindset and an attitude that sends a psychological cue to the Prospect. This behavior by the Agent psychologically cues the Prospect that something is different about the Agent. This difference creates an environment that is not sales-focused but client-centered.

This **"Casting the Marketing Net"** visualization exercise is used to focus the Agent on relating to a client in such a way as to gather client knowledge and capture the Client's attention long enough to form a foundational relationship. This foundational relationship allows the Agent to determine whether the Prospect is really a Prospect. This could be called qualification but is different because it does not qualify them for the purchase or sale of real estate, but rather, for a relationship with the Consultative Agent.

It is an important concept about the attitudes of a Consultative Agent when first meeting or talking to a Prospect. This state of mind is a "Consultative" rather than a product sales-oriented state of mind. Mindset means the established set of attitudes held by someone. In this mindset, the Agent visualizes a Prospect standing in front of them and the Agent casting a very client-caring and friendly net over the Prospect to interact with them long enough to make such a benefit-laden presentation that the Prospect feels safe and compelled to share information with the Agent. This requires that the Agent be likable, interactive, and connected with the Prospect visually and mentally. It also requires immediate disclosures by the agent, symbolizing the removal of the mask to elicit similar reciprocal disclosures from the Prospect.

Many of the Keystone Concepts presented in this book may be used interactively with the "Net" concept by the Consultative Agent. Most of the marketing dollars of a Practices budget are spent to allow the agent an opportunity to "Cast a Net" over and capture a Prospect. The agent may only have one opportunity or one minute to do so.

The concept of the "Net" primarily involves Prospects, yet it is still important to relate to Clients. Because a client has already been captured in the "net" to some extent as they have signed a representation agreement of some type at some time in the past. It is not as difficult as it is with a Prospect who hasn't committed to the Agent.

The concept can also be used when visualizing the Capture of a Geographic Target Market Prospect. Where a selected group of people with a common interest are being targeted for contact, the Agent can use the "Net" to capture a Prospect and glean future business. Eye contact and a smile are the first actions that cross the divide between a Prospect and an agent.

Immediate eye contact and a smile, followed by a handshake, represent the Net.

Picture a frightened Prospect unsure of what might be said or done; making them feel comfortable and safe is a priority for the agent. Often Prospect's primary fear is having to commit to an Agent without knowing the details of the commitment and to whom the commitment is being made. Trust is not given but earned by the Consultative Agent. Demonstrating that the client can trust them is often done through the Agent's disclosures and reciprocal disclosures and the removal of the mask.

A Prospect doesn't know the Agent, is not sure what the Agent might say or do, and as a result, is on guard and cautious. They must be reassured and made to feel comfortable. This is done by eye contact, smile, handshake, posture, and disclosure. The first words uttered after "Casting of the "Net" over the Prospect completely are significant. If the "Net" is cast in the spirit of selling something, much can be lost as the Prospect will sense that the Agent is no different from the other Agents they have met or spoken to in the past. Their fear may return.

By disclosing first, the Agent sets up the self-disclosure & reciprocal disclosure strategy. Most Prospect believes that the Agent will try to sell them, and when they realize that the Agent will not do this, they relax. Don't sell… Relate to, collaborate with, connect with, and, most importantly, listen carefully to what the Prospect says. Do not act like a salesperson but rather a consultant seeking knowledge to help solve a problem. This is called Consultative Selling.

For example:

"Hello, my name is Smart Agent. I am with the Renaissance Group. It's nice to meet you. How can I help you today?"

The immediate disclosure of your name and company starts the removal process of the mask, allowing the Prospect to see the Agent. The Prospect almost always has "Resistance to Disclosure," and the task for the Agent is to reveal themselves to the Prospect, allowing them to see and like the Agent. This is the genesis of creating a climate of trust and confidence. A small piece of the Mask must be removed, allowing the Prospect to reciprocate before the relationship can continue to form. The Prospect will psychologically feel the need to reciprocate if the Agent is willing to trust the Prospect and be seen.

The Agent should not be anxious or in a rush, as relationship building takes time and patience. Nothing destroys a consultative relationship faster than a product-oriented qualification process and an agent in a hurry. Having the Prospect in the net allows the Agent to be patient while letting the relationship develop. This provides the Consultative Agent time to gather client knowledge to solve problems and thus benefit the Prospect.

Reciprocal Disclosures Must be Heard

Disclosing is important. Listening for disclosure from the other party may be even more important. Disclosing words are words that tell you that a vital disclosure is coming. Listening for disclosures from a Prospect is the cue to reciprocate with a similar disclosure as soon as reasonably possible.

Certain disclosing words are more important than others. The words "I feel," "I want," "we need," and similar words reveal that the Prospect is getting ready to say something that should be actively listened to while demonstrating sincere interest. An Agent thinking about the next qualification question will be disqualified by the Prospect as the Prospect will notice that the Agent is more interested in talking than listening.

The Agent must be prepared to reciprocate with a similar disclosure of the same level of importance. "I need to find a home right away; I am going through a tough situation and must find a place to live." This is an example of a significant disclosure by the Prospect that trusts the Agent.

The Agent must return the trust by disclosing something of similar importance. "Wow, I went through a divorce, and it was tough. I feel for you! I was lucky and found a perfect home in weeks."

Since a Prospect opened the window and there is reciprocation, the onion skin is being peeled away, and the mask is coming down in similar steps by each party to the communications. Be careful, however, not to disclose too much private information too quickly as it could cause the Prospect to be suspicious of motives and withdraw. Disclosure of information too quickly and too private can be complicated and confuse the other party. People get uncomfortable with early disclosures of a private nature, and it seems inappropriate to many.

What happens if, despite disclosures, a Prospect fails to reciprocate on even the simplest and less personal level? Be careful in this situation. When people fail to reciprocate, it makes the other party in the communication suspicious and uncomfortable and prevents them from removing their masks and showing themselves to others. It is not always the case, but sometimes the other party is not disclosing because they are hiding something. Perhaps they, or someone they know, is an Agent, and they have no intention of getting too close to another Agent. Remember, the goal is to reach them. Move forward to get them to relax and share their story. However, there is a need to be aware that they might not reciprocate and may not be reachable to capture. While in the "Net," the Agent has little to lose and much to gain by spending time with the Prospect.

"The Net" – and an Open House Event

The following is an example of dialogue at an "Open House" where an Agent is a host for the Listing Agent, and, therefore, the sitting Agent is not bound to the Seller by a representation agreement. A Prospect enters the home, and the Agent wants to identify whether they are a Prospect that might become a client. It is important to determine if they have a relationship with an Agent. In this situation, a Prospect may have a relationship with an Agent but not a signed agreement with that Agent and therefore is still a potential Client.

As the Prospect enters the home, the Agent focuses only on the Prospect, makes immediate eye contact, and flashes a brilliant smile while the "Marketing Net" is lifted into place. This is called the "Marketing Net" rather than the "Sales Net" is that this has little to do with selling anything. It has to do with connecting with people. It involves demonstrating skills, talent, and a collaborative problem-solving mentality. The interaction is not about homes. It is about the comfort and trust that an agent can create with a Prospect.

When approaching the suspect, not a Prospect, there is a Portfolio in the Agent's left hand. The Agent reaches out with their right hand to introduce themselves to the Prospect, saying, **"Hi, thanks for dropping by today. My name is Smart Agent with the Renaissance Group. I'll be showing you the home today."** People often respond with their first names only. Shaking the Prospect's hand and greeting them positively symbolizes the "Net" being cast, but the Prospect is not yet secured in the "Net" and can escape or be released by the Agent. There could also be holes in the "Net" that allow a prospect to escape. Those holes could be a lack of preparation by the Agent, an unwillingness to reveal themselves to the Prospect, or a general lack of skills when talking to or working with a Prospect.

While handing the portfolio and pen to the Prospect, the Agent asks politely, **"If you don't mind, could I get you to sign the guest register, please?"** Although this is phrased as a question, it is an implied requirement of the Prospect as the agent hands the guest register to the Prospect. There is a passive psychological message that completing the sign-in sheet is required. If the Prospect hesitates, the Agent can explain that it is a homeowner requirement as they want to know who has visited their home today. This is another effort to cause disclosure by the Prospect and is important for breaking down their "Resistance to Disclosure."

The guest register has a space for their name, phone number, and email address. The Prospect wants to see the home. They stopped, locked the car, and dropped in to tour the home. The Agent can provide access or not. The Agent has the ability and power to show the home, so the Prospect feels compelled to fill out the Guest Register. They want information about the home, and the Agent is standing in their pathway at the gate, so they reluctantly agree to sign the register. They often do so without filling in the phone number, as they are reluctant to disclose and can hide behind an email address they can provide without fear.

When the Prospect returns the Portfolio, it is sometimes missing the telephone number, to which the Agent should say, **"Oh, Bill, I need your phone number for my records. If you don't mind, I promise not to call you and drive you crazy!"** This comment by the Agent is also a disclosure in that the Agent is letting the Prospect know that they respect their privacy. The Agent needs the phone number for their CRM, which will provide the ability to follow up with a Prospect. The Agent is never sure if the email address is real, so it is essential to get the phone number.

The Prospect, wanting to see the home, provides the number. They want something, and the Agent has the power for the moment. The Agent usually wins this request for information. The Agent follows up with, **"So, John, I am holding this home open for the Listing Agent and specialize in this neighborhood. What caused you to stop and want to see this particular home?"**

The Agent now has a name, email address, and phone number. The breaking down of the "Resistance to Disclosure" has begun. The Agent has delivered a "Magic Minute," and the Suspect, himself a salesperson, thinks this Agent is good.

The Prospect replies, **"Well, I love the neighborhood, and the landscape of this particular home captured my attention. How large is it, and how much are they asking?"** The Agent now has a choice to make. Should they provide early disclosure of the information that gives power away or attempt to withhold it and remove more of the mask?

The Agent decides to make a "Perception Sale" by "Demonstrating Proficiency," **"I agree, this is a super neighborhood, and the landscape is outstanding as it was the model home in this neighborhood about three years ago. The builder was Strident Homes, one of the best builders in the DFW Metropolitan Area. I have worked with them several times as a REALTOR® for several years. Where do you work, Bill?"**

The Agent has now set up the following reciprocal disclosure. The Agent's disclosure is basic, and there is little risk for the Prospect in disclosing where he works, and another piece of the mask is removed when he does so. The Prospect may or may not notice that the list price of the home has still not been disclosed by the Agent, and the Agent has taken control of the conversation. Holding the information and being ready to satisfy the Prospect's need for that information at the right time will allow the Agent to buy time and work on trust building.

The Agent continues, **"Oh, let me provide you with a package of information about the home."** The Agent turns and escorts the Prospect to the "Heart of the Home!" The "Heart of the Home" is the most impressive area of the home that will possibly make a marvelous impression on most Prospects. The large open family room, with a view of the Chef's Kitchen, is a great place to start, as it is almost perfect. The home's exterior made a great first impression, caused the Prospect to park, enter the home, and provide important follow-up information.

A "Magic Minute" was delivered, and the Agent wanted to keep the positive impression going by escorting the Prospect into the home, demonstrating control. However, the Agent needs to continue to build the relationship and gather client knowledge while the Prospect is in the "Net."

The Agent must know if a Prospect is working with another Agent, as no Smart Agent wants to solicit another Agent's client. Entering the open family room, kitchen, and breakfast area, the Agent provides additional disclosures.

This satisfies some of a Prospect's needs. **"This open-concept family room, breakfast room, and open kitchen are popular with those who see the home because it facilitates significant family involvement. It makes a great statement. The home has over 2800 square feet, four bedrooms, and a spacious Owners Suite. I particularly like the way the family room is accessible to the kitchen and the great cooktop, which makes it great for entertaining.**

I live in a Strident Home, also not far from another great neighborhood. By the way, are you working with an Agent? I respect the relationship between a client and their Agent and want to ensure that I do so…."

This demonstrates professionalism to most Prospects and seeks to answer a fundamental question for the Agent.

The need for information has been partially satisfied, and the Prospect has disclosed some information about themselves. The Agent is now asking for reciprocity regarding a commitment to another Agent. Most often, the answer will be honest because a good reason for needing to know has been disclosed. More of the mask has been removed, allowing the Prospect to like and trust enough to feel comfortable with a disclosure. If the answer is no, then all is clear for further disclosures. If yes, a positive impression has been made as professionalism has been demonstrated by respecting the relationship with another Agent.

This dialogue shows how to "Cast the Net," capture a Prospect, and determine if the Prospect can be your client or if they are committed to a prior agent. You also can see from the dialogue how many concepts covered in this material can assist in the capture activity. <u>An Agent that cannot capture a Prospect</u> will have difficulty surviving in the real estate jungle.

The "Marketing Net" could have holes, and the Prospect could escape… Otherwise, a Prospect is in the "Net" and is ready to be converted into a client and a "Raving Fan." The possibility that the Prospect could escape is accurate, and there may not be a second chance if the Prospect gets away. To avoid this, be fully and wholly prepared to disclose, make additional "Perception Sales," and use the "Information Is Power" concept to cement the relationship with the Prospect.

<u>Here is an example:</u>

"Bill, thank you for sharing that information. I appreciate you trusting me enough to let me know your situation. Let me show you the rest of the home and answer any questions. First, let me say that the home is Listed at $625,000. That's what the seller wants, and I have comparable properties for the neighborhood that I will share with you to see how it compares to others. Few, however, have this former model home's upgrades."

Listen for disclosures at this point, as the Prospect has been rewarded with some significant information, and the comments and disclosures show that trust is being returned. Wait and listen carefully for disclosing words that indicate that the Prospect is about to disclose. The Prospect might say, **"Well, I'm afraid that $625,000 is a little much for me!"** This significant disclosure says the Prospect feels comfortable with the agent. The mask is almost down. Does Bill have a family, and what is his timing for making a move? Getting him to talk by listening and reciprocating with disclosures whenever appropriate will be easier now as the "Resistance to Disclosure" has been diminished. Do not hijack the conversation by talking too much or becoming a product salesperson, causing the Prospect to stop sharing more. This is Client knowledge, gold for real estate Professionals. The Consultative Agent is calm, patient, and, most importantly, Client-Centered.

"Casting the Net" on a Property Call… is another important skill an Agent must master. The most important thing to remember is, don't sell!

A Prospect Call Scenario

Here is a scenario for the following script and dialogue session. The caller has driven by a home and liked the look of the home. They tried to use their cell phone to get information but were frustrated because the street's name was a little unusual, and they did not know for certain that they were getting the correct information. Their desire for information was strong. They were impatient for immediate satisfaction, as many Prospects can be.

Sarah wants information about 4340 Woodbine Lane in Prosper, TX. The home appears lovely and is in an area where she has been watching for the right property to come on the market. This is the first time she has seen this one up for sale, and she wants to know the price, square footage, and number of bathrooms. She also wants to know about the pool, as was indicated by the pool swinger hanging on the yard sign.

She is a qualified buyer of up to $950,000 but would prefer to spend no more than $825,000. She does not have an Agent but doesn't want to sign with an Agent until she has found the right home and is ready to sign a contract on the home. Sarah is a rather strong-willed person and likes to get her way. Sarah doesn't want to work with a listing Agent; she wants someone who only represents her and not the Seller. Sarah is single with two teenage children. She has owned several homes and has been looking for the right property for three months.

The Agent is fully proficient with the concepts in this book and has been preparing for an opportunity to meet Sarah. She is on phone opportunity time at the front desk. The property at 4340 Woodbine Lane is listed by an Agent within the same Agency. The Agent has a solid background in Teaching at the Middle School level. She has her "Net" ready and is waiting patiently to become a STAR!

Watch for and make a note of which Concepts were used by the Agent during the tour while reading the dialogue.

The Agent's cell phone rings, **"This is Smart Agent, the Renaissance Group. Can I help you?"**

"Yes, this is Sarah, I was driving by a home, and I want to find out some information about the home. Can you help me?" Says Sarah.

The agent responds, **"Of course, Sarah, I will gladly help you. My name is Smart Agent, and I am a Broker at the Renaissance Group. If you don't mind, could I have the property address you want information about?"**

Sarah responds, **"Yes, it is located at 4340 Woodbine Ln., and the sign says it has a pool."**

"Excellent. Is that address in Prosper?" Says Smart Agent, who knows that the home is in Prosper but wants to break Sarah's resistance to disclosure. Every tiny bit of information extracted from Sarah will start breaking down resistance and open communication channels.

"Well, I think it is," Sarah says. **"… but I'm not sure."**

"That's fine. Let me check and confirm. While I am looking that up, if you don't mind, could I get your last name, please."

Sarah wants to know about the home and agrees to disclose her last name, Jones. Smart Agent, wanting to break down the disclosure resistance even more, ask her, **"Is that J o n e….?"**

Sarah finishes the word for Smart Agent with **"Jones."**

Smart Agent replies, **"Thank you, I have the number that comes up on my system. Is this your cell phone, and is it the best number to get back to you?"**

"Yes, it is my cell," says Sarah, wanting more information now. Increasing a Prospect's need for something is a good strategy and can be done if managed thoughtfully.

Smart Agent decides to meet some of her needs and says, **"Well, Sarah, the home is in Prosper in a wonderful neighborhood called Windsong Ranch. It does have a pool and spa and a fantastic backyard. Where are you moving from and are you working with an Agent?"**

Sarah responds, **"No, I don't have an Agent as I just moved here for a new position… I will need a place to live and want to be near great schools and would like a neighborhood with walking trails."**

"Great, where will your office be, and what is your company's name?" Smart Agent said.

"I'm with a large accounting firm, and my offices are in Plano near the Tollway," she replied.

Knowing that if the price is disclosed and is too high, a Prospect could be lost, Smart Agent decides to focus on obtaining client information and only give the price when required.

"Great," Smart Agent says, continuing to satisfy the Prospect's needs, **"This home has five bedrooms, is 4800 square feet, and has five full baths and two half baths. It is about five years old, and I have toured the home as it was a former model home in Windsong Ranch. Strident Homes built it, and is one of the best home builders in the Metroplex. It has three garage spaces and shows beautifully. You should see the two-story family room. It is located 3 miles from the Tollway and is an easy drive to North Plano."**

This demonstrates Smart Agent's proficiency and awareness of the marketplace, particularly this home. He continues, **"Does this sound right for you and your children?"**

"It may be a little large for us, but it depends on the price. How much is the home?"

Smart Agent replies, **"Well, it is in the $900's, and being a former model home, it should sell quickly. Is this in your price range?"**

"It's quite a bit higher than I wanted to pay… but it depends."

Smart Agent continues to disclose, **"Certainly, everyone has a budget. When I moved here about eight years ago, I had to compromise on a few things, but I came out great, getting a lot of value for the money. This home is in the Prosper school district, which is highly rated, and the neighborhood is a master-planned community with miles of walking trails, a private lagoon for homeowners, and many amenities. It is certainly worth touring if it is still available. The good news is that other villages in the same neighborhood have homes priced lower than this. There might be a few at a little lower price. What price range are you hoping to be in at the end of the day?"**

Sarah responds, **"A lagoon. What do you mean?"**

Smart Agent continues to disclose, **"Well, the lagoon is a 5-acre Cabo Style lagoon with all amenities and is private to the homeowners and visitors. It's also a very safe neighborhood and quite scenic. How old are your children?"** Smart Agent asks.

At this point, Smart Agent hasn't tried to sell and has focused on obtaining as much information as possible while avoiding an exact sales price. It may be time now to earn trust from Sarah.

"My girl is 13, and my son is 15, and they are great students. How much is the home?" Sarah asks.

"The home is priced at $950,000, but while we have been talking, I see two other homes close by that are under $900,000. Sarah, if you have time, I could show you all three. The home you called about is still available. Which would be better for you, this afternoon or tomorrow?"

Smart Agent has "Cast the Net," and Sarah is inside the "net." Smart Agent must now ensure that she doesn't escape. The goal is to meet Sarah in person, make her like them, and further develop the relationship.

Prospect Capture Requires Discipline

The visualization exercise of "Casting the Marketing Net" helps to understand that capturing a Prospect requires listening, using information, Demonstrating Proficiency, and obtaining sufficient client knowledge. This allows for placement of the "Net" and gives the Prospect enough reasons to trust and rely upon the Agent to assure that the "Net" holds the Prospect securely. The Smart Agent knows that information is power and that providing information slowly rather than quickly allows the Agent to have enough time to earn the trust of a Prospect. Smart Agent also understands that Demonstrating Proficiency is the fastest way to show a Prospect that Smart Agent is ready and able to deliver results.

The visualization concept is compelling in self-development and for perfecting the Consultative Selling way of doing business. Learning the language of consulting is essential. Knowing the language of real estate, when combined with the social science language behind solving client problems with real estate solutions, is a powerful combination of talents. When an Agent thinks of themselves as a consultant, talks like a consultant, and focuses on Client success, the outcome can be extraordinary. The ability to differentiate themselves from other Agents allows the Consultative Agent to stand alone in a ballroom filled with hundreds of other Agents who are product sales oriented and seem noticeably different to Prospects.

When Prospects become clients, they not only relate to the Consultative Agent as a trusted resource but also become sponsors as they believe in the power of the Consultative Agent to solve problems for themselves and others. While clients may believe that their Consultative Agent is better, they may not say so publicly unless encouraged. The Agent must build trust and confidence to convince Sarah that Smart Agent is the right person to assist her. That takes time, and the "Net" holds the Prospect closely while buying the Agent time to build a future relationship with the Prospect.

CHAPTER 20 | KEYSTONE CONCEPT: CLIENT AFFIRMATION

Affirmation means "the action or process of affirming something or **someone**. 2. Providing emotional support or encouragement."

When clients write or say good things about an Agent because of their performance or actions, they affirm their belief in that agent and the value the Agent brings them. This is a form of emotional support or encouragement.

When a client writes a testimonial letter or provides a positive quote about an Agent, they affirm their belief in the Agent, and the psychological impact of this is twofold. First and foremost, they express their positivity about the Agent but embed their opinion in their psyche. In short, they become psychologically supportive and believers in their own words. The client is more likely to defend the position they have stated.

Secondly, suppose a client writes a glowing statement about performance. In that case, the process of writing the statement combined with the public distribution of the information causes the Client to be fully committed to their story and become even more entrenched in their beliefs and what they have written.

A "Raving Fan" who proclaims to the world that they are a "Raving Fan" becomes even more of a "Raving Fan."

For this reason, getting Clients to say anything positive or put their positive comments into writing makes them even more loyal and committed. When they tell their friends to utilize the Agent, they are more profoundly and psychologically committing themselves to the Agent. A handwritten note or letter is the most powerful, and it is the most personal. A typed or emailed quote or letter is good but not as strong as a personal note or letter. Saying something positive to someone else about the Agent is an affirmation but not quite as powerful as some other methods of affirmation unless this statement is made in front of a group or crowd. In that case, the public affirmation to a Group of people is psychologically binding.

Obtaining Client Affirmation

A client appreciation party where clients stand in front of a crowd and profess their admiration or respect for an Agent binds the client to the Agent indefinitely and significantly.

Most clients will say positive things to an Agent before, during, or after the closing of a real estate transaction. It is not unusual for a client to say, **"Smart Agent, you are the best Agent I have ever worked with, and I have worked with several."** This is a powerful statement. Yet, when the Client memorializes that comment in writing, it has a deeper meaning and affirms what they are saying, making it even more true to them.

Clients saying good things in writing is more powerful than the Agent saying good things about themselves to a Prospect. The third-party testimonial is more believable because almost all highly successful Agents have confidence, believe they are good at what they do and are willing to profess this publicly to anyone who will listen.

Convincing a client who says good things to put their comments into writing takes tact and a willingness to ask for help. The most appropriate time to do this is right after they have said something nice. For example, John, a very satisfied client, says, **"Smart Agent, you are the best Real Estate Agent I have ever worked with. And believe me. I have worked with several."**

The immediate response could be as follows: **"John, that makes me feel great. I know that you have a lot of experience, and coming from you, this is quite a compliment. Would you be willing to do me a small favor?"**

John, of course, says, **"Sure, what can I do?"** Following a remark of this type, it is difficult for a client to say then, **"Well, no, I don't want to put that in writing."**

Smart Agent replies, **"Well, I am posting letters, testimonials, and quotes on my new website, and I would love to have your comments in writing so I can post them there. It would mean a great deal to me, and this would help me immensely. Would you mind?"**

John believes what he has said, saying, **"Sure, I'll be glad to do that."** Smart Agent replies, **"Wonderful, that is so nice of you. I appreciate you doing this for me."**

Shortly after receiving John's letter of endorsement, testimonial, thank you, etc., a thank you note is sent to John. In the thank you note, appreciation is expressed to John for his comments, and the Agent tells him once again how great a client he is and how much the letter means to Smart Agent. The Agent further affirms the words by enclosing a copy of the quote. Enclosing a small token of appreciation further reinforces the feeling that the Client was justified in praising the Agent. This could be a gift card or another small gift. It cannot be enormous, as that would appear unreasonable. The thank you note includes a copy of the letter the Client wrote or a screenshot of Smart Agent's website page where the Client's quote is displayed. All this is to make him feel good about what he did for the Agent. After all, he is a "Raving Fan."

John is now more of a Fan than before because he has affirmed his belief in Smart Agent and is ready for the next step by Smart Agent in further building a long-lasting relationship with John. It has been three months since John moved into his new home. He has been contacted several times in the three months by mail, email, and maybe a personal note. However, the most important step in Client relations has yet to occur. Assuring Satisfaction needs to be completed and is the bridge step to the next opportunity to serve the client or someone in the client's sphere of influence!

The Circular Sales Process

Assuring Satisfaction is an essential part of client management and also represents an opportunity to continue building the relationship with a "Fan." The Client is a "Fan," as he has written that he was. However, he hasn't been the "Raving Fan" in a way that the Agent wishes he was. The client needs to share access to his sphere of influence. That would represent real fandom.

This interview is the transition step to the next sale with John or a referral from another party likely to do business in the future. The next transaction with John could be five to seven years away, but preparing to serve the client again is revenue planning. The "Assuring Satisfaction Interview" is a formal step in securing the Client's long-term loyalty.

The Interview Explained

A call is made to John. The call should be at a time that will likely benefit John. Caller ID will probably show him who is calling, **"Well, Smart Agent, I am pleased to hear from you. What's going on?"**

"John, it is so great to talk to you. Thank you for taking my call. I realized that it has been three months since you closed on your new home and just wanted to make sure all is good with the world and you."

John replies, **"Well, come to think of it, I didn't realize it's been three months, but things are going well. Julie and I love the home and are so glad that you helped us decide to get this home."**

The Agent responds, **"Super, I am pleased to hear that you are happy, but I want to ensure you are also satisfied with me. I value your opinion and want to ensure you are satisfied in every way. Is there anything I can do for you, and is there any way I could have done a better job, as I am always looking to improve the services I provide?"**

John is surprised. He is surprised because it never entered his mind that the Agent would be concerned about him being happy with the service. The fact that he would be called three months after the closing and be asked for his advice on service performance is a compliment and re-affirms his belief in Smart Agent as the most professional Agent he has ever worked with. He responds, **"Smart Agent, you were great to work with, and I can't think of a single thing you could have done to be better than you were. You were fantastic."**

"Well, in my notes, I saw that one of the repair items was replacing the upstairs bedrooms' HVAC system. I know that you were considering using Jake's HVAC. I believe that I referred them to you. Did they do a great job for you? I don't want to continue referring people to my clients unless I know they do a superior job."

John replies, **"Yes, they were good to work with, but we did have to have them out a couple of times to finish things that weren't quite right. It all worked out well."**

"Super, do you think you would recommend them in the future? More importantly, do you think I should continue to recommend them?"

"Sure, they did what they promised to do, so I would say go ahead and recommend them in the future. I would, of course, call them again if I needed assistance."

"Excellent. You know it also occurred to me that your parents are living in Chicago, as I recall. Do you know if they have thought about moving to be closer to you? If they moved here, I would treat them great and represent them superbly."

"No, I don't think so, but you never know what the future brings, do you?"

"That is for sure, but I want you to know that if I can ever help anyone you know, I will do my absolute best to take great care of them, as I did for you! We will have a VIP Appreciation Event at the end of this year, and we hope you and Julie will attend. We will send out invitations in a few months, so watch your mail as we would love to see you there. Please let me know if there is anything I can do for you."

The Assuring Satisfaction Interview is an excellent way of staying in touch, confirming satisfaction, and asking for future business if the Client is satisfied with the services previously provided. If not, something must be addressed, and satisfaction earned. This early warning system indicates that more work needs to be done to keep a "Raving Fan" endorsement from the Client.

Oops… They are Not Happy

The client expressing dissatisfaction, or a lack of happiness, is similar to being jailed in a game of Monopoly. You do not get to pass, go, collect $200, and you cannot continue moving forward until you escape jail. This is why Assuring Satisfaction is so important. Many clients will not tell you that they are unhappy. You must probe and assure their satisfaction before you can proceed past go and tap into their sphere of influence.

Many agents assume the happiness of a client. Judi and I completed an almost perfect transaction in selling a home for a great client. When I contacted him several weeks after closing, I asked if he was happy with our services. We had closed on his property in a very short period, and he had received an offer for the total asking price for his home. I had erroneously assumed that he would be happy with us. What he told me stopped me in my tracks. I asked him if he was happy with our services, and he said, "Well, not really. I have sold several homes, and every time I have sold a home, the REALTOR® brought a closing gift to the closing. You didn't. Even a bottle of wine would have been nice."

This may seem petty, but the results were still the same. The client clarified that it was too late and that we had lost him. As a result of this $50 mistake, we lost a client and access to his sphere of influence forever. This was a loss of innumerable value to us. A small price for the gift was overshadowed. You can be assured that we will never make that mistake again. When you sell many homes per year, the budget for closing gifts must be planned and funded.

An Essential Component

The concept of "client affirmation" is essential to marketing and client care. Testimonials, reference letters, and quotes are some of the best evidence regarding an agent's expertise level. Testimonials are practical marketing tools because they illustrate the agent's expertise and provide social proof that they can provide value to the Prospect. Testimonials can come in various formats, such as reference letters or quotes, and they can be presented in various ways.

For instance, if a client sends a reference letter regarding an agent's work and how happy they were with their services, the agent may use that letter as a marketing tool to attract new Prospects. The letter provides an account of the agent's performance, and prospective Prospects are more inclined to put their faith in an agent who can demonstrate a track record of completing transactions with delighted clients.

Prospects feel more valued and appreciated when their words, in the form of quotes or letters, are used in marketing materials. This makes a Prospect value the Agent even more. This helps the agent build a stronger relationship with the Prospect and increases the likelihood that the client would recommend them to their friends, family and associates.

Chapter 21|Keystone Concept: "Team Selling Concepts"

What is Team Selling in the Real Estate Industry? This is a difficult question for the aspiring real estate Agent because the <u>Agent frequently thinks there is no team for them to manage</u>. There are many Teams in real estate with highly successful Practices, with employees or 1099 independent contractors, and as such, the ability to have Team Selling in Real Estate does exist. The Smart Agent can build a team to support a Team Selling program in several ways. It just takes knowledge and motivation.

Why there is a need for a TEAM

Team and Collaboration are closely related. The Chapter on Collaboration provides many answers to this question. The Smart Agent often competes with a more extensive and more successful Team or Group Agent with more resources, experience, and success to promote themselves. In addition, having a Group of people that a Prospect can connect with, as they share similar values, adds a dimension to the Agent/Client relationship that can be a strong differentiator to a Prospect.

Compared to real estate agents with a support team behind them, independent real estate agents who do not have a team may be at a competitive disadvantage. Since they don't have the resources and backing of a team behind them, individual agents could give the impression that they are less powerful when meeting prospective clients. While speaking with other agents with teams, some may stress the benefits of having a team, such as improved Prospect service.

Consider the following scenario: A potential client is interested in purchasing a home and is meeting with two agents. The first real estate agent is a sole proprietor who works alone. Still, the second agent is part of a real estate team comprising a marketing expert, a transaction coordinator, and an assistant.

During the interview, the second agent might bring up how their team can provide better support for the client throughout the entire process of buying a home. This might include scheduling property viewings, managing paperwork, and coordinating with lenders and inspectors. Conversely, the agent working alone might not have as much expertise or access to as many resources as the second agent to provide the same assistance.

Consequently, the potential client can get the impression that the second agent is more powerful and better equipped to fulfill their requirements. This competitive disadvantage for an individual agent is why they may need to develop different competitive strategies, such as emphasizing their personal expertise, providing services that are one of a kind, or utilizing technology to provide superior experiences for their clients. A careful reading of Competitive Strategies in a later section of this book provides additional ideas and information on this subject.

Behind the 8 Ball

This situation places the individual real estate agent at a disadvantage and could result in a lack of confidence in a competitive situation. When competing against a more successful Agent, the new or aspiring Agent needs all the help they can muster. An Agent can level the playing field by adding a Team Selling program to their capabilities. This could cause the agent to be seen as a more viable option. When the agent is highly professional and is liked by the client, success against the larger Team or Group is not only possible but likely as the new and aspiring Agent can utilize these resources in a more involved way than the larger competitor does. This chapter will explain how.

Building a team gives an Agent more credibility in competitive situations and is an excellent positioning strategy. There are additional benefits from the creation and development of a Team. The ability to provide superior service to Clients is one. There are also opportunities for cross referrals between the Team Members if they are Strategic Marketing Partners and joint funding of marketing activities when practical.

The Smart Agent can benefit significantly by building a Team of like-minded people who are not employees or subcontractors of the agent but have common goals and objectives of great client care and promotion. The ability to build a Team sometimes depends upon the Brokerage Agency with which the aspiring real estate Agent is affiliated. The Brokerage Agency and location that staff with a full-time Office Manager, and an Office Assistant and Listing Coordinator provide excellent opportunities for Team Selling as there are possible Team members who can be recruited as non-paid participants. Building a Team with Strategic Marketing Partners is also possible when the Agent is willing to work collaboratively. These Strategic Marketing Partners work as team members and bring value to the Client.

The Principal Broker or Office Manager is often very busy recruiting new Agents and therefore depends upon the staff of the real estate office to assist the Agents in most matters. The Office Administrator and Listing Coordinator are frequently skilled in the business of real estate, and many are licensed agents. Their daily activities provide little opportunity to interact with clients and develop their potential, and frequently they would welcome an opportunity to assist in collaboration with a client.

Provided an opportunity to participate, many office staff members can be highly motivated to assist the Agent in the Team Selling Concept for the Agent's Practice. Many Agents in an office do not utilize these staff members, as they have yet to learn the benefit of doing so and, as a result, pay little attention to the availability of these resources. Some Agents have their own Team Members and don't need to take advantage of these available resources, and office staff resources are often under-utilized for their skill sets. This sometimes leaves these staff members in a thankless position where many Agents demand help and assistance but don't motivate and encourage personal growth for the office staff members.

An Agent who involves the staff members in such a way as to provide an opportunity for self-growth and development motivates them to work for the Agent's benefit. Recognizing and meeting the psychological needs of the office staff members can create allies and part-time Team Selling participants while benefiting them simultaneously. These staff members frequently become a part of the Team Selling process and realize substantial self-worth because of their inclusion.

Compensation—Team Members

Even if the Agent does not directly compensate Team Members, they still need to be motivated and rewarded for their support and involvement. To achieve this, the Agent needs to identify ways of rewarding these Team Members through recognition and personal rewards.

For instance, the mere opportunity to work directly with a client and provide excellent service can be a reward to a staff member who typically does not interact with clients. When Staff Members are introduced to the client by the Agent and recognized as essential team members, they feel appreciated and gratified.

In addition to this, recognizing the staff member publicly in an office meeting or sending a letter of recognition to the Office Manager commending the staff member for their efforts can be greatly appreciated by the staff member. When the Agent acknowledges superior service, the staff member feels valued and encouraged to continue providing excellent service and support to the agent.

Another way of rewarding Team Members is by inviting them to a Team Selling luncheon with other Team members. Such events can be enriching, and the staff members feel valued as part of the team.

Simple thank-you notes can be powerful motivators. When the Agent takes the time to express gratitude for the staff member's efforts, the staff member feels appreciated, which can increase their motivation to continue providing excellent service.

Little, however, is as powerful as the staff member's opportunity to feel empowered by being involved in a Prospect or Client meeting where they are given a leadership or presentation role of any type. This often awakens the staff member's desire to do more, improve, and prove their worth. One example is allowing the staff Team Member to make a presentation, perhaps on "Showing Instructions" or how listing a property works. Another topic might be the Internet activities the Brokerage will do to assist in selling a listed property. Sharing this presentation subject with a staff member for client interaction will require training and practice, and this process with the Agent will help bond the staff members with the Agent as they will see a genuine effort to assist them in their personal development. Very few other Agents in the office will expend the time and effort to do this, and the Smart Agent has therefore created an inside track to building a Team Selling program within the office.

A Brokerage where there is a Broker of Record and no Office Manager or other support staff requires the Agent to look for other Agents within their brokerage office or select Strategic Marketing Partners to be on the Agent's Team. This is more challenging and involves some competitive risk for the Agent, as other Agents who become a part of the Team Selling program will be provided information that the Agent might prefer to be kept private. The Aspiring Agent might be well served by selecting an Agency to affiliate with where there is a support staff and the Broker of Record.

Conflict of Interest

Many of an Agents closest friends will come from fellow Agents and require discretion when sharing what might be called "trade secrets" with these real estate friends. It is not unusual for several Agents in the same office to compete for a Prospect simultaneously. It is also possible that another Agent's prior client might call upon the Agent to represent them and thereby disenfranchise the other Agent.

A potential problem exists when an Agent recruits a friend who is an Agent to be a part of the Team Selling process. The friend/Agent might be given information that could be copied or otherwise used and might present problems for the Agent in the future relative to the friendship. Caution should be taken when an Agent in the office is to be used to participate in a Team Selling process. The Agent should be sure that there will be no conflict that could arise. An example is a Prospect who lives in the same neighborhood as a friend selected to be a Team Selling participant.

Numerous possible Team Members can be recruited for the Team from Vendors and other professionals in and around the real estate world. These participants could have a common goal of obtaining new clients and providing excellent client care. These possible Team Members include but are not limited to Title Company associates, Mortgage Brokers, Insurance Agents, Financial Planners, Estate Planners, Inspectors, Vendors, and Print Media providers.

One of the important benefits of building a Team of Strategic Marketing Partners is to create a Decentralized Sales Organization (DSO) to further the real estate Agent's public relations and marketing reach to realize Market Coverage.

Participants in a Collaboration Hub & Team work together, and there is the opportunity for the Agent to create "Raving Fans" from the people within the Group that are not Prospects and who can become a Decentralized Sales Organization.

The Decentralized Sales Organization is a group of participants who don't necessarily realize they are considered a DSO. When a Vendor, such as a Paint Contractor, tells everyone they know they have a Star Real Estate Agent friend who promotes the Agent's business, they serve as a DSO. Having five or ten other business owners carrying the Flag of the Agent and promoting the Practice is always a worthy goal of an aspiring real estate Agent. This also extends the Agent's marketing reach to the DSO's sphere of influence when the DSO is adequately supported. For example, the Agent writing a letter to the Vendor thanking them for their great job with a particular client might be shared with the Vendor's sphere and therefore reach contacts that the Agent may not know.

Team Selling in Action

What does Team Selling in the Real Estate Industry look like in an office with a Manager, Listing Coordinator, and Administrative Assistant Team Member? How does it work, and why is it important to the Smart Agent?

The Team Selling program will work when the Team has been recruited, trained, and motivated to support the Agent. The Agent, when talking to a Listing Prospect about visiting the home for an appointment, might use the following script:

"Mr. and Mrs. Prospect, thank you for calling and inviting me to visit with you about your home. What I would like to do, if it is ok with you, is visit your home first and gather the information that would allow me to assess your home's value properly. I want to collaborate with you about your home and what would be most appealing to a Prospective Buyer. This usually takes about forty-five minutes, depending upon the questions you have for me when I visit. This will allow me to work with my Team and prepare a presentation for you. I always consider a home's square footage and fundamentals when I do my analysis. Still, I also include other information, such as floor plans, the condition of the property, and anything that I believe makes the home special. This visit allows me to do a thorough analysis of your home. Does this sound agreeable to you?"

Two Steps to Success!

Once the Agent schedules a Listing Appointment with a Prospect to meet at the office, Smart Agent, using a Two-Step Listing Approach, has already been to the Prospect's home to do a survey, tour the home, identify repair and improvement items, gather data about the property, and has returned to the office to create a unique marketing plan for the client's home. This includes a complete and detailed Comprehensive Market Analysis and marketing information to make a "powerful presentation, filled with such benefit and value that the Prospect will feel compelled to select the Agent." This was Step One of the Two Step Listing Process.

Step Two requires the Agent to plan to involve all of the office Team Members in the Prospect presentation by having each provide a "Magic Minute" to support the Agent. Smart Agent has prepared the Team by providing the name and basic information about the Prospect and giving them a brief one-paragraph summary of what they are asked to present. The Agent's mentor or other trusted friendly Agent could also be invited to be introduced as a Team member and resource or back-up to the Agent.

This presentation approach is augmented with a planned presentation that considers the Prospect's need for inclusion and interaction in a collaborative meeting. In his book *brain rules*, John Medina writes about the need for educators to consider the audience's need for reasons to stay attentive. He writes,

> *"Divide Presentations into 10-minute segments… Remember my students who said they got bored only 10 minutes into a mediocre lecture? The 10-minute rule, which researchers have known for many years, provides a guide to creating presentations people can pay attention to." (2014, p. 120)*

The collaborative and Team Selling Environment is particularly helpful in this regard. Not only is the presentation divided into less than 10-minute segments, but it also provides the Prospect physical movement in the office and a varied group of presenters who each have an important role in the overall presentation. All understand that the Stars of the show are the Prospects themselves.

Inviting various Team Members to present gives a Prospect different personalities and styles they can connect with, along with varied material and information. The presentation can be enhanced when the Team Members are asked to participate in the presentation by interacting with the Prospect. This approach at the office, rather than at home, provides an entirely different experience from what a Prospect expects or has experienced when dealing with Agents who usually meet them at their homes.

Baiting the Hook and Attention

In *brain rules*, Medina recommends "Bait the Hook!" Keep in mind the previous discussion about the Prospect's emotions and the ability of the Agent to capitalize on those emotions to create the Prospect's attention during the presentation. He writes,

"They need something so compelling that they blast through the 10-minute barrier—something that triggers an orienting response toward the speaker and captures the executive functions, allowing for efficient learning." (2014 pp. 121-122)

This is where the Consultative Agent's prospect knowledge and understanding of the prospect's emotions can help the Agent extend the prospect's attention span. Having the prospect be involved in the presentation by interacting with the Agent and the Agent's Team is a positive factor. Moving from one general area to another in less than 10 minutes can assist in the rapid change necessary to boost the attention of the Prospect. The relevancy of the comparable properties and how they compare to the Prospect's home can certainly tap into the Prospect's emotional spectrum. Explaining why a home didn't sell can also gain their attention. This understanding of the client and the situation allows the Consultative Collaborative Agent to make a powerful, personalized, and benefit-laden presentation that will cause the Prospect to be compelled to choose the Agent.

A Working Example of Team Selling

Team Selling is a powerful tool for the Aspiring Real Estate Agent. An example of how this strength can be maximized would be before leaving the Prospect's home after the initial visit. In Step One of the Listing Approach, the Smart Agent says:

"I want to thank you for allowing me to visit. I have gathered a lot of information to prepare for a detailed meeting with you. If it is all right with you, I would like to do the presentation at my office near here to introduce you to my support team and where we have access to our Collaboration Hub for our meeting. This will allow me to show you the competition on the market now and, of course, the sold properties that will be used to provide my recommendations to you.

Pause

Would that be all right with you?

Pause

Great, would Tuesday or Wednesday be better for you? Super! Tuesday it is. Would you prefer to meet in the morning or afternoon?

Pause

Excellent, Tuesday at 3 pm? Thank you. I'll be ready to present any recommendations my Team has on repairs or updates, which we also recommend. Do you have any additional questions?

Pause

Our presentation usually takes about an hour, and we will have plenty of time to answer your questions. Thank you so much, and I'll see you on Tuesday!"

Sitting in the office's lobby, the Administrative Assistant, Sally, will first greet the Prospect when they arrive for the appointment. She is ready and watching for the Prospect to arrive. Sally makes immediate eye contact with the Prospect upon their arrival. Sally has a great smile and stands to greet Mr. Prospect by name, saying, **"Mr. Johnson, I am Sally, the office OA, and it is so nice to meet you. The Collaboration Center is reserved for your meeting; let me show you to the room and get you a cup of coffee or a glass of water. Smart Agent will be right in, and I hope to visit with you more. Thank you for coming by."**

The Agent and the Office Manager, Thomas, enter the Collaboration Center immediately and greet the Prospect with handshakes and friendly smiles. Smart Agent thanks the Prospect for taking the time to come by and visit. The Office Manager, Thomas, says, **"Mr. and Mrs. Prospect, thank you for allowing us to visit with you. I know that Smart Agent will provide a great deal of information, and as the Office Manager, if I can help you or Smart Agent in any way, I will be very pleased to do so."**

Smart Agent thanks Thomas, and Thomas leaves as Smart Agent begins the presentation. There are pastries and soft drinks or water available for all. The Collaboration Center has a Smart TV, Internet access, and all the Agent's tools. Smart Agent begins the presentation and, at the appropriate time, asks the Prospect to accompany Smart Agent on a brief tour of the office, where the Listing Coordinator is introduced to the Prospect. The Listing Coordinator greets the Prospect by standing, shaking hands if appropriate, and briefly presenting how the Listing Coordinator assists and supports the Smart Agent in the office. The Listing Coordinator answers any questions the Prospect has, which are usually minimal.

Upon returning to the Collaboration Center, Smart Agent proceeds with the Listing Presentation.

This Team Presentation of Team Members has delivered multiple "Magic Minutes" for the Prospect to see and started the Prospect down the pathway of positivity. The Agent will reinforce this positivity throughout the presentation, and from the positive first impression, the Prospect is likely to look for positive things in the remainder of the Presentation. People support their first impressions, increasing the likelihood of success for the Agent. It also establishes that the Agent has the resources and the ability to provide great Client Care. It also shows the Prospect that the Agent has prepared for the meeting and has garnered the support of the Team, which is a demonstration of proficiency by the Agent. The Agent feels more empowered because of the Team interaction and has started the presentation in a position of power and prestige, setting the stage for the overpowering presentation that is to follow.

Salutary Benefits of Team Selling

The benefit of the Team Presentation is that the Agent is held in higher esteem by the entire Team and, particularly, the Office Manager. While the Agent does not report to the Office Manager in a typical real estate office, it never hurts to be favored by the Office Manager.

The Team's involvement and the later "Thank You Note" that Smart Agent will send to each Team Member motivates them and reinforces their commitment to support the Agent in the future. Being involved often motivates the Office Staff, particularly the OA. Later, when successfully capturing the Prospect and signed representation agreements, the Smart Agent should send a minimal gift card to each Team member along with a "Thank You note." This is another way of motivating them to work harder for Smart Agent. Recruiting, Training, and Motivating Team Members is a responsibility and privilege of the Team Leader. Later, when Smart Agent asks for a collaboration meeting with the Team Members or asks them for support or special attention on this or other matters, it is likely to be given when possible. Other office Agents seldom use Team Selling in this way. The client and the Team will likely become fans and possibly "Raving Fans."

Competitor Weakness

When the competitor Agent meets with the Prospect and explains how powerful and successful they are, the Prospect will remember that Smart Agent also has a friendly team, the experience they demonstrated, and the fact that they have personally met them. Since most Agents do their Listing Presentations at the client's home, seldom are Team Members used to assist in the presentation. The fact that Smart Agent brought the Prospect to the office, involved the entire team and has delivered multiple "Magic Minutes" differentiates the Agent from others and establishes a higher expectation in the mind of the Prospect. This makes it harder for the competitor Agent to live up to the standards that Smart Agent and his Team have established in the Prospect's mind. The entire method of presentation is different, and while at the Collaboration Hub, the Agent and Team demonstrate superior skills.

When meeting with the Client at the office is impossible, and the presentation must be made at the Client's home, the Team Selling concept can be utilized by video-conferencing technology. Although this is not as impressive as in person, it differentiates the Agent from the competitor. When the competitor is a well-recognized Agent or Group, it helps to level the playing field for the Smart Agent.

Team Selling and the "Buyer"

Team Selling is immensely powerful when working with a client hoping to find a suitable home to purchase. It is very image-building when a buyer asks for information. I call my office on speakerphone while driving, ask one of the Team Members to assist in getting the information, and request them to call me back immediately.

When they call back in just minutes, and I can answer questions or just provide information to my client on the spot, they are duly impressed at the support Team's efficiency. These additional "Magic Minutes" support the perception that our Team is highly coordinated and well-managed. When my assistant is also personable and highly professional, it is even more impressive. This is much more impressive than telling my client that when I get home after showing, I will try to get the information and get back to them. Invariably, something happens, and I am delayed in giving them a response until the next day.

A thorough understanding of Keystone Concepts is beneficial when integrating the concepts with Team Selling training. Combining all the Keystone Concepts creates a true differentiator for the Agent when Prospects compare Agents to make an Agent selection. It shows a sophisticated level of competency that causes the Client to become a "Raving Fan." A "Raving Fan" recommends their Agent to others because they want others to have a positive experience as they have had. An Agent's secret to long-term revenue generation is causing a client to become a "Raving Fan" and a Decentralized Sales Organization member. It unlocks the door to the client's sphere of influence.

CHAPTER 22|KEYSTONE CONCEPT: TELECONNECT – PERSONALIZED MARKETING

Sometime around 2010, we attended a meeting at a large hotel in Frisco, Texas. We were in the main ballroom with several hundred agents. A speaker presented emerging technology trends that would change the landscape of providing real estate services. He began his presentation by explaining that we would all be out of business in a few years if we didn't get on board with the new technologies that were emerging.

He inferred that we were Dinosaurs.

He described a world where real estate agents would be reduced to taxicab drivers because the information age would make them obsolete. Clients would no longer need agents, and we would have to find a way to be relevant. His presentation was insightful, frightening, and completely wrong. He forgot the most important equation in the business of real estate, and that is people wanting to collaborate with other people.

One might think from my comment that I am not a proponent of new technologies, but this is not the case. We were very high-tech in the business of real estate. However, our direction in using technology was to choose technologies that improved our communications with our clients and helped us stay in touch with and pay attention to them. We were using technologies that would improve our service level and make moving or buying a home less stressful for our clients.

As we left the three-hour meeting that day, I turned to Judi and said, **"Well, we learned a great deal today, didn't we?"** She asked, **"What do you mean?"**

"We learned that our competitors who listened to that speaker today and do what he says will provide less personalized, more automated services to the marketplace. Let's do the opposite. We should choose technologies that bring us closer to the client, not farther away."

That day, we took his message to heart and began migrating how we worked to a more client-centered strategy. We embraced the time-tested practice of talking to people and relating to them. We used technologies to be more people-oriented. We moved away from text messaging and email marketing and depending upon a website to reach our target markets.

Over the next ten years, our Practice experienced ten years of unprecedented success. We were among the top ten Groups at Ebby Halliday Realtors for ten years. This was no small feat, as there were 1,500 to 1,800 agents at Ebby Halliday during this period. We were voted "Best of Dallas by D Magazine" in all those ten years. This is an essential lesson for REALTORS. When you hear something forward-thinking and scary, ask yourself a fundamental question. Will this bring us closer to our client or take us further away?

During my entire business career, when working with numerous clients, I was astonished that so many people have injured their fingers. They can't seem to use them to push the buttons on their telephone, yet they can text. Occasionally, they have lost their voices and cannot call by voice command. Call reluctance is a dangerous disease. If afflicted with this disease, call me for immediate help.

Immediacy is critical to consider as a highly professional and responsive agent. While touring or previewing homes or neighborhoods, a Team Assistant might call to tell me that a client or prospect has called the office and wants to speak to me. Not having broken fingers and and having a working voice allows me to make responsive and demonstrating contact with the clients we serve. When a client called my office and didn't find me available, my assistant would hang up and immediately call me.

When told that I am out of the office, many clients assume it could be several hours until they are called back. After immediately calling them back, it is not unusual for them to say, **"Wow, that was fast. Thank you for getting right back to me. I have a question."**

A prospect has even less patience with the Agent when they want something. When I instruct my Team Member to call the Prospect back and explain that I will call them in five to fifteen minutes and to confirm the number they can be reached at, they are even more impressed. You could think that all of this is relatively "small stuff," but I can assure you that the difference between Good and Great is often the **"small stuff."** The cumulative value of "small stuff" adds up to "winning stuff." When a prospect tries to decide between Agents, all the little things can bring them to a "Tipping Point." They most often tipped in my favor when tipped over with great responsiveness. This also encouraged them to share me with their friends and associates because they believed I was different.

TeleConnect Meets the Need for Personalization

Let's talk about small and large ways of making a case for professionalism and excellent client care. The agent's secret weapons in the war for real estate success are the index fingers and the voice command on the cell phone.

TeleConnect is the integrated and systematic application of telecommunications, electronic transmission, public relations, research methods, management, sales, marketing systems, and computer systems (particularly a Prospect Relationship Management program) to optimize the marketing communications mix. It is utilized to reach Prospects and Strategic Marketing Partners, Vendors, Influencers, and others to maintain market coverage and provide superior client care to Prospects.

Most people have defined "telemarketing" as the use of the telephone to make random and unplanned sales calls to prospects who do not necessarily expect a call. As used herein, the meaning is a much broader concept called "TeleConnect Marketing!"

When Telemarking was first utilized, the cell phone did not exist, and the Telemarketing Concept referred to marketing by the business telephone. With the demise of personal landlines in many cases and the diminished use of business line telephone service in many industries, the cell phone has made the business landline a backup service rather than a primary tool for business communications. With the advent of business communications systems that allow for caller identification, even the business communications methods are vastly different from the older type systems.

The primary method of communication for an Agent in the real estate profession is by cellular telephone. In the real estate Practice, TeleConnect refers to numerous methods of communicating with the real estate Agent's target audience. Primarily the use of the cell phone has been by voice-to-voice communication augmented using the cellular telephone for email and text messaging by the Agent. In recent years, Agents have moved toward email and text communications by cellular phone, and many prefer this over voice-to-voice communication. This chapter explains why this trend of primary contact by **email and text is not the most effective way to communicate** in the real estate business, and, in some cases, I believe that it falls short of meeting the Agent's fiduciary responsibilities.

TeleConnect is a highly sophisticated marketing system for the real estate Practice. It goes much beyond simply using a Smart Phone to stay in touch. TeleConnect is used by all Practice Team Members but mainly by the real estate agents themselves. TeleConnect relies on the premise that contacts called in this manner may recognize the cell phone number and most likely will not be offended by receiving a call from the Agent. This is far different from contacting someone who does not know the caller.

Client, Prospect, and Contact are considered synonymous terms in this chapter. While there are situations where calls are made by an Agent to an unknown party, in almost all circumstances, these are not random calls but are based upon some information or knowledge that there is a need by the called party for some form of real estate assistance. We also anticipate that most contacts that are called have some form of caller identification and can determine who is calling and decline to answer if they so desire. We also should consider that many people whom an Agent or an Agent's Team calls are somehow involved in or interested in real estate and would be receptive to receiving a call. An Agent seldom calls a homeowner in what might be considered a "cold call" or "solicitation call."

A fundamental philosophy of the Consultative Agent is to avoid being perceived as a product salesperson but rather as a Consultative Agent. This directly opposes the historical ways that Telemarketing was used and is sometimes still used today. All activities using TeleConnect are carried out with client benefit as the primary goal. The client benefits from the responsiveness and speed of execution of the Agent and their Team.

When a Consultative Agent makes a TeleConnect contact for the client's benefit or a problem-solving solution for the client, the client will receive the call and react quite differently from when the call is made for the Agent's benefit. Confidence in the client-centered reason for the call causes the Agent to overcome "call reluctance" and "fear of rejection" and be positive in making calls, as the call will be client-benefit-oriented. This approach can reduce call reluctance.

Personal is Better

TeleConnect retains a highly personalized and individualized contact interaction while attempting to satisfy Prospect's needs and wants. TeleConnect voice-to-voice calls are far superior to email and text marketing programs because voice-to-voice calls retain personalized contact interaction and most often do not run the risk of the alienation of a Prospect, as it promotes benefit and problem resolution and allows for warmth and caring to be communicated through the voice. The friendly voice on the telephone disarms the contact receiving the call and eliminates contact apprehension.

A review of the material presented in the book *PRODUCTIVITY The Human Side*, written by Robert R. Blake, and Jane Srygley Mouton, will help to explain the significant differences between personal communication, such as voice-to-voice communication, and non-personal communication, such as email. It also demonstrates why voice-to-voice contact is superior as it allows the Agent to connect emotionally and with personality when talking to the contact. Email and Text Messaging do little in this regard.

"People tend to like others whose ideas, attitudes, and opinions, and actions are similar to theirs and to dislike those whose attitudes, opinions, feelings, and actions are significantly different." (1981, p. 35)

While I certainly use text and email in business, it is hard to imagine how one can effectively communicate attitudes, feelings, and opinions via text or email. These contacts are frequently brief, to the point, and cold rather than warm. While I use text messaging and email in many ways, I have found that they are best confined to simple communications that do not require dealing with problems and emotions. When a person feels the need for understanding and empathy, texting often fails dramatically and produces negative results.

The use of text and email when negotiating a contract with another Agent is a clear example of an Agent failing to provide the services they were retained to provide. Is there a correlation between using text and email as a favorite form of communication and the poor revenue results presented in the NAR information? This seems to me to be a real possibility. When an Agent communicates with a client by voice to voice, they allow emotions and personality to surface and a human connection to be made. Real estate service is about human connection rather than delivering cold information without feeling.

Fifty years of experience in the Practice of Real Estate convinces me that most Agents use email and text most frequently. Following is the language of an actual text received in a negotiation where I represented the Buyer on purchasing a two-million-dollar home in Dallas. The text is shown as written.

"This is Kimberly. The seller wants to counter your offer at 2.1 m. They want 500 in escrow. No opt per. Please, respond."

Imagine receiving this text, providing it to the client, and explaining the counteroffer.

This is how I typically respond to a text like this. I replied by text. **"Kimberly, I left you a voicemail. I need to discuss the counter-offer you texted me at 11 AM. My client insists that I speak to you personally. Please listen to my voice message or call me on my cell. Time is of the essence. Thanks, Sonny."**

The voice message that I left was as follows,

"Hi Kimberly, thank you for your text and counter-offer information. I really need to speak to you about your text counteroffer, as my client requires that we talk so that I can understand the counteroffer fully. I have several questions and want your opinion about several things and the best way to proceed to get a deal done. Please get back to me by telephone as I await your call. I want to talk to my client asap. Thanks, Sonny"

It was implied that things would go no further unless we talked. When I did get to talk to the other agent about the counter-offer, I insisted that the counter-offer be returned in writing with the required signatures and on the appropriate promulgated forms. This ensured that there was no misunderstanding of the terms and that my client could see, understand, and respond in writing. I would only negotiate without this approach if my client insisted I do so.

When agents accept texting or email rather than the appropriate way of negotiating a contract, they may not fulfill their fiduciary responsibilities.

I believe it is always necessary to use all my skills, talents, and capabilities to present my client's wishes and terms to the other parties in a negotiation. I do not think the client is represented professionally when texting or providing abbreviated information. I have found that I can only represent my clients to my fullest capabilities by demanding interaction.

When I tell my clients that I prefer to talk to them rather than use text or email to communicate, I send them a message about my efforts to personalize the service for them. This recognizes their importance. Naturally, if a client wants to send me a text or email, they can do so, but I would prefer to call them back unless instructed otherwise. Why?

This allows me to speak directly to clients, inquire about their families, or be warm and friendly. These are missed opportunities for many Agents to personalize the services they provide. Each opportunity to connect gives the Agent a greater personal connection with the client.

This utilization of TeleConnect improves the likelihood of Agent success because it is a more personalized and intimate form of communication that allows an Agent to sense or feel the emotion in the Prospect or Client's voice rather than just reading words in a text or email. This more intimate communications method, still not better than personal face-to-face contact, can differentiate the Agent and provide a greater opportunity for building client relationships and causing a prospect to like the Agent. The more contacts an Agent has with a client, the more likely familiarity is directly linked to likeability.

Because text and email are often brief and may sound terse, it is far better to communicate by telephone or in person than by electronic transmission. When composing text or email, most people trying to stay brief often fail to use language and grammar properly, sometimes abbreviating comments and presenting a poorer picture of the Agent's mental capacities to a Prospect. This does not build confidence or relationships.

There is another more emphatic reason that text and email fall short in representing a client in a negotiation. In *blink*, Gladwell writes about the face in The Naked Face section.

> *"What Ekman is saying is that the face is an enormously rich source of information about emotion. In fact, he makes an even bolder claim—one central to understanding how mind reading works— and that is that the information on our faces is not just a signal of what is going on inside our minds. In a certain sense, it is what is going on inside our mind." (2005, p. 206)*

This contention that the face is the brain is instrumental in understanding why face-to-face contact is so important. It also makes video conferencing even more valuable in the absence of face-to-face contact as it allows the Agent to see the other party and, in a way, read their minds. Yet this is also a revelation in that it allows the Agent to understand that the client can read their mind, improving communication between all. This being true, the Agent is not only able to "put on a Poker Face" but also to put on a "Consultative Face," "Happy Face," "Concerned Face," or an empathetic face if what they are thinking and feeling is automatically transmitted to their face via their brain. This could also include an Agents angry, frustrated, disappointed, or uncaring facial presentation.

This could pose a challenge to the agent if they cannot control their facial expressions and, without realizing this, communicate visually to the client their discomfort. Gladwell expands on this thinking and provides an excellent overview of how and why this works. When talking face-to-face with another agent being negotiated with, an agent can intentionally send a non-verbal message by presenting a facial expression that makes a profound statement.

This idea takes Self-Disclosure & Reciprocity to a different level. It demonstrates that the Agent can not only disclose through what they say but also what they think as demonstrated by their facial expressions. For this reason, the Agent cannot pretend to be a consultant or collaborative Agent. They must become one. Therefore, the agent might need brain rewiring if they are accustomed to being a product salesperson.

Most REALTORS® agree that the client buying or selling a personal residence has great emotion in their decisions. It is much more personalized to have the ability to hear and see a Prospect or Client when determining how to support them. The voice and face carry meaning, intent, emotion, and nuances that can only be heard by telephone or seen during voice-to-voice contact, videoconferencing, or person-to-person contact.

TeleConnect positively impacts the Prospect's perception of the Agent and the positivity of their experience with the Agent or Team. This allows the Agent to be connected and productive and improve Client Care while achieving Market Coverage. TeleConnect is essential in Account Protection efforts with the Prospect as it allows for frequent personalized interaction by the Agent and their staff with the Prospect and multiple decision makers and influencers within the Prospect's account, thereby avoiding competitor inroads with the account.

TeleConnect is executed in the Real Estate Industry to assure market coverage, maximize high-profit resources (the Real Estate Agent), and limit costly face-to-face resource expenditures on marginal (low risk/low opportunity) accounts.

To simplify, it emphasizes the Agent's face-to-face and voice-to-voice contact with high-potential accounts. It targets lower-cost resources to provide face-to-face and voice-to-voice contact with lower potential accounts.

A Way of Life for the Agent

In its optimum environment, TeleConnect is the way of life for the real estate Agent. This way of life begins with early morning "get in touch calls" to Prospects and "return calls" when appropriate. Activities in TeleConnect continue throughout the workday by reaching out to other parties to answer questions, elicit information, or solve problems. It continues to the end of the day and, when necessary, into the evening and weekends to return calls and meet prospects' needs and wants. It is essential to schedule Assuring Satisfaction Interviews and open new opportunities with new and existing Prospects.

When TeleConnect is appropriately integrated into the real estate operations and Practice CRM, it will become the nerve center for the sales and marketing effort within a Practice. A nerve center is a group of closely connected cells that perform a particular function. In this case, the function is the sales and marketing programs. The TeleConnect program is enhanced with a Client Relationship Management Program (CRM), and both become essential productivity tools for the Agent.

It is almost impossible to coordinate the complex activities of a sophisticated client management program without using a CRM regularly. TeleConnect requires a CRM to capture contact activity via the telephone.

CHAPTER 23 | KEYSTONE CONCEPT: INTEGRATING TELECONNECT

Dan and Donna Faucett were moving out of state and listed their home for sale. We first met with them while their three young girls played in the backyard. This was an adorable family. They were moving and asked us to help them. They knew of us because of our Neighborhood Target Marketing program. This included frequent mailings and the distribution of our magazine to their home. Shortly after listing their home, we received a call from a prospective buyer's agent about the home. There was a situation.

The agent and buyer had toured the property and were excited about seeing the home and were considering the home along with two other homes. The agent explained.

"When we arrived to tour the home, someone had written a message in pink chalk across the sidewalk in front of the home. The message read, "Do not buy this home. It is a "bad home," and you should not buy it."

The agent laughed with us and said that if the children loved the home that much, the buyer felt it was probably meant for them. They purchased the home, and Dan and Donna relocated out of state. Our primary method of staying in touch with them was by mail, but we supplemented this with occasional TeleConnect calls to say Happy Birthday or stay in touch. It isn't easy to stay in touch with people as the years pass. However, we did.

When a client moves away, it is sometimes difficult to prioritize resources to stay in touch with them. We created a code in our CRM for this purpose. While our highest priority local clients were labeled P-1, those that had moved away were coded P-1 Moved Away. For several reasons, it is difficult to commit resources to a client like the Fawcett's.

- They could meet new agents that replace us in their minds as the best agents.
- They might not find a reason to refer others from their sphere of influence.
- They may never move back into the area.

Over seven years later, I received a call from Dan. He had secured a new position and was moving back to our area. He wanted to know if we could/would help him. After visiting about their needs, they arrived for a home tour visit, and we got to work. The girls were now college-age, and we laughed about the funny situation and the pink chalk. They still remembered the story, and we were all connected in a unique way through the children.

They had a difficult time finding a home, and we had looked at everything in their price range as they were beginning to get frustrated. They contacted me on a Monday morning and explained that they had toured an "open house" and were sure it was the right home for them. It was well above their price range and had not been on our list.

They had "blinked" upon seeing the home. We arranged to see the home together, and they were delighted and made an offer. We successfully negotiated a contract. They were ecstatic and thankful for our support. The fee earned was more than $25,000.00. After closing, I jokingly asked myself if the time and money to stay in touch had been worth the expense and effort. You know the answer. Now they are back, happy, and fans to this day. We now have additional opportunities to serve them, their children, and their sphere of influence.

TeleConnect marketing is the most cost-effective and personalized way to stay in touch with clients that move away.

"TeleConnect Marketing" is an invaluable personalization tool in that it enables the agent to effectively:

- Monitor Prospect needs, wants, emotions, and concerns.
- Provide Progress Reports about Agent activities and results achieved.
- Provide current intelligence data about homes and property status changes.
- Isolate service problems that have been encountered or could happen.
- Evaluate marketing effectiveness in communications with Target Markets
- Conduct marketing and service research in selected areas.
- Gather information about Competitor activities and assess marketing systems.
- Expand knowledge about a client's family and sphere of influence
- Encourage referrals and increase Client collaboration and involvement.
- Build a relationship with the Client through involvement in their lives.
- Make Perception Sales passively.
- Create likability by relating to the Client's feelings, opinions, and attitudes.
- Stay in touch personally with people who are your fans but live in distant locations.

"TeleConnect Marketing" is inextricably linked to "Marketing." TeleConnect is used in concert with the CRM to build client information and has magnified benefits from frequent client interaction. The real estate professional uses TeleConnect to collaborate, inform, educate, and perform other activities with callers and the PROSPECT who is called. It is rarely used in the real estate practice to call unknown parties suspected of being buyers or sellers. Most of the time, when an Agent uses TeleConnect to make calls, it is to someone they have a reason to know and with whom they have at least a passing relationship.

"TeleConnect Marketing" in the real estate industry is a marketing method used to assure, among other things, "Market Coverage." The marketing term market coverage means assuring that all Prospects are contacted in one form or another regularly and consistently. Implementing market coverage techniques enables a Practice to stay in touch with its existing Clients and Prospects to prevent competitive loss or erosion, provide superior client service, and perhaps primarily help the Agent and Client or Prospect remain highly productive. It also enhances the ability to stay in touch with prospective clients and Prospects to improve future results. Good market coverage protects expected current revenues, anticipates client needs, and addresses sales and service opportunities, including potential referrals.

Market coverage works in concert with the 80/20 rule of business. This rule of business states that 80% of the clients generally provide twenty percent or less of the revenue of a typical real estate business. In comparison, the remaining 20% of the Prospects provide 80% or more of the revenue over some time. Within the Client Hierarchy, the 80/20 rule of business is used to target the face-to-face contact and time of the Agent on the 20% of the clients with the most potential.

In the real estate industry, Agents often face resource scarcity when executing a comprehensive contact program to ensure Market Coverage. To overcome this challenge, many Agents turn to low-cost and impersonalized methods such as standardized card mailers, email, or text messaging. However, these methods often fall short because they fail to recognize the importance of personalization in marketing.

For example, standardized newsletters, card mailers, email, and text messaging programs can appear less personal and are, therefore, less effective. Emails and texts, in particular, can be easily misunderstood due to the brevity of the message. Moreover, since these messages are often composed spontaneously, they may contain errors or poor communication, which can leave a negative impression on the client.

Are All Agents the Same?

Most standardized forms of messaging do not personalize the message, reinforcing the idea that all Agents are alike. This lack of personalization fails to differentiate the Agent and the Practice, which can hurt their image and branding.

To avoid these issues, Agents should focus on personalizing their messages to clients. For example, an Agent could include a client's name in a personalized email or send a customized thank-you note to show appreciation for the client's business. By taking the time to personalize their communications, Agents can build stronger relationships with clients and establish a more positive image for themselves and their Practice.

Successful real estate agents frequently have clients they have worked with for years. Market coverage assists in monitoring all clients in the Client Base, representing the greatest sales opportunity for the Agent and the highest risk if these clients are lost. Combining "TeleConnect Marketing" with other contact methods can solve many of these concerns. It is a cost-effective way of maintaining contact with people who have moved away or are not convenient to visit personally. It is more personalized than a letter, email, or text and demonstrates an effort to maintain the relationship that has existed in the past.

Personalizing contact also allows for constantly reevaluating the Client Base to identify which accounts will change places with one of the other accounts in the Client Hierarchy. Market coverage allows a Practice to monitor the ongoing shifting between high and low-potential accounts and attempts to identify those shifts between groups to avoid Client loss and capture future business cost-effectively. Monitoring the Client Base allows for more effective targeting of resources, advertising, and marketing dollars.

Managing a Complex Environment

Account Cycling is a market coverage method for a Practice with numerous clients to provide for the systematic and ongoing contact of accounts in a planned and programmed way. The need for Account Cycling is created because of the Practice's success in obtaining and maintaining Clients as the Client Base expands.

Based upon an analysis of each Client, a contact code is assigned in the CRM, and the system specifies a Treatment Grid that prescribes how each type of account should be contacted with each contact method to achieve market coverage and manage accounts. The treatment grid establishes the nature and frequency of contact required for different classifications of Clients in the Ranking System.

Activity Assessment & Assignment of Resources

There are three broad categories of "TeleConnect Marketing" activities. Each of these categories has numerous applications within its specific area of operation. There are numerous potential "TeleConnect Marketing" applications in a typical real estate Practice environment. The following is a list of examples of frequently used applications.

Order Processing Examples – Limited Skills Necessary

- Referral Management – Need for Vendors or Agents in Other Areas
- Simple Request for Client Support – Need for Materials
- Request for Changes in Home Showing Rules & Addressing Home Showing Problems
- Details regarding home showings or scheduled open houses, etc.
- Provision of Information, i.e., Property Tax Data & Active or Sold Properties

Client Service Examples – Moderate Skills Required

- Marketing Results – Showing Feedback & Follow-Up Results
- Vendor Follow-Up, Problem resolution
- Market Research – New Listings or Property Availability, Price reductions, etc., Pending Sales
- Complaint Handling, Dealing with Client conflicts, building affinity.
- Notification of Opportunities for Buyer Prospects

Account Management Examples – Expert Skill Required

- Complete Client Account Management Data Gathering & Procurement of Information
- Contract Management & Scheduling Contract Presentations, Closings
- Collaborative Selling – Looking for Ideas & Suggestions in Marketing
- Inactive Account Reactivation – Re-capture of Inactive Accounts
- Perception Selling to Protect Client Relationships
- Creating Affinity with the Client
- New Account Capture/Prospecting for Business via Referral or Target Market Activity
- Opening Client Spheres of Influence

Attributes of Highly Successful TeleConnect Agents

The Agent utilizing "TeleConnect Marketing" must possess strong communication and interpersonal skills. The Agent must be flexible in that they possess the ability to react and evaluate information quickly while on the telephone and avoid falling into a product sales approach. The Agent should not sell but instead support, advise, solicit information, and collaborate. This is what changes a typical Agent into a Consultative Agent.

Because of the skills involved, applicants for positions on the Agent's team who utilize TeleConnect as described should be evaluated to ascertain the applicant's ability to assist in TeleConnect calls. Without assessment by the Agent, Team Members frequently will not be involved in this "TeleConnect Marketing" program in specific areas unless they are trained and skilled at the appropriate level.

As a result, only lesser-skilled applications of the "TeleConnect Marketing" System should be assigned to Team Members until they have demonstrated the ability to perform at a higher level on TeleConnect activities. Careful evaluation should occur before being assisted in higher-level activities such as Account Management. An example of lower-function activities for TeleConnect would be calling a client to determine if they need marketing supplies in their home. This would also mean that the real estate agent will likely be assigned more complex "TeleConnect Marketing" activities such as problem resolution responsibilities and Account Management activities. This is consistent with the practice of assigning higher-skilled projects to higher-skilled resources. This further demonstrates the need for assigning lesser-skilled resources the lesser-skilled activities so that the Agent can spend the necessary time and energy in direct contact with Clients and Prospects. Effective execution of a "TeleConnect Marketing" Program provides critical benefits to the Practice, such as:

1. Improves Client Perception & Client Care
2. Reinforces Clients Prior Opinions About the Practice & Agent
3. Protects Important Clients from Competitor Efforts to Capture
4. Improves Utilization of Higher Skilled Resources to Higher Function Activities
5. Reduces Cost of Operations by Accomplishing More with Less
6. Increases Market Stimulation in a Cost-Effective Manner
7. Identifies Client Opportunities not yet Known

As a part of the marketing mix, "TeleConnect Marketing" provides the Practice with a cost-effective method of contacting the target audience, thereby impacting the staffing plan by improving the TEAM's productivity. The addition of TeleConnect impacts almost every area of the marketing plan.

The "TeleConnect Marketing" System is the primary method that the Agent must use to reach the target audience. TeleConnect can result in significant revenue and profit because it points the highest skilled resource directly at the revenue opportunity. An Agent that cannot use TeleConnect will find it challenging to succeed in real estate because they cannot stay in frequent contact with the P1 group and build account plans by adding important client information. While the Agent might use email and text messaging, their use is limited when the Agent seeks to differentiate themselves from competitors.

The team member assigned to the "TeleConnect Marketing" effort must be a highly confident, detail-oriented, and respectful person who enjoys working in the CRM. The Agent or Team Member making the contacts needs to be prepared to discuss ideas and solutions that most clients will appreciate. The Team Member must be an excellent listener who is tuned in to the client's needs and wants and can anticipate likely questions and problems presented by the client or prospect. The Team Member should frequently ask for input, ideas, and suggestions, thus fostering collaboration.

Procedures should be followed when contacting Clients and Prospects via voice-to-voice calls.

The call should target the right contacts at the right time and be disciplined enough to wait to speak to the targeted contact patiently. Calls should not be made to contacts at times that are likely to interrupt them and make it difficult for them to be open to discussion. The Team Member should always ask, "Is this a good time to talk."

The Team Member must be patient but persistent until the right person is reached without alienating anyone. They should always leave a message or, when speaking to a different person than the targeted, make them feel comfortable with who they are and give them the reason for the call, stressing the benefit of talking to the desired person.

For example: **"Hi John, this is Karen with Smart Agent's office. I wanted to talk to Kim about the open house this weekend to make sure it is all set and remind her of the time we will be arriving. Could you please let her know that I called?"**

When listening, the Team Member should remember that the call is always about the client. They should always have a defined goal and purpose for the call. They should have pre-planned the call and avoided making calls spontaneously without preparation.

They should always determine the customer's availability to talk to avoid disruption. If the client is busy or appears unable to talk, apologize for the interruptions and tell them they will call back at another convenient time. For example,

"I am so sorry to interrupt. I would be happy to call back later today when it is better for you to talk. Is this ok?"

The call should always ask for Prospect feedback, listen to their response, and document what was learned so that a follow-up plan can be developed from the call.

The **Team Member** must remember not to sell. They should not fall into the trap of trying to present a complex idea via the telephone unless the Client requires this to be done. If something is too complex, a meeting should be scheduled for a video conference, in-office meeting, or at the Client's home.

The caller does not want to fall into a pattern of sloppy speech or tone that tells the Client that the caller is not prepared or is calling without a purpose or need. For this reason, the contact call should always be scripted and rehearsed not to sound like the call is scripted. Scripts cannot be used during the call itself.

The Agent and Team Member should never assume anything before making the call. They should not assume that the contact will be happy or unhappy, friendly or unfriendly, available or unavailable. The Agent needs to be prepared to talk about several issues while keeping in mind the primary purpose of the call. The caller should never fail to deliver a brief and client-benefit-focused message. While making the call, the Agent should never miss an opportunity to serve, teach, inform, and support the Client in any way reasonable. When making a TeleConnect contact, the call is all about the Client.

The Agent must be cautious about trying to solve a problem for the Client if they suspect or doubt they can solve it. Over promising and failing to deliver is risky. If uncertain, the Agent should offer to think about it and get back to the Client with any ideas that the Agent can uncover. The Agent should seek to come up with an alternative solution or identify other resources if the client's needs or wants cannot be met at the time of the call or upon further evaluation. The Agent should consider situations like this as an opportunity to make a Perception Sale and position themselves positively with the Client.

When faced with a problem the Agent is unsure they can solve, they might say, **"You know, that is a complex problem. I want to consider it and confer with a few of my associates. Do you mind if I do some research and get back to you?"**

Before making any call, the Agent should review the CRM records and refresh their memory about essential things in the client's file. This will allow the Agent to say,

"By the way, isn't it Karen's birthday next week? I thought so... Please tell her I said happy birthday!" or the Agent could say, **"I just realized you have been in your home almost two years. Congratulations. Are you still loving it?"**

Above all else, the Agent should never put their call agenda ahead of listening to what the Client says. Listening and positively responding is essential in making the call a positive experience for the Contact. If the Agent is successful, the client will think, **"That was nice of them to call: they stay in touch with us!"**

The phone call and anything learned from the contact will be wasted intelligence if not adequately documented in the CRM. The notes field in the CRM is where the fundamental Account Plan is developed and maintained. Failure to document critical information for further follow-up or discussion wastes resources and opportunities.

Embrace TeleConnect and Win

TeleConnect Integration into the Real Estate Practice takes effort and commitment. TeleConnect Marketing is one of the most remarkable low-cost, effective ways to expand the use of resources in organizations with limited resources. It is the most important daily tool for the superior Agent.

CHAPTER 24|KEYSTONE CONCEPT: THE REVERSE SALES PROCESS

The Reverse Sales Process was derived from the understanding and study of the concept of "Differentiation." Earlier in this book, the analogy was made where there were 399 salespeople in a room attending for the same purpose. They were all dressed in gray, looked alike, talked the same storyline, and even smiled the same way. They all had the word **"Salesperson"** stamped across their foreheads in Red.

Understanding the Reverse Sale Process begins with the same storyline, except the number of salespeople attending has been reduced to twenty-five. The setting is a Chamber of Commerce Meet & Greet. Usually, the twenty-five people who attend this meeting are financial planners, insurance agents, bankers, REALTORS®, and others who are there to Network and find business Prospects. A few who attend are from the Chamber of Commerce, who supervise the event and keep order among the salespeople.

Most often, the people there bring their business cards and have their eyes peeled to find a Prospect. Some smart individuals have packets of information and they are ready to provide these to anyone who smiles or shows any interest. All those attending are hungry… but not for the food served at the event.

The attendees don't realize they all have the word **"Salesperson"** stamped across their foreheads. This is known because of their behavior. They look like salespeople, walk and talk like salespeople, and think like product salespeople based on their sales-oriented behavior. Even financial planning experts call what they offer products. Everyone has their script ready to present, and their pitch has been practiced and honed so that it is instantly ready for delivery, even to those without interest in hearing a sales pitch.

Many salespeople attending have been in or around sales most of their lives and possess a smooth delivery. Some have been in sales for a short time and were told by someone to come to this meeting to meet Prospects. Unlike seasoned professionals, they are anxious to tell their stories, filled with enthusiasm and excitement. Let the games begin…

One smart salesperson is dressed in blue and has a different strategy. Unlike the other salespeople there, they have a different plan that will differentiate them from the crowd. This is to utilize the "Reverse Sales Process" to find Connectors. This Smart Agent does not have **"Salesperson"** printed across their forehead. Instead, printed in "Blue," this Smart Agents label says, **"I am Interested in You!"** They do not wear a badge announcing their salesperson's pedigree and are not stalking Prospects.

This Smart Agent doesn't have a pitch ready to sling! They do not walk around like a product salesperson but rather as someone interested in others. Their eyes are not searching for Prospects. They just want to meet people and make them like them. They don't have a salesperson's smile plastered across their face, but rather, an exciting look, like they are attending a fascinating class on human behavior theory and are people watchers. They are a student of human behavior… and are searching for "Connectors."

When approached by others, the Smart Agent does not hastily qualify them as not being a Prospect and ignores them if they do not seem likely to be buyers. The Smart Agent is there to meet people, connect, relate, and get to know others.

Smart Agent is approached by Bob, a Financial Planner with a Financial Planning Practice, and Smart Agent patiently waits while actively listening, refraining from reciprocating with a sales message. The Smart Agent is "ALL EARS," and their antenna is tuned to what Bob says. Smart Agent wants to learn from Bob and about Bob. Bob may ask a favorite question to qualify Smart Agent like,

"Hi, my name is Bob Gibson. What do you do?" When asked, Smart Agent does not begin with a real estate pitch and says, **"Oh, I work in the real estate industry. How about you, Bob? What is it that you do?"**

Smart Agent quickly discovers that Bob is a Certified Financial Planner on the hunt for a few good clients. The onslaught of information follows as Bob begins his sales pitch to see how his target reacts. In the first three minutes, Bob drops at least two prominent names. He references products that he offers, like estate planning. Smart Agent reacts with interest, asking follow-up questions and mentally recording important information. Bob may soon tire as he has determined that Smart Agent is not a Prospect, and his eyes will shift to others in the room as he searches for a real Prospect. Smart Agent can tell he is searching because he stops making eye contact and looks over Smart Agent's shoulder for another person to approach. Soon, the inevitable card exchange happens, and Bob politely starts to move on, but Smart Agent says,

"Bob, it was great to meet you, and thank you for giving me interesting information! It sounds like you do an excellent job for your clients. Let's stay in touch. Don't forget my name, 'Smart Agent."

Having repeated his name several times aloud and repeated his business name, Smart Agent has established that Bob is a "Connector." Smart Agent makes a mental note to remember that Bob seems a little product-oriented rather than consultative in his methods. Smart Agent quietly makes a few notes on Bob's business card after Bob leaves and thinks about how Bob will be approached the next time they talk, which will be soon… right after entering Bob's information in the CRM. His contact type will be coded as.

- Connector
- Financial Planner
- Strategic Marketing Partner Prospect
- Chamber Meet & Greet

Bob will remember Smart Agent as the friendly, interested non-buyer that he was. They may visit again for a few minutes as Bob surveys the landscape to find a Prospect-looking attendee. Bob is blind to the red stamped label on the other attendees' heads.

This sales dance continues through the evening as Smart Agent makes mental notes that three of the stamped foreheads belong to real estate salespeople and likely competitors. Smart Agent has listened intently to them also and made them like Smart Agent as much as possible. They will not spend much time with Smart Agent, but Smart Agent is willing to listen to them and gather market intelligence by observing their approach, pitch, tenor, and skills. If they hand out materials or information, Smart Agent quietly collects the information for competitor files that are being assembled. Smart Agent is learning from them and listens carefully. Smart Agents may learn what to do and what not to do from these competitors.

With as many cards as could be gathered and notes on each card, Smart Agent ends the evening re-laxed and feeling good because there is a plan of action. This evening was not a waste of time, as three "Connectors" were identified by Smart Agent among those attending the event. As soon as possible, Smart Agent begins adding the contact names and information from those collected at the meeting into Smart Agent's CRM (Client Relationship Management). Memory is fleeting, so time is of the essence for this smart real estate Agent.

When entering information into the CRM, all relevant information is included, and in the notes section, expanded beyond the cryptic notes that were made on the business cards collected. Observations were made about them, their story, and how they responded to the meeting with them. Even the real estate Agents were documented for competitive intelligence reasons, and where they live was noted if obtained to avoid mailing information to them. Smart Agent tries to recall one important thing they said about themselves. This will allow Smart Agent to reach out to them to connect and build a relationship or gain more market intelligence.

Each record is categorized in the CRM as follows,

Types of Contact:

- Insurance Agent
- Influencer
- Chamber Member
- Chamber Meet & Greet Attendee
- SMP Prospect

Before making any TeleConnect calls, Smart Agent reviews the notes in the CRM and scripts a call to Bob and the others that were selected to be followed up with from the meeting. Those not to be called were scheduled to be sent a "Nice to Meet You Card" from Smart Agent.

Smart Agent hopes that Bob will remember their name, but if he doesn't, Smart Agent has the notes to remind Bob of their meeting and can reference several things that Bob said. This will likely make Bob feel great as everyone appreciates being heard and remembered.

Smart Agent adds Bob's name and his critical information to their cell phone unless it is already synced to their CRM. Smart Agent hopes this information will appear on Bob's cellphone when called. When calling Bob, Smart Agent remembers that this is not a sales call but rather a friendly call from someone interested in Bob and his services and how they can collaborate to help build each other's businesses. Smart Agent may also have a small gift for Bob. Something that will really make him remember Smart Agent!

When Bob answers, Smart Agent says: **"Hi Bob, this is Smart Agent with the Renaissance Group. We met last Tuesday at the Chamber Meet & Greet. I enjoyed meeting you and wanted to speak a little more about you and your business. I was particularly interested in your description of how you provide a blueprint for retirement for your clients. I have a few questions for you and would appreciate your help. I am in the real estate business, which is not why I am calling. I wanted to get more information about you and your services and invite you to my office for a short follow-up meeting. Would you be interested in getting together?"**

Bob will be surprised as almost no one follows up on these Meet & Greet sessions. He must have made a real impression on this Smart Agent. He will probably agree to meet as he wants to explore and see if Smart Agent is a Prospect after all. Smart Agent may need to give him an incentive!

Smart Agent does not mislead Bob and simply says, **"Bob, I hope to connect with several high-net-worth individuals to work with in real estate. I wanted to get to know you better so that I can refer you to my clients or associates if there is a need or opportunity to do so. I will only send referrals to people that I have gotten to know well enough to feel confident that they will manage the referral tactfully. I am particularly interested in what you do in estate planning."**

This approach is not just an excuse to get together. It cannot hurt to know about Estate Planning when dealing with high-net-worth individuals regarding real estate. Knowledge gained can allow Smart Agent to demonstrate proficiency in other areas to Prospects. Smart Agent also sees an opportunity to make friends and for the contact to refer business to each other and possibly work together in a Strategic Marketing Partner relationship. As a "Connector," Bob can be a good person to know. Smart Agent can learn from Bob and certainly share contacts when appropriate. Smart Agent fully intends to build a relationship with Bob as Smart Agent likes his style and experience. He also may have many contacts who may also be "Connectors."

When Bob arrives at the office, the Smart Agent is not wearing a Real Estate Badge and doesn't have **"Salesperson"** stamped on their forehead. Smart Agent is still interested in Bob. Smart Agent wants to understand who he knows, what he does, obtain more details, how he does it, and learn what marketing programs and strategies he utilizes. Smart Agent is still a student of human behavior and begins the meeting focused on knowing as much as possible about Bob and his business strategies and tactics. Perhaps Smart Agent can learn from Bob and possibly teach Bob a few things that might help him.

Smart Agent waits for the "Invitation to Present" from Bob, but if no "invitation to present" comes, Smart Agent is comfortable with just visiting and exploring the possibilities. Smart Agent might even have an opportunity to illuminate some possibilities for Bob.

Being Invited to Present is a Cue

The "Invitation to Present" concept is important to understand in numerous situations. The concept is that many people are unreceptive to hearing a sales message unless they invite the other party in the communication to present their message. For example, a salesperson should wait for an invitation from a potential client before presenting their product or service. If they just start talking about it without being asked, the potential client may be less interested and not listen as closely. When they invite a presentation of information, they listen differently than when they don't invite the presentation. Sometimes, without an invitation, they just "don't want to hear it" unless they ask someone to share information.

Listening to the "Invitation to Present" requires great discipline and has nuances that the Consultative Agent must consider. The secret to hearing the "Invitation to Present" is to have large ears finely tuned to what the other party being communicated with is saying. Visualizing that they have very large ears, finely tuned in to the other person, causes Smart Agent to pay closer attention and avoid talking. These super-large ears the agent visualizes as being theirs hear everything, and Smart Agent's eyes seem focused solely on the other person they are speaking with.

Most people who share information (See Self-Disclosure & Reciprocity) and talk about themselves at some point expect a reciprocal disclosure of a similar nature. Someone sharing information about their business will expect a reciprocal disclosure of a similar nature from the other party. Failing to do so can be negative and often will be seen as such by the disclosing party. They might become suspicious of why there are no reciprocal disclosures.

The Keystone Concept – Self-Disclosure & Reciprocity is fresh in Smart Agent's mind. "When disclosed to, people have a psychological need to reciprocate. This is not a want. It is a need… Likewise, they fully expect a reciprocal disclosure of a similar nature from someone they are disclosing to." Allowing someone to disclose and patiently listening often invites and causes the "Invitation to Present to be delivered."

When this reciprocal disclosure doesn't happen, the disclosing person begins to suspect that the person disclosed to is hiding something. Perhaps they can't be trusted, or they might have ulterior motives. They may think the other person is not interested in them and become uncomfortable. They expect the other party to disclose; when they don't, they often request disclosure to test the situation. Disclosing information of a similar nature, thus demonstrating that they are being heard, and trusted, makes others feel more comfortable.

This need for reciprocal disclosure is very powerful. After listening to a person talk, disclose, and share, listen for the Invitation to Present. A pause might disguise it or be as open as, "What do you think?" It doesn't have to be verbal; a physical cue could indicate that it is time to reciprocate, but it is easy to sense that the other party is looking for a response because "huge elephant ears" pick up signals. The human eye often sees more than one might think. It is good if they invite disclosure, but listening carefully for disclosing words can be a cue that it is time to reciprocate with a similar disclosure at a similar level of disclosure. This can be as simple as the **"What do you think?"** or the **"How about you?"** statement. They could also say, **"Well, now that I have told you a little about me, what do you do, and how do you help your clients buy or sell real estate?"**

Regardless of how it happens, when it does, the door is open for reciprocal disclosure with similar disclosures as those that the other party has disclosed. Be careful about disclosing too much personal information when the other party has disclosed non-personal information. When reciprocating, avoid a sales pitch or language that causes the contact to think they are talking to a product-oriented salesperson. Relate what is being said to what the other person disclosed.

Such as:

"Bob, like you, I focus my efforts on assisting my clients to realize their dreams in real estate. I use a collaborative approach, allowing me to work with my clients in a partnership. You know, I don't sell real estate. I help my clients make good decisions in real estate, and as a result, they buy or sell real estate."

Let's Work Together

"We have many things in common and should try to help each other provide great client care. How about you? Why don't we continue to talk, share ideas and information, and see how we can work together? I enjoyed our meeting and look forward to talking again. Any ideas on how we can work together? Oh, by the way, I know a real estate Associate that might benefit from your services. She is a very successful Agent. Can I give you her name? I mentioned your name to her yesterday but cannot guarantee that she will give you a meeting. Your thoughts?

I do know that she isn't completely satisfied with her financial plan, as she indicated to me. You can tell her I provided her name."

The relationship has progressed, and developing and partnering to build a possible referral network among other professionals who provide superior client care is appropriate. Be careful who is partnered with; they must have a similar mindset, or trouble could be the next stop. You may have to teach them about consultative selling in a non-aggressive way.

This concept is used where an agent might contact prospective clients in several places. The "Reverse Sales Process" forces the Consultative Agent to think and act like a consultant. This consultative attitude opens the doors to relationships that are problem-solving in nature. When the Agent becomes a problem solver, people listen more. This enables the Agent to build relationships with others and find "Connectors."

CHAPTER 25|KEYSTONE CONCEPT: STRATEGIC MARKETING PARTNERS

A Practice can use Strategic Marketing Partners (SMP's) to expand its marketing reach to prospects in Target Markets. This allows the Agent to reach more Prospects professionally and personally at a lower cost. This is often a strategy to augment the Agent's limited resources and can impact the ability to reach target audiences by four or five times the ability the Agent otherwise has.

Strategic Marketing Partners are selected because of their synergism with the Agent. Often these businesses aim to reach similar Target Markets and Groups but do not have the skills or resources to reach them independently. These SMPs could be financial planners, Insurance Agents, Mortgage Brokers, trade vendors such as painters, interior design professionals, professional stagers, landscape companies, and outdoor environment companies, as well as many others. They may not understand the Strategic Marketing Partner Concept and must be shown how these programs can help them expand their businesses. It is also helpful to the aspiring Agent because they are established and successful businesses willing to collaborate with the Agent in joint development activities.

One of the benefits of this program to an SMP is the value of reaching target markets that they could not otherwise reach without a third-party implied endorsement from the Agent and Practice. The Agent must, therefore, carefully screen possible partners to ensure their trustworthiness, operating practices, and quality of service.

With the help of an SMP, an Agent and Practice can expand its marketing efforts and position itself to compete with more established Agents in the marketing areas where the Agent seeks to build a presence. Where a competitor is publicly active with their marketing and promotional efforts, this strategy can give the Agent instant credibility and marketing reach.

While developing partnerships takes time and effort, the financial rewards can be substantial to both the Agent and the Strategic Marketing Partners. An ancillary benefit is the likelihood of forming a referral network between the SMPs and the Agent. This referral network called a **"decentralized sales organization"** (DSO), can be seen by the Agent as an additional way to reach more Influencers, Prospects, and "Connectors" with a resource that is a third-party endorsement for the Agent and the Practice. When effectively implemented, this can provide Prospects to the Agent consistently while the relationships with SMPs evolve and all participants win.

Strategic Marketing Partners are often identified using **"the Reverse Sales Process"** concept. At "Meet and Greet" events, Chamber of Commerce Events, Business Fairs, and other venues, the Agent will have an opportunity to meet and assess the potential of various vendors to become an SMP and should never discount a call or approach from a vendor like these as they may be potential partners. All vendor calls to the Agent should be taken seriously, and their information added to the CRM as these calls represent an opportunity for outreach to possible connectors and the spheres of influence they might have.

For this reason, the Agent should encourage contact and relationship-building with the principals of these potential partners. These executives will see the Agent as a Gateway to Prospects just as the Agent sees a Vendor as a shared resource in the marketing and a possible source of referrals.

The following is a real example of a Strategic Marketing Partnership project that was successfully implemented. It details the program and the benefits derived by the Renaissance Group, formerly the O'Dea Moyers Group.

The Starwood Times Magazine

The Renaissance Group wanted to expand its marketing to include more homes outside the Starwood neighborhood in Frisco, TX. It had been mailing a basic newsletter to its primary target market of about 1,000 homes for three years. The Managing Partners wanted to challenge another Agent in new markets and expand the Magazine distribution to approximately 5,000 homes. The plan was to improve the magazine's quality, expand its size to twelve pages, and distribute it each quarter. The Managing Partners saw the magazine as a Market Coverage vehicle to reach and identify prospects that may be turned into Clients.

The magazine would be a quarterly publication, so 20,000 magazines would be distributed to homes annually. The magazine would also be sent to all Clients and Prospects currently in the Client Hierarchy and all VIP contacts that Renaissance wanted to stay in contact with regularly. The Group did not have the resources to accomplish the objective without sacrificing other programs deemed essential by the Managing Partners of the Practice.

The envisioned magazine was a professionally printed and bound magazine that was 8.5 X 11 inches in size and would be folded in half for mailing by first class postage to the Geographic Target Markets in neighborhoods where the Renaissance Group sought to compete aggressively for Listing and Buyer opportunities.

The magazine would additionally allow the Group and Managing Partners to publish articles about real estate in general and, as a result, make Perception Sales to the homeowners in the target market areas. It would be a branded magazine establishing the Brand Name, The Renaissance Group.

Four thousand homes had been added to the CRM by targeted geographic neighborhoods. The Managing Partners had the writing ability, design ability, and material and content to develop the magazine. The name "Strategic Marketing Partner" was used to eliminate the term "Advertiser" when communicating with the SMPs. Outreach programs had been developed to reach the key contacts of vendors and providers that were believed to be good SMPs candidates selected for consideration.

We believed these other companies would also be interested in directly reaching the selected geographic target markets through a third-party endorsement approach. By placing an ad in the magazine, the vendor would link their name to the powerful name, The Renaissance Group.

A prototype marketing piece was developed that created a Magazine name to expand the Magazine circulation. The Prototype Magazine was printed and sent to the original neighborhood of 1,000 homes, and a copy of the Magazine was used to promote the SMP Program with the targeted SMPs.

The selected Strategic Marketing Partners' key contacts were targeted and approached with a written proposal. The SMPs selected already had a high opinion of the Managing Partners because of their active involvement in the Homeowner Association in the neighborhood where the Managing Partners lived. They also saw the Managing Partners as highly influential people from their involvement in Community Service work with the Frisco Association for the Arts, where one of the Managing Partners served as Board President.

Each SMP was promised exclusivity in the Magazine by Vendor Type. Each SMP was promised space in the Magazine for as long as they continued to be an SMP and would not be bumped by another SMP in a similar business. The advertising space was limited to 8 placements of 2 different size advertisements. Each SMP would be given several hundred copies of the Magazine to distribute to their clients or have available for distribution in their offices. This extended the magazine's reach to non-targeted individuals that the SMP might know but was part of their sphere of influence. This expanded the number of Magazines printed each year to 25,000 copies.

Every Strategic Marketing Partner was treated as a valuable resource in the project and was allowed to occasionally write content for the magazine. They were selected because of their reputation and service mentality. It was believed by all that each SMP would realize great benefit from the project.

The relationship was bound by a simple written agreement and envisioned Practice success as well as the success of partners. As a result of the SMP program, the magazine was published by the Group, producing an income for the Practice that covered all out-of-pocket expenses for the printing and distribution of the magazine. The magazine's development time, design time, and content were the Practices expense for the project. The SMPs entirely covered the printing and distribution costs of the Magazine.

During the project's life, all SMPs received and gave referrals to the Managing Partners. Because of this, all SMPs were very comfortable with their participation and the cost incurred through their involvement in the project.

Strategic Marketing Partner Stimulation

Marketing Partner Stimulation is an ancillary economic engine in the real estate brokerage business. Stimulation is done actively to cause a Strategic Marketing Partner to do business with the Agent, refer business to the Agent, or partner with the Agent in the future. When the Agent stimulates action by the SMP, revenue potential and profits follow and enhance the Agent's reputation. This activity also reduces Practice expenses or increases awareness of the Agent and the SMP in the target market area.

One of the most effective ways to motivate an SMP to work on the Agent's behalf is to provide the SMP with a referral from the Agent that expands their business. This is done by collaborating with clients to identify their needs and link them to an SMP that will provide superior service and competitive pricing. The results can be magnified when an SMP is also a "Connector" with a large sphere of influence.

By including the SMP in proactive outbound marketing efforts such as direct mail programs, advertising programs, and Client Appreciation Events, the Practice expanded drip marketing programs, generated referrals, shared information, and offset marketing costs for both the Practice and the SMPs.

Each SMP was offered an opportunity to participate in a project by sponsoring a Group VIP Appreciation event. This became another program between the SMPs and Group. As a result, at one VIP Appreciation Event, over $15,000 of prizes were given to the 100-plus VIP clients who attended the event. Other non-SMP vendors also participated in this event and were able to experience the power of the program. The event focused on the Managing Partners by having the Managing Partners distribute the prizes and be seen with numerous "Raving Fans." The "Raving Fans" also communicated with each other during the event, sharing their mutual respect for the Group and affirming their belief in the Group and the Managing Partners.

Each SMP was invited to the event, given a high-profile public introduction and recommendation by the Managing Partners, and privately introduced to many of the clients who attended.

The program was highly successful and resulted in substantial revenues for the Group. It also demonstrates that a Practice working in this manner can extend its marketing reach when a lack of resources limits it. Strength in numbers and collaboration with others is the lesson to be learned in the program described above.

Part Three

Framing the Practice

Adding Shape, Form & Substance
to the Foundation!

CHAPTER 26 | INTRODUCTION:
THE FRAMEWORK OF THE PRACTICE

You read about Muhammed Gerani earlier. He learned about us through our outbound marketing program in his neighborhood. You will remember Ali is a physician with a large physician group at one of the major hospital systems in Dallas. He is a gregarious friendly man who likes everyone. He was a "CONNECTOR" who loved to talk to anyone about anything, anywhere, on any subject that was interesting to the other person. He is a people person. Ali and his wife Simran had one small child and were expecting another. We did not live in his neighborhood. Most of his family still lived in Iran.

Our first meeting with Muhammed did not include his wife, as she was also with the hospital system and was at work. We spent almost ninety minutes touring his home and discussing his plans, notably his love of fruit trees. We felt the meeting went great and later learned that everyone who met with Ali was made to feel great. He was that kind of man.

Muhammed wanted to sell his home and find another home in the same general area. He loved fruit trees, and his current property had a large backyard with room for ten or more fruit trees. This was his hobby. He wanted a home with large open areas for his trees and explained that his wife wanted a home she could choose. He had owned the current home before they were married.

We scheduled a meeting with Ali and asked that both he and Simran be present for the meeting. He agreed, and we set a date and proceeded as planned. When we met with Ali and Simran, we found that he knew many REALTORS®, and we were able to differentiate ourselves and win the opportunity to list and market his home. The sale of his home went smoothly, and he was more than satisfied with our performance and told us so. They moved in temporarily with Simran's parents while we sought a home to meet their needs.

Finding the right home for Simran and Ali took time, patience, and focus. **They disagreed on what they wanted in a home**. He wanted room for fruit trees. She wanted a perfect kitchen and a home for their long-term future. We worked with them for two years and finally found the right home that satisfied them. During this time, we became close friends, and the young daughter, about three years old, asked her mother, Simran, an interesting question.

A Special Connection

She said, **"Mommy, how did Mr. Moyers get so many houses?"**

She thought that all the homes I showed them were mine. Events like this create a lasting memory with clients and are invaluable in keeping an agent especially connected with clients. We laughed about this for years to come. We found a home for them with a large backyard that backed up to a beautiful large green-belt area. The kitchen and home were outdated. We provided them with a reference to a local builder, and after finalizing a contract, Simran and Ali were delighted that we had accomplished both objectives. They moved into their home, and the real story begins. After learning more about the framing of a real estate Practice, we will continue our story about this wonderful family. Ali and Simran explain much about client management and the workings of a modern real estate practice.

A Framework of the Real Estate Practice

The framing of the Practice adds shape, form, and substance to the foundation that the Agent has created. The foundation is the support structure upon which the Practice is built. The framework describes how the Practice operates. It specifies how it communicates with and relates to Clients, Prospects, Strategic Marketing Partners, and the public in general. It prescribes how it will position itself with the public and institutions in the marketplace. The public and institutions include Target Markets that the Practice believes will provide access to Prospects and Clients in the future.

An Agent's fundamental ideals, principles, and abilities are the foundation for their professional work and make up the firm framework that supports it.

The "Framing of the Practice" is how the agent operates their practice, such as their marketing strategies, communication styles, and branding. This provides the foundation, structure, form, and solidity it requires.

The foundation of a real estate Agent's business may include delivering excellent client service, having a solid understanding of the market, and having extraordinary negotiation abilities. Their profession could be framed around a concentration on digital marketing, a robust presence on social media, and a particular specialty or area of expertise, such as luxury homes or first-time home buyers.

The framework considers how agents present themselves to the marketplace and concentrate their efforts on a certain demographic or geographic area. The way an Agent will use a particular strategy for connecting with homeowners, prospective clients, and strategic marketing partners to develop a consistent and easily identifiable brand follows. What the Practice looks like to the Public must be considered.

For this reason, the way clients and the Public see the Practice is kept in mind during the framing and construction. The framework adds further understanding to connect the theories and philosophies to the practice.

Like the Framework of the Practice is attached to the foundation, the foundation serves as a constant reminder of how the framework should be constructed to perform as the Agent desires. The framework is constructed in such a way as to allow certain operating functions to be executed in keeping with the goals and objectives of the Practice. The framework and foundation become one as the Practice takes shape. When completed, separating the frame from the foundation may be difficult because they are built under a unified plan with specific goals. The plan is not meant to be perfect and allows for adjustments during construction. The plan is always imperfect, and there must be revisions and corrections as the Practice comes to life and changes in the marketplace occur.

The framework, when properly constructed, adds structural integrity to the home. Like a home's structural integrity is assured with materials such as nails, wood, steel, brick, and mortar, the Practice's structural integrity comes from the integration of various procedures, concepts, and methods that assure the structural integrity of the Practice.

All Structural Elements to follow are essential in their own way. However, they work together systematically to provide connectivity with the foundation and Keystone Concepts, therefore, adding Structural Integrity to the Practice. They are not discussed in exact order, but an attempt is made to present them logically to allow you to understand the total picture of the Practices construction.

CHAPTER 27|STRUCTURAL INTEGRITY ELEMENT: COMPETITIVE STRATEGIES

The prospect was Muhammed Gerani, and he was a tough negotiator. It took about thirty minutes after the first meeting for Muhammed to drop at least three neighbors' names. He had a dazzling personality. He was a doctor and lived in a gorgeous home. He was charming, super friendly, and within seconds, I knew he was a "**Connector.**"

My presentation goal was to make such an overwhelmingly professional presentation that the client would be compelled to choose me. Despite this, there was a problem. A competitor agent offered to list his home for a reduced professional service fee of four and one-half percent of the sales price. I took a chance and, without tipping my hand, asked the following question,

"I am not surprised that someone would offer this discount. Do you mind telling me the name of the other agent that has offered to reduce their fee?"

Muhammed was surprised at my direct question and gave me the agent's name while being off balance. Time is always on your side when you ask a question like this, as the prospect doesn't expect you to be so bold. It was an agent that I knew a lot about as we had competed with her often and frequently won. I also understood the agent's offering well and how they compared to our offering. The competitor was a "**giant**" in real estate.

My professional service fee was a complete _% of the final sales price. Muhammed, with a warm, friendly smile, told me he wanted to choose me, but he just couldn't reconcile the difference in the fee being charged. I felt pressured to reduce my fee to overcome his objection to the fee structure to win the account. What made it even more imperative was that the prospect was a well-known person in the neighborhood where the home was located, and his home was one of the most well-maintained homes in the area.

I considered a strategic decision to reduce my fee and buy the business for the opportunity it might provide. However, the idea that he might disclose the reduced professional service fee to the other people that he referred to us in the future was a concern. My brand was to be a full-service broker, not a discounter, as I believed my services were the best in the marketplace.

I decided to go for it and let the cards fall where they may. An agent who believes in their capabilities must be willing to walk on the edge of the abyss while looking down into the darkness below.

My strategy began with a fundamental rule I have always believed in during my career. When in doubt, restate the benefits. First, I had to quantify the value we were negotiating.

When in Doubt—Restate the Benefits

I told Muhammed we expected the sales price to be about $800,000. He agreed that the number was reasonable, in his opinion. I computed that one and one-half percent of the sales value would be $12,000 in fees. Explaining that the most he would gain would be $12,000 if he chose the other agent and established a number that would be a starting point in the negotiation.

I reminded him that we provided a mini-home book available online via our website and the website where REALTORS® search for properties to show, MLS. I asked him if the competitor would do something similar. He replied that he wasn't sure, but I knew the competitor didn't. I suspected that Muhammed knew also, but I proceeded as planned.

When I asked him if the other agent had reviewed their marketing plan with him in detail and discussed the sales strategy that would be used to differentiate his property from others of a similar type, he was evasive. I began to suspect that he knew that she didn't go this deeply into the details as I knew that she allotted thirty to forty minutes for her listing meetings as she was busy. She was the number one agent in our Brokerage firm. I assured him I would be available when he wanted to talk or collaborate.

I was sure she was too busy to give Muhammed the time he wanted. She had participated in a round-table presentation at the office, where she had shared many of her secrets with the office. I attended and took copious notes. She boasted that she had allotted thirty to forty minutes, and that was all she could allow for a listing presentation as she was always very busy.

I then reminded Muhammed that I had an agent list of the twenty-five agents that did the most business in his area. After we listed a property and it was ready to go into MLS, it was my practice to TeleConnect the twenty-five agents and speak to them personally. I had all their cell phone numbers. If unavailable, I would leave a detailed message about his home. I further explained that most top agents pay attention to other top agent calls and that we didn't want to wait for them to find his property in MLS or on the Internet. This was described as an example of our personalized marketing program to get his home sold. Muhammed looked puzzled as I spoke, and I began to believe that the tide was turning in my favor. We were now ninety minutes into our meeting.

We will talk further about this competitive case later. For now, let's talk about giants…

In his book *David and Goliath*, Malcolm Gladwell takes on competing against impossible odds and winning the battle. He begins with the story of David and Goliath, and this is where this chapter on Competitive Strategies begins.

> *"David and Goliath is a book about what happens when ordinary people confront giants. By "giants," I mean powerful opponents of all kinds—from armies and mighty warriors to disability, misfortune, and oppression." (2013, p. 5)*

Most people have heard the story of David and Goliath. It is a part of many cultures and history and has often been used by many to make impassioned pleas for confidence for the world's underdogs. If David can win against Goliath, you can too. There is a great deal to be learned from the story about how the new and aspiring Agent must compete against the Goliaths in Real Estate. The aspiring real estate Agent begins their practice with at least three strikes against them.

First, many competitor Agents in the real estate business have already established numerous client relationships, have established connections to the communities they serve, and have proven success in supporting their claims and representations to a Prospect. They are both known and known about. They are the competition that no new Agent relishes competing against.

Second, they have the experience of handling difficulties, failures, and successes, some of the greatest lessons an Agent can learn. They have had the time and enough success to earn the money to invest in their advertising and marketing programs and expand their name recognition. They have more resources and capabilities than a new or aspiring Agent. They have learned what works for them and depend upon these learned behaviors to survive and prosper.

Third, they have peers and mentors around them who frequently reinforce their confidence, assuring them that they are in control of their real estate world. This gives them confidence and self-esteem to deal with tough times, unfavorable conditions, and changing real estate markets. Both colleagues and managers support them by telling them they are great.

In the story of David and Goliath, David had to deal with just this kind of situation. David had to fight a competitor in the arena who was bigger, stronger, more armored and had the confidence of a giant. Gladwell writes:

> *"Who could win against such a terrifying opponent?" (2013, p.5)*

Most people know that David wins the battle and slew the giant, sending the Philistines fleeing for their lives. This chapter is about the new and aspiring Agent's strategies and preparation to do battle in the competitive world of real estate. Gladwell writes:

> *"Giants are not what we think they are. The same qualities that appear to give them strength are often the sources of great weakness." (2013, p. 6)*

How does a newly licensed or aspiring Agent compete and win against the established competitors in the industry? To understand how to win, an Agent must recognize that a very small professional services company must compete with both smaller and larger competitors. Keith R. McFarland's book, *The Breakthrough Company*, may be helpful for advice in this area. In this excellent book, McFarland writes about competing against others. He writes:

> *"When we asked the executives from smaller companies with annual revenues between $1 million and $50 million what made them successful, we invariably heard the same thing: (1) we are better at giving the customers what they want; (2) we are able to respond more quickly: (3) we operate with a lower overhead so we can compete on costs." (2008, pp. 122-123)*

Many successful Agents fall into the trap of focusing on real estate volume in sales dollars and, as a result, are willing to discount their fees, believing that more revenue is better. This is often a result of an Agent seeing another Agent be recognized as a "Million Dollar Producer." New and aspiring Agents must keep these awards and recognitions in perspective and compute the actual net income they would net from a 3% professional service fee on a sale after deducting splits and expenses from that number.

Creating a Competitive Advantage

Early in developing our Practice, I struggled with finding a way to compete with larger, more successful REALTORS®. I realized we would need to catch up on volume and experience. We needed something to help us compete with Goliath and prove our value to a prospect. At an awards ceremony, I noticed a service award called the VIP Customer Service Award that was given out, and no one paid any attention to it, as it was not about volume or being "big."

I decided that we should win that award and set out to do so by ensuring everyone we served wrote a glowing letter about our services and sent it to our Office Manager, who was responsible for selecting the VIP Customer Service Award winner. During the following year, we received numerous letters of commendation, and they were read at office meetings while we were recognized each time. This created a belief with the Office Manager that we were amazing. We won the award for that year, and this was the beginning of my story about competing against others. When you don't have "skins on the wall," then you must find a way to have a skin for the wall.

Once we received the award, I made this award seem the most important award ever to be bestowed on an agent. Of course, it wasn't. Few in the public knew that the award was considered a minor award. All our letters, marketing, emails, and other messaging systems proclaimed us as the VIP Customer Service Award winners. Our website included a banner proclaiming our success in service to the world. We made it seem important, and as a result, it became important to those we communicated with. To make it important during listing presentations, I would say, **"Well, other people may do more business than us, but none take care of our clients as we do. We won the VIP Customer Service Award, which was a great honor. We were the only agent in our office of one hundred plus agents to receive this award"** We made it so important that it was perceived as very important and helped us compete against the Goliaths. Perception becomes a reality when you make it real. This points out that what is important to a prospect is often what you make important to them.

One day our Office Manager told me, **"Sonny, I can't believe what you have done with this VIP Award you received. You present it everywhere, all the time. Your marketing is amazing."**

Discounting Fees is a Failing Strategy

Successful Agents often have larger support teams that don't always operate efficiently. Agents sometimes realize that it is very difficult to cut their operating costs and need volume to offset their operation costs. Large Agents want to win in the derby of volume counting and are willing to discount their fee structure to achieve this volume. I have never measured our success in volume, choosing to measure profitability and client satisfaction instead.

There is an additional challenge for the new and aspiring Agent because the larger Agent can discount where the new and aspiring Agent doesn't want to discount and seeks to maintain their profitability. Sometimes Prospects see the lower professional service fee structure of the more prominent Agent, and they expect it to be universal. **"If this successful Agent will discount their professional service fee, why wouldn't you, they might ask."**

First, new and aspiring Agents must be able to maintain their professional service fees and not discount their fees when requested or expected to do so. The logical concern is, how does that happen without losing the business opportunity? Establishing value has been discussed significantly, and particularly the differentiation strategy presented is one way to justify the requested "FEE" for the Agent.

Second, the Agent must be disciplined enough not to "BUY BUSINESS" by reducing fees and reducing their profit just to realize revenues. This is challenging as many Agents are not disciplined in standing their ground and supporting their fee structure in fear of losing an opportunity. Agents often crumble under pressure and give in to the request for a lower fee and never know whether they would have lost the business or not had they not given in to the request for a lower fee structure.

Third, Agents frequently listen to the loud voices often in their heads, saying, **"Others offer discounts and give all kinds of concessions. Why don't I?"**

Fourth, Agents fail to recognize that the costs of acquiring a new client are higher and take longer than keeping an existing client and maximizing the revenue opportunities from the existing client and their spheres of influence. Proving a superior level of service is a way of supporting a fee structure. Demonstrating superior knowledge or marketing skill is a way of justifying the higher fee structure.

A Tough Nut to Crack

Muhammed still didn't crack. After explaining how we provided greater value in detail, he wanted to win more than I did. So, I let Muhammed win. I gave in and conceded.

I said, **"Muhammed, I know your goal is to sell your home within sixty days. You said you have a mortgage, and your taxes and operating expenses at the home are about $4,500.00 per month. So, if it takes you sixty days longer to get your home sold by not having our marketing program, it could cost you $9,000 in expenses. In addition, you and your family will have to live with viewings and tours, open houses, and other activities for another sixty days. I am confident that our marketing program provides an opportunity to sell your home more quickly than our competitors.**

I really want you to be my client. I know you will be a great person to know in the future, and I want your business. Here is what I will do. I will pay 50% of the Title Policy you provide the buyer. It is typical in our market for the seller to pay this fee. That will be approximately $2,500. But you must agree not to disclose this concession to others and that I will be your agent on the future home that you purchase. What do you think?"

This provided Muhammed a win and allowed me to capture a great client, a future "Raving Fan," and a real live "**Connector**." Muhammed asked me to call him Ali going forward, and we proceeded to sell his home and earn his business for years to come. This demonstrated a concept that I have taught for years. Always negotiate, but never give anything away. If you give something away, it has no value to the person you are negotiating with. The strong ego and high self-esteem individual must feel they won something of value for the victory to be satisfying.

Agents must be willing to prove their value and worth early in an opportunity by making such a powerful and overwhelming presentation filled with such benefit and value that the client is hesitant to ask for a discount because they inwardly see the professionalism and core competencies of the Smart Agent. The Agent must make the client think, **"This Agent is so good, so professional, and so competent, I am reluctant to ask for a discount as they are worth the costs. I will be lucky if I negotiate a lower fee, but this Agent is worth paying the price, he asks himself. Perhaps I should accept the higher fee."**

Sometimes this doesn't work, but when it doesn't work as planned, negotiate based on value and benefit, and if all else fails, let the client win by providing something less than they asked for, allowing them to save face. Ali wanted to win more than he wanted to save money.

Your Best Weapon to Compete

Agents with more business experience have advantages over a new or inexperienced Agent. This is where differentiation is the new Agents' best weapon. To level the playing field and improve their probability of success, new or less experienced Agents must find a way to create an advantage for themselves over their more successful competitors. Sometimes these advantages are real and demonstrable; other times, the advantages may only be in the client's perception of value and benefit. They both work to the Agent's benefit and eventual success.

Aspiring Agents must adopt and master competitive strategies and tactics to compete and win in the real estate Arena. The following material provides strategies for aspiring Agents to compete and win against larger and more successful Giants like Goliath.

You are not always what you are! To the Client, **you are what you convince the Client you are!**

Competitive Strategy 1: Emphasize Unique & Different

While the successful and established Agent has many advantages over the new or less successful Agent, the aspiring Agent can capitalize on their competitor's size and success to create a marketing advantage. Every issue that the large Agent or Group competitor uses to an advantage can be considered a disadvantage. A Group in the real estate business is generally an Agent with Buyer representatives and assistants that help them in the business. Differentiating services is not accomplished by disparaging the more significant agent and disparaging an agent is against the real estate code of ethics.

Bigger is Not Better; Better is Better

This is accomplished by positively pointing out the differences between the way the aspiring Agent conducts their business and serves their client and the way the competitor provides services. Not every Prospect believes that "bigness" equals higher service quality or success. The larger the competitor Agent has become, the more likely they will see their past success as the most crucial factor in competing rather than how the Prospect wants to be dealt with in the future. Often, their presentations focus heavily on the "success and size of their organization."

An Agent who fails to focus on what is important to the Prospect can easily fall into the trap of being self-centered rather than client-centered. Demonstrating the ability and willingness to provide what is vital to a Prospect is a far more powerful strategy than reciting past success or showing awards and recognitions to prove agent value. Sometimes self-aggrandizement comes off negatively to a Prospect.

Differentiating oneself completely and thoroughly from the larger competitors and creating a unique paradigm (business model) allows the aspiring Agent to emphasize how their business is conducted rather than how other people work.

The description of the Agent's commitment and the personal attention that is provided tells a story about how the Agent will deal with the Client. The more successful the competitor, the more likely they will rely upon and cite their success and experience while failing to relate to the Prospects' needs and wants.

For example, you might say to a prospect or client:

"While we are not as busy as some of the other Agents in the real estate world, this is how our Practice was designed, and we believe this is an advantage to you! You see, we focus on fewer clients and can focus more completely on a smaller number of important clients like you. We provide a level of service, communication, and professionalism that others cannot equal because we have the time to collaborate directly with you in a partnered way. We consider you the most

knowledgeable resource and the leader of our Teams effort. It is unimaginable for us to forget about what makes you happy and provides the greatest value to you when you are so important to our success. Our personalized attention to your needs sets us apart from other Agents. We do not claim to be better; we are different and unique in client care. While we could be larger, our goal is to be GREAT."

You might go on to say,

"Tom, we work extremely hard to personalize our service to each client. Every client is different and has their own special needs and wants. We listen to what you tell us about your home or your needs. We do our best to work closely and directly with you. If we must spend time working with many clients, your needs cannot be met as completely as we desire. "Most importantly, when you choose me to assist you as your Agent, you get me. I mean that I am not so busy that I must have assistants or less knowledgeable team members to contact you on important issues. You get me day, night, and during weekends. I don't have one of those messages on my cell phone that say, "If you are calling after 2 pm, I'll call you back tomorrow or the next business day."

Competitive Strategy 2: Customize to Meet Prospect's Needs & Wants

One of the challenges facing a larger Agent or Group of competitors is their self-perceived value of standardization. Many larger successful Agents try to convince a Prospect that their way of doing a particular thing in the real estate business is the only way it should be done. More experienced Agents like to standardize things around process and procedure because it is simpler, less expensive to provide service, and less challenging to train Team Members. Large Agent organizations tend to focus more on standardization and less on personalization.

Highly successful Agents focus a great deal on branding, and their Branding usually emphasizes sales volume, which is their size. This may appear to be positive for the more prominent Agent. However, it can be damaging. Clients are different, each with a unique personality and varying levels of ego. The likes and dislikes of individual clients are some of the most important challenges of delivering superior service. When organizations standardize, they often make services less personalized and customized. The failure to personalize and customize is where the aspiring Agent can differentiate their Practice powerfully and positively.

The smaller the entity, the more easily Branding can be achieved. Planning your Brand before progressing further down the development road can allow an Agent to brand their Practice with certain positive traits. If an Agent is smaller, they should standardize on personalization and customization. As the Practice grows, gains success, and becomes more extensive, they won't forget how standardizing excellent service helped them achieve the success that they now enjoy.

Once a larger Agent competitor is branded as big, autocratic, bureaucratic, insensitive, or non-client centered, it will be difficult to change their way of working and communicating. They usually get this branding through their actions and behavior, and these habits are hard to break. Agents must think carefully about the Brand they want to create. The Practice branding should be consistent with the Agent's vision of the service they want to provide their clients. It is also directly related to the decision to become a full-service superior provider of real estate services versus a discount Agent or Broker who offers minimal services.

Branding should always consider client receptiveness and value rather than just operational expediency or costs. What will the clients think of size versus personalized and customized attention? Is "bigness" consistent with good service in the real estate business, which usually deals with more personalized decisions and events? A case is easily built that personalized and customized client care is better than larger, more standardized methods and practices.

When communicating with a Prospect, here is how the Agent might differentiate themselves from a larger Agent competitor.

"Kim, we have built our Practice by prioritizing great client care. Our most important objective is your objective. We dedicate ourselves to personalized and constant communications with our clients. We believe in professional and customized service for our clients who are different from one another. We recognize that achieving your goals is the best way to prove our value."

When the Prospect asks, **"How do you schedule showings?"**

"We collaborate with you to create a showing plan based on your needs and wants. How would you like us to schedule tours? While we have several ways to schedule, give me an idea of how you would like us to work together to get more showings and sell your home quickly at a price that is great for you!"

Avoiding Text and Email—Training the Client

"We like to talk to you often and meet with you frequently to review progress. We can do this in several ways, but what do you think works for you in this regard? We want you to get as much information, updates, or just discussion time as possible based on your schedule. We can meet in person via Zoom, FaceTime, email, or telephone as you desire. We would like frequent collaboration with you on what is working best and any ideas that you might have. We value your opinion."

Regarding Marketing Materials for the Home...

"Susan and Jack, when we build your marketing materials for your home, we focus on the three or four things that make your home special. No one knows your home better than you, so can you help us? Having lived here for years, what do you think a Prospective Buyer would want to know about what makes this home a wonderful place to live?"

Competitive Strategy 3: "The Buck Stops Here!"

One of the advantages of size is the availability of resources. More resources (especially people) give the competitor Agent advantages. More people require more management, processes, structure, and a larger and more complex organization. Larger Agent competitors cannot become large without these processes, structures, and organizations. That can be a problem for them and make them appear disorganized.

Money can buy size more quickly than it can buy competence. In real estate, finding people to serve as Assistants is easy. There should be an objective to treat competence development equally with size development. Because of the many Agents' limited knowledge of multiple disciplines, their ability to create organizational size is more manageable than creating a highly competent organization. This deficiency exposes them to disorganization and poor communication practices.

While larger organizations have the advantage of size, they often lose the advantage of direct involvement by the lead Agent. When a Practice develops multiple layers of management between the Agent and the Client, personalized and customized Client care can be negatively impacted. This can turn "Raving Fans" into very unhappy and vocal critics of the Agent.

While it is certainly true that companies can retain Team Members, it is seldom true that these Team Members have the same level of commitment as a Practice Owner Agent. One way to get more commitment is to create compensation plans that reward Team Members for taking ownership of their jobs, but this adds costs and makes the more significant Practice even more focused on Sales Volume and size rather than excellent client care.

For example, we might tell a prospect:

"Well, Bill and Becky, I really like being able to talk directly to you rather than hearing your concerns through an assistant. I like to stay in touch with my clients. I cannot imagine trying to live up to promises made through assistants and team members conveying your thoughts and ideas to me. Big Practices have numerous listings and buyers that require much attention. When there are too many clients for an Agent to care for, something is going to be dropped through the cracks, and the client will be the one who suffers. I do not want that to happen to you."

OR

"Big real estate Practices often have more resources, but I have more time to collaborate with you and can assure you that you are being taken care of in a highly professional manner. I like the idea that you can call me, or we can meet for lunch and talk about how things are going or how they can improve. The Buck Stops right here, with me."

"Sometimes I think I would like more people to help me, but then I would need to spend much more time on management, training, and team member development rather than being available to collaborate with you. We are building our practice on great client care, so a big Practice environment would not work for me!"

"When working on a contract to purchase or sell real estate, I like to have all the time necessary to understand the offer, communicate with other Agents, and collaborate with you completely and with 100% of my attention. This isn't easy to do when too many things are going on, so my assistants are tasked with allowing me to work directly with you. They take all the non-client issues off my calendar. I cannot imagine how an overloaded Agent could provide the level of service that I seek to provide and that you want to receive! When you choose me, you get my full attention and are my highest priority."

The most important Asset in a Practice is <u>the Agent</u>. Assistants are present to allow the Agent to work with clients rather than pushing clients toward Assistants.

Competitive Strategy 4: Simplify the Clients Life - Maximize Client Satisfaction

One of the challenges of managing a large Practice is complexity. The larger the organization, the more complex the organization usually becomes. For this reason, an extensive Practice often has more rules, procedures, and guidelines. Client-friendly ways of doing business fall by the wayside.

Use simplicity as an advantage when competing against more complicated and less Client-centered Practices. Look at everything the client is asked to do and make it easier for them. Make it simpler and more client-centered. Make the Team easier to reach, easier to do business with, and make the client's life more satisfying. The perfect feedback from a satisfied client is, "Wow, my Agent just made it easy for us and took the pain out of selling our home!" Give the client a reason to become a "Raving Fan."

Take every form, procedure, and request, asking yourself, do we really need this? Or What is the value of this? Clean up your client communications to make it easier to handle unexpected problems for them. How do they like to be communicated with? If they prefer texting, you must train them to understand that text cannot always deal with complex issues. Develop a five-line rule in texting. What is that?

"If it cannot be said succinctly and clearly with a personal touch in five lines, don't text, call."

What is the best time for the Practice to reach out to them? These and many other questions and answers should be in the CRM so that you can see what is required from each Client to personalize and customize services while complying with their wishes. **It is all about them, their timing, needs, and most importantly, their wants.**

Catalog how you make it easier for Clients and make what you do to make it easier and better a part of your marketing and sales presentation. Point out to clients that you focus on their ease of selling or buying, not yours.

The script, for example:

"Jack and Sally, we like to keep things simple to make it easier for you to deal with the challenges of selling your home. Our entire Practice is dedicated to making your experience with us a pleasure, not a task. Your time is valuable, and because of that, we have streamlined all our business activities to make it easier for you to work with us in a collaborative manner. I am providing you with a "Communications Preferences Worksheet" where you share with us how you want to be communicated with on several items. Please complete it so we can save you a lot of time and frustration during the time we have to market your home.

Everything that is done, including showing instructions, feedback requests, progress meetings, and answering questions when you have them, is customized to the best time and ways for you. Therefore, we believe that our simpler way of providing great Client care is more valuable to our clients than asking you to do things for our convenience.

We recently reviewed all our procedures and practices and reduced them to practical methods based on our client's needs. We sought to become even much more responsive and easier to work with. We never stop trying to improve and listen to you for suggestions on how to do so.

Our TEAM prefers to work harder to make your life easier while you have your home for sale.

Rules and procedures are necessary; of course, we have rules, but we look at everything from your perspective. If you want us to do something for you, we will do our best to make it happen."

Competitive Strategy 5: Sharpen the Pencil - Add Value for the Client

Large Practices are sometimes guilty of seeking to squeeze additional revenues from their clients. Days are spent identifying new ways to reduce expenses and pass costs on to the Client. While this is an option in almost any business, look for ways to use this to advantage when competing against the more prominent Agent. Adding a fee because no one will complain or cutting service because no one will notice is not a client-centered approach.

When more time is spent looking for reasonable, cost-effective ways of adding value to our service offering, the ability to demonstrate to the client that our focus is on their success and convenience can be demonstrated. This can reduce client conflict and frustration, overcome Prospect's reluctance to accept the requested fee to the Agent, and allows collaboration to occur. This approach builds our relationship with the client and lessens the chance that another Agent will attract one of our clients. This increases loyalty while, at the same time, encouraging our client to become a decentralized sales organization for the agent and increases the probability that they will refer others.

For example,

"I am glad you asked about our professional service fee. There are many different Agents, each charge based on their program and the services they provide. As you have seen from our marketing presentation, no one does marketing the way we do. Our marketing materials are superior, and our professional photographer is one of the best in the industry. The time we spend marketing your homes is extensive. Posting your home online and our comprehensive outreach program to other Agents is unique and powerful. Our Team of support members, including vendors, inspectors, and advisers, is all part of the service.

Most importantly, you get me when you list your home with me. I do not turn you over to an Assistant as soon as the paperwork is done. I dedicate myself to selling your home and working with you collaboratively to ensure we are on the same page all the way to closing and the celebration afterward."

The following example is done only after the fee discussion has begun. It is not presented before making the marketing presentation.

"Like everything else with our Practice, our fee structure is very simple. There are no additional charges for photography, transaction fees, or other items that you need to worry about. We are highly motivated because the higher the price we sell your home for, the more you realize from the sale, and as a result, the more satisfied you will be with our services. The best thing we can accomplish for ourselves is becoming your long-term contact for all your real estate services. We also demonstrate that you would benefit your friends and family by referring them to us."

Or

"You may be wondering why we provide so many marketing services and tools for your home and manage to do so without extra fees. We work with a lot of clients. Some have homes that are less expensive than yours, and some more expensive. We provide great marketing services to all our clients; however, we customize our services based on your unique needs. George, we do this because we don't see you as a short-term client but rather as a relationship we hope to maintain for years. There may be several moves in your future. Time will tell. You may have several friends who need our assistance, and your referral to us is greatly appreciated. You are important to us and me, and for that reason, I will do everything in my power to make you happy that you chose us."

Competitive Strategy 6: Personalize the Relationship

As an Agent becomes more successful and busier, the Practice becomes more complex, and the Agent is more removed from day-to-day contact with the Client. It becomes easier to forget how personal the selling or purchasing of real estate is for the Client. Having many clients often reduces this personalized feeling of working with someone on their most important and personal project. Being too busy and worrying about all the other issues of the real estate business makes an Agent's relationship with clients less personal. As Practices become larger in numbers of transactions and Team Members, the Agent often forgets that the transaction for the Client is often the largest personal transaction they will perhaps have in their lifetimes.

This absence of personalization can be used to the aspiring Agents' advantage. Everything done for the client must be personalized. From birthday cakes to children's gifts, anniversaries of the home purchase to wedding anniversaries, the Practice needs to develop a comprehensive program to build personal relationships with clients. This will protect them from competitors attracting them and build a network of family members that have a connection with the Agent.

For example:

"Bob, it is so great that you could take the time to have coffee with me. How is the family...

After the Client responds.

"That is great to hear. I can't believe it has been two years since you closed on your home. Time really does go by quickly. I just wanted to visit and stay in touch with you. If I am not mistaken, next week is your birthday."

After the Client responds.

"Well, wonderful, Happy birthday early. I brought you a small gift just to let you know we appreciate you for being you! What else is going on in your world? Is there anything I can do for you?"

The client responds no, **"I am all good. Or, yes..."**

"I know that we referred a painter to you last year. How did he do?"

Knowing vendors and other resources is important to your service to the Client homeowner. Assuring their satisfaction by providing them referrals with those vendors is a way of saying, I care about you!

Every time an Agent Assures Satisfaction, they reinforce to the client that they care. Most people stop doing business with someone because they think the person doesn't care. Don't let that happen!

Relationships with clients must survive closings.

A client relationship must survive closing. When a problem is successfully solved, it is the perfect time to identify another of a client's needs or wants. By assuring satisfaction, the agent can begin solving the following problem. Think of the Assuring Satisfaction Interview as the bridge step to the next closing after meeting a client's needs. When an agent attends the closing of a sale of a property, it is not the ending but rather the beginning. The past is merely a prologue.

Competitive Strategy 7: Practice Readiness

Practice Readiness is a simple and important process. Practice Readiness is a state of preparedness to meet any Prospect; what must be done to demonstrate professionalism to a prospective client? The Practice Readiness checklist assures that the Agent has the materials and support tools readily available at a moment's notice so that Prospects can be met with a professional sales presentation and the likelihood of success increased.

In the early stage of a real estate Practice, each new client is significant as each client is like having a blood transfusion to a very injured patient. A larger Practice usually sees each client as less important because each client's contribution to revenue is a smaller percentage of the total revenues. This fact must be used to your advantage. Each Prospect means everything to you, and there can be no chance that you will not be ready to perform.

The list of Support tools includes but is not limited to the following:

- The "Finding a Home Guidebook" for Home Buyer Prospects
- Professionally Marketing Your Home – Presentation Leave Behind
- How Collaboration Works for Us? – Leave Behind Presentation Package
- Real Estate Forms and Documents Package
- Builder Packages from Neighborhoods that are Served
- Testimonial Letters & Quotes Package from "Raving Fans"
- Gifts for Prospective Clients

Frequently an Agent gets an unexpected opportunity to meet with a Prospect and is not prepared for this meeting. As a result, a competitive loss can occur. Losing an opportunity in the early stages of a Practice can be catastrophic to the Agent. Losing because the Agent is unprepared is a negative event, as the first client may be the hardest to capture and retain.

The **"Finding a Home Guidebook"** is an impressive presentation package describing what a Buyer needs to know to be successful in a home search. This "leave with the client" marketing piece presents the Agent's service plan and differentiates the Agent from others. It also explains and justifies the Buyer Representation process and removes the mystery of what the Buyer Agent does by providing specific concrete actions to be taken by the Agent for the client's benefit.

The **"Professional Marketing Plan for Your Home"** This is a written marketing plan that is customized based on the Client's knowledge and is a "leave with the client" marketing piece that explains the role of the Listing Agent.

"How Collaboration Works for Us!" It is a document about Collaboration and how the Agent Team collaboratively works with the Client. This demonstrates to the Client how the Agent is different and more collaborative in the client communications plan and how the client can be a vital part of the plan.

The **"Real Estate Forms and Documents Package"** is a group of promulgated real estate forms and contracts used for various purposes. This allows a client to have a preview of what will be used to reach the finish line, whether buying or selling a property.

The **"Builder Package"** is a document that provides information about all new neighborhoods and where Builders are building new homes. This allows the Agent to explain why the Buyer needs an Agent when working with a builder. It is not provided to a client until an Agreement for Representation is signed. In older markets where new home construction may have ceased, it might be information about gentrification areas or areas in a transition where many homes are being rebuilt.

The **"Letters & Quotes Package"** is provided to Prospect and provides various testimonial letters and quotes received from "Raving Fans." It allows the Agent to let someone else tell the Prospect why the Agent is GREAT. This third-party endorsement approach is generally very effective in causing a Prospect to seek further information.

Personal Contact & Professional Materials Tell a Story

All these information packages are very impressive when they are professionally prepared with Agent specific artwork and testimonials. However, nothing is more potent than an Agent making a face-to-face presentation accompanied by very professionally prepared materials to be taken by the client when they leave.

Competitive Strategy 8: Team Selling

The Agent in a more prominent and more successful Practice often has a difficult time building teams because most people were not hired or trained in a Team Selling environment. They may not have the communication skills to thrive in a Team Selling environment under a Team concept Practice. Larger Teams are more challenging to form, manage, and control. With a smaller Team, there is more communication and interaction among Team members. There is an ability to have more collaboration and less conflict.

The large Agent Practice has a challenge in this regard. Many Agents are too busy to manage, may not have the experience or skill sets in management, and often have few if any, procedures and practices for managing a Team of people. Personnel management is not often the forte of a highly successful Agent. As teams get more extensive and the span of supervision (span of control) gets more expansive, the time and effort required to manage a team also increase. While large organizations have more people, they are not necessarily better managed or more productive.

Less focus on management often results in more conflict between Team Members and occasionally between the clients and Team Members. The smaller organization, with a narrower span of supervision and more frequent communication, can more easily construct and maintain a team atmosphere and harmony with the client.

To compete against the large Agent Practice, the focus should be on TEAM building and strengthening the communications between team members and Clients. A collaborative environment where the client is involved often reduces potential conflict between the client and other collaboration partners. This will further support the claim that the Agent has a better group of Team Members who share the Agent's commitment that Clients are the priority.

Explaining Matrix Management

"Karen and Jim, a great deal of time has been spent selecting, training, and developing our TEAM. A cohesive group that works well with you to support your goals and objectives is imperative.

Our efforts to build a great team mean there is less conflict within our organization, and as a result, we can provide you with better service and more personalized attention. In the Collaborative Model that we use, Team building includes you! You can be involved as much or as little as you choose, but we always remember that we are here to support your needs and wants.

We train our Team members to understand your goals and objectives. Your ideas, suggestions, concerns, and opinions are of utmost importance. Because we are a smaller group, we can interact more frequently and respond more readily to your needs and challenges. We listen to you!"

Competitive Strategy 9: Drill Down on Client Knowledge

Goliaths are sometimes more consumed with themselves than with their opponents. Agents often, pressed with the day-to-day problems of operations and management, forget that clients are a Practice's greatest assets. Large Practices tend to evolve into a focus on the problems of daily activity and, as a result, push the sales and client work to the lowest priority level. They sometimes lose their voices and experience paralysis from call reluctance and fear, making them unable to call and talk to clients.

Success results in numerous invitations for the Agent to attend luncheons, participate in round table discussions at the office, mentor other agents, meet with Mortgage Lenders for lunch, attend real estate functions sponsored by vendors, and host non-sales activities. The time available to talk to and be in front of clients and Prospects shrinks, and the Agent gradually and incrementally moves away from sales activities and focuses more on operational needs. This is a potential concern as the percentage of Agent time spent on revenue-producing activities diminishes with the Agent not realizing this is happening. When an Agent does not have a plan to accomplish sales activities, it may appear to them that time is available to do other things rather than being focused on building the practice through client and Prospect interaction.

To compete and win against the larger Group Agent, there must be a concentration on client contact and knowledge. Client knowledge is an asset and a key that opens the doors to future long-term client relationships and business. Many large Practices with super busy Agents fail to take the time to gather, understand, and retain this valuable intellectual property, called Client knowledge. It is possible to find ways of helping and supporting the client when the Agents know and understand the client and the client's objectives.

Client knowledge is the secret to meeting clients' needs and wants. Typically, people pay more for what they want than they do for what they need. The strategy for outperforming the more established Agent is to obtain and absorb more client knowledge than they have. The CRM is the storage container for all this knowledge. Whether dealing with a prospect or an existing client, please get to know the client and their needs and wants.

Planting a Seed for the Future

"Jerry, thank you for allowing me to ask all these questions about your plans, needs, and wants. First and foremost, I want to understand your goals and how I can help you to achieve them. Selling your home is a crucial goal, but I suspect it is part of a larger plan for your future.

The effort to do so at a price and in a time frame acceptable to you is a priority for my Team. While many Agents may meet some of your needs, we take the time to understand what will help you achieve your lifestyle goals and apply all our resources to the task. This commitment takes time, but we genuinely believe in providing superior service."

Competitive Strategy 10: Willingness to Innovate for Clients

Many successful Agents become satisfied, happy, and sometimes careless. The drive to achieve success is often diminished as their success needs are satisfied. This may lessen their willingness to go the additional mile and innovate for clients. The phrase, **"This is what we do,"** often becomes their Anthem.

Working with Prospects is best done when an Agent is open to and looking for innovative solutions to the client's needs and wants. This requires an Agent to think outside the box and create new ways of providing great service. This can be done by finding a way to locate a property that is difficult to find when a client is looking to buy a unique or specialty property that is seldom available. It can also be looking for a new strategy that is outside common practices used in the industry to sell a listed property. It sometimes requires listening to a client's ideas and being open to a strategy or tactic that the Agent has not tried before.

While negotiating a contract for a Buyer or a Seller, the Agent willing to listen and collaborate with client involvement may find a strategy to get the contract concluded and make the client a "Raving Fan." Listening to the client about their ideas for something different from what the Agent has done in the past or might result from collaboration with a client that provides the Agent with a new real estate strategy and approach.

Creativity is often stifled by success. The adage that **"if it isn't broken, why fix it?"** holds the agent back from appreciating or hearing a new idea, an innovative activity, or a thought process that helps them get an advantage in achieving their goals and objectives. Perhaps the adage should be, **"If it isn't broken, always look for ways to improve it!"** When we were told that we would become dinosaurs unless we embraced technology, we rethought our action plans and asked ourselves, if it isn't broken now, what can we do to make it better for our clients?

Experienced and successful Agents often stick with what has worked for them. They can fall back upon habits that might not work in a changing or transitioning market. The Consultative Agent is open to new ideas regardless of where they come from and doesn't care who arrived at the idea but whether it might work for the client.

Some "ALL KNOWING" *Goliath* Agents have been here before and believe they know what to do, and may not include the Client in their plan, therefore, becoming the opposite of the collaborating Agent. Some sacrifice their relationship with a client because they are unwilling to bend, test, be flexible and listen to the client. The Smart Agent is most successful by listening to the client and, as a result, earns the client's trust and loyalty. Clients who feel unappreciated are more likely to look for other representation. For example,

"We haven't tried that idea before, but it may be a good strategy. Thank you for suggesting this idea. We will incorporate it into our discussion with Agents when we talk to them about your home. I'll let you know their reaction or response."

Or

"The marketing materials we place in your home are highlighted by benefits that the Buyer will derive when they purchase and live in your home. You showed us a list of events you held at your home over the past few years. If you have any photos of these events, we would like to see them and possibly include them in our materials. We think this is a great way to demonstrate to a Prospect the benefit you derived from living in this home."

Or

"The fantastic backyard that you have created is wonderful, but when we describe it, we will move from the fact that it exists to the benefit that the new owner will derive. We want your ideas about the best way to present your home."

Benefit before feature example:

"This amazing backyard for your family and children will provide wonderful memories that will last a lifetime."

There are many other strategies to compete with and defeat the Goliath that you might face. Do not fear the competition as it will teach you to win. As we continue in the next part of the book, we will begin with another story about Ali Gerani and how I competed with and defeated Goliath to win Ali's support and loyalty.

Winning isn't just about a transaction. It is about connecting with the hearts and minds of clients. It is about creating a relationship that stands the test of time, survives closings, and defends against competitor efforts to erode the relationships with your clients and wrestle them away from you.

CHAPTER 28 | STRUCTURAL INTEGRITY ELEMENT: SALES & MARKETING PHILOSOPHY

In his book, *The Tipping Point*, Malcolm Gladwell introduces a law that he calls "The Law of the Few." Ali and Simran will demonstrate why this law is vital in becoming a successful REALTOR®.

You may remember a story about Ali Gerani. This is another chapter in that story. Ali volunteered to be responsible for the social activities of the Doctors in the Practice he was affiliated with. He organized social events and brought the various physicians together at particular times during the year. In this capacity, he knew everyone, and everyone knew him. He was a social butterfly. He was socially dynamic, successful at networking, charismatic, and personally gregarious. His list of friends and contacts was extensive. His sphere of influence was large, and every new physician that joined the practice he worked with soon knew that Mohammed was the person to go to for help or information about almost anything. He was the perfect "Raving Fan" and "Connector."

Managing the relationship with Ali and Simran and having him provide access to his sphere of influence gave us innumerable opportunities to serve and assist high-income individuals that we would not have met without Muhammed. Why would (Ali), become such a "Raving Fan"? I'll explain after providing you with some information as to why managing the relationship with Ali was so important to our success. This begins with a complex and detailed explanation of Client Account Management.

Client Account Management

A thorough understanding of Client Account Management is warranted as this is an important consideration for the new and aspiring agent. A <u>Client Management Program</u> is a proactive, systematic, and ongoing process for managing existing and prior clients to ensure retention and maximize revenue and profitability. The Program helps a Practice maintain its relationships with existing and prior clients and through them, their families, and personal spheres of influence.

A Client may consist of one or more people, a family, or an entire organization that has been assisted in the past. They become a client by signing some form of a binding representation agreement. While this representation agreement may have expired, the positive relationship created by serving the Client has not expired. If the Agent's performance is superior and satisfaction is assured with the past Client, the relationship lives into the future. When the relationship is treated as important and managed professionally and personally, the relationship continues indefinitely.

So, if Ali is a client, then others in his family are also considered clients. If Ali is deemed the Key Decision Maker (KDM), then he is the primary contact, and the other family members are additional contacts. He might feel uncomfortable if the Agent contacts his wife, children, or others without his approval. In the early stages of building a relationship, it might be best to select a KDM like Ali and allow him to expand communications with other members of his family and their sphere of influence as he feels warranted. The client opens the door and invites the Agent to connect with others in the client's sphere of influence. <u>Anyone Ali can influence is, therefore, a part of his sphere of influence and perhaps reachable by the agent</u>.

In the book *Consultative Selling* there is a discussion about handling multi-level positioning within a large key account. A client's family and sphere of influence is to the Real Estate Agent what a large key account is to a large business enterprise. The authors write:

> *"A consultative salesman must penetrate deeply and widely throughout his customer organization. He must become a master of the art of crossing organizational lines without making the organization's leaders cross." (1973, p. 32)*

The Agent hoping to access a client's sphere of influence must consider the Client's family and associates, similarly as the salesman must work within key accounts to gain access to people without alienating anyone. Understanding the family and the family's relationships outside the immediate home must be considered. This is also true of the sphere of influence that a client might have. Maximizing potential from other family members and a client's sphere is essential for the successful Consultative Agent. It is difficult but not impossible to access a client's sphere if an Agent is a product salesperson. Why? Because few people want to turn an aggressive product-oriented salesperson loose upon their valuable sphere of influence contacts. They could be concerned about aggressive behavior on the part of the product-oriented salesperson.

A KDM (Key Decision Maker) is a contact who is believed to have been given or has taken power to be the decision maker regarding a decision in real estate. Depending on the subject being considered, there can be multiple decision-makers in a family. When it comes to a home, there are likely multiple decision makers and potentially many influencers up, down, and across the Client's family.

The analysis and decision regarding who is the primary **KDM** for the Client may change over time and depend upon the decision being made. The decision to purchase a personal home might result in the **KDM** being one partner in the family, while purchasing an investment property might result in a different **KDM** in the family.

It is also important for the agent to be known and liked by members of the Client's sphere across and up and down the contact spectrum. Anything said about the agent before their sphere of influence contacts can affect the relationship. At the beginning of a relationship, a careful evaluation of the hierarchy in the family can provide insight into who will be the primary point of contact and **KDM**. When purchasing or selling a home, the agent must be careful not to assume one person has all the power. Ali and Simran will provide insight into this multi-decision-maker aspect of real estate. Earlier, I asked the question as to why Ali would open the doors to his sphere of influence to me. Let me explain.

Earning Trust Requires Putting the Client First

While searching for a home, Ali, Simran, and the children accompanied me to a property they had requested to see. The home was priced at over $1,200,000. This was above the price range that they had been targeting. While touring the home, it was obvious to me that Ali had blinked upon entering the home. He was excited. This was a situation where the homeowner, a very outgoing middle-aged man, was at home and very involved in our tour of the property. Early on, he injected himself into the tour and made numerous comments while speaking directly to Ali. They primarily spoke in Ali's first language, and I did not know what was being said between them. I was able to perceive that they were getting along well.

After an hour of touring and visiting, I asked Ali for a private moment, and we walked through the property's backyard. He explained that he loved the home and thought they should make an offer. I brought his attention to the artificial stucco that the sides of the home were constructed with. I explained that the open crevices around the windows and doors indicated a lack of maintenance. I further explained that this could be a "**mold**" issue and that a mold inspector would most likely need to be consulted before signing a contract as "**mold**" was potentially a serious and costly problem. Ali listened intently and agreed with my recommendation that the seller obtain a mold inspection at the seller's expense and provide us with the documents to confirm that there were no mold issues before contracting for the home. It is always the best policy to put the client first. Never be tempted to do what is best for you. Putting the client first is what the fiduciary relationship in real estate is all about.

Ali and the seller spoke briefly, and we thanked the seller and left the property. In the car and on our way to the next property, Ali provided me with the following information:

Privately, the Seller had proposed that Ali terminate me as his Agent and that they agree on a contract price. The Seller would agree to reduce the sales price since I would not be involved. He suggested that Ali did not need an agent as he was very familiar with the contracting process. Listening to the Seller, Ali felt uncomfortable and said he had not intended to follow the Seller's suggestions. It was after this that we spoke about the mold issues. Ali and Simran ruled the property out of consideration, and we continued the search for another home. Ali said he did not want to purchase a property that had been so poorly maintained. He also felt uncomfortable with the ethics of the Seller. The Seller tried to contact Ali numerous times, but Ali did not take his calls.

Several months later, when writing an offer to purchase a different home, Ali confided in me by saying.

"Sonny, when you told me not to buy the other house with the mold concerns, you were putting me first. I was ready to buy, and you told me things, proving that you put me first and had my best interest at heart. If you were "burning" a sure contract for over $1,000,000, you must be an honorable man."

Ali began to refer his family and members of his sphere of influence. This brings us to the need to explain the **"Account Plan"** and how it impacted our future dealings with Ali and Simran and their family, friends, and sphere.

The Account Plan

In a large business enterprise, the client account plan could consist of several hundred pages of organization charts, structural notations, and multiple **KDMs**. The Client Account Plan may be maintained in a CRM or a separate secure document for the real estate agent. The Client Account Plan is a private, secure document that answers the question of who, what, where, when, why, and how about a client, the client's family, and their personal and business spheres of influence. It begins as a simple document with minimal details of others in the family and grows as time passes, and the relationship matures.

Account Plans are written for each client secured in a real estate practice. Some will be quite simple, and others quite complex. If three Clients are looking for a real estate solution, and five have been successfully assisted in the past year. If four Clients have been successfully assisted in prior years, there would be 12 Account Plans in the real estate Practice. If the business has been operating for ten years, there could be several hundred clients and several hundred Account Plans. Some of these could be quite simple, and some quite complex. Ali Gerani had a rather complex account plan.

With Ali, it soon became apparent that many people were in his sphere of influence, and therefore a more complex account plan would be created and maintained. An account plan begins by establishing a contact record in the CRM of a Practice. In the case of Ali and Simran, the first such family contact was their parents, whom they lived with while looking for a new home. They referred their parents to purchase a new home shortly after meeting them. They also owned multiple rental properties and were planning to move out of one of those properties after we found their dream home.

These parents became clients and purchased a personal residence and multiple investment properties as our clients. The parents represented the largest referral opportunity from within Ali and Simran's family at that time. This would prompt us to establish a new contact type in our CRM, **"Gerani Referral Network."** This would allow us to track and monitor his referrals and properly thank him in the future.

Kavya and Riya, their children, who are not yet college-age or older, would become the next family-related account plans to be established as separate records within the CRM. There would be many friends and associates who would later be added to the CRM and become clients. Those friends and associates who referred prospects from their family or sphere of influence would also be added to the CRM and become prospects or clients. This is the _growing tree_ of a real estate practice. It poses a great opportunity and great management challenges.

Inactive, Active, and Dead Accounts

Some of these accounts become inactive over time, and some are inactive but could become active again. A client that refers a person in their sphere of influence might be inactive, but the person they referred to us could be active at any time. Likewise, the person they referred to us could become inactive, and the original client could become active again.

All these accounts can be a source of additional business based upon the ability of the Practice to motivate clients to refer family, friends, and associates in their sphere of influence. Motivating them can be called Client Stimulation. Client stimulation is not just about a client buying and selling real estate. It includes those referred to the agent from their family and their sphere of influence.

Client Management Programs are utilized with accounts that are currently active and clients that have been serviced in the past but are currently inactive. An inactive account might be an account that in the past has been active but not currently looking to make a real estate move. The agent, therefore, seeks to remain connected as much as possible so that when an inactive account becomes active again, they are still connected to the client and have an opportunity to serve. Over ten years, the client may only be active for a total of six months. The other months have to be worried about when clients are inactive. They are more likely to forget about the agent or meet other agents who want to secure them for the future.

When a Prospect Becomes a Client

When does a prospect become a client in the real estate Practice? This would be once all parties sign a representation agreement of some kind. A prospect must have signed a consulting or representation agreement to be called a client. This gives the agent the legal authority to hold themselves out as the client's agent.

Our policy and practice is that an ongoing Client Relationship survives and continues after the expiration of the legal agreement signed with the Client. The assumption is that once a Prospect becomes a client, they remain a client until the Practice becomes aware that something has happened to cause the agent to believe that the Client no longer considers the agent a needed resource and is unlikely to do business with them in the future.

This is a departure from the usual practice in real estate regarding representation. The Agent takes the risk in this assumption that a client could utilize services and then fail to contract with the Agent in a transaction where the agent is providing ongoing assistance to them. **In our Business MODEL**, if a client has ONCE signed an agreement for representation, a client relationship is believed to exist until something indicates otherwise. This is done with full recognition that when a representation agreement has expired, the Practice has no legal right to represent the client. As a result, the Client would legally revert to being a Prospect. In our situation, the Practice takes the risk that the client will recognize the Agent as its representative after the expiration of the legal documents and will sign a new representation agreement with the Agent upon request or when necessary.

This philosophy states that it is believed that once a client becomes a client, they become a client for the future until something happens to cause the Practice to release them from the client relationship. A few things could cause the Practice to believe that the relationship has terminated. This includes but is not limited to the following situation.

1. A former client could purchase a new home or sell an existing property without the agent providing services to them.
2. The client could move away and retire and not be expected to move back into the area.
3. The client could explain that they no longer look to the Practice for support and therefore break off the relationship.
4. The client could sell their business, and the relationship could be terminated.
5. They could become deceased.
6. The Practice could terminate the relationship between the Client and the Practice for ethical, legal, or other practical reasons.

The Agent should be aware that once a relationship with a client has terminated, the ability to keep in contact with and maintain a relationship with their sphere of influence is negatively impacted. If a client disconnects from the agent, then some of his family and sphere of influence are likely to leave also. This makes keeping clients happy and connected of the utmost importance.

When between transactions with a client, it is our policy to continue the fiduciary responsibility to the client even if one doesn't legally exist. The Practice believes that a fiduciary responsibility still exists, and the Practice operates as if it does. This is a way of maintaining a trusting relationship with the Client.

If something comes to our attention, we will disclose the information to the client as if we were under a representation agreement. It should be recognized that this is not a legal standing but rather a business principle. In this situation, **THE FORMER CLIENT IS NOT BOUND OR COMMITTED** to the Agent or the Practice, and there is no reason to expect otherwise.

The representation agreement with Ali and Simran expired after purchasing their home and has never been renewed or resigned. Yet, we continued to work with them in a fiduciary relationship and have provided advice and counsel on numerous issues since purchasing their home. This relationship is paramount and far exceeds the binding of a signed agreement. It is bound by trust and competence.

The Law of The Few...

Our experience over a twenty-year period has been that client accounts and their sphere of influence could represent as much as 80% of the total Practice INCOME. This is especially true when a Client Account is defined as the client, their extended family, and their sphere of influence.

This concentration of potential revenue is the primary reason that each client and their sphere represent a significant opportunity for the agent. Losing one of these accounts is a major loss to the agent and the Practice. The need for Client Account Management is emphasized in the book *Sales Force Management* by Churchill, Ford, and Walker. They write:

"In response to the growing importance of major accounts—those very large customers who represent a disproportionate share of a firm's total sales volume—many firms are also developing explicit policies regarding how such customers should be handled." (1981, p. 84)

Ali Gerani and his family were a significant account to us. He and his sphere of influence represented a sizable portion of our revenues and profits over the years. Ali and others provide ample proof that the Law of the Few cannot be ignored.

The situation for a REALTOR®, if anything, has become even more dependent upon a small number of clients whose sphere of influence produces a very high percentage of revenues. This is largely due to the number of real estate agents competing for the client's business.

The number of clients to be managed will vary based on how long the Practice operates and the number of clients captured over the years who have signed a binding agreement of some type. It also depends upon how long the Practice and the Agent can maintain a relationship of trust and confidence with the client and develop referral opportunities within their client spheres. Here is an example.

Referral & a New Client Sphere

Ali called me and explained he referred a good friend and fellow hospitalist, Sunita. He had given my name to Sunita and had given him a glowing recommendation about us. I contacted Sunita immediately, and he was very positive, so we set a follow-up meeting. He was added to the CRM, and his contact types were coded.

- Gerani Referral Network
- Buyer Prospect

Sunita was single and wanted a home in the $500,000 plus range. He preferred new construction. We hit it off immediately, and Sunita chose to purchase a new home in a popular neighborhood in the area we served. In the future, Sunita will refer prospects to us also. Sunita and Ali would occasionally refer the same person, and both were called and thanked after sending a thank you note and a small token of our appreciation. Both were always invited to our VIP Recognition Events. At one point, several clients originated with a referral from Ali or Sunita at our events.

The coding in our CRM allowed us to track the number of prospects both Ali and Sunita referred. This is how we could see the financial impact of a client like Ali, a "Raving Fan."

Working by Referral

Many seminars and training programs are available to the Agent that teach how to prospect for referrals. These programs are sometimes shortsighted in that they emphasize the client being a provider of referrals rather than someone who continues to buy or use real estate services in the future. Working by referral often falls short of fully explaining the profound income potential possible when the Practice adopts and executes a more comprehensive Client Management Program.

Few of these programs are designed to protect existing clientele from erosion and loss, thereby, an inability to secure possible future revenues from those clients. Many referral programs constitute reaching out to clients and asking them if they know someone in the market for a home or are contemplating a real estate transaction. This is a product-oriented method of requesting a home buyer. It usually involves a referral request but no real effort to build a continuing relationship with the client.

Most do not envision a plan to ensure future business in a planned way through an Account Plan process over decades. Many do not consider developing a program to capture the client's sphere of influence by creating an Account Plan that documents and manages the client to realize additional Practice revenues. Most do not envision the Assuring Satisfaction step as a natural step in developing future business with a client.

Tools for Implementation of Client Account Plans

The primary tools for managing the Client Management Program involve using a CRM and implementing "TeleConnect Marketing" concepts. Many inactive clients might be reluctant to engage in face-to-face meetings when they are not actively looking to make a real estate change. <u>They might not understand why this is even necessary.</u>

The "TeleConnect Marketing" Program is a cost-effective, personalized, and exceptional way of maintaining a relationship with a client without infringing on their time. When intermingled with other less personalized contact methods such as direct mail, email, or text messages, the communications mix (varied ways of contacting clients) allows for effectively keeping a contact engaged and committed to the Agent and Practice after they become inactive, assuring that the client remembers the Agent and the services they provided. The goal of the program is not to let them forget you. Finding a particular event or some emotional fact or detail can sometimes provide a memory to a client that will remain over time and provide a connection to you that will sustain the passing of years.

brain rules, by John Medina, provides some insight into the reason for constantly staying in touch with a client. He writes,

> *"Some memories hang around for only a few minutes, then vanish.*
> *Others persist for days or months, or even for a lifetime." (2014, p. 130)*

Expanding The Understanding of Opportunities with Clients

A client sphere includes all family members, business associates, and acquaintances. The Client Management Program anticipates that the client could meet someone and influence that person to utilize the Practice's services. Client Management Accounts can be seen as Influencers and, therefore, can be a conduit to future clients based upon whom the Client encounters daily. A client is not expected to carry a sign or placard for the agent advertising the agent. However, it is incumbent upon the agent to motivate the client to refer and recommend the agent's services through frequent contact and relationship building.

A client can be motivated to cause someone they meet to use the agent's services. A supervisor, subordinate, or fellow team member at a client's business is an excellent example of where a client can serve as an **Influencer** to cause others to use the agent's services in the future.

Client Management is much more than just working on referrals from clients. It is a systematic, ongoing process of managing and working with existing and prior clients to develop new opportunities. Through clients, the agent can reach and develop opportunities for other clients and prospects within the contact's spheres of influence and people the client meets in the future. Clients may need to be motivated to refer people to the Agent, and the marketing programs provide such incentives to inactive and active clients within the legal constraints of the real estate licensing act. It is also important to recognize that some "fans" may not recommend anyone. This does not mean they are unhappy, but it could indicate that they are not "Raving Fans" or "Connectors."

Assuring Satisfaction – The Required Step to Secure Referrals & Future Business

Client Management is a structured program for working with people who already know and believe in the Practice. If the relationship is properly maintained, their clients would likely utilize the agents' services again, refer other people they know, refer their family, friends, and associates, and recommend the Agent to others when given a prompt of some kind. It is working with clients who like the Agent and are likely to do business with the Agent in the future. People buy from people they know and like, and their experience with the agent is an important goal in expanding future business opportunities. This is one reason it is important to assure satisfaction, as a client is unlikely to refer an Agent if they are not completely satisfied with the agent's services in the past. With Ali Gerani, not only did I call to thank him for his referrals, but I also confirmed that the person he referred was happy with the services we provided. He appreciated this, and it gave me one more opportunity to Assure Satisfaction with him and set the stage for the next referral.

When an existing or previous client refers a Prospect to the agent, and that Prospect does business with the Agent, the revenue is categorized as **CLIENT STIMULATION REVENUE** in the accounting system of the Practice. Tracking revenue generation by referred party is valuable as it allows the Agent to identify the highest-value clients in the CLIENT HIERARCHY.

Decentralize Sales Organizations

The Business Model in the real estate Practice considers existing and past clients as Marketing Partners in that they can become an uncompensated <u>decentralized sales organization</u> for the Practice. If the Agent has successfully made them "Raving Fans," then they are likely to refer others in the future. It is understood that even though they are "Raving Fans:" they are not likely to carry a sign that says, **"Retain Sonny Moyers for your real estate needs."** For this reason, the Agent must be fresh in their minds so that when prompted by someone, they will think of the agent. When asked to write a testimonial letter, sometimes with assistance, a script has been created for them to use when referring friends, family, and associates. They might be encouraged to write, **"They are so professional and stay in touch with us frequently. They listen to us, will take great care of you, and always put you first."** This would be a powerful third-party endorsement for the Agent.

Creating Memorable Slogans, They Cue Referrals

Slogans can be created, such as "Clients First, That's What We Do!" and "We Appreciate You," which are slogans and psychologically powerful statements used frequently in client communications. In many client conversations and at the end of letters, emails, and texts, it is constantly written or said, "We Appreciate You!" Over time, clients frequently begin to say, **"We Appreciate You"** when talking to our team members or us. This demonstrates the unconscious or subconscious connection that a client can form with an agent through consistent and timely communication.

When an existing or prior client is motivated to refer others and to work to create business "opportunities for the agent actively, they have effectively become a "decentralized sales organization." To accomplish this, the Agent and Practice must cause them to believe in the services provided so much that they want to assist in the agent's sales efforts. They must want others to benefit as they feel they have benefited from the agent's services. This is the state of mind that is necessary to build long-term relationships. The client must believe that the agent is so valuable that they want to share their agent with others. They must get intrinsic rewards as the agent could never compensate them fairly for their endorsement.

Reward Systems

Properly managed, many clients will do business with the agent for years. Because these clients are not paid to refer family, friends, and associates, they must be motivated to speak boldly and positively when communicating with their friends and associates about the services the Agent provides to their sphere.

Ali Gerani, when sending referrals to us, was intrinsically rewarded because he believed he demonstrated his value to us. While we provided occasional gifts as rewards, they were nice and indicated to him that we saw his efforts to help us as a sincere desire to support us. Early on, we realized that client gifts weren't just thank-you items. They were cues to remembering our involvement in important events in their lives. We chose to give memorable, not necessarily expensive, gifts that would be kept over the years rather than gifts that would be forgotten quickly.

Motivating clients to send referrals can be done with or without a reward. Sometimes the reward is simple, **"We Appreciate you; thank you for giving us this referral. This is the biggest compliment I can ever receive. Thank You!"** A Client management program includes plans and resources to fund tactics to motivate the client to keep the agent in mind when they can mention the agent's name and give a referral. Many will refer their agent because they like the agent and want to help the agent succeed. A VIP Appreciation Event, quiet business lunch, or some other special event might be the trigger to cause the referral action to begin or continue.

The Revenue Pipeline

Consider the possibility that some clients will move every five to seven years. Once they have been captured and secured as a client and adequately managed with excellent follow-up, there is a high probability of earning future business for the entire client relationship. The longer the relationship is maintained and nurtured, the more revenue will be generated.

Based upon this likelihood of referrals, the contact plan is frequently adjusted to maximize contact with those clients who are believed to be more likely to bring future business and send referrals. Clients are ranked and placed in the Client Hierarchy accordingly. This is accomplished by assigning a P1 ranking to the highest potential accounts and a P4 ranking to the lowest potential accounts. This is not to say that a P4 account is worthless. They could be priceless in the future. P2 and P3 accounts are ranked somewhere in between these two baselines.

Remember, clients are constantly re-ranked based on their activities, referrals, goals, and family situations. The agent needs to communicate <u>frequently enough and in such a manner</u> as to recognize when a client's ranking needs to be changed and the communications mix utilized with them adjusted.

The ability to benefit from a client relationship over many years is directly related to the likelihood for the Practice to stay in the real estate business for a lengthy period. A client named Brown, who purchased a home with the Agent's assistance in 2020, is likely to sell that home somewhere before 2027. Unfortunately, predicting when they will want to make a change is impossible. They do not have to outgrow a home, want to downsize or decide to change. Sometimes their life situation could change, and they might want something more or different in a home.

Quantifying the Value of a Client

They are likely to sell their current home and purchase another home in the future, whether in the same area or in another area outside the agent's marketing area. Some clients will sell their homes in the future and never buy another home based on their age or financial considerations. Most clients will sell and purchase a home every few years over many years.

Example: client Brown is 30 years old and upsizes or downsizes their home every seven years until 65 years old. There are potentially ten more transactions to occur in some manner (sell, purchase, or refer outside the Agent's area of operation) over the next 35 years of their life.

These clients will most often purchase a more expensive home than the one they sell every five to seven years. Quality information obtained by staying in touch with and communicating with the client will help determine the likelihood that the Agent will be engaged in these transactions. There could be as many as ten transactions during that time frame with an escalating market value. The number of transactions could also be either higher or lower depending on various clients' buying and selling habits.

Once a client has purchased a home, the Agent may have an opportunity to work with them when they sell it and buy another home. Each time the agent performs superiorly, they could become "Raving Fans" once again. This could ensure an opportunity to earn additional future revenues. Creating "Raving Fans" and future business and referrals is essential for expending great effort through the communications marketing mix with Clients. This is why a client purchasing a home of lower value than the target value in the agent's business model is still a highly valued account. The total of all their business added to the value of referrals could be substantial over time.

This opportunity to work with a client on multiple transactions makes the value of a client significant in the overall marketing strategy of the Practice. Learning that a Prospect converted to a client could represent $250,000 or more of revenue over several years is certainly motivation for an agent to be highly invested in providing great client care.

These opportunities to serve can be much more profitable to the Agent because a prior client who chooses to use services again does <u>not necessarily have to be convinced to do so</u>, understands the Agent's method of interaction, and generally trusts the agent explicitly. The **Value of a Client** is an all-important concept to keep in mind. Every client has a value that can be estimated with the understanding that the assumptions are just that; they are assumptions.

Scarcity Of Resource & Prioritization

The scarcity of resource concept is the primary reason the agent must have the time to evaluate, develop, and promote future business with Client Accounts. When a real estate agent is focused on non-sales development activities, their available time for this analysis is siphoned away, and revenues and profits are lost. In the early days of operation, an Agent has more time and fewer clients to manage and develop. This available time is reduced as the Practice grows directly proportional to the agent's success. A resource plan to maximize the available time of the most important resource, the agent, is essential to long-term success.

Expenditures to stay in touch with and keep a client is an investment by the agent in the long-term revenue stream that might be generated from a client. These numbers do not necessarily include any referrals from that client or family members, friends, and associates. This may be an opportunity to create another client and repeat the process described above. Some people are natural "**Connectors**" and referral machines, and others are difficult to motivate. Efforts must be made to motivate all. It is often easy to identify which clients are "Raving Fans" and which clients are highly expressive **"Raving Fans"** based on how much business they have done with or referred to the Practice.

When a client refers a new prospect, this is called Client Stimulation in the revenue tracking system of the Practice. When a client refers someone, and the Practice fails to capture them as a prospect, the Practice has lost the potential of a significant revenue stream over time. Failing to convert a referred Prospect could also diminish the Agent's reputation with the referring party.

If a client purchases a $500,000 home this year and subsequently purchases and sells ten more homes over 35 years, one can see the revenue and profit potential that can result over time from converting one new Prospect to a Client. Each call, each contact, and each exposure of the agent to a prospect is important.

The Engine for Future Revenues

Client Management is the nucleus of developing a real estate Practice. It should not be assumed that future revenue just happens. That is why a Client Management Program is created; it maximizes the potential revenue from existing clients over a long period.

An existing client who has become a "Raving Fan" adds value to the revenue stream, which could be substantial compared to a client only being somewhat satisfied with the services provided. Assuring satisfaction is essential to obtaining referrals and future business from a client. If a client is dissatisfied, the agent must find a way to restore their goodwill. If they can't, they are likely to lose the client.

For example, a call could be made to the client, saying, **"Ken, it has been three or four months since you closed on your home. How are things going? Well, good, so you are happy with your decision? Great, that is so good to hear. By the way, I want to make sure you are happy with the way we assisted you with your real estate needs. Can you give me an idea of how you feel about us and our services?"**

When a client becomes a Raving Fan, the revenue potential is likely to be substantial for as long as the Practice and Agent maintain that relationship and ensure that "Raving Fan" relationship with a client.

Continuous Contact & Interaction

Each time a client is contacted, the opportunity exists to maintain or upgrade the client's perception of the Practice and to make them a "Raving Fan." If a client has been well taken care of, but the Agent senses that something might be wrong, then the Agent must find a way to serve them again and cause them to become a "Raving Fan." This does not necessarily require that a real estate transaction be completed to change their perception. This can be done by providing them with great support after closing. An example of this kind of support could be as simple as assisting them with a tax protest, where important information is provided that allows the client to see the Agent as being a valuable resource. It could also be by providing the client with valuable information about the cost and challenges of building a pool or some other issue relative to their real estate needs. Perception can be changed by making the client aware of accomplishments and recognition in the community. This effort to upgrade them from Fan to "Raving Fan" is an objective of the Client Management Program.

The ability to hold on to a client even after they have been successfully supported this year is not solely based upon the Agent's performance this year. It is based upon continued communication with that client and efforts to be able to be there present in their minds when it's time for them to move, invest, or refer business in the future.

Frequent contact of a meaningful nature is required to recognize opportunities to serve and provide a meaningful method of maintaining a relationship. While Gifts, Cards, and other communications help to stay in touch, they do not provide Client Perception Changing opportunities. These Gifts and other communications say you are nice and that you care, but they often don't change the client's perception of their agent. They probably knew you were nice but might not know that you can provide advice and counsel in other important areas.

Suppose three new clients are captured this year, and a relationship is developed by successfully helping them purchase or sell a home. In that case, a future revenue stream over numerous years is within grasp. Grasping must, however, happen. There must be an effort to build and maintain relationships. An effort must be made to continue to impress and find ways to serve. A significant part of marketing expenses each year should be devoted to developing and protecting Client Accounts. Failing to do this could result in the erosion of Client relationships.

Facing the Competition & Protecting Future Revenues

Clients often move into a neighborhood or area where other REALTORS® are vying for their business. Other real estate agents may attend their places of worship or have school children in the same class or sports activity and, therefore, may have an automatic connection with them that the agent does not possess. This creates a competitive threat to the professional relationship with the client.

Not all REALTORS® have the same opportunity for contact. Diligent work must be undertaken to keep the relationships active and to protect the Client Account. Client Accounts are open to competition. A host of tactical plans must be funded to allow for the protection of Client Accounts.

Keeping in touch with clients so that the revenue stream can be realized by protecting them over time is a primary goal of the Client Management Program. The revenue stream that they can realize over the next 35 to 50 years is substantial, and efforts must be made to capture that revenue stream. Some of these clients will go away regardless of what is done, and losing an account doesn't always mean the program failed. Natural attrition happens, but a good protection program can minimize the losses.

Not an Ending, a Beginning

A well-designed and executed Client Management Program will allow the Practice to keep a large percentage of the Client Management Revenue Potential and the growth of the new business by accessing their sphere of influence. Client management is the mainstay for the future success of the Practice!

You may be wondering how the story with Ali ends. It hasn't. Ali and Simran are still **"Raving Fans"** and providing referrals to us. They have slowed down as Ali is no longer in charge of the social network at his group. But he is still a **"Connector."** So far, the relationship with Ali and Simran and all of the referrals of family and sphere of influence contacts have resulted in over $500,000 of revenue for our Practice. The $2,500 I offered to allow him to win and secure his business was an excellent investment in the relationship with Ali. Perhaps, best of all, we have maintained the relationship and still talk frequently. The children are now college-age, and we hope to help them with future real estate opportunities or challenges.

P1 opportunities would be the highest revenue and timing opportunities, while P4 would be the lowest. Ranking each of these accounts is a subjective opinion based upon the Agents experience and the information available from the referring contact.

Chapter 29|Structural Integrity Element: Client Revenue Stimulation

Steve and Kimberly were referred to us by another client. They very badly wanted to relocate from New York to Texas and called to ask for information and advice. The entire relationship was built over TeleConnect for over one year. At the end of about one year, Steve and Kimberly traveled to our area for an overview visit, and we spent three days looking at neighborhoods and areas with them. This was a wonderful experience, and we all became fast friends and related well. It was during this period that we cemented our relationship with them. Yet, no representation agreement was signed as they were not yet ready to purchase. They needed to sell their home in New York first.

We stayed in touch with Steve and Kimberly for the next year regularly. At one point, they asked us for additional advice. They had a hard time selling their home, and Steve was holding out for a price that he felt was fair. On a conference call, I had a very sensitive conversation with Steve. I asked Steve if he and Kimberly were still emotionally attached to their home in New York. He said no, it was just a problem.

I helped Steve solve his problem by getting him to recognize that his problem in New York needed to be dealt with like a business problem. The home no longer provided any emotional value to them and, as such, was only an asset that needed to be disposed of reasonably and prudently. He agreed, and I reminded him that while waiting for the right price, his life and family were on hold as they sought to move to Dallas. The cost of waiting might be greater than the cost of reducing the price and solving the problem with the non-performing asset in New York. He listened and did not agree or disagree, but he heard what I was saying and did not take issue with my comments. He trusted me.

Approximately six months later, Kimberly informed me they were ready to move. We never revisited the issue of the home in New York. The decision had been made, and we looked toward the future. After two and one-half years, they were ready.

Client Revenue Stimulation

Client Revenue Stimulation **is the primary economic engine** of the real estate Practice. It is easier and faster to stimulate revenue or obtain referrals from existing clients than to identify new Prospects without referrals, convert them to Clients, and meet their needs. Stimulation is something that is done in an active way to cause a previous or existing client to do more business with the Practice. Future revenues and profits are increased when contact efforts stimulate activity or referrals by the previous or existing client. Since these clients know and like their Agent, there is a high probability of securing additional business. This is especially true when the Agent has assisted them with a highly successful result from previous transactions and satisfaction has been assured.

Client Revenue Stimulation doesn't always require specific action by the agent. Some clients purchase or sell again and refer others without being asked. This is the exception rather than the rule. Actively staying in contact or bringing something to the Client's attention can stimulate activity and referrals. This happens most often when the agent is positioned correctly within the client as the "go to" person that the client thinks of when they are stimulated to do anything regarding real estate.

Stimulating activity is meant to "encourage interest or activity." What is done to encourage interest or activity is described in the Marketing Plan as a Tactical Plan. Without some action on the Agent's part, the Agent is just hoping for "something good to happen." This is an entirely passive strategy on the agent's part and occasionally happens in the real estate business. It is more likely to stimulate activity and cause the client to think of contacting the agent because it provides a better opportunity to be selected for assistance by the client. Bringing ideas or opportunities to the client's mind can cause them to contact their agent for advice or service. Client Stimulation Revenue is revenue from existing or past clients and referrals to the Practice. These clients are ranked in the Client Hierarchy and receive attention based on their potential.

Client Revenue Stimulation is causing the Clients that have been secured to take some positive action that includes but is not limited to; buying or selling a home, referring someone, sharing information about someone who might use the Practice services in the future, or simply just saying good things about their Agent in public or in print.

When a client refers a friend or associate, getting the referred person's contact information is more complicated than it might seem. A client that tells their agent about a friend or associate will usually say, **"Sonny, I gave your name and number to an Associate of mine who is thinking about selling their home!"**

Here is a way to ask diplomatically and professionally for contact information. Smart Agent could say: **"Bob, thank you, I really appreciate you telling me this. A comment like this is music to my ears. I will send you a couple of business cards, and if you are talking to someone about real estate, perhaps you could do me a favor and give them my card or, if possible, send me their contact information; that would make my day. I promise to treat them great and tell them how much I appreciate you telling me about their interest."**

This makes a reactive situation into a proactive situation when the name of the contact is known. A call can be made, a letter can be sent, and action can be taken.

It is essential that the agent recognizes the client for their effort and further motivate them to recommend the Agent in the future by sending them a small token of appreciation. While a gift is not required, remember that these clients can become a decentralized sales organization (DSO) for the Agent, and the Agent needs to reward them and motivate them to repeat this referral process. A gift card to their favorite restaurant, movie tickets, etc., may be the perfect way of thanking them. A luncheon in the future might be an ideal way to continue building relationships and motivating them further. A call to say, **"Bob, you were so thoughtful to recommend me to Susan Jackson. We had a brief conversation, and I am waiting to hear back from her about an appointment. I appreciate you for doing this for me, and I would like to visit with you and catch up. I hope you will join me for lunch at the Capitol Grill at your convenience. When would be a good day for you?"**

This allows the Agent to accomplish several objectives. First, appreciation is shown for the effort expended by the client, and an opportunity to gather more data about the client is presented. A short conversation about the client's family, friends, associates, job, etc., could further build the relationship. If the client is reluctant to meet for lunch, it could be because they are afraid an effort will be made to sell them something. It must be clearly established that they are appreciated for what they have done and that this is the reason for the invitation. If a client mentions that they love their home and have no intention of ever selling the home, then in dealings with that client, the message should be focused on things to improve his life and finances with his current home; never indicate a desire to convince the client to move or make changes.

The CMA—A Great Conversation Starter

A Comprehensive Market Analysis (CMA), for example, could be sent to the client for their home with the rationale that knowing the home's value would allow them to review their insurance coverage and ensure that the home is not underinsured. All of this has the client's best interest in mind without consciously pursuing a direct sales opportunity. The CMA would include more information about the Agent and make a Perception Sale to demonstrate the Agent's concern for the client's well-being.

A luncheon meeting with a client should be focused on the client. The Agent must listen closely and avoid making a sales pitch or appearing to be looking for a sales opportunity. By not trying to sell anything, the Agent can open the doors to better dialogue and discussion. The Agent should understand and mentally document everything learned about the client during the meeting. Later, when time is available, the agent can add the information to the CRM and update the Account Plan for the client.

The Account Plan has been discussed previously but is a written document that details everything known about a client and how the Practice can assist them, connect with them, and build a relationship with them. The Account Plan is the **"Roadmap to Service"** with the client and their family, associates, and sphere of influence. It is the starting point for developing long-term plans while serving the client. Assuring Satisfaction is the **"Starting Over"** or bridge-step to continuing the sales cycle. In a Circular Sales Cycle, everything starts again after the sale, and the Assuring Satisfaction Step moves the Agent forward to the next opportunity to serve the Client. Moving forward to the next opportunity is difficult if Assuring Satisfaction has not been confirmed with a client.

A stimulation opportunity from a Client Account Plan might be analyzing and presenting the current value of their home, or sending them information about the market for rental properties in their area. Anything that awakens an unrealized need or wants causes the Client to consider a change in real estate that could be the impetus to create more business for the Agent. Moving their family members closer to them or buying a home large enough to accommodate relatives or guests is another example of stimulating activity. Illuminating the possibilities in an investment opportunity in real estate is another example of expanding opportunities with existing clients. This also cues them to refer you to their sphere when they learn that someone in their sphere has real estate needs and wants.

Client Stimulation can be accomplished in several ways; it all begins with creating a personalized marketing message targeted to the unique client or group of clients with similar characteristics and delivered to them creatively. This personalized, customized message considers the Client Accounts' economic status, location, age, number of children, other family members living with them, and many other factors. Each message is not entirely different from messages to other clients, yet there are subtle changes in design and messaging that consider the audience. Very seldom do broad-stroke messages without a personal connection stimulate client action.

This varied delivery system is called the Marketing Communications Mix. It could include messages delivered in person, by telephone, text, or email, or by personal letter, signs, brochures, billboards, websites, blogs, and other ways. The type of delivery system for the message is customized to reach the targeted contacts most effectively.

Consultative Selling

Taking a Consultative Selling stance with the client avoids taking a sales-first approach. Messages are client-centered, demonstrating a collaborative problem-solving approach rather than an "I want to sell you something position." Communicating a product-centered approach to selling real estate will often taint the message. The goal is to help a client solve a problem, meet a need, or reach a goal. The natural result of assisting the client in doing this is the resulting sale of a product such as a home. Selling a product is not the best way to build a long-term relationship with a client and cause that client to refer you to his family, friends, and associates. Selling a product often reduces the Agent to ubiquitous rather than a unique and special Consultative Agent.

Selling real estate is selling real property, including brick and mortar, stone, and steel products. The product is not always the most important reason the client purchases a home. They purchase a home to fulfill a lifestyle need, feel good about themselves, provide shelter for themselves or their family, and secure a safe environment. Occasionally, they do so to impress others. (See Buyer Seller Hierarchy) The product will likely be exchanged for a different home or solution when it no longer satisfies their needs and wants. Seldom do people purchase a home because of the product alone. While it must appeal to them, they purchase the product to meet their needs and wants, both known and unknown. This would include their self-esteem and how they feel about themselves. Helping them sort through these needs and wants to make the best decision is a consultative role rather than a product sales role.

Sacrificed Alternative Concept

This brings up the concept of sacrificed alternatives. The concept of sacrificed alternatives is that most people cannot have everything they need or want and must choose between needs and wants by prioritizing their choices. A person who chooses a career in residential real estate may not be able to have weekends off to enjoy their family. The sacrificed alternative concept forces one to decide and prioritize needs and wants. This is also true of clients. A client who wants to preview and tour homes on the weekend will likewise give up attending a family member's activity or watching their favorite team play.

This prioritization is a natural part of life for most people. Few can have all they need and want all the time without sacrificing something by prioritizing what is most important to them. When purchasing a home, a client has needs and wants and psychologically chooses what is most important by prioritizing the choices. Seldom is a home perfect for a client, even if they say or think it is when they decide to buy. Soon after signing the contract, they begin to have cognitive dissonance. Cognitive dissonance is the psychological conflict between simultaneous attitudes. This often occurs when a person's behaviors and beliefs do not align. If a client chooses to purchase a home and does so for specific reasons, soon after making the decision, they begin to compare and try to align the action of buying with their beliefs. This often creates conflict within the person, resulting in distress and emotion. The Consultative Agent deals with emotion calmly and patiently to help the client reconcile the prioritization of their needs and wants.

Client Stimulation is the concerted effort to stimulate and capture opportunities referred by existing and prior Clients from their spheres of influence or someone they have recently met. Revenue potential can be maximized in this manner. These programs must be executed over a long time and with patience and targeted messaging to be most effective.

The Client Care Service Funnel

Client Stimulation is an essential part of the marketing strategy of the Practice. Picture a funnel with Prospects being pushed into the funnel by clients who are "Raving Fans." Marketing messages should clarify to existing clients that the Agent wants and needs referrals, as the client may often think that the Agent is so successful that they do not want or even need referrals. Many clients believe their Agent makes lots of money and doesn't need their assistance. When an agent places "Million Dollar Producer" on their business cards or email signature line, the client may think this is incredible when it is not. When an Agent drives a beautiful car, provides superior client care, and takes a client to lunch, the client may often assume that the agent is very successful and does not want or need assistance.

Client Management Programs provide a mechanism for motivating clients to refer Prospects from their sphere of influence. This motivation is not financial. When the Agent creates reasons to connect and communicate in a way that provides the client value, they motivate the client to refer others because the client feels rewarded. Each time a referred Prospect tells the client they were treated wonderfully and are very happy, the "Raving Fan" position is further cemented.

The systematic process of staying in touch with and developing business opportunities with existing or prior clients keeps the client engaged and encourages them to remember to refer and share their satisfaction with others.

Maximize Client Satisfaction & Practice Revenues

Brooklyn and David Beale have two children, Bobby and Mike. Their mother and father also live close by. All these contacts are included in the same Account Plan for Brooklyn and David Beale. They have a sister and brother living in the area, and they would also be added to the CRM system. The goal of managing the account is to increase knowledge of all these contacts. For example, one of the children is Bobby.

The Agent would want to know Bobby's birthday, special interests, and anything else that could help in cementing a relationship for future opportunities with Bobby. Bobby will grow up and become an adult and could become a Prospect. The birthday cards sent to Bobby will please the parents but will also establish the Agents name in Bobby's mind either consciously or subconsciously. The contact made with Bobby through the parents will allow the Agent to build a relationship with Bobby in the future. This could take a long time if Bobby is only twelve years old, and the Agent will have to stay in contact with Bobby until he is out of college or buying age. His parents may even be the influencer or the instigator for Bobby to purchase a home with the assistance of their Agent.

The Agent, learning that Bobby will attend the University of Texas, could suggest to the Parents that purchasing a second home in Austin might be a good idea. Bobby could live there while attending the University, and the parents would have a place to stay when visiting. It is noted in the CRM that the parents are interested in investing in real estate, and this might serve as an opportunity to help them and solve the problem of Bobby's housing in Austin. Keeping notes and information in the CRM in an Account Plan might provide the impetus for the Agent and the Client to work together again.

As you can see, the management of an account could create as many as one to twenty-five contacts from within this family that require contact over some time to maximize the revenue opportunities from the account. These contacts are "warmer" rather than "cold" as a referral contact is associated with them.

Brooklyn, a Connector, and David know many people within their companies, respectively. The goal is to create a relationship with Brooklyn and David so that they would refer other friends and associates in the future. These referrals are of high value because the Agent is referred from a trusted source. The Agent could have the inside track on securing the business opportunity from the newly-referred contact. Brooklyn and David may refer Margaret Johnson, and when they do so, a new Prospect would be added to the CRM, and the origination of that new account would be noted as coming from David and Brooklyn.

That Prospect, when converted to a client, would be a Client Account that stands on its own and would add Margaret's husband, Margaret's children, parents, and anyone else who is thought to be an important prospect into the Account Plan for Margaret Johnson.

When a real estate agent has 10 or 12 accounts in the management system, and each average a referral of five other Prospects over several years, and each of those accounts refers an average of five or more contacts within their sphere, it is easy to see how an Agent can expand their Prospect contact list and grow targeted contacts in the Practices CRM. This is far better than expanding the CRM contacts with people with whom the Agent still needs to meet and has no direct connection.

Many other contacts were added to the CRM because of learning about a client's different buying needs and wants, and timing. As a result, a steady stream of potential business can be created, and this is how the real estate marketing system adds contacts and works to provide substantial revenue potential for the Agent.

Building an Account Plan is best done with a Client Relationship Management System (CRM). The CRM System allows an Agent to expand and link parties to each other yet have standalone records. Brooklyn and David would be set up on one account. And all the contacts that are related to them would be included in their Account Plan, but each would have separate records in the CRM, and the process would continue to add new contacts to the system.

Brooklyn and David may refer five people, and those five may each refer five additional people; therefore, the Practice has substantially multiplied the number of contacts to be considered. These referral contacts should be contacted regularly as part of the Agent outreach program while seeking to qualify them for an upgrade to a Prospect status in the Client Hierarchy.

It is reasonable to ask how an Agent will be able to manage and maintain relationships and contacts that are in the CRM. The CRM will allow the Agent to do so in an organized and structured fashion using the Treatment Grid and low-cost marketing techniques, mainly TeleConnect Marketing, as it is the most cost-effective and personalized method. The CRM is integrated with a marketing system that contains letters, emails, and suggested content and provides additional methods of cost-effectively reaching out to new contacts added to the CRM.

The management process of maximizing contacts and maintaining relationships with many contacts over time is an important reason to use a CRM. It is also important to remember that these contacts will be ranked within the CRM with various codes indicating potential future business. David and Brooklyn would be ranked P1 because they have done business with the Agent in the past and have referred other Prospects that will be doing business with the Agent if the Agent continues to build the relationship. Brooklyn and David, being known and liked by the referred prospects, make them more easily reached and converted to future clients. Their endorsement further supports the agents' efforts to convert these contacts into prospects. Parents and grandparents represent excellent development opportunities because they have a reason to move close to their children and grandchildren. They also frequently have large spheres that can add to the value of connecting with them.

A letter to a family member of Brooklyn and David might begin with the following sentence. **"My name is Sonny Moyers, and Brooklyn, and David mentioned you when I assisted them in finding their home in Plano, Texas. They mentioned that you might be interested in moving here or having a property as a second home in the area. I want to introduce myself and let you know that I would welcome an opportunity to provide information about the area and possible options if you desire."**

When enclosing a letter or a quote from Brooklyn and David, the Agent provides a third-party endorsement trusted by the family member being communicated with.

A person who is referred but not ready to buy at the time of initial contact but is a future prospect might be classified as a P3 or P4 opportunity in the CRM system. A typical classification system would include P1 through P4.

CHAPTER 30 | STRUCTURAL INTEGRITY ELEMENT: TARGET MARKET SIMULATION

Charles and Maria Nissen were homeowners in a neighborhood we were marketing to in Plano, Texas. Our marketing efforts were successful, and Charles contacted us about buying another home to occupy as their primary residence. They intended to keep their current home as a rental property. This began a long relationship with them and is an example of how marketing to a "target market neighborhood" pays big dividends to an agent.

The Nissens are very private people. They are quite social but do not mix business with their private relationships. They became **"Raving Fans"** rather quickly. They selected us from a list of many REALTORS® that we're marketing to them. We believe it was because we were different from other REALTORS® in our messaging. Our messaging emphasized our superior marketing skills, collaborative approach, and personal service orientation.

When we found them a home, they purchased it and rented their previous home rather quickly. They were very happy with our services. Several years later, they contacted us about selling the property they had been renting, and we could get it sold in short order. It wasn't until four years later that we once again had the opportunity to assist them with selling their home when they moved to California for a job opportunity. We primarily stayed in touch with them through TeleConnect while they were in California, and seven years later, they called us to ask for help relocating back to the Dallas area.

Finding a home for them was challenging as the Buyer's market was difficult, but we were able to do so, and they closed on their home here. They were ecstatic about being back in Dallas, and we were so pleased that they had been loyal to us. All the mailings, phone calls, and happy birthday wishes had certainly been a part of their choosing us again. All these transactions added up to over five million dollars in sales volume. Most of the target marketing is finding the few who can become clients like Charles and Maria Nissen. We are certain that they will contact us when they need to make their next move.

Selecting Target Markets and Target Market Stimulation

Target Market Stimulation is the **real estate brokerage business's <u>second most important economic engine</u>**. Stimulation is something that the Agent does in a proactive way to cause a Suspect or Prospect that they do not personally know who is targeted in a Target Market Program to contact the Agent for information or assistance. A Target Market Program is a tactical activity such as a direct mail piece or other marketing communication sent to a target market area. It rarely includes a non-solicited telephone call.

It isn't easy to stimulate activity in this group of Prospects, as most often, the Agent doesn't know who the contact is, and in most instances, the Prospect doesn't know the Agent. The Contacts are contacted because of the market stimulation activities of the Agent. These activities are known as Tactical Plans and are identified in the Practices Marketing Plan.

There is often no marketing intelligence indicating a direct need for assistance. There is a supposition by the Agent that some in the Group of people might need assistance now or in the future. It is believed that frequent contact by the Agent by various methods will build awareness of the Agent with the contact so that when a need arises, the Agent will be remembered and contacted. This is a long-term marketing strategy and tactic and, as a result, requires a disciplined and consistent effort on the Agent's part. While it can produce immediate results, the commitment to a long-term effort to reach the contacts in the Target Market is made.

In his book *Identity Branding*, Robert Krumley quotes Michael Boylan, author of *The Power to Get In*, and writes,

"Marketing is not selling. Marketing is not prospecting. Marketing is about getting the prospect attracted to you before the first contact is initiated. It is about getting prospects to knowingly want you to contact them." (2000, p. 14)

The Agent designs a Tactical Plan to motivate the Prospect to initiate activity if there is a real estate question or need. The agent's goal is to differentiate themselves in such a manner as to create a reason for a client to pick them rather than a competitor who is also contacting them in some manner.

Target Market Revenue Stimulation refers to a target audience from whom the Agent hopes to capture Prospects. Perhaps the Agent's involvement in the community has caused the potential Prospects to identify the Agent. They may have attended an Open House, been reached by other marketing outreach programs, been involved in an HOA, seen a sign that the Agent placed in the neighborhood, or received some other outreach message from the Agent. The Agent might have advertised or been active on social media or a website, which the Prospect may have been exposed to.

Likely, the Prospects in this group do not know or remember the Agent. For this reason, the methods and approaches used to encounter them are more expensive, time-consuming, and less likely to be fruitful than contact with Clients whom the Agent has already met and supported their real estate needs. Capturing Clients requires an effort to reach new people to replace those clients that are Inactive or, for whatever reason, decide not to use the Agent's services in the future. This is called Account Attrition.

A Target Market Stimulation Program is a proactive approach to targeting an audience that the Agent wants to reach because it is believed that there are Prospects in the Target Market who might need real estate assistance. It is believed that contacting the Target Audience through mixed methods will motivate them to reach out to the Agent and request information or assistance. The Target Market must be large enough to allow the Agent and Practice to identify and capture Prospects over time.

Target Market Stimulation Revenue is income to the real estate Practice. This is income generated from an activity with a new client that was discovered because of marketing activities in a Target Market where the client resides or works.

Target Market Revenue Stimulation is a revenue center in the Practice's financial accounting systems. Target Market Stimulation is outreach beyond existing or prior clients to a Geographic Target Market or a Group of Contacts identified as a Target Market.

Contacts in any of these Target Markets are generally those contacts where there is no prior personal relationship with the Agent or the Practice. These contacts are suspects in that the Agent suspects there is potential and hopes that the contacts will become prospects and clients. Tactics are initiated to result in opportunities to serve to come to the surface, allowing the Agent to communicate and capture contacts with strategies that will convert these prospects into clients. Because the Agent cannot know which contacts are likely to need support soon, all must be contacted regularly to give the Agent the best chance of harvesting opportunities from the Target Market.

Referrals of new Prospects developed from Client Accounts provide the highest probability of success and usually cost less money to convert. Prospects gleaned from Market Stimulation Activities by the Practice expand the Practice and add to the growth of the Practice. Prospects must be identified even when they are more costly to find. The absence of enough clients to grow the Practice will likely result in initiatives to be funded by the Practice to identify unknown contacts to stimulate new business opportunities.

Likely, other Agents also target the contacts in the Target Markets selected. One way to increase Practice revenues from Target Markets is to provide the contacts in the Target Market with an opportunity to see the agent differently from the way the Contacts see other agents in a target market.

Sending information to a Target Market about neighborhood market values and shifts, property tax information, and major events that affect the neighborhood, vacation homes, or farm and ranch property nearby can make a perception sale about the Agent. This is called a perception sale and illuminates the opportunities to the client by bringing attention to an idea or fact that they may not already know or realize. Differentiating themselves from these Target Markets allows the Agent to stand out from the numerous other Agents seeking their business. Positioning oneself as a Consultative Agent using a collaborative approach and a Neighborhood specialist stance is an excellent marketing strategy.

A Perception Sale is a sale that doesn't necessarily result in Agent income but changes the perception of the Prospect, allowing the Agent to be seen as a valuable resource that could help the Prospect in the future. When speaking to or assisting someone without compensation, the Agent may make a Perception Sale that will substantially impact the Practice's long-term revenue. While a Perception Sale can produce income and profit, the goal is to position the Agent with the contact better. Looking for opportunities to improve Perception while simultaneously providing great service is a winning formula!

Target Market Stimulation activities are those actions (tactical plans) that seek to create new opportunities for real estate transactions. Target Market stimulation methods include but are not limited to:

- Publication advertising
- Internet Marketing
- Direct mail activities
- Homeowner Association involvement (volunteerism)
- Participation in nonprofit activities
- Attendance at various Neighborhood events
- Local School Involvement, such as PTA
- Outlet advertising-School Magazines or Publications
- Institutional advertising by Branding, such as Supermarket Baskets

Target Market stimulation activities are distinctly different from Client Stimulation activities. The messaging is very different as the Agent has not established a reputation with the contacts to depend upon to open the doors to discussion. When Target Market Stimulation actions and activities are successful, revenues and profits are increased. To track them and determine how successful various marketing activities are, they are categorized as an income category called Target Market Stimulation Income in the Practices financial reporting system.

Successful Target Market stimulation activities create new prospects converted into new clients. The question is unanswered as to when this might happen. Tactics are funded and executed continuously for this reason. Some might call this "drip marketing." It is also predicted that at any given moment, only a few of the contacts in the Target Market could be actively interested in real estate activities.

The goal of frequent contact by the Agent and Team via various methods and messages is to reach contacts when they become active and thus capture them. They have familiarity with the Agent's name because of numerous exposures to the Agent's name and the interest-creating information provided by the Agent. This entire process relies upon the adaptive unconscious and adaptive subconscious concepts. When a contact sees the Agent's name, signs, ad, banner, or other information, the contact unconsciously or subconsciously remembers the Agent.

They might say, **"I think there is an Agent named Sonny Moyers who does a lot of business in the neighborhood; perhaps we should call him!"**

Perhaps they might remember the name and photo but not know why they remember the Agent. They might have retained fliers, neighborhood data, school magazines, or other materials that include the Agent's contact information and can use the necessary contact information to recall the information and reach out for assistance. The Agent can then **"Cast the Marketing Net"** to capture the Prospect and begin the conversion of the Prospect into a Client.

These new prospects and future clients do not come from a friendly "Raving Fan" referral or source. They require that the Agent compete with other real estate agents for the opportunity to represent them, regardless of the type of service to be provided. It is also important for the Agent to realize that often a contact in a Target Market Area will be helping a friend or associate, someone in their sphere of influence, and refer the Agent to that person. The Agent may never find out how it all came about. This might be considered a form of institutional advertising.

All is done to identify a Prospect and convert them to a client, who will then sign a representation agreement. Obtaining a new Prospect in this manner is more expensive than getting a referral from a trusted client who is a "Raving Fan."

Some might say that marketing to a Target Market is like throwing a dart at the market and hoping to score a bullseye. This is not true if the Agent has done a thorough job of identifying and selecting the Target Market based on reasonable criteria and assessment of the neighborhood demographic information. The Agent who fails to do research and select Target Markets based on reasonable criteria will be betting on success rather than banking on success.

Market Segmentation is segmenting a market into logical sub-groups, categories, or types of Prospects. Markets can be divided based on several criteria. When selecting a Target Market of homes in a particular neighborhood, an Agent must not assume that all homes should be selected for targeting. Some homes offer more challenges for selling and, as a result, might be excluded. Segmentation of a Target Neighborhood in a residential community could be completed as follows.

- Large
- Small
- Irregular Homesite
- Interior Homesite
- Inferior Homesite
- Superior Homesite
- Recently Purchased
- No Sales in the Past Five Years
- Owned By a Real Estate Agent

An Agent might segment the neighborhood to avoid spending marketing resources on homes that are not highly desirable and might be challenging for the Agent to sell. An Agent might not refuse to list a home for sale but might not spend resources on marketing a home with challenges compared to others in the same Market Area.

An Agent might avoid marketing to homes on Inferior Homesites, Homes Owned by Agents, or homes that have recently changed ownership and are less likely to become marketable in the next three to five years. A Target Neighborhood of 300 homes might have 200 in the Target Market selected to receive marketing materials. This leaves resources for targeting another 100 homes that are more desirable for listing in another neighborhood or a different target audience. An Agent who has chosen to market to a particular neighborhood should carefully select the targets so they do not waste resources that could be applied to better opportunities.

Investing in the Long-Term—Target Market Prospects

The Prospects captured from Target Market Stimulation activities differ from those referred by a trusted source. The need for the Agent to be ready to present their attributes and compete professionally and strategically is paramount.

Prospects who have not signed an agreement are not expected to be loyal, and the expenditure of resources to support them without an agreement is costly and risky. This is no different, however than if the Agent is asked to provide a CMA and conduct a listing presentation to secure a listing with a Prospect.

Very few Agents would say, **"I'll spend two days preparing for a listing presentation, make several visits to your home, and provide you my recommendations, but only if you sign a listing agreement first."** This would be a losing strategy. The Agent works to obtain a listing opportunity, and they must work to capture a Buyer or Investor similarly. Drawing the line on where to stop supporting a Prospect of any kind without a signed representation agreement is an important strategic decision. Aspiring Agents often get confused when deliberating on how much to do to help a Prospect before an agreement for representation has been signed.

Most Agents would invest substantial time and energy in a listing opportunity to make a professional presentation and provide significant amounts of information to the Prospect to secure a listing. This is no different than spending some time and resources to secure a buyer representation agreement without an agreement for compensation or guarantee. The Agent should provide enough support to demonstrate competency and prove that they have the ability and the knowledge to assist a Prospect. This support might be limited in scope and time based on the Agent's current level of business activity.

An Agent, when deciding whether to begin an assignment with a Prospect derived from Target Market Stimulation activities, should remember that the revenue received in the first year of working with the new client is only the beginning of the potential revenue stream that may be derived from the client and their sphere of influence over numerous years. Some risk is therefore acceptable to the aspiring Agent as the opportunity is potentially quite large.

The marketing message used in the Target Market Stimulation effort differs greatly from the messaging used in Client Management activities. The target audience in the Stimulation Marketing activities is prospects that have not met or done business with the Agent; therefore, the messaging must be different. There is no history of working with the Agent, and they don't necessarily have a reason to like the Agent other than the message that they are receiving. The Agent must "Cast the Marketing Net" to capture them and make them want to interview the Agent. The "net" can only be cast if there is a message of benefit and value to the Prospect.

Institutional Advertising & The Agent Dilemma

When the Agent has an opportunity to introduce themselves and create a **"Magic Minute,"** they can create an ability to secure the Prospect and build the business. Target Market Stimulation can be seen as institutional advertising. It is trying to create an image and a compelling reason for the prospect to call the Agent and give them an opportunity for an interview.

The contacts that are being reached could be people who have no interest in making a change in their real estate holdings. They may have a REALTOR® that they like and trust. They may also have a friend or relative in the real estate business. These contacts would be difficult to capture. They could be interested in purchasing or selling real estate but are not necessarily focused on this activity. They could be open to capture if their former Agent is no longer in the Real estate business or has ignored them since their previous transaction and failed to assure satisfaction. In this case, they could be receptive and an excellent target for capture.

Target Market Stimulation produces results because an Agent has a refined message based upon analysis and research in a Target Market and executes a sophisticated marketing program over time, and with different messaging methods, to create awareness of the Agent in the Target Market.

Target market selection and stimulation require time, discipline, and money to invest in the business. Marginally profitable real estate Practices have difficulty sustaining a marketing program in identified target markets as it is easy to give up. The payoff is very large if the future investment is funded and consistently executed.

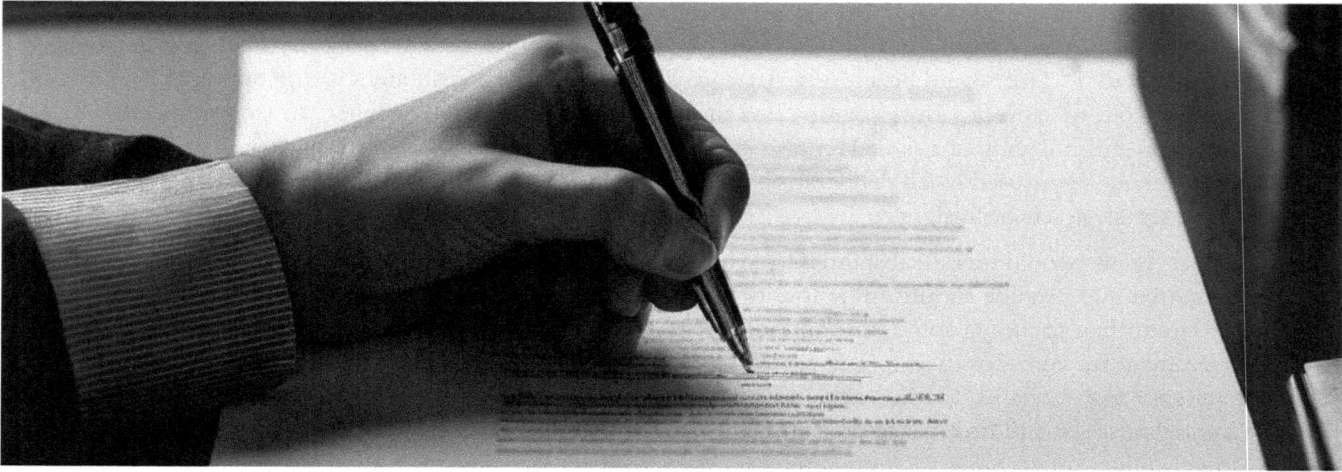

CHAPTER 31 | STRUCTURAL INTEGRITY ELEMENT: THE CLIENT HIERARCHY

What does Hierarchy mean in the world of real estate?

In the real estate practice, a hierarchy is a system that ranks individuals or groups based on their status, authority, or value to the organization. Specifically, Clients and Prospects are ranked based on their value to the agent and the practice. This means that clients who have signed a representation agreement with the agent are considered to have a higher value than prospects. This concept is fundamental in the real estate Practice, as it helps agents prioritize their efforts and resources toward those clients who are more likely to generate revenue for the practice.

When talking about Client Hierarchy, the Prospect who has not signed any agreement but who represents substantial opportunity would be placed in the Client Hierarchy even though they have not signed any representation agreement with the Agent. By placing a Prospect in the Client Hierarchy, the Agent is <u>committing resources</u> with the belief that the Prospect can be converted into a client by signing a representation agreement.

Have you ever wondered why some people receive more attention, care, service, and time than others? Although many people believe that everyone is to be treated equally, the reality is that a natural hierarchy tends to develop over time. In the real estate business, this hierarchy is particularly noticeable.

A hierarchy develops as the real estate practice evolves, and certain clients and prospects are elevated to the top. These individuals typically do the most business, refer the most business, or have the potential to generate the most business for the agent. This means that these high-value clients and prospects receive more attention and care from the agent.

For example, an agent has a client who frequently buys and sells properties and refers their friends and family to the agent. This client would be considered high-value and receive more attention and care from the agent than a prospect who has only expressed a vague interest in buying or selling a property.

A smaller, less profitable Client can be at the top of the Hierarchy and get more attention and resources; however, there is usually a logical business reason for this. Resources are otherwise squandered on low probability and profitability Clients, and this reduces the available resources for reaching and building relationships with those most likely to do continuing business or refer business to the Practice. The VIP is a significant person and is ranked and named a VIP to give them additional attention. Why?

Being Involved in Connector's Lives

In the years following their move to Dallas, Steve and Kimberly, both dynamic "**Connectors**," referred numerous people to us. They purchased investment properties and referred their friends to do so likewise. Steve was looking for a property for commercial purposes for his business and purchased a twelve-acre horse farm in the country that could be used for that purpose as well as providing living quarters for some of his workers.

Connectors like Steve and Kimberly are similar to potent magnets, except they attract people. It was only a matter of time before Steve decided to run for public office. He had been involved in his New York neighborhood and area and was a natural for becoming involved here. He asked us to support his campaign.

We made a reasonable donation and provided great support as Steve ran for office. When he invited me to speak at a campaign rally at his home that we had sold him, I was excited to do so. About one hundred people were present, and I spoke for only a few minutes, extolling the virtues and intellect of Steve and commenting about his wonderful family. The event went well, and the election went even better. Steve won the election. I had further cemented the relationship with them and the one hundred people who saw me speak at his rally. Opportunities like this seldom happen by accident. He constantly introduced us as his REALTORS® and friends.

People like Kimberly and Steve rise to the top of the client hierarchy, but it does not occur by happenstance. It didn't happen because we waited for them to discover they needed something. It happened because we were there, ready and willing to serve. We actively stayed in touch with them and introduced additional ideas as part of our account plan to support them. As a result, we were ready to meet their needs and wants. The client hierarchy is important to understand. Let's explore further why it is so important.

In the book *Consultative Selling*, the authors point out a universal fact about the relationship between a company and its accounts. They write,

> *"Every business rests on this kind of relatively small foundation of heavy, repeat customers who are its key accounts. These are the users who form the base of support for their suppliers, whose patronage accounts for the bulk of the earnings and profits, and whose needs define the nature of their businesses." (1973, p. 1)*

A very successful real estate Practice may have approximately 90% of the revenues and profits derived from about 10% of the Clients and their spheres of influence. Would it make sense to devote 80% of the available resources to the bottom 20% of the clients who are least likely to do business with the Practice? The authors of *Consultative Selling* go on to discuss key accounts.

> *"One discovery we have made over and over again is that successful companies concentrate their sales function on a relatively small number of key accounts." (1973, p. v)*

It is practical and sensible for the Practice to devote more time, energy, and money to the top of the Hierarchy. Some people at the middle or bottom of the hierarchy may be liked more by the Agent than others, and some might make a greater contribution to society, but they still might not receive as much attention as others. Should they be ranked at the top of the Hierarchy regardless of the business they do with the Practice? They may be because some people are so well known and impactful in society that they are selected because they are influencers, and therefore spending time with them is potentially of greater value to the Practice regardless of their revenue or profit contribution. However, the normal selection process would be to select Clients for the highest tier of the hierarchy who have or could produce the highest revenues and profits in the shortest period.

Time Management is Part of Client Management

An Aspiring Agent, when beginning a Practice, most likely has fewer Prospects than an established Practice might have. Fewer are likely to have a high probability for real estate activity in the first 180 days of the Agent's Practice. The aspiring real estate Agent has approximately 2,080 hours available for revenue and profit-generating activities in a calendar year of operation. If 80% of the Agent's time were devoted to sales and marketing-related activities, it would constitute 1,664 hours.

Anything that takes away from this pursuit of Prospects that can be captured and converted to Clients is likely to harm the success of the Practice in its early days of existence. The ordinary course of business provides countless opportunities for non-sales-related activities to be presented to the Agent. Prime time for the real estate agent is the time that is the best time for a client to be contacted or reached. Activities that take away from the primetime availability to produce revenue and profit contribution can delay results or put the new Practice at risk of running out of resources. Prime time for Buyers and Sellers is frequently during evenings, late afternoon, and weekends.

An Agent who devotes excess time to non-client activities during this early time frame is missing out on being available to clients and Prospects during the clients' and Prospect's most available times. Many Agents have a conflict with this and must reconcile their priorities to be available when the client or Prospect most wants the Agent's time. This requires a brief description of the sacrificed alternative concept.

When 80% or more of the Practices revenues and profits are likely to come from 20% or less of the Clients and their spheres, then it is practical for the Agent to commit to a goal of 80% of their time being devoted to sales and marketing activities on its key accounts. There should be careful consideration, of course, where the other 20% of their time is spent. 10% of the time could be best spent on management, education, business planning, and a host of other activities. The remaining 10% of their time might remain available for activities that the Agent has not planned or programmed. This allocation of the most valuable resource in the Practice to sales and marketing with key accounts is essential if the aspiring Agent is to sustain and grow the business in the early days or years of operation.

There may not be enough Clients or Prospects at the beginning of the practice for the Agent to spend 80% of available time on. Therefore, there must be a concerted effort to reach and capture them. Therefore, the Agent must spend any remaining 1664 hours available to search for Prospects to Capture. Target Market Selection is critical to the Agent's future success. Target Markets must be selected based on research, analysis, and criteria that indicate potential Prospects can be reached. The Agent must also be able to reach and identify Prospects in a timely and cost-effective manner with their available resources.

As the Agent captures clients and ranks these clients in the Client Hierarchy, the Hierarchy begins to take shape. The number of Clients and Prospects Ranked in the Hierarchy increases as the Practice matures and requires more selectivity in where the clients are ranked in the Hierarchy. As this happens, the Agent's time is more heavily focused on the top band of the Client Hierarchy since they represent the most potential. While the other bands of the Hierarchy are important, the Agent must focus on the Prospects who represent the highest potential to become Clients. Other tactics, methods, and resources are used to identify Prospects in the selected Target Markets.

Hierarchy Theory

Clients in the Hierarchy system are not generally spread equally throughout the tiers as the Agent must first ascertain which clients will most likely result in more revenue. This requires Client knowledge and careful attention to the Buyer and Seller Hierarchy of Needs and Wants which will be discussed in a later chapter.

The Agent determines the number of tiers in the hierarchy, which can be adjusted based on the number of Clients and Prospects in the Practice. Clients and Prospects move up and down the hierarchy based on current information and the availability of resources at any given time, but usually for a Plan Year. In the beginning, an Agent may have only Prospects in the Client Hierarchy, and it is important to remember that the conversion of a Prospect to a Client, by its very nature, could move that Client upward in the Client Hierarchy.

There may be numerous Clients that cannot be ranked in the top band of the Hierarchy because they do not meet the criteria of doing business with the Practice in the past, as the Practice has no history. There could also be a lack of information about them that prevents them from being ranked higher. These Prospects are therefore assigned to a lower tier in the hierarchy as determined by the agent. The search for clients to be in the highest tier is an ongoing process, and the system's objective is to concentrate all the Practice resources on the highest potential Clients.

The top tier includes the Clients the Agent has ranked as most likely to do business with the most immediate opportunity for future revenue and profit. The remaining Clients and Prospects might be considered a lower priority and therefore be in a lower tier. In the beginning, if an Agent has three Clients and the available time, all three could be in the top tier. However, placing a client in the top tier, and spending time on them when they are marginal, could result in time not spent looking for Prospects in the Target Market Groups. Clients are managed to determine at what point they might become more active or be re-classified upward within the hierarchy. Based on the Agent's assessment, they could also be a lesser priority and move to a lower tier. The Hierarchy is fluid in that clients and prospects may move up and down and occasionally out of the Hierarchy.

Client Protection Required—as Clients Attract Competition

The Practice must protect all Clients in the Practice to ensure that they are not lost due to competitor efforts to attract them. Client Retention is essential for the Agent to always keep in mind when funding tactical plans that expend resources. The Clients are always deemed to be at risk, and the Practice must implement tactics to assure client loyalty and retention. Clients move up and down within the hierarchy. Still, the Agent tries to ensure that they are not lost and only removed from the Client list when the Agent believes they no longer have potential, or it is apparent that they are lost to a competitor or lost for another reason. They are moved out of the hierarchy and coded as a **"Lost Account"** in the **CRM** when this happens to keep their information but eliminate any resource expenditure being targeted toward them going forward.

Focused on New Prospects

A new Agent must devote much of their sales time to looking for candidates to become Prospects and later clients. Prospects should always be evaluated for future potential based on their sphere of influence and whom they might meet in their natural course of business. The Client Capture System can be referred to as the **"Marketing Net"** and is designed to capture and qualify Prospects that are likely to be looking for a real estate agent to represent them in the future. At the beginning of the Practice, an Agent must focus more time on Target Market Stimulation to find Prospects who could ultimately become Clients.

The Client Hierarchy is utilized for this purpose. It guides the Agent and the Practice on where critical resources should be concentrated. It identifies the clients most likely to do the most business with the Practice and gives them the attention they expect and deserves (The Treatment Grid). It provides a mechanism for allocating resources to the highest probability accounts and away from the accounts that utilize valuable Practice resources but do not contribute greatly to the revenues and profits. At the same time, it provides enough attention and resources to protect the lesser probability accounts so that when they have higher potential, they are protected against competitive efforts in the future.

The Agent should always consider the cost of working with a Prospect that is a lower probability and failing to spend time working on identifying Prospects in a Target Market Group. When a real estate Practice is organized around the needs and wants of its most valuable clients and Prospects, the agent becomes highly adept at identifying and capturing opportunities, and resources are selected and developed for that specific purpose.

Objectives for the agent include:

- Maximizing revenue and profit from high-value clients.
- Protecting lesser-value clients from erosion or competitive loss.
- Constantly searching for Prospects to replace Clients with low potential.
- And driving the real estate Practice to maximize its revenue and profit potential.

Organizing the business around the Client Hierarchy and allocating limited and costly resources to the highest priority accounts requires structure and discipline. The Ranking System was created for this purpose.

The Client Ranking System

This client ranking system sorts the accounts by the highest probability of future business, referrals, and public support. The goal of the Ranking System is to allocate and target the highest level of Practice resources to those accounts that represent the highest potential for future business. In this example, Practice Clients and Prospects (Accounts) are ranked from P1 to P4.

Knowing their history, where would you have ranked Steve and Kimberly in the ranking system?

Accounts can be re-activated from inactive status if their situation changes. A major event could change their situation, such as a marriage or divorce. Contact is maintained with the clients over time for this reason. If a client is deemed to have no future potential, they should be rated as a **"Closed Account."** They would remain in the **CRM,** allowing for something in the future to happen that would allow for the reclassification back to a funded account or if there is a need to re-visit activities or transactions that had been completed with them in the past. Until something changes, they are no longer sent marketing information.

The ranking system establishes priorities for the expenditure of limited resources to assure profitability. Depending upon the resources available for a given plan year, the contact grid and plans could be changed each year. A plan year is generally twelve months. An account reassigned in the Ranking System and changed in the CRM during a plan year would automatically move to a different contact grid and receive more or fewer resources allocated to them after a reclassification.

It is not advisable to change classifications frequently in the Ranking System without a strong reason, as a reclassification of an account would change the resource requirements for a plan month, quarter, or year.

The Client Treatment Grid—Personalized Client Management

Once the Ranking System is completed and accounts are assigned a Rating in the CRM, the Treatment Grid needs to be created. To accomplish this task, the Agent must know what resources will be available during the Plan Year. The Treatment Grid will specify what kind of contact is assigned to each Account for a particular Plan Year. This will include the frequency and type of contact selected to achieve success with each client. The goal is to assign the highest skilled resources to the activities likely to create the most income and profit.

The Treatment Grid must be designed with activities that do not exceed the available resources to ensure the work will be completed. Resource availability and activities assigned must be balanced. Assigning 100% of the available resources for a Plan Year would be a mistake because situations are likely to change and require using resources of a particular type that was not anticipated during the planning process. Assigning only a pre-determined percentage of total available resources by category is wise.

The marketing activities and contacts with the P1 Clients and Prospect in the Target Markets may result in several accounts becoming Active and seeking to buy or sell a home and needing support and thus resources. The contact plan for the new clients would need to be reallocated, which might cause other resource plan changes. The additional resource requirements of new accounts could unbalance the agent's workload and require adjustments.

For a new Practice, fewer sales activities will likely occur, such as touring, researching, and negotiating contracts. The amount of time used by the Agent on Account contacts will be greater the longer that the Practice operates. As the business grows, the Agent must assign work to other resources to remain available to make account contacts and work on transactions. This will keep the Agent focused on higher potential Clients categorized as P1 and P2 accounts.

The Agent, achieving success, will have less available time and, therefore, must assign activities to other resources or re-classify some accounts to a lower ranking to avoid wasting resources on marginal accounts.

When an Agent commits large amounts of time during regular business hours on activities that are not client or marketing related, they start a downward spiral that often leads to failure. An Agent devoting large amounts of time during **"PrimeTime"** to activities that are not the most likely to result in revenues and profits may commit valuable resources to activities that do not produce income or profit. This could result in the Practice running out of resources and risk failure.

A goal is to target 80% of the Agent's time on revenue-producing or market development activities. An example of resource allocation of the Agent's time for the first three years follows:

New Practice, Year One

1. Client Management: 10%
2. Target Market Development: 70%
3. Other Activities: 20%

New Practice, Year Two

1. Client Management: 40%
2. Target Market Development: 40%
3. Other Activities: 20%

New Practice, Year Three

1. Client Management: 65%
2. Target Market Development: 15%
3. Other Activities: 20%

Existing clients are more likely to buy again, are easier to connect with, and sometimes refer their friends and associates. Because Target Market Development activities are targeted to possible prospects, they are less likely to produce results in Plan Year One.

Target Market Development, which may take months or years to produce results, may be shifted to other Team Members as the Practice and number of clients grow. The Agent must be involved in outreach marketing design, planning, and execution at all times to ensure that the marketing strategies are followed.

Examples of Ranking:

Priority One (P1) Accounts are the highest priority accounts in the Ranking System. They may or may not have purchased or sold a property in the past, and they are qualified Prospects for a future purchase or sale, are active or inactive clients now, and are likely to do business with the Practice in the future. They may have written a testimonial letter or quote expressing their satisfaction, have or would refer friends and associates, and are considered **"Raving Fans"** or potential to be **"Raving Fans"** and "Connectors."

Priority One (P1) Clients and Prospects will receive the most personal attention from the Agent and get the most frequent contact throughout the contact system in numerous and varied ways. Great effort should be made to increase the number of contacts in the account's family and sphere of influence to seed future business.

The following is an example Treatment Grid for an Agent who has been in the business for several years. It would vary greatly depending on how long the Agent has been in business. The example is from a mature Practice and is, therefore, more complex than a new Practice.

Treatment Grid for P1 Accounts

- Annual personal contact by Agent at lunch, coffee, or other in-person event.
- Quarterly contact from Agent by Telephone Contact.
- Monthly Direct Mail Contact with birthday cards, anniversary cards, announcements, market update information, or some other valuable information.
- Monthly newsletters from Practice in Print or Email format.
- Invitation to Annual VIP Client Appreciation Events
- Email & Text Messages when Information about them warrants contact.
- Level 1 Holiday Gifts Delivered.
- Instant Recognition Gift Card for Referrals or Special Action by Client

Priority Two (P2) Clients are the second highest priority accounts in the Client Hierarchy System. They may have purchased property or sold a property in the past, are inactive accounts but are likely to do business with the Practice in the future, have written a testimonial letter or quote expressing their satisfaction, have or would refer friends and associates, and are considered, "Raving Fans." They have the potential to be "Connectors."

Based upon this, the P2 Accounts will receive frequent personal attention from the Agent and get numerous contacts in the contact system. Great effort will be spent staying in touch with these accounts as they could become active or provide referrals at any time.

Treatment Grid for P2 Accounts

- Annual personal contact by Agent for coffee, tea, or other events.
- Two Contacts per year from Agent by Telephone Contact.
- Monthly Direct Mail Contact with birthday cards, anniversary cards, announcements, market information, or some other valuable information.
- Monthly newsletters from Practice in Print or Email format.
- Invitation to Annual VIP Client Appreciation Events
- Email & Text Messages when Information about them warrants contact.
- Level two holiday gifts delivered.
- Instant Recognition Gift Card for Referrals or Special Action by Client

Priority Three (P3) Clients Prospects are the third highest-ranked accounts in the Client Hierarchy System. They may have purchased property or sold a property in the past, show no signs of moving or selling, are inactive accounts, are possible future clients with the Practice in the future, have written a testimonial letter or quote expressing their satisfaction, would refer or have referred friends and associates but are at this point not considered, **"Raving Fans."**

Priority Three (P3) Clients and Prospects will receive less personal attention from the Agent and get less personal contact throughout the contact system in numerous and varied ways. Great effort should still be made to increase the number of contacts but without the agent's personal attention.

Treatment Grid for P3 Accounts

- Monthly Direct Mail Contact with birthday cards, anniversary cards, announcements, market information, or some other interesting information.
- Monthly newsletters from Practice in Print or Email format.
- Email & Text Messages when Information pertaining to them warrants contact.
- Instant Recognition Gift Card for Referrals or Special Action by Client

Priority Four (P4) Clients and Prospects are the fourth lowest ranked accounts and are likely to become dormant and move out of the Client Hierarchy system unless something changes. They have not purchased or sold a property in the past, may or may not show signs of moving or selling, and are inactive accounts. The Practice is uncertain whether those accounts will do business with the Practice in the future. They are not considered **"Raving Fans."** They will be contacted hoping to become active or refer others from the sphere of influence in the future. If an account is no longer ranked P1 through P4, it is categorized in the CRM as a closed account and has no ranking. An example of this type of Prospect is someone who has previously asked for CMA and/or tax data and demonstrated potential and was therefore added to the Client Hierarchy.

Based upon this, the P4 Accounts will receive little direct personal attention from the Agent but get some attention in the other areas of the contact system, such as direct mail or email, or text messages.

Treatment Grid for P4 Accounts

- Quarterly Direct Mail Contact with birthday cards, anniversary cards, announcements, market information, or some other interesting information.
- Monthly newsletters from Practice in Print or Email format.
- Email & Text Messages when Information about them warrants contact.
- Instant Recognition Gift Card for Referrals or Special Action by Client.

In summary, the ranking of many clients in the ranking system is purely subjective and at the agent's best judgment. Throughout this book, clients written about were primarily P1 accounts and "Raving Fans." Muhammed Gerani and Simran are excellent examples of P1 Clients. They purchased and sold homes with us. They referred family members to us. They referred numerous people from their sphere of influence to us. They spoke highly about us both in writing and in conversations with others. They supported us in every way, and we delivered tremendous value to them in various ways.

My Friend & Client, Ali

Ali loved being valuable to us. This gave him great satisfaction and fulfilled some of his self-actualization needs. He was the ultimate **"Connector,"** and we will always appreciate the relationship with Ali and Simran as they are not only great clients but great people. They have inspired me; perhaps someday, I will write a book just about him.

CHAPTER 32|STRUCTURAL INTEGRITY ELEMENT: THE BUYER & SELLER HIERARCHY

The Buyer & Seller Hierarchy for an agent's purpose is as follows: This hierarchy is based on a system or methodology in which a client's needs and wants are prioritized based on their values and ability to fulfill those needs and wants. By ranking clients and prospects accordingly, agents can focus their efforts and resources on those most likely to generate revenue for their practice.

Hierarchy of Needs

One of the most quoted people in the world is Abraham Maslow, the author who wrote about one of the best-known theories of motivation for human beings. His writings are well known by many, and his work is often called a **"Hierarchy of Needs."**

Maslow's concepts can be used to explain how the Smart Agent can better understand buyers', sellers', and investors' motivations. Exploring Maslow's philosophy of human motivation provides insight into how to work with various types of Buyers and Sellers depending on where they are in satisfying their needs and wants. What motivates them to be who they are and do what they do? It is helpful for the Agent to understand if a client is at a self-actualization stage or is still focusing on other basic needs to be met.

Maslow's Hierarchy of Needs is a model that organizes human needs into a pyramid with tiers arranged from top to bottom. At the top of the pyramid is the tier of Self-Actualization. This tier includes people who have surpassed the fundamental needs and wants of the lower tiers and are now striving toward self-fulfillment and completeness. For these individuals, the pursuit of self-actualization becomes a significant goal. They have a strong desire to achieve personal growth, creativity, and overall fulfillment, which they perceive as the ultimate level of achievement.

Clients at the self-actualization stage tend to be those who are fully aware of their need for satisfaction and tend to be less concerned about other needs as they have already met those needs and are more concerned about realizing their personal potential.

Maslow is reported to have said, **"What a man can be, he must be,"** Maslow explained this when referring to the need for people to achieve their full potential as human beings. This may be described as utilizing talents, capabilities, and potentialities and realizing the satisfaction of reaching that point of achievement in their lives. Said another way, they could be ready to enjoy just living and experiencing rather than working to achieve other things less important to them at the time.

At the bottom of the pyramid or Hierarchy, one would find the physiological needs for items necessary for survival. These include but are not limited to food, water, breathing, shelter, clothing, and other basic needs like eliminating waste.

Moving up the pyramid to the next tier, the need for safety and security becomes the items humans typically seek before moving to the next stage and eventually to the top of the pyramid, where they can find self-actualization. This is considered the highest level and, therefore, the most important to people who have met their other physiological needs.

When a client is financially sound, has safety, and has met those needs, they might be ready to move up the pyramid to the next level of need and are motivated to do so. This next stage can be called social needs. Social needs in this tier can be acceptance, love, friendships, community, and religion. Generally, it can be said that if a person is worried about survival or freezing to death, it might be difficult to worry about self-actualization. Yet, there are always exceptions to every rule. While we might not understand why, a homeless person who values his freedom from the world's cares more than feeling safe or warm is a possible example.

Esteem needs are placed next in the pyramid, moving to the fourth level by Maslow, and should not be confused with "pride," often referred to as one of the seven deadly sins. The need for self-esteem includes appreciation and respect and the need to achieve and accomplish what they most desire. People need to have their achievements recognized by others. Sometimes this one person, or in many cases, the recognition by the world around them, could be necessary. It is important to remember that this is not pride or ego but general acceptance that the person has a place in the world in which they live. This is often called self-esteem or self-worth. Most good parents strive to help their children feel this self-esteem and self-worth. My father did that for me.

It is commonly understood that individuals start at the base of the pyramid and ascend toward self-actualization. This is the point at which the conversation about how the agent applies Maslow's Hierarchy of Needs in real estate practice becomes pertinent.

What Makes People "Tick"

I learned very early in my life that what made me "tick" was recognition. Of course, I also needed everything, like food, shelter, safety, to be loved, etc. However, at age twenty-eight, while working for AT&T, I found little satisfaction working in a mundane job for people who were not highly imaginative and didn't challenge me to do more. I wanted to do great things and be seen as flourishing and impactful. These things were perceived as providing great value to others. This caused me to leave corporate life and pursue other ventures where I could be my own boss. Like Darren, the young man I spoke about earlier, I wanted to do something meaningful.

People generally pay more for wants than needs, once their fundamental needs have been met. Why? It could be said that a person needs transportation, such as an automobile, but they don't necessarily need a Mercedes Benz. They want one. One could undoubtedly find warmth and safety in a moderately priced home and not need a large one with a swimming pool to meet their fundamental needs.

Some Prospects feel safe, well-fed, and comfortable at a different point in life or stage of satisfaction than others. One person could be pleased in a small, modest home where they are comfortable, feel safe, and their fundamental needs are being met. They are then free to move on to the Self-Actualization Stage at a different point than others. Some people cannot reach the point of self-actualization until they are financially independent. Others need to have financial independence in the eyes of the world or be successful in the eyes of others to move into a stage of self-actualization.

As in most things in life, some people disagree with Maslow's theories and are quite vocal about their criticisms. Many people, however, tend to agree that the concept has merit. Admittedly it is difficult to test this theory in the laboratory of life.

It should be clearly stated that through observation and the development of close relationships with many clients over a period of more than fifty years, I have formed the opinion that Maslow's Theory of Motivation is well thought out and correct.

Needs and Wants Vary Depending on the Client

One misconception of many, however, is the premise that humans must satisfy each need entirely before moving to the next level. The Agent should be mindful that one person's view of safety is not always another person's. Therefore, interpreting another person's needs is, at best, difficult. Not all of my needs had been met at twenty-eight years old, yet I wanted to move on and satisfy other, more essential needs.

The operative word for this discussion is **"satisfy each need completely."** What is "completely" for different individuals is subject to interpretation but essentially resides within the individual. The client is the only one who knows his most important needs and wants. A person who is satisfied with most aspects of his life as far as basic needs may choose to have less worldly things than he currently has and seek to move on to satisfy his self-actualization needs and wants.

The artist is an example of this situation. <u>The artist might give up safety or shelter to satisfy their need for self-actualization to create art</u>. While this is difficult for many to understand, being an artist provides benefits of greater value than shelter for some individuals. An Agent working with a **"couple"** who are the clients can be complicated, as the two people may have differing views on where they are in having their needs and wants met before moving on to self-actualization. This can create conflict and great emotion that an Agent must cope with. This also represents an opportunity for the Agent to build relationships with the couple and the individuals.

The real estate agent serves the client by understanding the client's current stage of needs and wants at that moment. A client who purchases a home today may have different needs and wants in the future and therefore need to make a change to satisfy these different needs and wants. It is, therefore, incumbent on the agent to listen and understand what the client needs and wants to guide the agent in satisfying them. The agent who does so could win the <u>loyalty and trust of the client, which is the gold of the real estate business</u>.

He who has the client has the gold! Finding a few good clients who might also be "Connectors" is what marketing is all about.

What You Think Important—May Differ

This requires great patience and a willingness by the Agent to suppress their own opinions of value and to focus on what the client perceives as valuable to them. Most experienced agents have observed a change of mind by the client when proceeding down a particular pathway with a client where the agent felt they were on the correct pathway, only to find that the client changed direction. This should not be surprising if the agent has not correctly assessed their Client's Hierarchy of Needs and Wants at the moment they are interested in making a change. Based upon the **"sacrificed alternative concept,"** a Client may change their choices based upon a recent self-assessment of their priorities and realizing their inability to satisfy all their needs and wants. Frequently in the process of making a large decision such as buying or selling a home, the process itself can cause the client to reassess their values and goals along the way.

Agents sometimes project their opinion on a pathway acceptable to them and supplant the Prospect's value system based on their own perspectives. The Collaborative Selling Concept is valuable in that it introduces more opportunities for client interaction and, as a result, better communication about needs and wants with a client. When an agent takes on a Consultative Agent role, the agent's ideas and opinions take a back seat to the client's ideas and opinions, and the Agent is more connected to and listens more closely to the client. <u>The collaborative process frequently replaces the all-knowing agent with the all-caring agent.</u> This fosters an environment of listening and understanding, sharing, and learning, as well as joint decision-making, with the client being the direction setter.

The interpersonal communications theories discussed herein allow the Agent to understand the client's needs and wants fully and completely. To do this, the agent should understand the hierarchy of needs and wants of the Client. An investor seeking to purchase investment property has different needs and wants than a first-time home Buyer seeking to own a home.

The Hierarchy of Buying and Selling real estate also depends upon the financial capabilities of the Buyer, Seller, or Investor and where they are on their journey to self-actualization.

A Changing Client Creates Opportunity

The Buyer's and Seller's Hierarchy for decision-making in real estate is like Maslow's Hierarchy of Needs. When clients' needs have been met, they prioritize their decision-making differently regarding real estate decisions. A client who needs shelter has a high-priority need, which might drive the decision-making process. Where they have limited resources, they could prioritize having a roof over their head and food on their table. However, as the needs have been met and they move to the Self-Actualization stage, their most important **wants** tend to prevail in decision-making.

If the Buyer of real estate has sufficient finances to meet their fundamental needs, they may switch to their Buyer Wants Hierarchy in reaching a decision. Therefore, an Agent specializing in luxury homes will probably use a different set of priorities when searching for the right home for their client.

Just as an automobile buyer who is in the Self-Actualization phase might want a convertible or a Mercedes Benz, and therefore their wants would guide their decision making, a home buyer who has their basic needs met could choose to pay more for wants than the agent might expect. Therefore, the agent must listen to and understand, but not write in stone, what a luxury home buyer says is their buying limit. Their choice of a home may be more costly than the agent might have considered. This can particularly happen when a client realizes that a vital want is moving them closer to self-actualization.

Choosing Your Target Client

This is an important consideration for an Agent when choosing a Target Market. Selecting a luxury home Target Market will bring the agent in contact with a different group of clients with different motivations in many cases than a Target Market of more modest homes.

Many agents in the early stages are not focusing on buyers or sellers who are in a particular phase of life but rather on anyone who needs real estate assistance. There is an important consideration when considering the long-term targeting of where an agent wants to work. An Agent who chooses to focus on the luxury home market must focus more heavily on the Buyer's and Seller's wants rather than their needs. In this situation, the client's needs are easily identified as the client will tell their Agent, **"I need at least 4,000 square feet, five bedrooms, at least four bathrooms, and a large open floor plan with a nice backyard and a pool."**

It does not require a great deal of effort or skill by the Agent to obtain this information from a Buyer. It is easy and comfortable for the Buyer to relay this information. Identifying the unknown wants that will cause a client to reach self-actualization goals may require great skills, patience, and an understanding of Maslow's Theory of Motivation.

The Agent might find that the wants are more specific when exploring further. For example, **"I want a four-car garage to store my two collector cars, and I would like the back yard to have an outdoor kitchen, fireplace, and cabana with a nice sized heated swimming pool and spa. I would most like a beautiful view… I prefer a gated neighborhood, but that is an additional option. A media room on the first floor would be nice."**

An Agent targeting contacts in a higher income bracket should consider that they are frequently dealing with someone who has had their basic needs met and is therefore focusing their decisions more on what they want rather than what they need. The client may still want their needs met but will pay dearly for a property that meets or exceeds their needs and satisfies their wants.

Likewise, when working with a lower-priced home buyer, the Agent might be surprised by what the Buyer might need and want. It might be hard for an Agent to understand a buyer who purchases a home with bars over the windows and doors. With a Buyer who needs safety and peace of mind, this far outweighs any aesthetic opinion of how the bars look to someone else. An Agent working in an area where the home prices are in the lower price range must realize that the way they communicate and collaborate with the client will be different, as the understanding of meeting their needs could be of the highest importance to the client.

Projecting Needs of the Client

Moving into the realm of assisting clients in marketing and selling a property, the same concepts apply but are vastly different. Here is an excellent example of understanding the client's actual wants versus needs.

One of my clients, Brant, has indicated they wish to sell a large parcel of land for several million dollars. I proceed to analyze the project, estimate the land's value, and develop a Marketing Plan for that purpose. Several meetings are held in which he explains why the land is valued as it is and believes it should be sold. I agree with him about the comparable properties and estimated values. Yet, something didn't make sense. We have agreed on a list price for the land, but the client isn't willing to proceed.

Several meetings later, Brant repeats several comments that have been made previously. Brant appears highly conflicted about what to do with the land and the decision to sell. In a collaborative mode, after some delays, I listen carefully and hear a new want from the Seller. Brant says, **"The fact is, I am just sick of dealing with this property and want to be rid of it as soon as possible. It has made my life difficult, and I am ready to move on to other things. I want to be free of this…."**

The client did not have a problem with my assessment of the value being too low, but rather, it might be too high, and the property might not sell quickly enough to satisfy the Client. Learning this, I realized I needed to change my perspective to meet the client's wants and sell the property.

The client's wants were tilted toward moving on with their lives to accomplish something of greater value than money. This was an example of a client in a stage of "Self-Actualization."

This story demonstrates the need for an agent to have an open mind and base their decisions and opinions upon the Buyer or Seller's needs and wants. It is far better to understand these needs and wants and where the client regards needs and wants during the agent's presentations.

Taking the time to peel away the layers of the onion and unmask the client allows the Agent to fully comprehend and understand where the client is in their needs and wants Hierarchy. A meeting with a client solely focused on the client is an essential ingredient in the Agent working in a collaborative and consultative manner and demonstrating that the client is most important to the Agent. When an Agent assumes that money, high value, lower price, or commission rate is most important to the client, they can fall into an unforgiving trap. By focusing on price or commission rate, the Agent can make the client focus on those issues rather than what they want or need. The philosophy of the Consultative Collaborative Agent is to target needs and wants, both known and unknown, for the client and avoid talking about value and fee rate so as not to block open discussion of these critical needs and wants.

Understanding Goals Requires Asking

The following statement is an example of opening dialogue without driving the focus to money or fees.

After establishing rapport and thanking the client for the meeting, the Agent might begin with, **"Sam, why don't we take a few minutes, if it is all right with you, to talk about what you hope to accomplish in buying or selling a home. I want to understand your goals and how I can best help you achieve those goals."**

My preoccupation with avoiding money and price is based upon the belief that these topics block communications with the client and, therefore, should be avoided if the client is not alienated when doing so.

The Collaborative Agent who understands the importance of **"Client Knowledge"** will be able to work with most Clients because what the Agent is showing has little to do with brick, mortar, or lumber. It concerns Clients' needs and wants and where they are in their pursuit of "Self-Actualization." The product-oriented salesperson will likely experience difficulty satisfying a client moving toward self-actualization.

CHAPTER 33 | STRUCTURAL INTEGRITY ELEMENT: THE MARKETING MIX

There are many options when considering how a real estate Practice communicates with its target audiences. An artist combines paints of different colors to create a palette and original artwork, and the varied colors make the piece memorable or different. Different types and amounts of various marketing communication methods are selected to achieve the best mixture of contact methods and content that will produce the desired results. The marketing communications method selected for every target audience attempts to produce satisfactory results for the Agent. This mixture of contact methods could be different depending on the makeup of the target audiences. Choosing the appropriate messages and various contact types requires study, research, experimentation, and considering the likely reaction of the target group recipients.

How does an Agent cause an audience member to take action that results in a relationship? Does this happen by accident or strategy? Exploring how to motivate people to reach out and contact an Agent is essential for long-term Agent success. Learning more about what makes people listen, see, and remember is a central theme of this chapter.

A book about learning concepts provides some fascinating insight. Jeanne Ellis Ormrod wrote *human learning*. She writes,

> *"A behavior that is followed by a satisfying state of affairs (a reward) is more likely to increase frequency than a behavior not followed by a reward." (2012, p. 5)*

Going on, Ormrod also writes,

> *"People learn what they pay attention to. A reward increases learning when it makes people pay attention to the information to be learned." (2012, p. 5)*

The agent's communications with the target audience must produce results that the audience can see. The Agent must create engaging content that can be communicated to the target audience to generate interest and cause them to see the information as a "reward" or something that "satisfies them". Communication from a unique agent has value, and providing a reward will teach the target audience to pay attention to the Agent as a source of information resulting in a satisfying situation for the target audience members.

Instead of thinking or saying, **"I get mail from this Agent all the time."** The audience member says or thinks, **"I get really interesting and valuable information and ideas from this Agent, and I look forward to receiving their information."**

Many Agents believe that any contact is good. They often believe repetitive contact will produce results without considering the value of the information sent to the individuals receiving it. The recipients must remember something that results in future business for the agent for the marketing to have value to the agent.

The conversation or message that does not create interest and provide a reward falls short because it is much less likely to cause a contact to look for future messages and exciting content that offers rewards. Varying messages and communications methods provide diverse ways of reaching target audiences with stimulating and rewarding content that will result in behavior that increases the likelihood of the target audience reaching out to the Agent for support. Any contact from any audience member is an opportunity for the Agent to solve a problem, demonstrate proficiency, make someone like them, identify a "Connector," or help an audience member realize a benefit.

Having a strategy for messaging to target audiences that differentiates the Agent and provides value to the message recipient requires thought, planning, research, and excellent execution of the tactical plans by the Agent Team.

Target Audiences could be Existing & Prior Clients or Groups of contacts in a Geographic or Selected Contacts list. Each group could be assigned a different combination of contact methods and a different frequency of contact. For example, a P1 Group of Existing and Past Clients would most likely receive a more personal touch from the Agent and possibly fewer other types of contact than a P4 Group of contacts.

The resources utilized by each group are specified in the Client Treatment Grid. This Grid describes and defines the various types of contact methods and frequency of contact that will be used to provide market coverage to the Client Hierarchy and the Target Markets. Target Markets could be identified in the CRM as shown below.

- Starwood Neighborhood Homeowner
- City Council Member
- Arts Group Member
- "Connector Group"
- P1 Group

The distinct naming of Target Market Groups in the CRM allows for the efficient distribution of Target Group-specific messages. An audience contact could be a Starwood Homeowner and Arts Group Member member. Therefore, the messages sent to them could be varied and unique, increasing the number of contacts for a particular target audience member.

All contact methods other than personal contacts from the Agent have some required content that fulfills licensing organizations' licensing requirements. This includes non-solicitation language, logos, identifying labels required by the real estate licensing act or Broker, branding information, and differentiating content.

Many agents choose a contact method and content because of their limited resources, lack of creativity, simplicity of creation, or lack of time. These are poor reasons for selecting an ineffective contact method and often waste valuable time and money without producing meaningful results. Often these card mailers, social media posts, email messages, and other content do not provide interesting information or differentiating content, resulting in a minimal response from the target audience.

To be effective, contact methods should be target audience specific, contain the necessary legal components for licensing, and provide interesting and memorable Branding information. All messages must make it easy for a recipient to find the agent's contact information and also differentiate the Agent from their competitors. They should always provide some reward for the recipient and a "call for action" on the part of the recipient. It should not be forgotten that a professional logo, an attractive color palette, and a catchy slogan all provide prompts to help the prospect remember the agent.

One could argue that marketing poorly done, such as sending uninteresting information on a social media site or other methods that have no value to a contact, could result in damaging the Brand of an Agent or reinforcing the idea that the Agent is like all the other Agents that send non-beneficial information to a contact. Sending similar messages to what other agents send can be counterproductive. At least by doing nothing, the Agent still has the resources to do something better. Insignificant zero-value marketing can result in negative impressions.

Passive versus Active Marketing

What is passive outreach or passive marketing? It is accepting what happens or what others do without active response or resistance. Passive marketing is speaking to an audience without expecting them to pay attention and react to what is said. It is broadcasting a message without expecting anyone to hear it. It is posting a flier on a wall that faces inward to an empty space.

<u>Passive outreach is not as effective as it could be unless combined with other active contact methods.</u> Active outreach programs combined with passive programs can cause a Prospect to respond and accept a **"call to action"** by the Agent. When a Prospect receives mail from an Agent and later sees a billboard with the agent's photo, phone number, and a **"call to action"** on the billboard, there is value to both passive and active messaging.

Some may argue that social media posting is an active method of reaching contacts. One should considers the number of messages of zero value that are sent on social media. In that case, it isn't easy to imagine that this medium will be highly productive unless it is considered in context with the total marketing program or marketing mix. Social media marketing coordinated with other methods of reaching the target audience may produce results that cannot be quantified much of the time. Like most things in real estate marketing, it isn't easy to directly quantify an activity to catalog results. This is because when someone sees content, they may call their agent or someone they know who shows them a property, and the posting agent may never know that the post or other contact method produced results.

Relying upon a target audience to respond to a passive outreach message is ineffective and may waste resources. A billboard sign is passive because it requires someone to drive by to see it, but the person driving by the billboard must notice it and have time to comprehend the message presented. The message on the billboard may not be able to create interest or promise a reward as the contact passing by may not have time to read and understand the information on the billboard.

A card or letter sent to a contact is an active outreach method. Waiting for a contact to find a website would be a passive outreach method. Waiting for enough contacts in a target group to find and take the time to view a website is a **"sit back and hope"** mentality and passive marketing activity. Frequently, an aspiring agent who expends resources on passive methods of contact will run out of time and money before enough results are realized to allow them to succeed in real estate. Some passive activities could be destructive to the agent's brand if the message is one of a product salesperson. **There are thousands of agents to choose from with** "Salesperson" **printed in red on their forehead.**

Driving traffic to a website via an active contact method is the fastest way to get contacts to view the site. Waiting for a contact to call is a passive activity. Doing something that causes the contact to call is an active activity. This is often called a **"call to action"** in a marketing piece, regardless of the marketing message used. A **"call to action"** can be embedded in direct mail, email, text, or other form of advertising but should always be present somewhere in the message. Many text and email messages from Agents fail to include a "call to action" and interesting information that is beneficial to the contact and are, therefore, less effective in getting the contact to make a call to the Agent or even remember the Agent's name. Sending a card mailer to a group of contacts offering a free service or publication for an opportunity to talk is a way of driving contacts to the Agent in a personal contact way where they can be captured in the agent's **"Marketing Net."**

The Marketing Net & the Client Capture System

The reason for the "Marketing Mix" is that some contacts respond to email and advertising, some to written material, and others only to personal contact. Often any type of contact is more successful if combined with other forms that create a compelling reason for the contact to reach out to the Agent. Everything in real estate marketing is about driving personal contact to the Agent. Phone calls to the Agent allow an Agent to **"Cast the Marketing Net"** and obtain an appointment for a face-to-face meeting. When an Agent fails to convert a Prospect into a client, they have failed to capitalize on the many expenditures made to reach the target audience and motivate them to respond.

Many real estate offices ask agents to handle the incoming call desk, which is often called the "up desk." Being on the "up desk" at a Brokerage office is a Passive activity. The agent is waiting for someone to call or arrive at the office, and the Agent may have done nothing actively to cause a contact to call or visit the office. Sitting at an open house is another form of passive activity unless the Agent has done something to cause visitors to walk into the home. The purpose of an open house sign is to cause contacts to enter the home and meet the Agent in the open house, allowing the Agent to **"Cast the Marketing Net"** and capture the Prospect. It can also be an effective way for the Agent to meet neighbors who live in a market area where the Agent can add a face to a name or personally meet and deliver a **"Magic Minute,"** increasing the likelihood of capturing a Prospect.

Agents that hold **"open houses"** for other Agents in an area they do not know or have not done anything to build a presence in the neighborhood or drive traffic to the open house is a low-probability passive marketing activity and frequently squanders valuable resources. Sometimes agents schedule these open houses because they don't know what else to do and feel they must do something to get prospects.

Holding an **"Open House"** in a neighborhood that the Agent does not reach with other marketing methods is less effective than holding an open house in a neighborhood where the Agent has a differentiated identity through other forms of contact. Contacts seeing an Agent name on the "Open House" sign might remember the name and associate the name with the Agent branding and stop to visit. Signs that simply say **"Open House"** without providing the hosting Agent's name are less effective than when placed in a neighborhood where an Agent is actively marketing. Contacts who become Prospects often say, **"I don't know where I saw your name, but I know that you do a lot of work in the neighborhood because I see your name everywhere."** This name recognition doesn't just happen without some form of marketing. The marketing and tactical plans for a target neighborhood seek out opportunities to be present, visible, successful, and above all else, different.

All outreach programs and types of contacts are used together in an integrated way to motivate audience members to call or meet with the Agent.

The Treatment Grid

The Client Treatment Grid is used to specify the types and frequency of contact with the clients in the Client Hierarchy to maximize the benefit and value of the contacts by strata within the Hierarchy. A mixture of different contact methods is used depending on the contacts' ranking and the Agent's personal involvement in the contact methods used.

There must also be a Treatment Grid for Target Market groups.

The Strategy of Opposites

This strategy simply states; when all the competitors are dressed in blue, then dress in any color other than blue.

Conversely, suppose all the Agents in a market are sending postcards that all look like what other Agents are sending. In that case, an Agent should send something other than postcards or commit themselves to send cards that are unique and different enough to differentiate themselves and always include a call to action. A dilemma of the Agent is those card mailers often fail to provide enough space to create engaging information that provides value and, therefore, often fall short of accomplishing the objective of causing recipients to act to receive a reward.

Because card mailers and social media posting are easy, many Agents rely upon them exclusively and repeatedly send similar, uninteresting, zero-benefit mailers to their target audiences while thinking they are accomplishing something when they may not be doing anything of value. When an audience member receives four cards or information from four Agents with a similar message like, **"I am Great, I sell houses,"** the message is lost as it is considered noise.

Letters, newsletters, website content, and other methods, such as Magazines, provide more room to elaborate and, therefore, can deliver more interesting information with more value. In other words, go where the competition isn't, not where they are.

The Agent Must be Visible—Must be Seen!

The goal of the Agent is to stand out and be seen as different and better. When the contact methods make an Agent appear to be the same as other Agents, they can diminish their ability ever to be perceived as different or better than their competitors. This is the opposite of positive Branding. It is **"equal to"** Branding.

When something is done on social media, it must be different from and better than others and have value to the person seeing the information. One should keep in mind that because 5,000 people like you, it depends on where they are physically located as to whether or not you have reached the target audience where you can impact lives. Broad-based advertising methods such as social media marketing, radio, television, and the Internet do not necessarily reach your target audience and can be a large investment in a failing strategy. One presentation to the City Council where you live and work can often reach more people who are likely buyers or sellers than advertising to the masses. This is quite different from when there is a real estate agency that has many office locations or operates on a regional or national level and does this kind of mass-market advertising.

When an Agent simply writes, **"Sold in 90 Days,"** and all other Agents are writing, "Sold in 90 Days," there is no reason a contact would perceive that one Agent is better than the others. They simply think, so what?

When an agent sends a card that touts their greatness and volume, they are not speaking to the prospect that wants and expects personalized attention. Almost all agents claim to be highly successful and, as a result, sound a great deal like each other.

The information in a marketing piece can be specified, including a subliminal message and a direct call to action to increase the response rate. A subliminal message is sensory stimuli below an individual's threshold for conscious perception, in contrast to supraliminal stimuli. An example might be a quote from another satisfied client: **"I called Sonny, and that was the best call I have ever made."** This, combined with a "CALL TO ACTION" elsewhere in the message, may well result in a response that allows the Agent to "CAST THE MARKETING NET."

One purpose of sending memorable materials to a Target Audience is to create awareness of the Agent and make themselves memorable. By sending a mailer or email multiple times and the contact seeing the Agent's name, an Agent can create a subconscious memory of the Agent's name. In this example, impressions can be the number of times an individual sees a person's name and Logo. In real estate, it is not unusual for an Agent who has been targeting a contact in a Group of contacts over a long period to hear the following from a Prospect, **"I don't remember who told me about you, but I know that you do a lot of business in the neighborhood, and I wanted to get your opinion of value for our home."** When frequent contacts from the Agent include interesting information and a reward, the results are magnified.

When an Agent sends look-alike materials to contacts, they are competing with other Agents that send a similar look-alike message, and it is more difficult for contacts to remember one Agent over the other. While many organizations offer free marketing materials to an Agent that is standardized and simple to use, these programs seldom offer the Agent the ability to modify the material to individualize and differentiate themselves enough to create a recognizable difference in the marketing. Therefore, they are less effective and can be counter-productive to the Agent and the Practice. An Agent that **brands** themselves with a photo and poses like many other Agents' photo and pose reinforces the concept of **"equal,"** not different or better.

Emulating a successful Agent is a good idea if what is simulated is unique and different. Emulating another Agent when what they are doing is standardized is not a winning strategy. Publishing a magazine and sending it to homeowners is an effective way to reach many of them because few agents have the money and resources to emulate this strategy. When the magazine is different, mainly focused on content, not advertising, it will be well received and have a longer shelf life. The content-focused magazines that are sent result in better Branding and differentiation of the Agent. Most agent-created real estate magazines are guilty of being too product-sales-oriented and weak in reader-value-centered content.

It would be far better to contact fewer in a target audience with a more differentiated message than to reach more prospects in an audience with a message that will not reach the subliminal mind with its uniqueness and, therefore, not be remembered by the recipient.

The Marketing Mix can be thought of as a deck of cards. The Agent selects the cards most likely to appeal to the target audience and, when combined in an integrated way, creates an opportunity for the Agent to maximize revenue potential and minimize the use of high-cost resources on marginal accounts. In this manner, the Agent can design, personalize, individualize, and differentiate contact messages.

Additional Thoughts...

When aspiring Agent spends most of their time and money on Passive activities, they are likely to fail in real estate as they run out of money, patience, and motivation before they can realize success. When an Agent spends most of their time on passive activities and waits for results, they are waiting to fail.

Be Careful about Rewards & Discounts

One caution about rewards. Many agents erroneously assume that a discount for a client is required to obtain the business. They instantly assume that discounting their fees or offering a rebate to a client is the way to reward them and secure business. This is a dangerous precedent.

Once an Agent falls into the trap of discounting, they brand themselves in such a way as to assure limited profitability and a lack of loyalty from past and future clients. There are many better ways to reward clients for being loyal and utilizing the unique services provided. Once an Agent reduces themselves to a discounter role, that erodes any chance of being perceived as a consultant to the client. They ensure that the client will link the relationship to saving money on the agent's fee, and fifty-plus years of experience proves that this is not the way to build a highly successful real estate Practice.

Discounting the professional service fee sends a message to Prospects that the Agent is average and similar to all the other Agents who fail to value their time and efforts. All efforts must be made to make the Professional Service Fee reasonable considering the level of professionalism and the benefits the agent will deliver.

Chapter 34|Structural Integrity Element: Market Coverage

The term, Market Coverage means to assure that all Clients and Target Markets are contacted in one form or another regularly and professionally to assure client satisfaction, protect Client relationships, expand Client knowledge, identify new opportunities, and capture Prospects to convert into Clients. In Target Markets, Market Coverage seeks to build a "Brand Identity" for the Agent and Practice and identify and connect with contacts that need real estate services in the future. It is also used to develop relationships further, thus increasing loyalty and "Raving Fan" status within the Client base.

John Medina, a molecular biologist, wrote *The Genetic Inferno*. The book is an amazing discussion of the brain in context with Dante's Inferno. Don't be concerned about the *Dante's Inferno* connection now. Rather, focus on the process of learning and memory. Medina writes,

> *"Most researchers have concluded that learning is part of the overall concept of memory. Learning may simply be the process of acquiring certain kinds of memories, the process that occurs when information is first presented." (2000, p. 303)*

Medina discusses memory after relating this comment to *Dante's Inferno* and drawing an analogy.

> *"Memory may thus be defined as "what happens afterward," the gradual process of massaging information into a form that will be maintained over time." (2000, p. 304)*

One goal of Market Coverage is to reach target audiences with interest creating messages that cause the contacts in the Target Audience to remember them. The repeating process of teaching and providing new information and having these contacts learn from the material will inevitably result in a memory that allows contacts in the Target Audience who need real estate assistance to remember the Agent. They will do so because they remember the important information provided to them over time. Perhaps the greatest opportunity to have a client remember the Agent is when the Agent gives the prospect a reason to call or meet with the Agent in person. A seminar on tax protest strategies is an example.

In essence, this is a form of "Branding." Agents must motivate contacts in the Target Market to remember the Agent.

Market coverage applies to target markets where the Agent seeks to establish name recognition and compete for the Prospect's business when target market contacts first become aware they need real estate assistance. One goal of Market Coverage in targeted markets is to ensure that when a Prospect needs help in real estate, they can locate the Agent's name and contact the agent to request assistance. To accomplish this, the **Marketing Mix** is used to vary the message and increase the number of exposures to the target market contacts.

Implementing market coverage techniques enables a Practice to stay in touch with its existing (Accounts-Clients) and Prospects to prevent competitive loss or erosion. It also allows the Practice to stay in touch with prospective clients and contacts in target markets to improve future sales results. Good market coverage protects client relationships, protects potential revenues, anticipates client needs, and addresses sales opportunities, including potential referrals.

Market coverage works in concert with the Marketing Mix, Ranking Systems, Treatment Grid, and Client Hierarchy to enhance marketing effectiveness and good resource allocation.

Examples of Market Coverage Program Usage

Client Example – P1 Group

Description

Jack and his wife Kathleen are coded as a P1 Account in the CRM. They have sold and purchased a home with the Agents assistance. Jack and Kathleen have introduced the Agent to their son, Jack Jr, who is engaged to be married and is a future Buyer Prospect. Jack Jr. is also in the P1 group due to his relationship with the family and his pending marriage.

Jack and Kathleen are potential Commercial Real Estate prospects for office space for their business. They also own property in the country, where they maintain a vacation home and may want to acquire more land adjacent to that home.

All are on the Contact list and are scheduled for contact as follows:

Quarterly follow-up personalized call contacts by the Agent. Semi-annual personal luncheon or coffee meetings with the Agent to maintain and grow the relationship. These meetings might also bring attention to them to the office or land opportunities. Monthly letters, cards, or notes regarding numerous and varied issues will be sent. Newsletter mailings to all every quarter will enhance the relationship. Invitations to various events, including VIP Appreciation Events, will be mailed and followed up by the Agent and team.

This Target Market group is targeted for contact in the following manner:

All contacts, approximately forty, in the Target Market group are invited to various events for the Arts in Frisco. At the events, Agent, as Board President, will lead and serve as the Master of Ceremonies. This allows the Agent to be seen in a position of power and prestige in a non-REALTOR® role.

The Agent, as Board President, will make annual personalized contact calls to the various contacts of the Group to inform them of the planned activities of the Association.

As Board President, the Agent will occasionally (when warranted) speak at City Council meetings about issues involving the Arts in the City of Frisco when they warrant his presence.

All Group Contacts are invited to the Annual Arts Gala promoting the Arts in Frisco, where the Agent, Board President, recognizes the most influential group contacts.

As Board President, the Agent emails the group contacts about various Art events.

As a result of this involvement, Agent, as Board President, is invited to participate in the Collin County Arts Project, where he serves on the Governance Committee as a Committee Member. This group meets quarterly and includes high-profile citizens and leaders in the Collin County area.

Neighborhood Target Market

Description

In this example, 200 homes were selected from a neighborhood close to the Agent's office and home. The 200 homes were selected from a neighborhood of 300 or more homes. The 200 selected were prime properties within the neighborhood. The properties selected were not on busy streets and did not back up to commercial land, apartments, or anything that might be a negative marketing consideration.

The 200 homes were identified, and tax records were researched to determine property parameters, ownership, and other important factors, such as a swimming pool or other upgrades and additions that might make the property more desirable. Information that could be used to personalize marketing efforts to the homeowner was a priority in the research and documentation in the CRM.

In this example, the Agent selected the most likely to sell at a higher price, could be seen as outstanding properties when driving the area, and had ownership characteristics that could be identified as owners occupying the home.

The date of acquisition of each property was noted in the CRM so that contact with the homeowners could be personalized when communicating with the owners in whatever manner was selected.

This Target Market group is targeted for contact in the following manner:

The Quarterly Magazine will be distributed to the 200 homeowners with personalized addressing and mailed with first-class postage.

Card mailers or letter mailers with inserts distributed monthly during ten months of the Calendar Year. November and December were not selected as mailing months due to holiday implications. Mailers are to be personalized by personally addressing and mailing by first class mail. All content will be neighborhood specific.

When other agents list homes in the neighborhood, the Agent will seek to hold Open Houses for the listing Agent and market heavily to the neighborhood to increase Open House participation to meet homeowners.

A domain name featuring the name of the neighborhood and an email address with a similar name will be obtained. All contact with the neighborhood will include Smart Agent@WindmillEstateHomes.com and www.WindmillEstateHomes.com with this information and other information to Brand the Agent as a neighborhood specialist.

All information about the neighborhood HOA will be compiled, and the agent will remain knowledgeable about issues affecting the neighborhood's homeowners. Information about the HOA will be distributed to the neighborhood when warranted. The agent will advertise, when possible, in any neighborhood publications or magazines.

When and where possible, the Agent will participate as a sponsor in any events that would allow the Agent to meet and/or be seen at neighborhood activities.

Discussion About Market Coverage Examples

As seen from the example above, all targeted markets are approached using a Mixed Marketing Method, practically and cost-effectively. The personalized approach is a significant consideration in all contact methods.

All direct mail materials will be personalized to include the owners' full names and look for ways in the CRM to integrate property information in the Agent's possession in all marketing efforts. For example, the Agent could include information in the mailers that would allow the recipient to recognize that the Agent has specific knowledge of their property. For example, **"As a pool owner in Windmill Estate, you clearly take great pride in your home."**

Impersonal marketing materials and look-alike marketing materials will be avoided. The templates other agents use will not be used, as they perpetuate the idea that all Agents are similar. When using a Brand Name provided by a large Brokerage, such as "The Renaissance Group," the Agent must modify the mailers to make the marketing pieces different, more professional, and personalized than the Agency provides. They must create interest and provide a reason for the recipient to contact the Agent. The Agent should keep omnipresent the "Information is Power" concept discussed in an earlier chapter. The brand that is being built is you!

Bulk Mail permits will not be used as they do not allow mail returns, and therefore the Agent must keep the CRM updated with current information. It is also important for the recipient to believe they are the only ones who received the mail from the Agent. While this is not true, it doesn't benefit the Agent to look like they are mailing to everyone. It is not personalized to receive mail addressed to someone else. Mail should be personalized to establish that the Agent has knowledge and expertise greater than their competitors. I have found that one way to do this is to leave a space somewhere in the mailer where I can handwrite a short two or three-word message from me to the recipient. Of course, I signed my name under the note.

The unconscious brain recognition concept theorizes that when a homeowner glances at the mail that is personalized to them, the eye reading the information automatically transmits it to the recipient's brain. The recipient's mind is imprinted with the information to establish a familiarity with the party sending the information. This is important when considering the long-term impact of repetitive contact by Direct Mail. The brain seeing the name and number and recognizing familiarity will allow the recipient to subconsciously remember the Agent or the Practice in the future without immediate direct action on the part of the recipient.

This drip marketing approach will attempt to contact the homeowners frequently enough that when a homeowner decides to make a change, such as a move from their home, they will consciously or subconsciously remember the Agent that has been contacting them for several years.

Consistent Market Coverage Approach—Abandoned Marketing Dollars

It is far better for the Agent to market consistently utilizing a Market Coverage approach to assure greater acceptance than to expand marketing efforts and diffuse them by providing poorly designed, copied materials, replicating what other Agents might also be sent to the targeted area. Worse yet, it creates boring marketing materials that do not create interest or provide a reason for the recipient to contact the Agent. Materials that do not have a **"call to action"** can be wasteful due to a limited marketing budget. The Neighborhood Expert Approach demonstrates and differentiates the Agent, increasing the likelihood of being remembered and selected as the Agent becomes more relevant to a Prospect.

When an agent ceases marketing to Target Markets, they abandon the marketing dollars they have spent in the past.

Chapter 35 | Structural Integrity Element: Account Cycling

The modern real estate Practice is a complex business. In a collaborative agent model, a Matrix Management concept is appropriate. The reason is that the Team Member in the Practice has at least two managers. One is the Agent, and the other is the Client. It is understood that a client cannot take disciplinary action but can provide feedback about team member performance. All members require recognition of this fact of the Agent team as the Client is very much like a "Project Manager" and has enormous input and power over everything that happens as the Client controls the environment where the organization functions daily. While the Agent or Practice Manager is the primary manager of all Agent Team Members, the client (homeowner) is given project management responsibility to facilitate Practice success.

When the client (homeowner) is a seller of real estate, the client controls access to the property and everything that happens within that property. They greatly influence everything that happens in selling or purchasing a home. The client's continued happiness with the Agent Team is essential for the Agent and Team's success.

For a real estate buyer, the client controls the schedule and activities of the Agent and the Agent team. Without the Buyer's cooperation, organizational success will be less likely.

To comprehend the operational realities of running a successful real estate practice, it's essential to understand matrix organizational design. But what exactly is matrix management? The indeed.com website offers a straightforward and succinct explanation.

"Matrix management refers to the organizational structure used by companies to distribute employee responsibilities and have them report to multiple managers. The two main chains of command within matrix management are the project manager and the functional manager. In these matrix systems, the project manager has limited amount of authority. This could mean they have no one reporting to them. In a weak matrix, the power shifts to the functional manager, and project managers take on more of a project coordinator role." (2022, Indeed.com Website)

In the weak matrix system described herein, the Agent takes on the functional manager role and is the primary place of power. Because of this Matrix Management structure, there is a potential conflict between the Client and the Team Members, including the Agent. When Team Members don't do what the Client desires, the Agent is frequently brought in to resolve conflict. Managing the Team Members of the Agent becomes paramount to avoid this conflict by making the client happy and avoiding Agent involvement that takes the Agent away from other sales, marketing, and client care-related activities. This results in the utilization of the highest skilled resource in the organization to get involved with and solve simple operational problems and is destructive to the Agent's long-term success.

Therefore, an emphasis must be placed on superior management and training of the Team Members to avoid this situation. Andrew S. Grove writes about this in his book, *High Output Management*. He writes,

"Earlier: I built a case summed up by the key sentence: A manager's output is the output of the organization under his supervision or influence." (1983, p. 157)

One should note the last part of this quote as it mentions "under his supervision or influence." Because the Practice uses a Collaboration Model and a Consultative approach as well as subject area experts that are part of the collaboration team, the Agent and Client, in some respects, jointly manage these participants whether direct subordinates of the Agent or not.

Grove goes on to write,

"Put another way. This means that management is a team activity. But no matter how well a team is put together, or how well it is directed, the team will perform only as well as the individuals on it. In other words, everything we have considered so far is useless unless the members of our team will continually try to offer the best they can do." (1983, p. 157)

Why is all this discussion necessary since the title of this chapter is Account Cycling? Account Cycling requires a Team to accomplish results by using the highest-skilled resources in the Practice in the most productive way. This will allow the Practice to focus the agent's time on the highest opportunity accounts while at the same time being in frequent contact in an organized and systematic way to ensure great client care being provided to all clients.

Account Cycling—Resource Utilization

Account Cycling is used to execute a sophisticated and complex marketing plan and requires client relationship management software and people who know how to use that software.

Account Cycling schedules contact activities systematically to maximize the best use of resources, particularly for the real estate Agent. It works with Market Coverage to ensure that all accounts in the Client Hierarchy are contacted frequently enough and with the correct resource and message to maximize revenue potential.

Account Cycling integrates with the Client Hierarchy, Target Market Stimulation Programs, Market Coverage Program, and Client Treatment Grid, as well as the Ranking System, to ensure that Clients and Prospects are contacted in a systematic way to protect the Clients from competitor efforts to capture them.

Contacting Clients and Prospects systematically and practically assures that the Agent and Practice will remain active in the Clients' or Prospects' minds, increasing business opportunities. In short, it does not allow the Clients and Prospects targeted to forget the Agent and the Practice regarding their current or future real estate needs.

Account Cycling activities are made possible using a CRM where the Agent and the Agents Team Members can be prompted (reminded) of an assigned task on various client accounts regularly to ensure that the contact plan is executed in concert with the Treatment Grid. When a real estate Practice has a so-phisticated marketing system and seeks to reach Clients, Prospects, and Target Market contacts frequently, the process of doing so is greatly simplified with a robust CRM program.

The use of Account Cycling is best explained in the following examples, describing how it can be used.

P1 Accounts – Account Cycling Example:

At the beginning of the Plan Year, it was determined by the Agent that there are 25 P1 Accounts coded as such in the Client Hierarchy. Each account has, on average, two Key Decision Makers or Influencers. A goal was set in the Treatment Grid to contact each of the 50 Client contacts by "TeleConnect Marketing" four times per year.

The plan stipulates that each Client contact will be contacted once each quarter. This would result in 25 accounts with two contacts on average receiving four calls per year, totaling 200 calls from the Agent and Team. The average time estimated to prepare for each call and attempt to reach will average 30 min-utes per call. The time to properly document the CRM and schedule follow-up activities after each call is approximately 10 minutes.

The total time per call will therefore average 40 minutes per call. Two hundred calls at 40 minutes each is 8,000 minutes per year or 133 hours per year. This is an average of 160 minutes per week using a 50-week year for making calls. The Agent making the calls would average making four calls per week, and the calls could be made with some flexibility in timing as determined by the Agent. The Agent will receive a contact-specific reminder two days before each scheduled call. This is entirely automated in the CRM and designed to make the Agent highly productive and focused on these high-priority contacts likely to use services or refer prospects. The calls will help maintain the relationship with these high-priority accounts and protect them from competitors reaching out to these Clients by direct mail, email, or mass advertising. Sometimes, the client will encounter other Agents at activities in their neighborhood or place of worship. By coding an address as "Competitive Agent," the Practice can ensure that marketing materials are not being sent to competitors.

In the CRM, an automated Tactical Plan would be scheduled before the beginning of the plan year, specifying each call to be made weekly. This schedule will remind the agent of each planned call in the CRM and allow for preparing reports showing which calls were completed. Each call would be documented. The Agent will determine the subject or reason for each round of contacts before beginning the quarterly contact process.

Target Market Account Cycling Example:

The implementation of account cycling for managing the marketing to selected Target Markets is best managed with a CRM. The following example details how the Account Cycling Concept targets a geographic Target Market.

Geographic Target Market (Neighborhood Luxury Home Market)

Two hundred and fifty homes have been targeted in a neighborhood near the Agent's office and home. The plan is to contact these 250 homes semi-monthly by direct mail. This Drip Marketing approach is part of a tactical plan initiated by the Practice to increase agent awareness in the neighborhood targeted. It will be combined with other strategies and tactics, including HOA involvement and Community Service Involvement.

The homes will be contacted by card mailers, letters, and/or personalized notes from the Agent. A list of the 250 homeowners was entered into the CRM, and the Contact Type of these homeowners was selected to be Oak Knoll Homeowners Group. The tax rolls were used to obtain the names of the homeowners so that the mailer could be personalized. The Agent obtained a domain name to utilize for the marketing approach, which was www.OakKnollFamilies.com

The Agent obtained an email address of SmartAgent@oakknollfamilies.com, and the domain name and email address will be used to demonstrate the neighborhood specialization by the Agent.

The 250 homes will be mailed information six times during the plan year. Feb, April, June, August, October, and December were selected as the months of contact. All mailing pieces will target the neighborhood and include the neighborhood-specific domain and email names above. The mailing pieces will always include the domain name, email address, Agent name, Agent phone number, Agent Title, Practice, designations, and logo, as well as all required logos and notices necessary to comply with real estate ethics guidelines and rules. This plan will result in 1,500 mail pieces being sent during the plan year.

The benefit of Account Cycling is the ability to proactively schedule and manage skilled resources to assure that the Agent is highly productive and targeted on the highest priority accounts with the most potential for revenues and profits to the Practice.

In the early development of a Practice, the process is significantly simplified. As the system is implemented, it is organized to manage a more extensive contact program in ongoing years. Efforts spent on this process early will allow for a learning period and require an understanding and knowledge of the workings of the CRM, which is the practice's primary scheduling and management tool. The importance of CRM to the effective execution of a marketing plan cannot be overstated.

Where some real estate Groups utilize additional Agents who are Group Agents, it is not unusual for a top-producing Agent that is not part of a Group to have one or more Personal Assistants or other Team Members to assist them in maximizing Agent productivity. The Renaissance Group operation consisted of two real estate licensed Managing Partners, two assistants, and one licensed assistant. All these resources were tasked with maximizing the personal productivity of the lead Agent, Partner, and Broker. This allowed the lead agents to spend 80% or more of their time on consulting and real estate sales activities.

PART FOUR
LAUNCHING THE PRACTICE

CHAPTER 36 | DEVELOPING THE "BUSINESS MODEL"

Once the foundation, framework, and operating systems of the real estate Practice have been visualized by the Agent, the next step is to envision a Business Model that will serve as a guideline to move things forward. The Business Model is a conceptual blueprint that will provide the Agent with a clear approach. This will ensure the Agent effectively implements the necessary activities and efforts to achieve their dreams and aspirations.

To begin, the Agent must transform their vision into a written outline, which will be called the Business Model. This plan will summarize organizational, marketing, and client relations philosophies. The Agent can develop a comprehensive Marketing Plan, Marketing Budget and Business Plan from this model. These documents will provide a clear outline of the necessary steps that need to be taken to bring the Agent's visions to fruition.

The business model guides the agent to make the Practice a complete organizational plan ready to be put into words. The documents for creating the real estate practice can be written from these ideas and objectives. The Agent and their Team will be able to utilize the Business Model and associated plans to guide their efforts, ensuring that their Practice operates smoothly and efficiently. By taking these steps, the Agent will be well-positioned to achieve their goals and build a successful real estate Practice.

Definition of a Business Model

A Business Model is a written conceptual outline for how an Agent envisions a Practice will operate. It defines and outlines the goals and objectives as well as strategies of the business. It is a living and breathing conceptual document in that it will be modified frequently depending on the events, successes, disappointments, circumstances, and market changes that occur in the future.

The Business Model is essential in developing the Marketing and Business Plan. It establishes the nature and culture of the Practice. It identifies its reason for existence, primary strategies, sub-strategies, tactical plans, target markets, and profit centers that will be used to track and measure the Practice's success.

It puts into writing the philosophies, standards of performance, and general goals for the Practice at a point in time. It begins to change immediately after creation and is modified continuingly as other plans are created. This Business Model description explains the actions and plans that will be followed to achieve the Agents objectives.

The business model describes what the Practice does and what services it will provide to the targeted audiences of the Practice. It identifies where the Practice will operate, to whom it will provide these services, and how it will position itself to compete. It is a proprietary document.

The Business Model is the inspiration piece to outline the Marketing Plan, which can be created before the completed Business Plan. Allowing the Agent to create the Marketing Plan, which should be the most critical and costly element of operating a real estate Practice, enables an agent to understand what must be budgeted for and the staffing requirements necessary for executing the plan.

This allows for creating the budget, staffing plan, technology plan, accounting, financial management plan, and other essential pieces in the Business Plan document.

Without a Business Model, it is almost impossible to write coherent and specific Mission Statements, Financial Goals, Non-Financial Goals, and Marketing Plan that includes strategies, sub-strategies, and tactical plans to accomplish the business's mission. It indicates what legal documents will be needed to move forward.

Perhaps one should consider what the Business Model "Is Not" before proceeding.

The Model does not need to be a polished paper that is presented to investors for their examination and review of what the Agent plans. It may have ambiguity and questions that are left unanswered. It is for the Agent and is a malleable plan that anticipates frequent changes.

It does not need to be finite. It can be open-ended in some areas as long as the overall concept of what is envisioned is explained for review and modification by the Agent. These reviews and modifications are done annually. Through revelation and discovery, the Agent will evolve the plan to cope with the many changes of direction experienced.

The Business Model is a written statement of the vision of the agent.

While this book is written for others, the Business Model for an Agent is not written for investors, partners, team members, advisors, or others. It is written for the Agent. It is **never complete...**

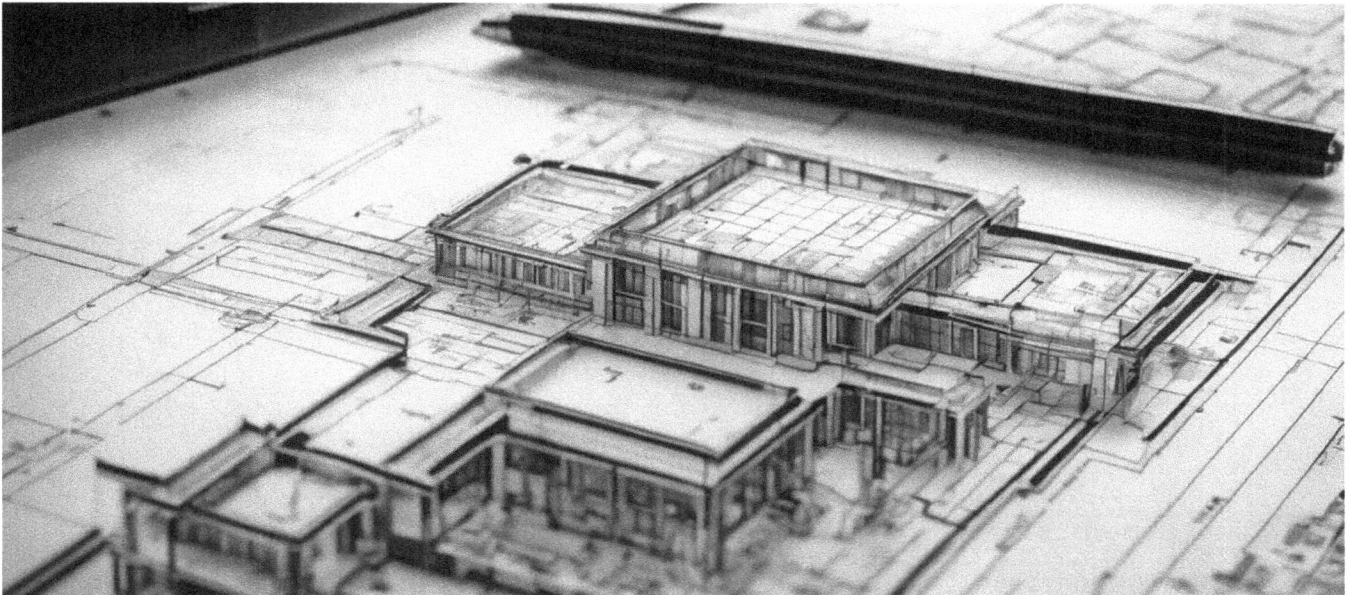

CHAPTER 37 | LAUNCHING THE PRACTICE: EXAMPLE BUSINESS MODEL

Sonny Moyers, dba, The Renaissance Group (TRG), formerly The O'Dea Moyers Group

The Renaissance Group provides Residential Brokerage Services, Commercial Brokerage Services, and Consulting services to clients in selected geographic and target markets in the DFW Metropolitan Area. The primary profit centers are Residential Real Estate Brokerage Income, Commercial Real Estate Brokerage Income, and Consulting Services Income.

Profit Center One

The Residential Real Estate Brokerage Profit Center includes Buyers and Sellers of homes and investment properties in the North Dallas, Plano, McKinney, Frisco, and Prosper areas. The homes sold will generally have a value greater than $350,000. The median home price listed in the target market area is approximately $217,000. Targeted neighborhoods include Starwood in Frisco, Willow Bend in Plano, Stonebridge Ranch in McKinney, and the Windsong Ranch Neighborhood in Prosper. Buyers, Investors, and Sellers will be targeted, and a marketing mix will be utilized to reach each Target Market audience.

While the Practice will not target Prospects outside this geographic marketing area, it will accept referrals and other business opportunities that come to the attention of the Practice through referrals, marketing, and public awareness.

Profit Center Two

The Commercial Real Estate Brokerage Profit Center area includes tenant representation of office space users leased in large office buildings. These clients will utilize office space greater than 15,000 square feet and seek offices in the Dallas North Tollway, Stemmons Freeway, North Central Expressway Corridors, and their connecting roadways in the DFW Metropolitan Area. The office space users in the shared office and business center industry will be targeted if they operate in the target areas.

Profit Center Three

The Consulting Services Profit Center provides advice to large companies and Commercial Office tenants or who seek assistance with Landlord lease problems and who maintain offices in the Corridors mentioned above. This mainly includes tenants who are shared office operators and business center operators where the Agent has established relationships with the owners or operators.

Client Benefit Statement One

Utilizing a single point of contact approach, this Practice is a provider who can be retained for obtaining real estate services in Residential and Commercial Real Estate and Real Estate Consulting. This allows the Practice to assist clients with their homes, investment properties, office space, and other real estate needs, including problem identification and resolution.

Client Benefit Statement Two

The advantage of the individual Managing Partners, Judi O'Dea and Sonny Moyers, and their varied and unique skills and abilities will combine with the added benefit of having both partners available to provide a higher level of services to the client than its competitors. This approach will be promoted in all marketing messages and presentations to the public. The Practice will be "The Singular Solution" for all its clients' real estate needs.

Client Benefit Statement Three

All marketing messages and presentations emphasize the ability to do all things in real estate while providing the most professional services available in the industry. The idea that a client can work with a trusted advocate in all matters regarding real estate and not have to depend upon multiple sources of support will be a primary marketing strategy. The Managing Partners' advanced education, experience, and different personalities will be emphasized to provide core competencies in all real estate matters where the Practice provides services.

Client Benefit Statement Four

The Practice will position itself in the marketplace as the superior marketing organization and emphasize a collaborative and consultative way of working with clients. This and superior marketing services will differentiate the company in quality representation and professionalism. Its Matrix Management structure will allow the Practice to provide a level of service that clients embrace.

Client Benefit Statement Five

Positioning itself with the public as the provider with a personal commitment to always putting clients first in all situations will differentiate the agent. This fiduciary relationship aspect of the service will be promoted in all written and verbal presentations about the Practice.

Client Benefit Statement Six

The Renaissance Group (TRG) is not a discount Broker. The professional service fee (commission) structure will be among the highest in the industry. The Practice will promote that while it is not the least expensive provider, it is the most valuable provider available to its clients. One marketing strategy of the Practice is to make an overwhelming and powerful marketing presentation so that the Prospect will feel psychologically compelled to choose TRG.

Client Benefit Statement Seven

A marketing strategy in Residential Real Estate for homeowners selling their homes will be to provide superior marketing tools that are differentiated from the competitors in the real estate industry. As a result, clients will expect and be willing to pay a substantial fee for the products and services offered by the Practice. It is recognized that providing these higher-level services will require TRG to invest in marketing systems and programs that are more costly and can only be paid for if TRG is not a discount broker.

Client Benefit Statement Eight

The marketing strategy in the Commercial Real Estate area will be built upon the ability to demonstrate that Sonny Moyers has a unique experience in consulting and providing real estate brokerage services to large tenants in large buildings and that his knowledge of leases and business concepts far exceeds those offered by Commercial Brokerage competitors. Sonny will prove this superior competence by demonstrating a deep knowledge of commercial building lease contracts and creative space design capabilities.

Client Benefit Statement Nine

The marketing strategy in the Consulting Area will be based upon the Managing Partner experience as a General Marketing Consultant with worldwide experience providing a unique insight into the strategies and tactics of marketing. A Consulting profit center is a developmental tool for creating other business opportunities.

Client Benefit Statement Ten

TRG's management and organizational structure will be focused on allowing the Managing Partners to spend a large percentage of their available time dealing with and working with clients. TRG will incorporate a Matrix Management Weak Structure concept into its organizational design to do this.

Client Benefit Statement Eleven

TRG will seek to position itself as an indispensable asset in helping clients and prospects solve problems regarding their real estate needs. The Consultative Problem Solver and Collaborative Agent approach will encourage the clients of TRG to refer members from their spheres of influence.

Client Benefit Statement Twelve

Community Service is an important element in the success of TRG as it will provide the opportunity to establish credibility in the markets served and further the relationship of the Practice with the principal Broker and The Renaissance Group. This Community Service area is not seen as a profit center but as a marketing tool to establish name identification in target markets where the Managing Partners do not have a developed reputation or brand recognition.

PRIMARY BUSINESS STRATEGIES

Primary Business Strategy 1. - Superior Client Care

A primary strategy is a commitment to superior Client Care while working in a consultative and collaborative manner. This is a constant consideration in every activity of the Practice. It is envisioned that the Group will provide services at a level that other competitors in the industry cannot equal in kind or quality. While personal contact and superior Client Care are disappearing, the Practice will return to placing "Clients First" and emphasize a return to excellence in personal service.

A commitment is made to providing superior service from every Team Member. This includes returning phone calls on the same day as received. When Clients are promised to receive materials, the promise will be kept. If scheduling an open house, a Team Member will coordinate activities closely with the Client and remind the Client before the event that there is an event scheduled. This includes complex activities such as following up on showing activity or providing Buyers with new information about properties in their search area.

TRG will provide continual contact by integrating TeleConnect Marketing on a regular and planned basis. When negotiating a contract offer, when representing a Client, the Practice Team will focus on providing personal communications with the Client regarding the progress of the contract offer.

Team Members within the Practice will be committed to ensuring a concerted, collaborative effort making everyone in the group part of the sales and service process. This Team Selling Concept will encourage Team Member interaction and motivate Team Members to feel they are essential to the Practice's success. Client contact and follow-up procedures will ensure that the Client receives frequent "contact" from various Team Members. This will allow the Team to increase the number of contacts from our organization with the Client and satisfy them with the overall commitment to Client Care that is provided.

All Team Members will use a collaborative approach when dealing with a Client to ensure Client involvement and satisfaction. This collaborative process will allow the Agent to involve the Client in more decisions and planning ideas to confirm that they agree with all activities and plans for meeting their needs and wants. This involvement will ensure client and prospect satisfaction and help them achieve their goals. TRG believes most clients quit working with a service provider because they feel unappreciated. TRG will make a concerted effort to demonstrate how much the client is appreciated, and TRG will constantly and frequently express its thanks for the opportunity to assist clients.

Primary Business Strategy 2. - Maximizing Profitability

The Practice is founded to operate at the maximum level of profitability while always putting the client first. TRG will focus on the highest profit income categories first but will not shirk responsibility to help a client if the client needs assistance in a less profitable area of real estate. The client's needs will guide the Team's actions, and the Team will trust that this loyalty to the client will be returned many times over.

In the real estate business, there are two primary measures of success: sales volume and profitability. The business model for the Group establishes that the primary objective and goal is profitability, and while volume is important, profitability would not be sacrificed solely to increase sales volume. The Practice culture will be established so that daily operations will focus on profitability, client satisfaction, and success.

The profit center areas of the Practice will be tracked separately to focus on the most profitable business first. By funding tactical plans based on their profit contribution in the high-profit areas and evaluating the cost of executing each tactical plan, the Practice will prioritize actions to ensure that the highest income and profit activities are completed first, thus assuring higher profitability.

Tenant representation in large buildings, a part of the Commercial Real Estate profit center, is predicted to be the highest profitability income category. The second most profitable business category will be the representation of buyers in residential real estate. The third highest income profitability area will be income from residential listing opportunities. It is recognized that residential listing opportunities often result in numerous other opportunities even though providing services to listings is less profitable in the total picture of profit contribution by category of business activity.

It is recognized that in the real estate industry, one opportunity for service might create another income opportunity in a related real estate profit center. When working with a listing opportunity and where success is achieved in selling a home, this success will open the door to representing the client on purchasing a new home through buyer representation. For these reasons, client service and needs will not be ignored when looking at profitability by income area. An opportunity in a lesser income category might open the door for a higher profit transaction in a different area. It is believed that capturing a client in residential real estate is less complicated than capturing a Client in Commercial Real Estate. When evaluating an account, looking at each income category will lead to developing other opportunities and stimulating new business in multiple profit centers.

Primary Business Strategy 3. - Maximizing Use of Skilled Resources

A Primary Strategy is a belief that every organization has critical high-skilled resources that must be maximized for the business to achieve maximum profitability. These highly skilled resources must be utilized in the best possible way if the Practice is to achieve the goal outlined in the business and marketing plan. It is believed that the Managing Partners are the highest skilled resources in the Practice and must be protected from involvement in non-essential non-sales activities.

This will allow them to be available to focus on client relationships and transactions. These highest-skilled resources must be assigned the highest-skilled activities and protected by not assigning lower-skilled activities to Team Members who do not have the essential skills and talents to be given the higher-skilled activities.

The Managing Partner's sales time will be maximized by utilizing multiple resources to keep the Partners from involvement in non-sales activities. It is accepted that the Practice has limited resources and therefore seeks to implement a Team Selling Concept to capitalize on shared resources from the affiliated broker. These resources are not an additional expense. It is believed that this can be accomplished by providing the Broker resources with motivational reasons to assist the Practice in its marketing and sales efforts.

Primary Business Strategy 4. - Business Ethics & Clients First in All Matters

A Primary Strategy and ethos of the Practice is the principle that the client will be served in a manner consistent with the highest real estate ethics. The client, and those dealt with daily, will be considered first in all the operations and activities of the Practice. This will be done by remembering that the Practice charges among the highest fees and that profitability will be maintained despite higher costs due to increased Client loyalty and more referral activity.

A slogan is created: "Clients First, Whatever It Takes, That's What We Do!" This concept is more than just a slogan but a guiding principle when considering Client Care. By putting the client first and communicating this message to the target audiences, the client is assured that whatever is in their best interest will always be chosen by the Practice rather than doing the best thing for TRG. In everything done, appreciation for and respect for the client is paramount. This approach is consistent with the real estate ethics and code of ethics within the National Association of Realtors and the Texas Real Estate Commission. It is theorized that when clients believe that the Practice places them first, they will be less reluctant to allow the Agent to represent multiple parties in a transaction.

Primary Business Strategy 5. - Premiere Marketing Organization

A Primary Strategy of the Practice is to focus every daily effort on ensuring that the Group is the premier marketing organization in the real estate industry and that the Practice and its principals will differentiate themselves from others. This will be accomplished through the professionalism and quality of the Practice's marketing systems, client deliverables, and communications system methods.

The concept that "Professionalism Is Synonymous with Value" will be a constant consideration in everything done. Client support materials, such as marketing booklets for each home listed for sale, must demonstrate more professionalism than those provided by competitors. The technology chosen will provide an advantage in this effort by offering capabilities that others don't have or fail to use effectively. Publishing software will create marketing materials for a home and the Internet that are superior to any of those that competitors have available. This will benchmark the practice's professionalism and differentiate TRG from its competitors, particularly in marketing and client care.

When dealing with clients seeking to purchase a home, the Practice marketing program will provide a customized "Finding a Home Guidebook" to the Client. This document will enable the Practice to span the differences between a product sale approach and the service first orientation of the Practice. The book will be used as a sales tool and incentive to a Buyer, causing them to sign a buyer representation agreement when requested.

The marketing materials, such as Letters, Mailer Cards, Flyers, and even emails and text messages, will be superior to our competitors in design and execution. They will not be like other Agents and, therefore, will seldom be the standardized materials from the Broker. Contact opportunities will not be wasted with poorly written communications that fail to present the right image of the Practice and its Partners. By gaining competitive intelligence about others, TRG will understand how to differentiate TRG from competitors. The materials will not be standardized industry documents that many agents use but customized, one-of-a-kind materials that personalize messaging with the client base. Each marketing message will present a specific Prospect benefit rather than just a braggadocios message, and each message will be targeted to the individually unique client.

The TRG website will be comprehensive and highly professional while demonstrating superior marketing skills. The website must appeal to existing and prospective clients and focus on client benefits and value. It will focus heavily on the use of testimonials and client comments and support. It is recognized that the Website is a Passive Marketing Activity. Nothing is accomplished unless someone visits the site. As a result, the Practice implements a Marketing Mix strategy to drive traffic to the website.

The website will be a vital strategy component to differentiate the Practice from competitors. The website will be used at the Collaboration Hub when making presentations to Prospects and Clients to establish marketing superiority over competitors.

Preparing marketing materials such as Property Brochures to be used in homes listed for sale will differentiate the Practice from competitors and demonstrate TRG's superior marketing skills. In addition, these deliverables will stimulate buyer interest in a listed property and demonstrate to Agents and homeowners the marketing expertise of the Practice. A goal for the Practice is to ensure that visitors, Buyers, and Agents will take marketing materials with them.

Primary Business Strategy 6. - Technology Innovator & Early Adopter

A Primary Strategy is a commitment to innovation and new technology when tested and proven to be a viable tool for the Practice. Technology will not be chosen because it is unique and exciting but rather because it can be shown to be effective or improve client care and productivity and increase profitability. Technology and innovation will be adopted to achieve the objectives and goals of the business. Careful review and analysis of all technological developments will allow the Practice to adopt meaningful ideas but not waste resources and money on ideas simply because they are new. While new technology will be embraced, it must be proven more profitable and provide better service. This would include adopting new technologies to achieve higher profitability while maintaining a superior level of Client Care.

TRG will be an early adapter of technology if it can be confirmed that technology will provide a benefit either in marketing, Client Care, or productivity. One piece of technology that will be a significant part of the sales and marketing strategy of the Practice is the Collaboration Hub that will be in the offices of TRG. This Hub will allow the Practice to differentiate itself from competitors in a high-tech way centered on great Client Care via collaboration. The Group can passively demonstrate its commitment to state-of-the-art technology by making presentations at the Collaboration Hub.

Primary Business Strategy 7. - Marketing Mix to Maximize Marketing Reach

A Primary Strategy of the Practice is the adoption of marketing mix concepts. The Practice will utilize strategic marketing partners to boost and maximize marketing reach and the ability to communicate with the target markets using varied methods and messages. Many target audience members are believed to be best reached with different messages over time rather than just one or two communication methods.

All methods of communicating with the target audiences will be considered, including direct mail, email, text mail, print advertising, personal contact (TeleConnect Marketing), association involvement, HOA involvement, school involvement, community service involvement, social media marketing, and other messaging methods that may be identified in the future in a concerted programmed way to maximize market coverage.

TRG will rank various contacts in a Client Hierarchy into categories and determine a treatment criterion in a treatment grid, assigning the types and frequency of contact to assure market coverage, thus ensuring that each contact is reached consistently to maximize their potential.

Primary Business Strategy 8. - Limited Resource Limitations Drive Decisions

The eighth Primary Strategy is the recognition that capital and resources are limited. No business has the resources and money to do everything; therefore, the Scarcity of Resources must be considered in selecting tactics and actions.

Funding every activity imaginable is impossible as there will never be sufficient resources to fund everything that could be tried. For this reason, scarce resources and capital must be expended based on the ability to immediately create more capital and obtain more resources while growing the company's profits.

With limited resources, it is necessary to precisely target marketing activities and tactics to maximize the revenue potential. By linking tactics and activities to the strategies that have been developed, the company will be able to avoid the expenditure of resources on risky tactics and activities that do not drive the Practice toward the achievement of objectives in the shortest amount of time.

The most effective and best resource will be used to contact clients regularly. If a Team Member is best suited to contact a client due to their knowledge or personality fit, it would be preferable to have that Team Member lead the contact efforts, thereby improving TRG's positioning with the client.

Primary Business Strategy 9. - Community Service Emphasis

Community Service is a bedrock of The Renaissance Group's success. It is a principle for "Giving Back" to the Community and improving the lives of its citizens.

The Strategy of a commitment to community service provides a platform upon which the Practice can reach clients, high-profile individuals, target market audiences, and the public to build the name and identity of the Practice. The community service strategy would be executed without an effort to promote or grow the Practice. In this manner, the Practice will avoid target audiences perceiving that Community Service is the practice's marketing strategy. The Practice will conduct Community Service activities with a blind eye to the promotion opportunity and an understanding that this would insulate the Practice and Agents from the claim that Team Members are solely doing something for the community for the benefit it would provide to the Practice.

It is believed that a business needs to have some involvement in community service in the communities and markets they operate within and that by doing so, there will be benefits that are derived without any effort to promote. The Frisco Association for the Arts was chosen to provide community service and build name recognition within the community. By volunteering first as a worker, TRG hopes to be allowed to rise in the organization and have a position of prominence. As a Board Member and then later a Board President, the Agent and Practice can be in the public view and be seen as a community-oriented business owner. By never commenting in any public forum about real estate or the Practice, the Agent can avoid community members believing that the efforts were made for the self-benefit of the Agent or Practice.

Communicating with the Association participants using a mixed message approach distinctly partitioned from the Association involvement will make it known that the Practice provides real estate services. The Renaissance Group will optimize this community involvement and, as a result, will be positively viewed by its target audiences.

Participating in Community Service activities will allow the Agent to be in public view and become known to observers.

Primary Business Strategy 10. - Sophisticated Sales & Marketing Management Approach

The Practice will use sophisticated interpersonal communications concepts and advanced account management programs to build the Practice. This approach will recognize the Client as the primary source of revenue for long-term results and will devote its efforts to capturing and managing client accounts to maximize the existing income and profit potential.

To accomplish this, the Practice will attempt to be highly visible to the audiences it seeks to reach. The Managing Partners must seek ways to be highly visible to Clients and the selected Target Market groups. The Managing Partners (Agents) do not have the connections with the marketplace that many competitor Agents have. We do not have children in the local schools. We do not have large extended families in the area and do not have many things in common with many of the targeted audience members.

There must be a way to find methods to be visible to the target audiences. Therefore, TRG must find ways of gaining visibility to ensure its targeted audiences can see it most favorably. TRG will be visible to the target audience and target Community involvement, HOA involvement, and Community Service to accomplish this objective. Serving on REALTOR® Advisory Boards for communities in the Target Market Area is another pathway to increase its visibility.

Summary

These are the concepts of the business model for The Renaissance Group. They will be used to write Public and Private Mission Statements, define short and long-term objectives, Create Marketing Strategies and Sub-Strategies, design Tactical Plans, and create a Marketing Plan that can be incorporated into the organization's overall Business Plan and budgets.

CHAPTER 38 | LAUNCHING THE PRACTICE: MARKETING CONCEPTS REFINED

Carol & The Cats

Carol Langston was a luxury property homeowner living in our neighborhood. We had never met in person. Carol called and spoke to our assistant, and upon being notified of the call, we called her back within the hour. She explained that she was considering selling her home and wanted us to visit with her about what she could expect to realize from a sale. She was very clear that she had not decided whether or not to sell but wanted to consider the possibilities. Many listing prospects say this as a way of reserving the right not to choose the agent or do nothing.

We met with Carol for the first time and presented her with a small package of Godiva truffles as a thank-you gift. This made her smile brightly. The visit was over one hour long, with much time spent talking about the market and her situation. She loved her home, yet for some reason, wanted a change of atmosphere. She provided us with a printed survey of the property, a list of upgrades she had made, and a brief description of what she felt were the most desirable aspects of her home.

Carol had been receiving our mail for several years. She had seen our many signs throughout the neighborhood and knew we were active in Starwood. She was a cat lover and had two beautiful cats that were her family. Carol was personable and had significant experience working in a large corporation as a high-level executive, and we clicked with her from the very beginning. We agreed on a follow-up meeting to share our analysis and provide a detailed presentation of our marketing program. We sought a meeting at the office, but Carol insisted that we meet at her home so she would not have to inconvenience the cats.

Several days later, we again met with Carol and began our carefully planned and personalized marketing presentation for her home. We included much of the information she provided us in our first meeting. Carol was open and engaging, listened to our presentation, and shared her thoughts and ideas with us freely and openly. She was a very talkative person, and we both sensed that she was very positive about us. After agreeing to list her property and signing the appropriate representation documents, I casually asked her about the other agents she had considered. She indicated that there had been little consideration of others. Taking a chance at her openness, I asked her what had caused her to choose us.

She removed our *Starwood Neighborhood News Magazine* from a folder she had gathered about various agents and showed us our dog's photo. In the folder were copies of prior marketing pieces we had sent, as well as tax information we sent each year. The folder was several inches thick.

She answered, **"Well, I knew from receiving the marketing pieces you sent that you were very professional and successful in Starwood. I saw many of your signs and visited several open houses for properties you were selling. The Starwood News Magazine that you sent to Starwood also got my attention. I read the article in your magazine about your dog, Paris. Her picture was so cute, and I felt that we would get along well and that you would be the kind of people I would enjoy working with. How old is Paris?"**

Connecting with People

Marketing is about messaging and connecting with people on a human level. Marketing is branding and creating a persona about you. In our case, we were seen as highly professional, accomplished, and above all else, human.

Carol became a great friend and client, provided testimonial letters to support us, and the fee we earned from selling her home funded our marketing programs in Starwood for more than a few years. Her referrals and support were instrumental in our continued success in Starwood. We never failed to thank her when we spoke to her. She was invited to our special VIP Appreciation events, where we could stay in touch with her. She still lives in the same home she purchased after we sold her home in Starwood.

Marketing requires talent, discipline, planning, creativity, and a keen understanding of the target market to be spoken to. Empathy for others and their life situations and circumstances is of great value. Success in real estate ultimately depends on applying human creativity and skill in relating to others. The skill required to match the agent's personality to the marketing message is essential. The construction of a Practice should create a unique and differentiating approach to providing services and value to clients. This differentiated image is combined with the personal magnetism of the Agent and causes people to reach out and connect.

Marketing systematically provides multiple exposures to a target audience that reveals the agent's knowledge and unique skills, brand, and personality. Marketing increases Practice revenues and profitability while building long-lasting relationships.

Timed interrelated strategies and actions are designed to ensure a thorough understanding of the likely prospect's needs and want. This allows the consultative Agent to provide solutions that benefit the client and justify the Agent's existence. This is directly tied to the Mission Statement in the agent's marketing plan.

Profitability Measured

We aimed to generate maximum revenues at a minimum expense while providing superior services with the highest professional business ethics. Our goal was to establish client trust, achieved through personalized efforts and dedicated integrity as a real estate Agent.

Marketing requires awareness of prospect needs and wants and the changing real estate market and macro trends that emerge over time. Responses to those changes and the resulting marketing requirements needed are identified and communicated promptly. Marketing demands constant personal improvement of those individuals working in the Practice, thereby improving the services provided while always seeking to become and remain "Great." It is not enough to be just Good at satisfying Clients...

Three Beliefs

I.   Every Prospect and Practice Team Member has a unique potential for self-improvement, development, and contribution, which will help lead them to self-actualization.

II. The Agent must understand their own self-actualization goals to find happiness and reward in providing excellent client care, even when the agent has no immediate and direct financial benefit.

III. Each Client has distinct needs, wants, and unique communications preferences, and the Agent must bend to the Client's needs and wants to maximize the relationship that can be nourished. At the same time, the Practice strives to maintain the highest ethical standards as specified by the Real Estate Code of Ethics.

"But what makes the salesman himself tick is vital self-intelligence. Without it, the salesman can easily become his own worst enemy. It will not be his customer's resistance that defeats him, it will be his deficiencies." Hanan, Cribbin, Heiser– Consultative Selling, (1973, p. 54)

Through collaboration and communication, an environment is created where the Client is comfortable and trusting of the Agent, and, as a result, this positions the Agent as a Consultant to the Client rather than a salesperson.

"When the salesman reveals his authentic self, he permits his customer to feel comfortable with him. He also puts the customer under subtle pressure to respond in kind. This creates reciprocity and reinforcement, which are vital to negotiation. Every time the salesman and his customer tradeoff feedback freely and openly, they reinforce the team basis of the consultative relationship." Hanan, Cribbin, Heiser– Consultative Selling, (1973, p. 60)

The Ultimate Goal

The primary objective of any marketing effort is to achieve three things: to be noticed, respected, and remembered. This way, when a prospect needs the services offered by the Agent, they will be able to recall the Agent's name and reach out to them. Without accomplishing this goal, the Practice risks wasting both energy and money on marketing activities that do not produce the desired reputation.

All marketing activities must answer the following questions.

1. Does the marketing activity differentiate the Agent from other providers?
2. Will the Agent be respected because of the marketing message?
3. Is it likely that the prospect will remember the Agent and know how to contact the Agent in the future?

The consultative collaborative salesperson must see the prospect and client with their eyes and brain and listen to the prospect and client with their ears and heart.

PART FIVE
Moving On And Moving Up…

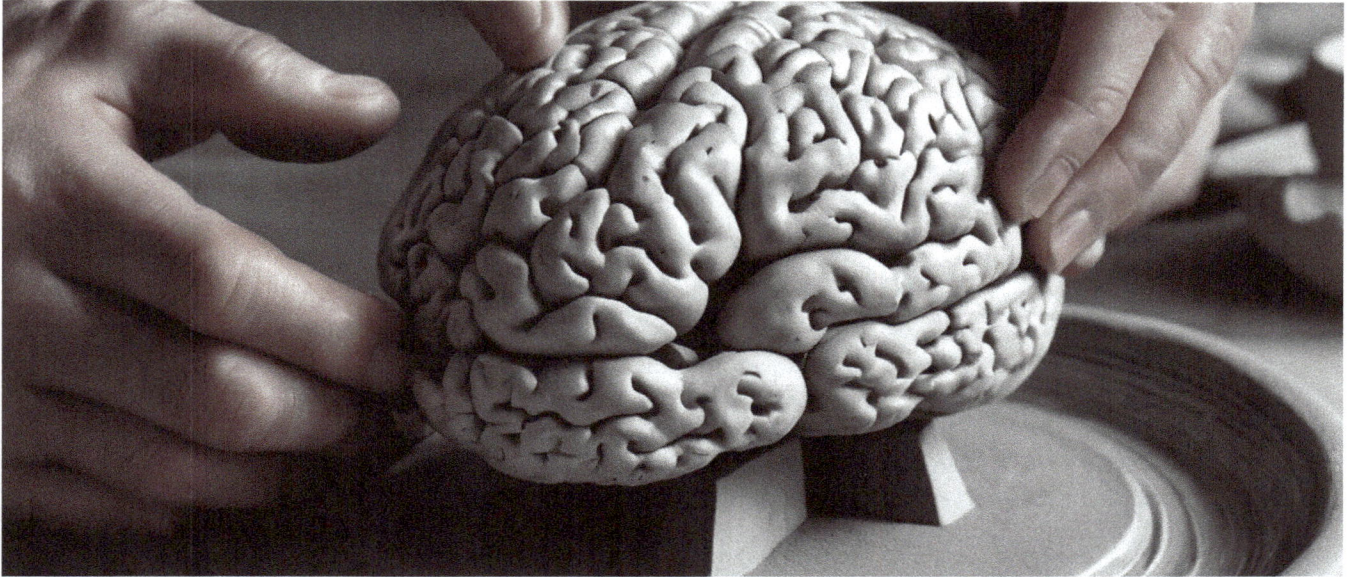

CHAPTER 39|MOVING ON:
CHANGING THE MALLEABLE BRAIN...

I wrote in earlier chapters that after understanding more, many might find it necessary to rewire their brains to find a different way of relating to and communicating with their clientele. What do I mean when I write, "REWIRE THE BRAIN?"

The book, *Rewire Your Brain* by John Arden is particularly insightful in this discussion. Rewiring the Brain will allow you to effectively reach more people in a "people first" way.

In the book *Rewire Your Brain*, John Arden writes,

> *"This system includes mirror neurons, spindle cells, the orbital frontal cortex, and the anterior cingulate. I'll describe how these neural systems help to build relationships and empathy." (2010, p. ix.)*

Social conditioning in our society regarding how a salesperson works is a significant reason that rewiring the brain may be necessary. Rewiring the brain takes knowledge and discipline but can be vastly rewarding. This rewiring helps correct the way the typical Agent works as a product-oriented salesperson and enables them to work in a manner that will build better relationships, connect with people in a personal way, differentiate themselves from competitors, and establish a brand and identity that is perceived as collaborative and consultative.

Learning about the brain and how to rewire it will allow you to understand how to cope with the competition, stresses, challenges, and emotions prevalent in real estate. Arden writes,

> *"You'll learn about the calming yet vitalizing role of attention, your prefrontal cortex, and attitude. The subtle power of parasympathetic meditation can increase your tolerance of stress and your sense of peace." (2010, p. x.)*

This will help you change how you work to become more client-centered and avoid believing that real estate sales are about selling homes. It will help you work with people to solve problems in a consultative, collaborative way.

Arden also writes about how to do this.

> *"The PFC enables you to develop and act on a moral system because it allows you to set aside your needs and reflect on the needs of others. The PFC is part of a system that provides you with the capacity for empathy." (2010, p. 5)*

These ideas are consistent with the Real Estate Code of Ethics in putting clients' needs and wants first. It is essential to meet fiduciary responsibilities to clients by always doing what is best for them rather than what is best for you, the Agent.

This book's consultative, collaborative approach is client-centered, problem-solving-focused, and service-first-oriented.

A great deal of this book has been about the human brain's conscious, subconscious, and unconscious nature. I consider myself a behavioral theorist. I like to explore why people think what they think and why they feel as they feel. This demands an understanding of the conscious, unconscious, and subconscious mind.

Arden writes,

> *"Implicit memory is often thought of as unconscious memory. It reacts to the emotional intensity of events and situations; when the situation is dangerous, it activates the fear system in your body." (2010, p. 15)*

The total of all a person has seen and heard, as well as felt, makes up their way of dealing with the world. This is why the following discussion about recognizing when a person has reached a tipping point is important.

Tipping the Prospect Toward You!

The Tipping Point by Malcolm Gladwell is a brilliant book about a concept I believe is game-changing. Reaching the tipping point with a client is a significant step toward self-actualization for me. When this happens with a client, I am profoundly renewed and reinvigorated. There is nothing in real estate more rewarding to me than the moment when I realize that a Prospect has reached the tipping point and is going to select me!

I have written several times in this book that you must make **"such a powerful and benefit-oriented presentation that is so personalized that the Prospect surrenders and feels compelled to choose you!"**

How does this happen? How do you bring a Prospect to the tipping point so they feel psychologically compelled to select you as their Agent? How do you know when this is happening?

In *The Tipping Point*, Gladwell presents an argument for accomplishing this objective by examining various situations when a "tipping point" was reached. None of these situations have anything to do with real estate, but they all answer the questions above.

Occasionally the difference between good and great is a vast ocean, and frequently it is only a small divide that must be crossed in a Prospect's mind. The accumulated power of good information, ideas, and attitudes, presented in a highly professional consultative, and collaborative way, crosses the ocean or divide and positions the Agent such that the Prospect feels psychologically compelled to select the Agent to represent them. They reach the tipping point...

In *The Tipping Point*, talking about a measles epidemic, Gladwell writes.

> *"These three characteristics—one, contagiousness; two, the fact that little causes can have big effects; and three, that change happens not gradually but at one dramatic moment." (2002, p. 9)*

Gladwell goes on to write,

> *"Of the three, the third trait—the idea that epidemics can rise or fall in one dramatic moment—is the most important because it is the principle that makes sense of the first two and permits the greatest insight into why modern change happens the way it does. The name given to that one dramatic moment in an epidemic when everything can change all at once is the Tipping Point." (2002, p. 9)*

In the example of the client presentation, the "tipping point" is brought about from the accumulation of impressions, ideas, and information so great that the client cannot imagine anyone else providing the level of service you will provide. They must think, **"No one could do this better than this special person."** The fact that little things can cause major effects is brought about by accumulating numerous small differences or differentiating factors that cause the client to see the agent as unique, different, and better. The third is that when all of this is presented highly professionally, the client feels an avalanche of value and benefit and surrenders mentally, if not physically, by saying, **"I choose you!"**

Recalling the previous discussion about the unconscious mind and how unconscious thoughts can be brought forward to the conscious mind, an agent should remember that placing a lot of information in the mind of the prospect that supports the decision to choose the agent can affect the outcome or action taken by the prospect. It can also allow thoughts and opinions to accumulate and, when brought forward to the conscious mind, cause a landslide that results in the prospect doing something they did not expect, like tipping over.

Frequently this psychological surrender can be seen in the Prospect's eyes, non-verbal feedback, or smile. This is when an Agent can experience one of life's most significant non-financial rewards. The client says or thinks, **"You are the solution for me. I want you."**

Gladwell, in *The Tipping Point*, writes that the possibility of sudden change is one of the most complex concepts to accept. He writes,

"This possibility of sudden change is at the center of the idea of the Tipping Point and might well be the hardest of all to accept." (2002, p. 12)

Numerous times during my career, I have been interrupted by a Prospect and told, **"I thought I had my mind made up, but you are making this very difficult for me."** This statement tells me the client was prepared to choose someone else but is at a tipping point and wants to choose me. They may need to be tipped a little more to make this happen. This is when I might say, **"Well, I hate to create additional stress for you, but of course, I would love to be your first choice and would appreciate the opportunity to help you win. We are in this together…. We can be partners in your success."**

Often the resistance to tipping over comes down to a prospect's reluctance to change direction and give other Agents unpleasant news. Yet, psychologically they know, not think, that they must. Sometimes, letting the Prospect off the psychological hook can be the answer. Providing a solution might be required. I might say, **"Well, this is a business decision for you and has little to do with personality; you should choose the Agent that you feel can best work with you and will provide you the best chance of success in the time frame you have."**

In *The Tipping Point*, Gladwell wrote,

"But the world of the Tipping Point is where the unexpected becomes the expected, where radical change is more than a possibility. It is—contrary to all our expectations—a certainty." (2002, pp. 13-14)

Regarding radical change and rewiring the brain, one must consider another radical idea in real estate.

The Client Hierarchy & Connectors

To understand where this is going, I will quote Gladwell once again.

He writes,

"I'm going to introduce three fascinating kinds of people I call, Mavens, Connectors, and Salespeople, who play a critical role in word-of-mouth epidemics that dictate our tastes, trends, and fashions." (2002, p. 14)

While Gladwell is certainly not talking about real estate, his ideas have an enormous impact on becoming a SuperStar in the real estate jungle. We will focus on the "Connector" concept for a few minutes.

In an earlier chapter, I wrote about the 80/20 rule and the P1 client. It was also pointed out that a small number of REALTORS® do a large percentage of the business in the real estate industry. The NAR statistics cited earlier certainly confirm this hypothesis.

The point was that some who are "Raving Fans" can be responsible for significant amounts of an Agents revenues and profits over a long period. In this regard, Gladwell introduces a concept he calls "The Law of the Few." He writes,

"The Law of the Few says the answer is that one of these exceptional people found out about the trend, and through social connections and energy and enthusiasm and personality spread the word about Hush Puppies." (2002, p. 22)

In his book, *The Tipping Point*, Gladwell names a few "Connectors" that he felt were important. Paul Revere, the messenger who changed the world by delivering important news to the Colonies, was one of them. Real estate goals are to find a few Paul Reveres and make them "Raving Fans." Because Paul Revere was a renowned "Connector," you will want to find people like him. A "Raving Fan" that is a "Connector" is the secret weapon in creating high income and long-term profitability for you.

Gladwell writes of Paul Revere,

"Paul Revere's ride is perhaps the most famous historical example of a word-of-mouth-epidemic." (2002, p. 32)

Paul Revere reached the right people and connected with them to help start a Revolution. Perhaps you can also. You may have heard many profess that word-of-mouth advertising is how they get their business. In Paul Revere's case, he just needed a message to share and to be turned loose upon the world to make magic happen.

Further, Gladwell writes,

"The answer is that the success of any kind of social epidemic is heavily dependent on the involvement of people with a particular and rare set of social gifts." (2002, p. 33)

This person, Gladwell calls a "Connector." What makes a person a "Connector"?

Gladwell explains,

"The first—and foremost obvious—criterion is that Connectors know lots of people. They are the kinds of people who know everyone. All of us know someone like this. But I don't think we spend a lot of time thinking about the importance of these kinds of people. (2002, p. 38)

A Dynamic Connector & Raving Fan

Jennifer was a client referred to us who worked in a massive corporation in a lower management position. She did not have much power in the corporation but knew everyone. She collected acquaintances like some people collect antiques. She had a sparkling personality and a dazzling smile and quickly became a fan. When working with my wife and partner Judi, she instantly became a "Raving Fan," but we did not yet know that she was also a "Connector." Following her closing after purchasing her new home, we realized she was special as she immediately referred a prospect who worked with her.

Jennifer and her family were quickly added to the P1 list in the Client Hierarchy. She and her spouse purchased a moderately priced home in an area where we specialize. Her connections with people in her sphere proved that all you need is a few people like Jennifer to start an epidemic of business. Her friends and associates soon began calling and telling us that Jennifer said to "call Sonny and Judi." Anyone she knew who would listen to her about us became prospects immediately as she knew other "CONNECTORS."

Over the next several years, Jennifer referred over twenty real estate buyers and sellers in her sphere of influence. This included her direct family, and this referral business accounted for over $400,000 of income to the Practice during the ensuing years. The total amount of money and profit created by Jennifer was impossible to calculate as many of her referred friends and associates were "Connectors" and referred others who referred others. It seems to us that Connectors mainly connect with other Connectors to share connections. This is an excellent shortcut to other Connectors.

She and her relationships were instrumental in my being nominated for the Best REALTOR® in Dallas by the Dallas Builders Association. I won the McSam Award from the Dallas Builders Association and was the only REALTOR® in Dallas to receive that Award that year.

A "Connector" active on any social media site is one of the most valuable assets an Agent can ever acquire. All marketing efforts by a Practice are intended to find one or more "Connectors" that can be captured in the "Marketing Net."

A final note about Connectors before moving on: Gladwell writes,

"Sprinkled among every walk of life, in other words, are a handful of people with a truly extraordinary knack of making friends and acquaintances. They are Connectors." (2002, p. 41)

The Client Marketing Programs and Target Marketing Programs of a Practice are all about finding that handful of people who are Connectors. Everyone needs a few name-droppers in their group of past clients. They should be respected and rewarded as they are most often Connectors.

Connectors are sometimes found in places where agents might not frequently go. This could be on the City Council, School Board, or another group such as an Arts Group or non-profit organization. Agents must find the Connectors wherever they may be located. The root purpose of all Agent marketing is finding these special people we call "Connectors." A Connector with "pride" in their Agent is priceless.

Solving Problems by Serving as a Consultant & Opening the Door to Relationships

Sean Murphy was an acquaintance from my earlier career in real estate consulting. He had boyish good looks, a smile that could melt the masses, and an engaging and sincere personality. In the past, despite my best efforts, I had never been able to capture Sean in the "Net." I could not convert him from a prospect to a client. When our real estate Group was established, I refocused my efforts on capturing him and contacted Sean numerous times. I suspected that Sean was a Connector. He politely told me each time that he had several commercial real estate agents and didn't need my help. I refused to accept this answer and sought a way to differentiate myself and prove my worth. I knew that Sean was a high-potential Prospect and that if I could find a way to get him into my "Net," then I would benefit both him and me greatly. Finally, the opportunity presented itself because I was willing to listen and empathize.

I called Sean and again asked if there was anything I could do to help him. He again told me he was all set, had several commercial real estate agents he was working with and was quite satisfied. He also explained that he had no signed agreements for real estate representation with anyone. I asked Sean to share the most significant problem he had in his business. He thought momentarily and replied, **"Well, my commercial rental rates are high, and the current market in my business has not kept up with the increases in our rental rates. My Commercial Real Estate Agent, who represented me on the three locations' leases, told me he couldn't help as he did not want to alienate the building personnel by suggesting a renegotiation of the leases I had on the buildings."**

Sensing that this was a problem for Sean and knowing that each location constituted over 20,000 square feet of office space, I realized this was a severe threat to his future. It threatened his ability to continue in his business. I offered to renegotiate the leases for him and further agreed to accept as compensation a monthly payment equal to 10% of the rent I could save him each month. This meant he could pay me from the monthly rental rate savings that I could negotiate with the building owners. Sean was sure I couldn't do much, but because he had no risk, he agreed to let me help as he was desperate for a solution. He did not sign a consulting or representation agreement at this point.

Searching for Solutions

Over the next several months, I worked with his building owners in a collaborative, consultative way and was able to renegotiate the leases for Sean. It resulted in substantial savings for Sean, and my monthly savings check for 10% of the saved rental amount was more than $3,500.00 per month over the years. The total consulting fees I earned were more than $200,000. Sean was ecstatic! His savings were substantial. I was on my way to creating a "Raving Fan," and Sean was almost securely in my "Net." I was different. While always concerned about what people think of me, I was first committed to Sean. Being willing to work on the bet that I could solve his problems and earn the right to become his exclusive Agent gave me an advantage over others.

During the ensuing months, I stayed in touch with Sean and frequently asked him if I could represent him as his Tenant Representative. He was now less reluctant but still did not believe that I could do anything more than what his other non-exclusive Commercial Real Estate Brokers were doing. I once again asked him what his biggest problem was in his business. He told me he needed a specific location in Dallas's highly popular Preston Center Submarket. He explained that space in that submarket was unavailable, and multiple Brokers confirmed this fact. I once again asked if I could help him solve the problem, and he reluctantly and pessimistically said, **"I know you can't, but knock yourself out...if you want to!"**

Michael Bradley was a building representative for a large building owner in Preston Center. I had met Michael while touring for another client and had stayed in touch with him. Michael was a Connector. I contacted Michael and inquired about a full-floor lease in one of his buildings. He explained that the Preston Center Market was highly occupied and that no full-floor leases were available. He said getting five thousand square feet of space would be difficult, and twenty-five thousand and a full floor would be impossible.

I told Michael, **"Michael, I know you can find something. Just do me a favor, look at your "Stacking Plan" and determine who is moving or downsizing in the next two years and let me know if you find anything."**

A Stacking Plan for a large building is a map showing every tenant and their lease term by floor. It is how a building representative manages a building to high occupancy. Michael was skeptical but promised to take a look. Several days later, Michael gave me a call. There was a floor that might be coming available in eighteen months.

I informed Sean that a 25,000-plus square foot floor in the Preston Center Market area in a Class A. building might become available in about 18 months. He was surprised and agreed to look at the property. After asking him three times if I could be his REALTOR®, he agreed that I could represent him if the space met his needs. Sean signed a representation agreement for that property only, and following that successful negotiation and a new lease, I became his only Tenant Representative in Commercial Real Estate. Over the next sixteen years, I represented Sean, and my professional service fee income from Sean's business activities was over two million dollars. He was my largest client, and my relationship with Sean grew as I became an indispensable asset to him because I understood his needs and wants and put him first. In a consulting capacity, I solved another problem for Sean. I recommended an organizational structure that would protect him from future risks like the ones he had faced on the leases I had renegotiated.

For many years, this client and several other Connectors allowed us to become one of the top 4% of all REALTORS® in the United States.

Sean was a client whose problems were solved on numerous occasions. I enhanced the relationship with Sean each time and kept the other Commercial Brokers at bay. Sean and I became good friends, and we often commented on how we communicated with landlords as a Team as if we were one person.

I was a consultative collaborating real estate agent who always prioritized my client, concerned myself with client success, and let the results happen. I did not sell or lease buildings; I solved problems. In our initial interview, a great client asked me the following question.

"Sonny, are you a "giver" or a "taker?"

Joe Callahan was a giver and quite a gentleman, and marvelous client. He made his fortune as a janitor. He was polished, professional, and impressive in appearance and demeanor. He had sharp eyes and a charming smile. His company cleaned buildings, and he employed over two thousand people. The first question he asked me upon meeting him was; Sonny are you a giver or a taker? **So, I ask you, are you a "giver" or a "taker?"**

CHAPTER 40 | PROLOGUE

A GREAT MAN ONCE WROTE TO ME, "SONNY, WHAT IS PAST IS PROLOGUE...."

Inspiration... Coach Wally Bullington stood in front of the meeting room in 1971 and boldly announced to the team that Steve would be <u>starting at my position</u> in the upcoming big game. He explained that Steve had been working at the defensive tackle position for a week and playing like he had played it his entire life. I was embarrassed and dismayed.

This was the first time I had been benched in my football career. I did not understand why and felt betrayed and ashamed. Why would Coach Bullington humiliate me like this? We were playing a nationally ranked team with an All-American offensive guard I would have played against. I was looking forward to the challenge. The opponent was better than anyone we had ever faced during my time at ACU. I wanted to leave the room, and it was difficult for me to sit there as Bullington went on and on about Steve and his amazing talent. I felt sick.

Learning to win often requires losing. It often requires jolting situations that rock you to your core. I somehow managed to maintain my composure, control my anger and disappointment and survive until game time. As I watched the first half of the game from the bench, I saw Steve outplayed at Defensive Tackle as the other team rolled up thirty-five points and established their clear superiority over our team.

At halftime, Coach Bullington approached me in the locker room and told me I would start the second half at defensive tackle. It was difficult not to say more, but I didn't. I just said, **"Thank you, Coach."**

Steve was moved back to his previous position to finish the game. We went on to lose, but I went on to win. I played well, and we stopped the inevitable slaughter and finished the game while still failing at the end. I learned a great deal from the experience of being demoted and embarrassed. It inspired me to strive for excellence! Later, while preparing to leave school and move to begin my business career, Coach Bullington approached me and asked if I would consider staying on as an assistant coach. I explained that with two children, I needed a position that paid a little more than a beginning coach. He smiled and wished me the best of luck. We remained friends for the rest of his life. Many years later, I visited him at his home and introduced him to my son, Jeff.

I began this journey with you talking about Inspiration... Inspirational moments, people, places, and events. All inspirational moments touch our lives and make us blink at the pure illumination of inspiration. I often found inspiration while just living through a regular day. Occasionally I had to dig deeper to find inspiration and needed help in being inspired. People usually came along to provide that inspiration.

By stepping outside of your body and looking at yourself through a prism of reality, one can see the fantastic things about you and those things about you that need improvement.

Moving Forward from Here

George Bernard Shaw wrote:

"You use a glass Mirror to see your face; You use works of art to see your soul." (2001, Dallas/Ft. Worth Home Book p. Inside Cover)

In an earlier chapter, I wrote that new and aspiring Agents could visualize receiving their first professional service fee check from a real estate transaction. I also asked a question. Are prospective agents beginning their real estate careers with misconceptions?

My fifty-plus years of experience in seeing, observing, and competing against other real estate Agents convinces me that the answer to that question is yes.

Life in real estate brings a person into contact with amazing, exciting, awe-inspiring people and places. There are many opportunities to experience life uniquely. These are the non-financial benefits of being a successful real estate agent. Looking inward and recognizing that self-improvement is required allows a person to reach self-actualization.

Aspiring Agents must accept that the quality of contact is more important than the quantity of contact. Agents must see the business as **serving the few rather than the masses**. They must have a plan, strategy, and an understanding of how they will differ. They must create their own "brand" centered around their own **"personality."**

Having read this book, you should be prepared to visualize a Business Model for your Practice and answer the questions of how you will work and how you will attract Prospects and Clients. The provided Business Model will serve as your outline to create your own personalized Business Model.

Numerous times I have noted that Agents often see the emotions of clients and prospects in the real estate industry as the enemy. I believe that the Prospects' and clients' emotions are a close friend and an opportunity for the aspiring Agent to connect emotionally and intellectually. Visualize that a client is afraid, and their fear is causing them to want to run or fight. When the Agent calmly and empathetically solves a problem and alleviates the fear, they position themselves in a highly positive and partnered way with a client. You can be the hero, and that position can make your client a "Raving Fan." When this "Raving Fan" is also a "Connector," you will have found the fountain of income.

The overall message for a reader of this material is that the way of working proposed in this book begins the process of rewiring the brain to a different way of working. It drives the Agent to become a Consultative Agent, a collaborator, and a trusted client confidant.

I hope you can now visualize the form and substance of your real estate Practice and construct a Business Model. If you can, I have partially achieved my goal of helping you! I want to solve a problem for you and help you achieve your desired results in your real estate career. This is how I seek to become **a valuable resource to you** and a problem-solver you can rely upon in the future.

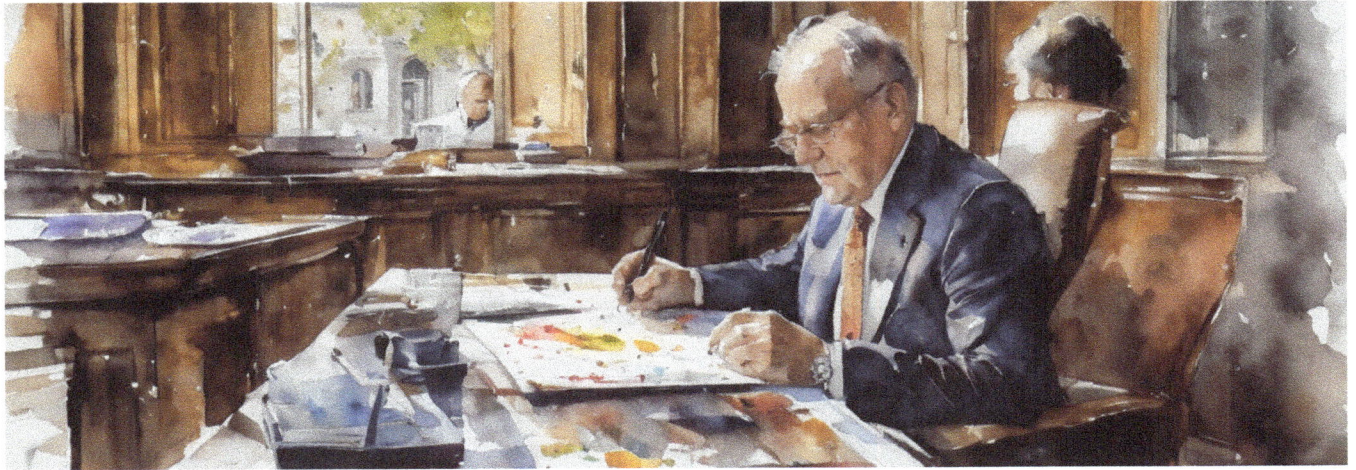

ABOUT THE AUTHOR

Sonny graduated from Abilene Christian University with a Bachelor of Science Degree in Management & Communications and a Master of Science Degree in Psychology, emphasizing Human Behavioral Theory, Interpersonal Communications Theory, Organizational Design, and Research Methods. He obtained his Texas Real Estate Sales License in 1971 and his Texas Real Estate Brokers License in 1988.

He is an award-winning agent who has achieved great success in the real estate industry in the DFW area. Between 2004 and 2018, Sonny was in the top 4% of all real estate agents nationwide. Depending on the index used, Sonny was in the top 1% of all real estate agents in Texas for numerous years.

Sonny is President of The Renaissance Group, a Real Estate Brokerage, Consulting, and Publishing Company in the DFW area. The Brokerage firm that the Sonny and the O'Dea Moyers Group was formerly affiliated with was Ebby Halliday Realtors, located in Dallas, TX. The O'Dea Moyers Group was at the top of the 1,800-plus Agents for over 15 years. They were in the highest production plateau for 15 of the 20 years from 1998 to 2018. Sonny was named D Magazine Best of Dallas for sixteen straight years and was named by D Magazine as a Top Producer Agent in Dallas for over ten years.

Sonny was presented the McSam Award and named the REALTOR® of the Year in Dallas by the Dallas Builders Association in 2015. Sonny was the only REALTOR® of thousands in the DFW Metropolitan Area REALTORS® to receive this award. Sonny was interviewed by a panel of experts who made the decision and was selected from the three finalists as the Best REALTOR® in DFW. In his book, Sonny credits his experiences, psychological concepts, and philosophies for his success.

Prior History

After completing his undergraduate degree at Abilene Christian University in 1973, Sonny began his professional career in the Sales & Marketing Department at Southwestern Bell Telephone Company. He held the Account Executive-Major Accounts-Utility Industry position and later was named Industry Manager for the Wholesale Distribution Industry in North Texas. As a result of his innovative management and writing skills in this position, he was promoted to the Texas State Staff as a specialist in Revenue Planning & Quota Setting Methodologies.

He created a proprietary method for tracking prior results, assigning quotas, and measuring the sales organizations in Texas for SWBT. He named this revised study process the **Hybrid Information Transfer Study Methodology**.

He helped develop and write an Advanced Data Processing Sales Course for AT&T in Denver, Colorado. In this project, Sonny assisted in creating selling strategies for selling to highly analytical decision-makers and partnering collaboratively to establish long-term business relationships.

He led a project developing and writing a Financial Analysis & Competitive Strategies course for Southwestern Bell Telephone Company at its Headquarters offices in St. Louis, MO. In this project, Sonny collaborated with the other team members and Professors at St. Louis University to teach the Account Executive at Southwestern Bell and AT&T how to utilize Team resources best to connect and partner with high-level financial managers. This is where Sonny first identified the enormous power of Team Selling Concepts and how to utilize highly specialized costly resources better and more effectively to improve sales productivity. He also began an in-depth study of Matrix Management systems at this time.

In 1984, he was asked to review and rewrite marketing sections of the Texas Business Plan for Southwestern Bell Telephone Company. He authored the presentation used by the Executive Vice President of Marketing of Texas to present new strategic marketing concepts to Southwestern Bell Telephone Company officers.

Demonstrating a wide-ranging background in all business management and sales disciplines, he attracted several high-level executives' attention with his writing and speaking skills. This is where he first evaluated and improved on Client Management, Client Stimulation, Target Market Selection, and Market Stimulation.

Sonny taught sales at Tarrant County Community College in Ft. Worth, Texas, during this period. This inspired him to focus on teaching and consulting in the future and resulted in him seeking opportunities to expand his education and experience.

Upon leaving Southwestern Bell Telephone, Sonny served as an on-staff Marketing Consultant for a Unit President at Ericsson Network Projects, Inc. He assisted ENPI in implementing a new marketing system for the US markets. Using the Hybrid ITSM that Sonny had previously used, he studied the sales organization of Ericsson Network Projects, Inc. He developed a reorganization plan for the Unit to make the organization more in tune with the American markets, selling highly technical systems and networks using fiber optic facilities. The project was adopted and implemented by ENPI. The plan featured a Matrix Management approach to manage highly skilled resources.

Sonny left Ericsson to pursue a leadership role at ShareTech, a joint venture between AT&T and United Technologies. He became the Southwest United States Regional Manager for ShareTech. When that joint venture was disbanded, he was asked to serve as the National Dissolution Manager and reported to the Chairman of ShareTech while overseeing the close-down of that Corporation. In this capacity, he negotiated settlements with clients and vendors of ShareTech and was the last employee of ShareTech.

After completing his assignment at ShareTech, Sonny formed a Marketing & Management Consulting firm. Management Consultant Services, provided consulting services worldwide for 14 years. As an Enterprise Consultant, he worked on numerous projects involving business planning methodology practices for AT&T, Ericsson Network Project, Inc, and Zurich Corporation managers.

As a Consultant for ZCRES, a division of Zurich, Sonny wrote a comprehensive sales reorganization plan. In this project, he again used the Hybrid ITSM to review and identify weaknesses in sales processes at ZCRES. Then he developed and authored a plan to revise and replace sales and marketing systems with a more client-centered collaborative approach. Upon completing this assignment, Sonny expanded into an area of consulting that allowed him to specialize and test many of the philosophies and theories he had developed in his prior career, and this led to new approaches and concepts being identified.

In early 1988, he began a Research Project on the use of "shared office space," "incubator space," and the operation of Business Centers and Executive Suites. This niche market was unsophisticated, and few Consultants focused on the industry.

This research project led to 150 reviews of business operations in five major markets in the United States, where he assessed these organizations' sales and marketing proficiency. Utilizing the Hybrid Information Transfer Study Methodology, he developed new systems and methods for the industry to overlay the sales and marketing practices prevalent in the industry, allowing him to author new "Sales & Marketing Methodologies" for the industry. By the end of 1989, Sonny was recognized as a renowned marketing expert in the Business Center-Shared Office Industry and began consulting with companies in most of the United States, Canada, and Europe.

In this capacity, Sonny then began consulting with organizations worldwide on real estate, site selection, sales and marketing, and lease matters. This would later lead him to provide real estate brokerage services to Commercial Real Estate clients in Texas.

Sonny has presented his concepts and ideas at multiple industries' National Conventions. He has spoken in most major cities in the United States, Vancouver, Calgary, and Toronto in Canada. He has spoken in London, Paris, Salzburg, Frankfurt, Mulhouse, and other European cities as he consulted with clients in Europe and Asia. He has consulted with Clients in more than twenty countries and most major markets in the United States. He conducted sales and marketing-related seminars for real estate-related companies throughout Europe and South America. During this period, he wrote his first book, "The Complete Reference Manual for the Shared Office Industry."

He became a recognized expert in developing Business Centers, Collaboration Centers, Virtual Office environments, and Co-Working environments. Sonny wrote the Business & Marketing Plan that led to the development of The Alliance Business Centers Network, a joint venture of two of Sonny's clients from Philadelphia and New York. The Alliance Business Centers Network became a Worldwide Marketing organization, and Sonny implemented the marketing and development plan for the venture as he continued to lecture and teach worldwide.

Sonny then founded the O'Dea Moyers Group, affiliated with Ebby Halliday Real Estate, with his wife and Partner, Judi O'Dea Moyers. The unique and novel approach to the Business Model for this firm resulted in the Practice specializing in Residential & Commercial Real Estate and Consulting Services. This single point of contact concept resulted in a blended business with several profit centers, allowing the Group to achieve high profitability and noteworthy success in the real estate industry. Sonny made groundbreaking innovations in operating a Real Estate Practice by introducing Matrix Management Concepts in the real estate industry.

He was also the first Agent who installed and utilized a Collaboration Hub in his private offices in the DFW Area. This was done in 2012 in concert with Steelcase Corporation and numerous workplace studies that indicated Collaboration as a future method that showed substantial promise in the real estate Industry. His book, *The Architecture of the Real Estate Practice,* is one of the only books about how social sciences are used to provide real estate brokerage services.

His understanding and use of the interpersonal communications theory, Self-Disclosure & Reciprocity are one of his notable contributions to the industry.

Sonny consulted with an international client and collaborated with Steelcase Corporation to design a 24,000-square-foot Executive Collaboration Center in Addison, Texas. This project also resulted in Sonny's incorporation of collaborative selling concepts into the operation of the O'Dea Moyers Group, where he utilized a Collaboration Hub for sales and marketing presentation and client management with real estate clients and prospects. This innovative approach to the sales process in the real estate industry served as a differentiation factor and is a Keystone Concept to his real estate sales and marketing strategy.

Sonny's extensive experience in developing co-working and collaboration environments within sales organizations and his use of the concepts resulted in being asked to present to the Ebby Halliday Real Estate Management Team. This presentation on innovative facility design and the incorporation of Hub Concepts in Collaboration along with co-working concepts was made to the Executive Management Team of Ebby Halliday Real Estate, Inc. Sonny was singled out and recognized by Ms. Ebby Halliday, the founder and leader of Ebby Halliday Realtors and Ebby Halliday Real Estate, Inc. as an outstanding contribution to the future of real estate sales.

In 2012, Ebby Halliday wrote:

"Sonny, Congratulations, you did a great job on your presentation this morning, really the best I've ever heard and the concept you will be working on is great! You did a beautiful presentation Sonny. Warmest Regards, Ebby"

The concept was implemented within most Ebby Halliday office locations within several years, with collaboration rooms at each location.

Sonny has authored numerous papers, made hundreds of presentations, and developed marketing, sales, and interpersonal communications theories courses. He took many concepts and sales and marketing theories he had taught worldwide and applied them to the real estate industry at the O'Dea Moyers Group. Using the Hybrid ITSM he had created, he studied and researched the sales and marketing practices of Agents in the real estate industry. He created a proprietary marketing system for the O'Dea Moyers Group at Ebby Halliday Real Estate, Inc. Many of these concepts are the basis for his book, *The Architecture of the Real Estate Practice.*

Sonny's approach to implementing new methods and practices in the real estate industry resulted in Sonny and Judi becoming highly successful REALTORS® in the very competitive DFW area. While operating The O'Dea Moyers Group, he taught professional marketing courses at the Ebby Halliday Real Estate Career Development Center. In this way, he spoke with and interviewed numerous new and aspiring real estate Agents. Sonny and his Group have received numerous recognitions in the real estate industry. This included Ebby Halliday Realtors and many other organizations, such as D Magazine and the Dallas Builders Association. Sonny served on the REALTOR® Advisory Boards for numerous large neighborhoods and developments in the DFW Area.

Community service was an integral part of the O'Dea Moyers Group mission. While serving as Managing Partner of the O'Dea Moyers Group, Sonny volunteered to help develop the Frisco Association for the Arts in Frisco, Texas and later served as the Board President of that non-profit organization for three years. The Frisco Association for the Arts realized unprecedented growth and success under Sonny's leadership, and he was invited to serve on the Governance Committee for developing the Arts in Collin County, Texas.

Craig Hall of Hall Financial Group was a sponsor and essential ally in developing the Arts in Frisco. He is a prominent real estate developer who at Sonny's request was the Keynote speaker at the first Gala for the Arts. Ebby Halliday of Ebby Halliday Real Estate, Inc. was a Keynote Speaker at the Frisco Association for the Arts Gala. They had a close relationship with Sonny, sharing a common love and appreciation for the Arts. Baxter Brinkmann, a prominent developer and landowner, also spoke at the Arts Gala at the request of Sonny Moyers.

Sonny is uniquely qualified to write a book of this type. After separating from Ebby Halliday Realtors, he founded his current company, Sonny R. Moyers, dba, The Renaissance Group. and developed strong support for the Arts in Frisco by partnering and building relationships with people with common interests.

REFERENCES

Alexander, A. A., & Muhlebach, R. F. (1990). Managing and leasing commercial properties. John Wiley & Sons.

Altman, I. (1973). Reciprocity of interpersonal exchange. Journal for the Theory of Social Behavior, 3(2), 249–261.

Altman, I., & Taylor, D. A. (1973). Social penetration: The development of interpersonal relationships. Holt, Rinehart & Winston.

Archer, R. L., & Burleson, J. A. (1980). The effects of timing of self-disclosure on attraction and reciprocity. Journal of Personality and Social Psychology, 38(1), 120–130.

Arden, J. B. (2010). Rewire your brain: Think your way to a better life. John Wiley & Sons.

Beckwith, H. (2003). What Clients Love. Warner Books.

Behrenfeld, W. H. (1979). Accounting Desk Book (6th ed.). Institute for Business Planning Inc.

Berscheid, E., & Walster, E. (1974). Physical attractiveness. Advances in experimental social psychology, 7, 157-215.

Blake, R. R., & Mouton, J. S. (1964). The managerial grid: Key orientations for achieving production through people. Gulf Publishing Company.

Blanchard, K., Bowles, S., & Mackay, H. (1993). Raving fans: A revolutionary approach to customer service. William Morrow and Co.

Braaten, L. J. (1961). The movement from non-self to self in client-centered psychotherapy. Journal of Counseling Psychology, 8(1), 20–24.

Branch, A. Y. (1974). Until we meet again: Anticipation of future interaction and self-disclosure (Doctoral dissertation, Harvard University).

Cacciatore, J. (2017). Bearing the unbearable: Love, loss, and the heartbreaking path of grief. Simon and Schuster.

Collins, J. C. (2001). Good to great. Harper Business.

Cozby, P. C. (1972). Self-Disclosure, Reciprocity, and Liking. Sociometry, 35(1), 151–160.

Cozby, P. C. (1973). Self-disclosure: a literature review. Psychological Bulletin, 79(2), 73-91.

Crowne, D. P., & Marlowe, D. (1960). A new scale of social desirability independent of psychopathology. Journal of consulting psychology, 24(4), 349-354.

Davis, J. D., & Skinner, A. E. (1974). Reciprocity of self-disclosure in interviews: Modeling or social change? Journal of Personality and Social Psychology, 29(6), 779–784.

Derlega, V. J., Chaikin, A. L., & Herndon, J. (1975). Demand characteristics and disclosure reciprocity. The Journal of Social Psychology, 97(2), 301-302.

Derlega, V. J., Harris, M. S., & Chaikin, A. L. (1973). Self-disclosure reciprocity, liking, and the deviant. Journal of Experimental Social Psychology, 9(4), 277-284.

Dion, K., Berscheid, E., & Walster, E. (1972). What is beautiful is good. Journal of Personality and Social Psychology, 24(3), 285–290.

Doster, J. A., & Strickland, B. R. (1971). Disclosing of verbal material as a function of information requested, information about the interviewer, and interviewee differences. Journal of Consulting and Clinical Psychology, 37(2), 187–194.

Feigenbaum, W. M. (1977). Reciprocity in self-disclosure within the psychological interview. Psychological Reports, 40(1), 15-26.

Gladwell, M. (2000). The Tipping Point: how little things can make a big difference. Back Bay.

Gladwell, M. (2005). blink: The Power of Thinking Without Thinking. Back Bay Books/Little, Brown & Company.

Gladwell, M. (2008). Outliers. Little, Brown, and Co.

Gladwell, M. (2013). David and Goliath: Underdogs, misfits, and the art of battling giants. Little, Brown.

Goffman, E. (1963). Behavior in Public Places. FreePress.

Gouldner, A. W. (1960). The norm of reciprocity: A preliminary statement. American Sociological Review, 25(2), 161-178.

Grove, A. S. (1983). High Output Management. Random House Inc.

Hanan, M. (2011). Consultative selling: The Hanan formula for high-margin sales at high levels. AMACOM.

Himelstein, P., & Kimbrough Jr, W. W. (1963). A study of self-disclosure in the classroom. The Journal of Psychology, 55(2), 437-440.

Himelstein, P., & Lubin, B. (1966). Relationship of the MMPI K scale and a measure of self-disclosure in a normal population. Psychological Reports, 19(1), 166.

Hocker, J. L., & Wilmot, W. W. (1991). Interpersonal conflict (3rd ed.). William C. Brown Publishers.

Holiday, R. (2017). Perennial Seller: The art of making and marketing work that lasts. Penguin.

Holtz, H. (1983). How to succeed as an independent consultant (1st ed.). Wiley.

Hood, T. C., & Back, K. W. (1971). Self-disclosure and the volunteer: A source of bias in laboratory experiments. Journal of Personality and Social Psychology, 17(2), 130–136.

Jones, E. E., & Davis, K. E. (1965). The attribution process in person perception. Advances in Experimental Social Psychology, 2, 220-266.

Jones, F. C. (2008). How to Wow: Proven Strategies for Presenting Your Ideas, Persuading Your Audience, and Perfecting Your Image. Random House Publishing Group.

Jourard, S. M. (1964). The Transparent Self: Self-disclosure and well-being (Vol. 17). Van Nostrand.

Jourard, S. M. (1970). The beginnings of self-disclosure. Voices: The art and science of psychotherapy, 6(1), 42-51.

Jourard, S. M. (1971). Self-disclosure: An Experimental Analysis of the Transparent Self. Wiley-Interscience.

Jourard, S. M., & Friedman, R. (1970). Experimenter-subject "distance" and self-disclosure. Journal of Personality and Social Psychology, 15(3), 278–282.

Jourard, S. M., & Jaffe, P. E. (1970). Influence of an interviewer's disclosure on the self-disclosing behavior of interviewees. Journal of Counseling Psychology, 17(3), 252–257.

Jourard, S. M., & Lasakow, P. (1958). Some factors in self-disclosure. The Journal of Abnormal and Social Psychology, 56(1), 91–98.

Jourard, S. M., & Richman, P. (1963). Factors in the self-disclosure inputs of college students. Merrill-Palmer Quarterly of Behavior and Development, 9(2), 141–148.

Kahneman, D. (2015). Thinking, Fast and Slow. Farrar, Straus and Giroux.

Krumroy, R. E. (2000). Identity branding: Distinct or extinct. Lifestyle Press.

Kubr, M. (1976). Management consulting: A guide to the profession (Vol. 4). International Labour Office - ILO.

Latane, B. (1970). Field studies of altruistic compliance. Representative Research in Social Psychology, 1(1), 49–61.

Levin, F. M., & Geren, K. J. (1969). Revealingness, ingratiation, and the disclosure of self, Proceedings of the 77th Annual Convention of the American Psychological Association, 4 (Pt. 1), 447-448.

Lubin, B., & Harrison, R. L. (1964). Predicting small group behavior with the self-disclosure inventory. Psychological Reports, 15(1), 77–78.

Marlatt, G. A. (1971). Exposure to a model and task ambiguity as determinants of verbal behavior in an interview. Journal of Consulting and Clinical Psychology, 36(2), 268–276.

McFarland, K. R. (2008). The Breakthrough Company: How Everyday Companies Become Extraordinary Performers. Currency; Illustrated edition.

Medina, J. (2000). The Genetic Inferno. Cambridge University Press.

REFERENCES

Medina, J., & Conn McQuinn, P. S. E. (2014). brain rules (Updated and Expanded). Pear Press.

Miller, A.G. (1970). Role of physical attractiveness in impression formation. Psychonomic Science, 20, 241–243.

Miller, R., Strombom, D., Iammarino, M., & Black, B. (2009). The commercial real estate revolution: Nine transforming keys to lowering costs, cutting waste, and driving change in a broken industry. John Wiley & Sons.

Mouton, B. (1981). Productivity: The Human Side. Amacom.

Ormrod, J. E. (2012). human learning (6th ed.). Pearson Education, Inc.

Rosenthal, R., & Rosnow, R. L. (2009). Artifacts in Behavioral Research. Oxford University Press.

Rubin, Z. (1973). Liking and Loving: An Invitation to Social Psychology. Holt, Rinehart, and Winston.

Rubin, Z. (1974). Disclosing oneself to a stranger: Reciprocity and its limits. Journal of Experimental Social Psychology, 11(3), 233-260.

Rubin, Z. (1974). Lovers and Other Strangers: The Development of Intimacy in Encounters and Relationships, The American Scientist, 62(2), 182–190.

Schuller, R. H. (1984). Tough times never last, but tough people do! Bantam.

Sermat, V., & Smyth, M. (1973). Content analysis of verbal communication in the development of a relationship: Conditions influencing self-disclosure. Journal of Personality and Social Psychology, 26, 332–346.

Shonk, J. H. (1982). Working in teams: A practical manual for improving work groups. Amacom.

Simmel, G., & Wolff, K. H. (1950). The Sociology of Georg Simmel: By Georg Simmel. Free Press.

Stern, C. W., & Deimler, M. S. (Eds.). (2006). The Boston consulting group on strategy: Classic concepts and new perspectives. John Wiley & Sons.

The Ashley Group. (2001). Dallas/Fort Worth Home Book (1st ed.). Ashley Group.

Thibaut, J. W., & Kelley, H. H. (1959). The social psychology of groups. J. Wiley & Sons.

Truax, B. C., & Carkhuff, R. R. (1965). Client and therapist transparency in the psychotherapeutic encounter. Journal of Counseling Psychology, 12, 6–9.

Vondracek, W. F. (1969). Behavioral measurement of self-disclosure. Psychological Reports, 25, 914.

Vondracek, W. F. (1969). The study of self-disclosure in experimental interviews. Journal of Psychology, 72, 55–59.

Walker, O. C., Ford, M. N., Gilbert, A., & Churchill. (1981). Sales Force Management. Richard D. Irwin Inc.

Wegner, D. M. (2002). The illusion of conscious will. Massachusetts Institute of Technology.

Weston, J. F., & Brigham, E. F. (1973). Managerial finance. Holt Rinehart and Winston.

Worthy, M., Gary, A. L., & Kahn, G. M. (1969). Self-disclosure as an exchange process. Journal of Personality and Social Psychology, 13(1), 59–63.

Zankel, M. I. (1991). Negotiating commercial real estate leases. Dearborn Trade Pub.